The *New* Daily Study Bible

The Gospel of
Luke

The *New* Daily Study Bible

The Gospel of
Luke

William Barclay

WJK WESTMINSTER
JOHN KNOX PRESS
LOUISVILLE · KENTUCKY

Originally published in 1953 as *The Daily Study Bible: The Gospel of Luke* by Saint Andrew Press, 121 George Street, Edinburgh EH2 4YN

Revised and updated by Saint Andrew Press, 2001

Published in the United States by
Westminster John Knox Press
Louisville, Kentucky

Cover design by McColl Productions Ltd., by courtesy of Saint Andrew Press

Library of Congress Cataloging-in-Publication Data

Barclay, William, 1907-1978.
  The Gospel of Luke / William Barclay.—Rev. and updated ed.
    p. cm. — (New daily study Bible)
  ISBN: 978-0-664-22487-5 (alk. paper)
    1. Bible. N.T. Luke—Commentaries. I. Title. II. Daily study Bible series
(Westminster Press)

  BS2595.3 .B29 2001
  226.4'077—dc21   2001045375

To the Kirk Session of
Trinity Church, Renfrew,
over whom God called me to preside
from 1933 to 1946
and in particular to
M.R. and J.B.K.,
Men of God

CONTENTS

SERIES FOREWORD
(by Ronnie Barclay)

My father always had a great love for the English language and its literature. As a student at the University of Glasgow, he won a prize in the English class – and I have no doubt that he could have become a Professor of English instead of Divinity and Biblical Criticism. In a pre-computer age, he had a mind like a computer that could store vast numbers of quotations, illustrations, anecdotes and allusions; and, more remarkably still, he could retrieve them at will. The editor of this revision has, where necessary, corrected and attributed the vast majority of these quotations with considerable skill and has enhanced our pleasure as we read quotations from Plato to T. S. Eliot.

There is another very welcome improvement in the new text. My mother was one of five sisters, and my grandmother was a commanding figure as the Presbyterian minister's wife in a small village in Ayrshire in Scotland. She ran that small community very efficiently, and I always felt that my father, surrounded by so many women, was more than somewhat overawed by it all! I am sure that this is the reason why his use of English tended to be dominated by the words 'man', 'men' and so on, with the result that it sounded very male-orientated. Once again, the editor has very skilfully improved my father's English and made the text much more readable for all of us by amending the often one-sided language.

It is a well-known fact that William Barclay wrote at break-neck speed and never corrected anything once it was on

xiii

paper – he took great pride in mentioning this at every possible opportunity! This revision, in removing repetition and correcting the inevitable errors that had slipped through, has produced a text free from all the tell-tale signs of very rapid writing. It is with great pleasure that I commend this revision to readers old and new in the certainty that William Barclay speaks even more clearly to us all with his wonderful appeal in this new version of his much-loved *Daily Study Bible*.

Ronnie Barclay
Bedfordshire
2001

GENERAL INTRODUCTION

(by William Barclay, from the 1975 edition)

The Daily Study Bible series has always had one aim – to convey the results of scholarship to the ordinary reader. A. S. Peake delighted in the saying that he was a 'theological middle-man', and I would be happy if the same could be said of me in regard to these volumes. And yet the primary aim of the series has never been academic. It could be summed up in the famous words of Richard of Chichester's prayer – to enable men and women 'to know Jesus Christ more clearly, to love him more dearly, and to follow him more nearly'.

It is all of twenty years since the first volume of *The Daily Study Bible* was published. The series was the brain-child of the late Rev. Andrew McCosh, MA, STM, the then Secretary and Manager of the Committee on Publications of the Church of Scotland, and of the late Rev. R. G. Macdonald, OBE, MA, DD, its Convener.

It is a great joy to me to know that all through the years *The Daily Study Bible* has been used at home and abroad, by minister, by missionary, by student and by layman, and that it has been translated into many different languages. Now, after so many printings, it has become necessary to renew the printer's type and the opportunity has been taken to restyle the books, to correct some errors in the text and to remove some references which have become outdated. At the same time, the Biblical quotations within the text have been changed to use the Revised Standard Version, but my own original translation of the New Testament passages has been retained at the beginning of each daily section.

There is one debt which I would be sadly lacking in courtesy if I did not acknowledge. The work of revision and correction has been done entirely by the Rev. James Martin, MA, BD, Minister of High Carntyne Church, Glasgow. Had it not been for him this task would never have been undertaken, and it is impossible for me to thank him enough for the selfless toil he has put into the revision of these books.

It is my prayer that God may continue to use *The Daily Study Bible* to enable men better to understand His word.

William Barclay
Glasgow
1975
(Published in the 1975 edition)

GENERAL FOREWORD

(by John Drane)

I only met William Barclay once, not long after his retirement from the chair of Biblical Criticism at the University of Glasgow. Of course I had known about him long before that, not least because his theological passion – the Bible – was also a significant formative influence in my own life and ministry. One of my most vivid memories of his influence goes back to when I was working on my own doctoral research in the New Testament. It was summer 1971, and I was a leader on a mission team working in the north-east of Scotland at the same time as Barclay's Baird Lectures were being broadcast on national television. One night, a young Ph.D. scientist who was interested in Christianity, but still unsure about some things, came to me and announced: 'I've just been watching William Barclay on TV. He's convinced me that I need to be a Christian; when can I be baptized?' That kind of thing did not happen every day. So how could it be that Barclay's message was so accessible to people with no previous knowledge or experience of the Christian faith?

I soon realised that there was no magic ingredient that enabled this apparently ordinary professor to be a brilliant communicator. His secret lay in who he was, his own sense of identity and purpose, and above all his integrity in being true to himself and his faith. Born in the far north of Scotland, he was brought up in Motherwell, a steel-producing town south of Glasgow where his family settled when he was only five, and this was the kind of place where he felt most at

xvii

home. Though his association with the University of Glasgow provided a focus for his life over almost fifty years, from his first day as a student in 1925 to his retirement from the faculty in 1974, he never became an ivory-tower academic, divorced from the realities of life in the real world. On the contrary, it was his commitment to the working-class culture of industrial Clydeside that enabled him to make such a lasting contribution not only to the world of the university but also to the life of the Church.

He was ordained to the ministry of the Church of Scotland at the age of twenty-six, but was often misunderstood even by other Christians. I doubt that William Barclay would ever have chosen words such as 'missionary' or 'evangelist' to describe his own ministry, but he accomplished what few others have done, as he took the traditional Presbyterian emphasis on spirituality-through-learning and transformed it into a most effective vehicle for evangelism. His own primary interest was in the history and language of the New Testament, but William Barclay was never only a historian or literary critic. His constant concern was to explore how these ancient books, and the faith of which they spoke, could continue to be relevant to people of his own time. If the Scottish churches had known how to capitalize on his enormous popularity in the media during the 1960s and 1970s, they might easily have avoided much of the decline of subsequent years.

Connecting the Bible to life has never been the way to win friends in the world of academic theology, and Barclay could undoubtedly have made things easier for himself had he been prepared to be a more conventional academic. But he was too deeply rooted in his own culture – and too seriously committed to the gospel – for that. He could see little purpose in a belief system that was so wrapped up in arcane and complicated terminology that it was accessible only to experts. Not only did he demystify Christian theology, but he also did it for working people, addressing the kind of things that mattered to ordinary folks in their everyday lives. In doing so, he also challenged the elitism that has often been deeply ingrained in the twin worlds of academic theology and the Church, with their shared assumption that popular culture is an inappropriate vehicle for serious thinking. Professor Barclay can hardly have been surprised when his predilection for writing books for the masses – not to mention talking to them on television – was questioned by his peers and even occasionally dismissed as being 'unscholarly' or insufficiently 'academic'. That was all untrue, of course, for his work was soundly based in reliable scholarship and his own extensive knowledge of the original languages of the Bible. But like One many centuries before him (and unlike most of his peers, in both Church and academy), 'the common people heard him gladly' (Mark 12:37), which no doubt explains why his writings are still inspirational – and why it is a particular pleasure for me personally to commend them to a new readership in a new century.

John Drane
University of Aberdeen
2001

EDITOR'S PREFACE

(by Linda Foster)

When the first volume of the original *Daily Bible Readings*, which later became *The Daily Study Bible* (the commentary on Acts), was published in 1953, no one could have anticipated or envisaged the revolution in the use of language which was to take place in the last quarter of the twentieth century. Indeed, when the first revised edition, to which William Barclay refers in his General Introduction, was completed in 1975, such a revolution was still waiting in the wings. But at the beginning of the twenty-first century, inclusive language and the concept of political correctness are well-established facts of life. It has therefore been with some trepidation that the editing of this unique and much-loved text has been undertaken in producing *The New Daily Study Bible*. Inevitably, the demands of the new language have resulted in the loss of some of Barclay's most sonorous phrases, perhaps best remembered in the often-repeated words 'many a man'. Nonetheless, this revision is made in the conviction that William Barclay, the great communicator, would have welcomed it. In the discussion of Matthew 9:16–17 ('The Problem of the New Idea'), he affirmed the value of language that has stood the test of time and in which people have 'found comfort and put their trust', but he also spoke of 'living in a changing and expanding world' and questioned the wisdom of reading God's word to twentieth-century men and women in Elizabethan English. It is the intention of this new edition to heed that warning and to bring

xxi

William Barclay's message of God's word to readers of the twenty-first century in the language of their own time.

In the editorial process, certain decisions have been made in order to keep a balance between that new language and the familiar Barclay style. Quotations from the Bible are now taken from the New Revised Standard Version, but William Barclay's own translation of individual passages has been retained throughout. Where the new version differs from the text on which Barclay originally commented, because of the existence of an alternative reading, the variant text is indicated by square brackets. I have made no attempt to guess what Barclay would have said about the NRSV text; his commentary still refers to the Authorized (King James) and Revised Standard Versions of the Bible, but I believe that the inclusive language of the NRSV considerably assists the flow of the discussion.

For similar reasons, the dating conventions of BC and AD – rather than the more recent and increasingly used BCE (before the common era) and CE (common era) – have been retained. William Barclay took great care to explain the meanings of words and phrases and scholarly points, but it has not seemed appropriate to select new terms and make such explanations on his behalf.

One of the most difficult problems to solve has concerned monetary values. Barclay had his own system for translating the coinage of New Testament times into British currency. Over the years, these equivalent values have become increasingly out of date, and often the force of the point being made has been lost or diminished. There is no easy way to bring these equivalents up to date in a way that will continue to make sense, particularly when readers come from both sides of the Atlantic. I have therefore followed the only known yardstick that gives any feel for the values concerned, namely that a *denarius* was a day's wage for a working man, and I have made alterations to the text accordingly.

One of the striking features of *The Daily Study Bible* is the range of quotations from literature and hymnody that are used by way of illustration. Many of these passages appeared without identification or attribution, and for the new edition I have attempted wherever possible to provide sources and authors. In the same way, details have been included about scholars and other individuals cited, by way of context and explanation, and I am most grateful to Professor John Drane for his assistance in discovering information about some of the more obscure or unfamiliar characters. It is clear that readers use *The Daily Study Bible* in different ways. Some look up particular passages while others work through the daily readings in a more systematic way. The descriptions and explanations are therefore not offered every time an individual is mentioned (in order to avoid repetition that some may find tedious), but I trust that the information can be discovered without too much difficulty.

Finally, the 'Further Reading' lists at the end of each volume have been removed. Many new commentaries and individual studies have been added to those that were the basis of William Barclay's work, and making a selection from that ever-increasing catalogue is an impossible task. It is nonetheless my hope that the exploration that begins with these volumes of *The New Daily Study Bible* will go on in the discovery of new writers and new books.

Throughout the editorial process, many conversations have taken place – conversations with the British and American publishers, and with those who love the books and find in them both information and inspiration. Ronnie Barclay's contribution to this revision of his father's work has been invaluable. But one conversation has dominated the work, and that has been a conversation with William Barclay himself through the text. There has been a real sense of listening to his voice in all the questioning and in the searching for new words to convey the meaning of that text. The aim of *The New Daily Study Bible* is to make clear his message, so that the distinctive voice, which has spoken to so many in past years, may continue to be heard for generations to come.

Linda Foster
London
2001

INTRODUCTION

(by John Drane)

William Barclay never prefaced his writings with extensive literary analysis of the Bible books. He believed that the main focus of his attention should be the text itself, and he always aimed to allow the original writers to speak for themselves. Had he been writing today, he might have felt it necessary to say a little more about the fact that Luke's gospel is just one section of the two-volume work of Luke–Acts, and to have paid more attention to the various ways in which Luke's story of the life of Jesus is similar to, yet different from, the other New Testament gospels. Certainly, that has been a major pre-occupation of scholarship over the last twenty years. Of course, Barclay was not unaware of such questions; and, though he never uses words like 'redaction criticism', he was obviously happy with the concept (that each of the evangelists placed their own distinctive spin on the stories which they record).

One of the major characteristics of Luke's gospel is its stories. It contains some of the most striking of Jesus' parables, not found in other gospels – stories like the Good Samaritan and the prodigal son (or, as Barclay preferred, 'the good father'). One of Barclay's own skills was the ability to think in pictures, and his comments on Luke are full of graphic descriptions of human life, both in the first century AD and in the world he himself knew. Throughout, he writes with ease about the social and historical background of the life of Jesus, but always combining his considerable intellectual knowledge with corresponding insights into human nature which are as true today as they were when he first wrote. On Luke 5:36–9, he comments: 'We should never be afraid of adventurous thought . . . of new methods . . . Any business which had lost as many customers as the Church has would have tried new ways long ago – but the Church tends to resent all that is new.' And on 14:25–33, 'It is possible to be a follower of Jesus without being a disciple'. Comments like that (and not only on that topic) ensure the continuing relevance of Barclay's work. Like the writer of Luke – and indeed of Jesus – he has the knack of cutting through irrelevance to address the most fundamental questions of all: how can we be good, live closer to God and be more spiritual people?

John Drane
University of Aberdeen
2001

INTRODUCTION TO
THE GOSPEL OF LUKE

A Lovely Book and its Author

The Gospel according to St Luke has been called the loveliest book in the world. When once an American asked him if he could recommend a good life of Christ, the theologian James Denney answered, 'Have you tried the one that Luke wrote?' There is a legend that Luke was a skilled painter; there is even a painting of Mary in a Spanish cathedral to this day which purports to be by him. Certainly he had an eye for vivid things. It would not be far wrong to say that the third gospel is the best life of Christ ever written. Tradition has always believed that Luke was the author and we need have no qualms in accepting that tradition. In the ancient world it was the regular thing to attach books to famous names; no one thought it wrong. But Luke was never one of the famous figures of the early Church. If he had not written the gospel no one would have attached it to his name.

Luke was a Gentile; and he has the unique distinction of being the only New Testament writer who was not a Jew. He was a medical man, a doctor by profession (Colossians 4:14), and maybe that very fact gave him the wide sympathy he possessed. It has been said that a minister sees men and women at their best; a lawyer sees them at their worst; and a doctor sees them as they are. Luke saw men and women and loved them all.

The book was written to a man called Theophilus. He is called *most excellent Theophilus* and the title given him is the normal title for a high official in the Roman government. No doubt Luke wrote it to tell an earnest inquirer more about Jesus; and he succeeded in giving Theophilus a picture which must have bound his heart closer to the Jesus of whom he had heard.

The Symbols of the Gospels

Every one of the four gospels was written from a certain point of view. Very often on stained-glass windows the writers of the gospels are pictured; and usually to each there is attached a symbol. The symbols vary but one of the commonest allocations is this.

The emblem of *Mark* is a *man*. Mark is the simplest and most straightforward of the gospels. It has been well said that its characteristic is *realism*. It is the nearest to being a report of Jesus' life.

The emblem of *Matthew* is a *lion*. Matthew was a Jew writing for Jews and he saw in Jesus the Messiah, the lion of the tribe of Judah, the one whom all the prophets had predicted.

The emblem of *John* is the *eagle*. The eagle can fly higher than any other bird. It is said that of all creatures only the eagle can look straight into the sun. John is the theological gospel; its flights of thought are higher than those of any of the others. It is the gospel where the philosopher can find themes to think about for a lifetime and to solve only in eternity.

The symbol of *Luke* is the *calf*. The calf is the animal for sacrifice; and Luke saw in Jesus the sacrifice for all the world. In Luke above all, the barriers are broken down and Jesus is for Jew and Gentile, saint and sinner alike. He is the Saviour of the world. Keeping that in mind, let us now set down the characteristics of this gospel.

2

A Historian's Care

First and foremost, Luke's gospel is an exceedingly careful bit of work. His Greek is notably good. The first four verses are well-nigh the best Greek in the New Testament. In them he claims that his work is the product of the most careful research. His opportunities were ample and his sources must have been good. As the trusted companion of Paul he must have known all the great figures of the Church, and we may be sure that he had them tell their stories to him. For two years he was Paul's companion in imprisonment in Caesarea. In those long days he had every opportunity for study and research and he must have used them well.

An example of Luke's care is the way in which he dates the emergence of John the Baptist. He does so by no fewer than six contemporary datings. 'In the fifteenth year of the reign of Tiberius Caesar [1], Pontius Pilate being governor of Judaea [2], Herod being tetrarch of Galilee [3], and his brother Philip being tetrarch of the region of Ituraea and Trachonitis [4], and Lysanias tetrarch of Abilene [5] in the high priesthood of Annas and Caiaphas [6], the word of God came to John' (Luke 3:1-2, Revised Standard Version). Here is a man who is writing with care and who will be as accurate as it is possible for him to be.

The Gospel for the Gentiles

It is clear that Luke wrote mainly for Gentiles. Theophilus was a Gentile, as was Luke himself, and there is nothing in the gospel that a Gentile could not grasp and understand. (1) As we have seen, Luke begins his dating from the reigning *Roman* emperor and the current *Roman* governor. The *Roman* date comes first. (2) Unlike Matthew, he is not greatly interested in the life of Jesus as the fulfilment of Jewish prophecy. (3) He very seldom quotes the Old Testament at all. (4) He has a habit of giving Hebrew words in their Greek equivalent so that a Greek would understand. Simon the *Cananaean* becomes Simon the *Zealot* (cf. Luke 6:15; Matthew 10:4). *Calvary* is called not by its Hebrew name, *Golgotha*, but by its Greek name, *Kranion.* Both mean *the place of a skull.* He never uses the Jewish term *Rabbi* of Jesus but always a Greek word meaning *Master.* When he is tracing the descent of Jesus, he traces it not to Abraham, the founder of the Jewish race, as Matthew does, but to Adam, the founder of the human race (cf. Matthew 1:2; Luke 3:38).

Because of this Luke is the easiest of all the gospels to read. He was writing, not for Jews, but for people very like ourselves.

The Gospel of Prayer

Luke's gospel is specially the gospel of prayer. At all the great moments of his life, Luke shows us Jesus at prayer. He prayed at his baptism (3:21); before his first collision with the Pharisees (5:16); before he chose the Twelve (6:12); before he questioned his disciples as to who they thought he was; before his first prediction of his own death (9:18); at the transfiguration (9:29); and upon the cross (23:46). Only Luke tells us that Jesus prayed for Peter in his hour of testing (22:32). Only he tells us the prayer parables of the friend at midnight (11:5–13) and the unjust judge (18:1–8). To Luke the unclosed door of prayer was one of the most precious in all the world.

The Gospel of Women

In Palestine the place of women was low. In the Jewish morning prayer a man thanks God that he has not made him 'a Gentile, a slave or a woman'. But Luke gives a very special place to women. The birth narrative is told from Mary's point of view. It is in Luke that we read of Elizabeth, of Anna, of the widow at Nain, of the woman who anointed Jesus' feet in the house of Simon the Pharisee. It is Luke who makes vivid the pictures of Martha and Mary and of Mary Magdalene. It is very likely that Luke was a native of Macedonia where women held a more emancipated position than anywhere else; and that may have something to do with it.

The Gospel of Praise

In Luke the phrase *praising God* occurs oftener than in all the rest of the New Testament put together. This praise reaches its peak in the three great hymns that the Church has sung throughout all her generations – the *Magnificat* (1:46–55), the *Benedictus* (1:68–79) and the *Nunc Dimittis* (2:29–32). There is a radiance in Luke's gospel which is a lovely thing, as if the sheen of heaven had touched the things of earth.

The Universal Gospel

But the outstanding characteristic of Luke is that it is the universal gospel. All the barriers are down; Jesus Christ is for all people without distinction.

(a) The kingdom of heaven is not shut to the Samaritans (9:51–6). Luke alone tells the parable of the Good Samaritan (10:30–7). The one grateful leper is a Samaritan (17:11–19). John can record a saying that the Jews have no dealings with the Samaritans (John 4:9). But Luke refuses to shut the door on anyone.

(b) Luke shows Jesus speaking with approval of Gentiles whom an orthodox Jew would have considered unclean. He shows us Jesus citing the widow of Zarephath and Naaman the Syrian as shining examples (4:25–7). The Roman centurion is praised for the greatness of his faith (7:9). Luke tells us of that great word of Jesus, 'People will come from east and west, from north and south, and will eat in the kingdom of God' (13:29).

(c) Luke is supremely interested in the poor. When Mary brings the offering for her purification it is the offering of the poor (2:24). When Jesus is, as it were, setting out his credentials to the emissaries of John, the climax is, 'The poor have good news brought to them' (7:22). He alone tells the parable of the rich man and the poor man (16:19–31). In Luke's account of the beatitudes the saying of Jesus runs, not, as in Matthew (5:3), 'Blessed are the poor in spirit', but simply, 'Blessed are you who are poor' (Luke 6:20). Luke's gospel has been called 'the gospel of the underdog'. His heart runs out to everyone for whom life is an unequal struggle.

(d) Above all Luke shows Jesus as the friend of outcasts and sinners. He alone tells of the woman who anointed Jesus' feet and bathed them with her tears and wiped them with her hair in the house of Simon the Pharisee (7:36–50); of Zachaeus, the despised tax-gatherer (19:1–10); of the penitent thief (23:43); and he alone has the immortal story of the prodigal son and the loving father (15:11–32). When Matthew tells how Jesus sent his disciples out to preach, he says that Jesus told them not to go to the Samaritans or the Gentiles (Matthew 10:5); but Luke omits that altogether. All four gospel writers quote from Isaiah 40 when they give the message of John the Baptist, 'Prepare the way of the Lord; make straight in the desert a highway for our God'; but only Luke continues the quotation to its triumphant conclusion, 'And all flesh shall see the salvation of God' (Isaiah 40:3–5; Matthew 3:3; Mark 1:3; John 1:23; Luke 3:4, 6). Luke of all the gospel writers sees no limits to the love of God.

The Book Beautiful

As we study this book we must look for these characteristics. Somehow of all the gospel writers one would have liked to meet Luke best of all, for this Gentile doctor with the tremendous vision of the infinite sweep of the love of God must have been a lovely individual. F. W. Faber wrote the lines:

> There's a wideness in God's mercy,
>   Like the wideness of the sea;
> There's a kindness in his justice,
>   Which is more than liberty.
>
> For the love of God is broader
>   Than the measures of man's mind;
> And the heart of the Eternal
>   Is most wonderfully kind.

Luke's gospel is the demonstration that this is true.

LUKE

A HISTORIAN'S INTRODUCTION

Luke 1:1-4

> Since many have set their hands to the task of drawing
> up an account of the events which were completed
> among us, telling the story just as those who were the
> original eyewitnesses and who became the servants
> of the word handed it down to us, I too made up my
> mind to carry out a careful investigation of all things
> from the beginning, and to write to you, Theophilus,
> your excellency, an orderly account of them, so that
> you might have in your mind a full and reliable account
> of the things in which you have been instructed.

LUKE's introduction is unique in the first three gospels because
it is the only place where the author steps out upon the
stage and uses the pronoun 'I'. There are three things to note
in this passage.

(1) It is the best bit of Greek in the New Testament. Luke
uses here the very form of introduction which the great
Greek historians all used. Herodotus begins, 'These are the
researches of Herodotus of Halicarnassus.' A much later
historian, Dionysius of Halicarnassus, tells us at the beginning of his history, 'Before beginning to write I gathered
information, partly from the lips of the most learned men

9

with whom I came into contact, and partly from histories written by Romans of whom they spoke with praise.' So Luke, as he began his story in the most sonorous Greek, followed the highest models he could find.

It is as if Luke said to himself, 'I am writing the greatest story in the world and nothing but the best is good enough for it.' Some of the ancient manuscripts are very beautiful productions, written in silver ink on purple vellum; and often the scribe, when he came to the name of God or of Jesus, wrote it in gold. The story is told of an old workman who, every Friday night, took the newest and shiniest coins out of his pay packet for Sunday's offering in church. The historian, the scribe and the workman were all filled with the same idea – only the best is good enough for Jesus. They always gave their utmost for the highest.

(2) It is most significant that Luke was not satisfied with anyone else's story of Christ. He must have his own. Real religion is never a second-hand thing. It is a personal discovery. Professor Arthur Gossip of Trinity College, Glasgow, used to say that the four gospels were important, but beyond them all came the gospel of personal experience. Luke had to rediscover Jesus Christ for himself.

(3) There is no passage of the Bible which sheds such a floodlight on the doctrine of the inspiration of Scripture. No one would deny that the gospel of Luke is an inspired document; and yet Luke begins by affirming that it is the product of the most careful historical research. God's inspiration does not come to those who sit with folded hands and lazy minds and only wait, but to those who think and seek and search. True inspiration comes when the searching mind joins with the revealing Spirit of God. The word of God is given, but it is given to those who search for it. 'Search and you will find' (Matthew 7:7).

A SON IS PROMISED

Luke 1:5–25

In the time of Herod, the king of Judaea, there was a priest called Zacharias, who belonged to the section of Abia. His wife was also a direct descendant of Aaron and her name was Elizabeth. Both of them were good people before God, for they walked blamelessly in all the commandments and ordinances of the Lord. They had no child because Elizabeth was barren and both of them were far advanced in years. When he was acting as priest before God, when his section was on duty, in accordance with the custom of priestly duty, it fell to him by lot to go into the Temple of the Lord to burn the incense. The whole congregation of the people was praying outside at the hour when incense was offered. The angel of the Lord appeared to him, standing at the right side of the altar of incense. When Zacharias saw him he was deeply moved and awe fell upon him. The angel said to him, 'Do not be afraid, Zacharias, because your request has been heard and your wife Elizabeth will bear you a son and you must call him by the name of John. You will have joy and exultation and many will rejoice at his birth. He will be great in God's sight; he must not drink wine or strong drink and, even from the time he is in his mother's womb, he will be filled with the Holy Spirit. He will turn many sons of Israel to the Lord their God; and he himself will go before his face in the spirit and the power of Elijah, to turn the hearts of the fathers to the children, and the disobedient to the wisdom of the just, to get ready a people prepared for the Lord.' Zacharias said to the angel, 'How will I know that this is going to happen? For I am an old man and my wife is far advanced in years.' 'I am Gabriel,' the angel answered, 'who stands before God, and I have been sent to speak to you and to tell you this good news. And – look you – you will be silent and unable to speak until the day these things happen, because you did not believe my words which will be fulfilled in their own time.' The people were waiting for Zacharias and they were surprised that he was lingering so long in the Temple. When he came out he was not able to speak to them and they realized that he had seen a vision in the Temple. He kept making signs to them but he remained unable to speak. When the days of his time of service were completed he went away to his own home. After these days Elizabeth his wife conceived; and she hid herself for five months. 'This is God's doing for me,' she said, 'when he looked upon me to take away my shame among men.'

ZACHARIAS, the central character in this scene, was a priest. He belonged to the section of Abia. Every direct descendant of Aaron was automatically a priest. That meant that for all ordinary purposes there were far too many priests. They were therefore divided into twenty-four sections. Only at the Passover, at Pentecost and at the Feast of Tabernacles did all the priests serve. For the rest of the year each course served two periods of one week each. Priests who loved their work looked forward to that week of service above all things; it was the highlight of their lives.

A priest might marry only a woman of absolutely pure Jewish lineage. It was specially meritorious to marry a woman who was also a descendant of Aaron, as was Elizabeth, the wife of Zacharias.

There were as many as 20,000 priests altogether and so there were not far short of 1,000 in each section. Within the sections all the duties were allocated by lot. Every morning and evening sacrifice was made for the whole nation. A burnt offering of a male lamb, one year old, without spot or blemish was offered, together with a meat offering of flour and oil and a drink offering of wine. Before the morning sacrifice and after the evening sacrifice incense was burned on the altar of incense so that, as it were, the sacrifices might go up to God wrapped in an envelope of sweet-smelling incense. It was quite possible that many a priest would never have the privilege of burning incense all his life; but if the lot did fall on any priest, that day was the greatest day in all his life, the day he longed for and dreamed of. On this day the lot fell on Zacharias and he would be thrilled to the core of his being.

But in Zacharias' life there was tragedy. He and Elizabeth were childless. The Jewish Rabbis said that seven people were excommunicated from God and the list began, 'A Jew who has no wife, or a Jew who has a wife and who has no child.' Childlessness was a valid ground for divorce. Not unnaturally Zacharias, even on his great day, was thinking of his personal and domestic tragedy and was praying about it. Then the wondrous vision came and the glad message that, even when hope was dead, a son would be born to him.

The incense was burned and the offering made in the inmost court of the Temple, the Court of the Priests. While the sacrifice was being made, the congregation thronged the next court, the Court of the Israelites. It was the privilege of the priest at the evening sacrifice to come to the rail between the two courts after the incense had been burned in order to bless the people. The people marvelled that Zacharias was so long delayed. When he came he could not speak and the people knew that he had seen a vision. So in a wordless daze of joy Zacharias finished his week's duty and went home; and then the message of God came true and Elizabeth knew she was going to have a child.

One thing stands out here. *It was in God's house that God's message came to Zacharias.* We may often wish that a message from God would come to us. In George Bernard Shaw's play, *Saint Joan*, Joan hears voices from God. The Dauphin is annoyed. 'Oh, your voices, your voices,' he said, 'Why don't the voices come to me? I am king not you.' 'They do come to you,' said Joan, 'but you do not hear them. You have not sat in the field in the evening listening for them. When the angelus rings you cross yourself and have done with it; but if you prayed from your heart, and listened to the thrilling of the bells in the air after they stop ringing, you would hear the voices as well as I do.' Joan gave herself the chance to hear God's voice. Zacharias was in the Temple waiting on God. God's voice comes to those who listen for it – as Zacharias did – in God's house.

GOD'S MESSAGE TO MARY

Luke 1:26–38

> In the sixth month the angel Gabriel was sent from God to a town of Galilee called Nazareth, to a maiden who was betrothed to a man called Joseph, who belonged to the house of David. The maiden's name was Mary. He came in to her and said, 'Greetings, most favoured one. The Lord is with you.' She was deeply moved at this word and wondered what a greeting like that could mean. The angel said to her, 'Do not be afraid, Mary, for you have found favour in God's sight. Look you – you will conceive and you will bear a son and you must call him by the name of Jesus. He will be great and he will be called the Son of the Most High; and the Lord God will give him the throne of David his father; and he will rule over the house of Jacob forever, and there

will be no end to his kingdom.' Mary said to the angel, 'How can this be since I do not know a man?' The angel answered, 'The Holy Spirit will come upon you and the Spirit of the Most High will overshadow you, and so the child who will be born will be called holy, the Son of God, and – look you – Elizabeth, too, your kinswoman has also conceived in her old age; and this is now the sixth month for her who is called barren, because there is nothing which is impossible with God.' Mary said, 'I am the Lord's servant. Whatever he says, I accept.' And the angel went away from her.

MARY was betrothed to Joseph. Betrothal lasted for a year and was quite as binding as marriage. It could be dissolved only by divorce. Should the man to whom a girl was betrothed die, in the eyes of the law she was a widow. In the law there occurs the strange-sounding phrase, 'a virgin who is a widow'.

In this passage we are face to face with one of the great controversial doctrines of the Christian faith – the virgin birth. The Church does not insist that we believe in this doctrine. Let us look at the reasons for and against believing in it, and then we may make our own decision.

There are two great reasons for accepting it.

(1) The literal meaning of this passage, and still more of Matthew 1:18–25, clearly is that Jesus was to be born of Mary without a human father.

(2) It is natural to argue that if Jesus was, as we believe, a very special person, he would have a special entry into the world.

Now let us look at the things which may make us wonder if the story of the virgin birth is to be taken as literally as all that.

(1) The genealogies of Jesus both in Luke and in Matthew (Luke 3:23–38; Matthew 1:1–17) trace the genealogy of Jesus through *Joseph*, which is strange if Joseph was not his real father.

(2) When Mary was looking for Jesus on the occasion that he lingered behind in the Temple, she said, 'Your father and I have been searching for you in great anxiety' (Luke 2:48). The name *father* is definitely given by Mary to Joseph.

(3) Repeatedly Jesus is referred to as Joseph's son (Matthew 13:55; John 6:42).

(4) The rest of the New Testament knows nothing of the virgin birth. True, in Galatians 4:4 Paul speaks of Jesus as 'born of woman'. But this is the natural phrase for any human being (cf. Job 14:1, 15:14, 25:4).

But let us ask, 'If we do not take the story of the virgin birth literally, how did it arise?' The Jews had a saying that in the birth of *every* child there are three partners – the father, the mother and the Spirit of God. They believed that no child could ever be born without the Spirit. And it may well be that the New Testament stories of the birth of Jesus are lovely, poetical ways of saying that, even if he had a human father, the Holy Spirit of God was operative in his birth in a unique way.

In this matter we may make our own decision. It may be that we will desire to cling to the literal doctrine of the virgin birth; it may be that we will prefer to think of it as a beautiful way of stressing the presence of the Spirit of God in family life.

Mary's submission is a very lovely thing. 'Whatever God says, I accept.' Mary had learned to forget the world's commonest prayer – 'Your will be *changed*' – and to pray the world's greatest prayer – 'Your will be *done*.'

THE PARADOX OF BLESSEDNESS

Luke 1:39–45

> In those days Mary arose and went eagerly to the hill
> country, to a city of Judah, and went into the house of
> Zacharias and greeted Elizabeth. When Elizabeth heard
> Mary's greeting the babe leaped in her womb and
> Elizabeth was filled with the Holy Spirit, and she lifted
> up her voice with a great cry and said, 'Blessed are you
> among women and blessed is the fruit of your womb.
> Why has this been granted to me – that the mother of
> my Lord should come to me? For – look you – when
> the voice of your greeting came to my ears the babe in
> my womb leaped with exultation. Blessed is she who
> believed that the things spoken to her from the Lord
> would find their fulfilment.'

THIS is a kind of lyrical song on the blessedness of Mary.
Nowhere can we better see the paradox of blessedness than
in her life. To Mary was granted the blessedness of being the
mother of the Son of God. Well might her heart be filled with
a wondering, tremulous joy at so great a privilege. Yet that
very blessedness was to be a sword to pierce her heart. It meant
that some day she would see her son hanging on a cross.

To be chosen by God so often means at one and the same
time a crown of joy and cross of sorrow. The piercing truth is
that God does not choose a person for ease and comfort and
selfish joy but for a task that will take all that head and heart
and hand can bring to it. *God chooses us in order to use us.*
When Joan of Arc knew that her time was short she prayed,
'I shall only last a year; use me as you can.' When that is
realized, the sorrows and hardships that serving God may
bring are not matters for lamentation; they are our glory, for
all is suffered for God.

17

When Richard Cameron, the Covenanter, was caught by the dragoons they killed him. He had very beautiful hands and they cut them off and sent them to his father with a message asking if he recognized them. 'They are my son's,' he said, 'my own dear son's. Good is the will of the Lord who can never wrong me or mine.' The shadows of life were lit by the sense that they, too, were in the plan of God. A great Spanish saint prayed for his people, 'May God deny you peace and give you glory.' One great preacher said, 'Jesus Christ came not to make life easy but to make men great.'

It is the paradox of blessedness that it confers on a person at one and the same time the greatest joy and the greatest task in all the world.

A WONDROUS HYMN

Luke 1:46–56

> And Mary said, 'My soul magnifies the Lord, and my spirit has exulted in God, my Saviour, because he looked graciously on the humble estate of his servant. For – look you – from now on all generations shall call me blessed, for the Mighty One has done great things for me and his name is holy. His mercy is from generation to generation to those who fear him. He demonstrates his power with his arm. He scatters the proud in the plans of their hearts. He casts down the mighty from their seats of power. He exalts the humble. He fills those who are hungry with good things and he sends away empty those who are rich. He has helped Israel, his son, in that he has remembered his mercy – as he said to our fathers that he would – to Abraham and to his descendants forever.'

HERE we have a passage which has become one of the great hymns of the Church – the *Magnificat*. It is steeped in the Old Testament; and is closely related to Hannah's song of praise in 1 Samuel 2:1–10. It has been said that religion is the opiate of the people; but it has also been said that the *Magnificat* is the most revolutionary document in the world.

It speaks of three of the revolutions of God.

(1) *He scatters the proud in the plans of their hearts.* That is a *moral* revolution. Christianity is the death of pride. Why? Because if people set their lives beside that of Christ, it tears away the last vestiges of their pride.

Sometimes something happens to us which with a vivid, revealing light shames us. The American writer O. Henry has a short story about a boy who was brought up in a village. In school he used to sit beside a girl and they were fond of each other. He went to the city and fell into evil ways. He became a pickpocket and a petty thief. One day he snatched an old lady's purse. It was clever work and he was pleased. And then he saw coming down the street the girl whom he used to know, still sweet with the radiance of innocence. Suddenly he saw himself for the cheap, vile thing he was. Burning with shame, he leaned his head against the cool iron of a lamp standard. 'God,' he said, 'I wish I could die.' He saw himself.

Christ enables us to see ourselves. It is the death-blow to pride. The moral revolution has begun.

(2) *He casts down the mighty – he exalts the humble.* That is a *social* revolution. Christianity puts an end to the world's labels and prestige.

Muretus was a wandering scholar of the middle ages. He was poor. In an Italian town he became ill and was taken to a hospital for waifs and strays. The doctors were discussing his case in Latin, never dreaming he could understand. They suggested that since he was such a worthless wanderer they might use him for medical experiments. He looked up and answered them in their own learned tongue, 'Call no man worthless for whom Christ died.'

When we have realized what Christ did for each and every one of us, it is no longer possible to regard anyone as being beneath us. The social grades are gone.

(3) *He has filled those who are hungry – those who are rich he has sent empty away.* That is an *economic* revolution. A non-Christian society is an acquisitive society where people are out for as much as they can get. A Christian society is a society where no one dares to have too much while others have too little, where everyone must get only to give away.

There is loveliness in the *Magnificat* but in that loveliness there is dynamite. Christianity brings about a revolution in individuals and revolution in the world.

HIS NAME IS JOHN

Luke 1:57–66

When Elizabeth's time to bear the child was completed she brought forth a son. When her neighbours and kinsfolk heard that the Lord had shown great mercy to her they rejoiced with her. On the eighth day they went to circumcise the child and it was their intention to call him Zacharias after his father. But his mother said, 'No; he must be called John.' They said to her, 'There is no one in your connection who is called by this name.' They asked his father by signs by what name he wished him to be called. He asked for a writing tablet and wrote, 'John is his name.' Immediately his mouth was opened and his tongue was loosed and he kept on praising God. And great awe fell upon all the neighbours, and all

these events were talked about in all the hill country of
Judaea; and all those who heard them kept them in their
hearts and said, 'What will this child turn out to be, for
the hand of the Lord is with him?'

In Palestine the birth of a boy was an occasion of great joy.
When the time of the birth was near at hand, friends and
local musicians gathered near the house. When the birth was
announced and it was a boy, the musicians broke into music
and song, and there was universal congratulation and rejoic-
ing. If it was a girl the musicians went silently and regretfully
away! There was a saying, 'The birth of a male child causes
universal joy, but the birth of a female child causes universal
sorrow.' So in Elizabeth's house there was double joy. At last
she had a child and that child was a son.

On the eighth day the boy was circumcised and received
his name. Girls could be named any time within thirty days
of their birth. In Palestine names were descriptive. They
sometimes described a circumstance attending the birth as
Esau and *Jacob* do (Genesis 25:25-6). They sometimes
described the child. *Laban*, for instance, means *white* or
blonde. Sometimes the child received the parental name.
Often the name described the parents' joy. *Saul* and *Samuel*,
for instance, both mean *asked for*. Sometimes the name was
a declaration of the parents' faith. *Elijah*, for instance, means
Yahweh is my God. Thus in a time of Baal worship Elijah's
parents asserted their faith in the true God.

Elizabeth, to the neighbours' surprise, said that her son
must be called John and Zacharias indicated that that was
also his desire. *John* is a shorter form of the name *Jehohanan*,
which means *Yahweh's gift* or *God is gracious.* It was
the name which God had ordered to be given to the child
and it described the parents' gratitude for an unexpected
joy.

21

It was the question of the neighbours and of all who had heard the amazing story, 'What will this child turn out to be?' Every child is a bundle of possibilities. There was an old Latin teacher who always bowed gravely to his class before he taught them. When he was asked why, he answered, 'Because you never know what one of these pupils will turn out to be.' The entry of a child into a family is two things. First, it is the greatest privilege which life can offer a husband and wife. It is something for which to thank God. Second, it is one of life's supreme responsibilities, for that child is a bundle of possibilities, and on parents and teachers depends how these possibilities will or will not be realized.

A FATHER'S JOY

Luke 1:67–80

His father Zacharias was filled with the Holy Spirit and prophesied like this: 'Blessed be the Lord, the God of Israel, because he has graciously visited his people and wrought deliverance for them. He has raised the horn of salvation for us in the house of David, his servant – as long ago he said he would through the mouth of his holy prophets – even deliverance from our enemies and from the hand of all who hate us, in that he has shown mercy to us as he did to our fathers and has remembered his holy covenant, the pledge which he gave to Abraham our father, to grant to us that we, being delivered from the hands of our enemies, should fearlessly serve him, in holiness and righteousness before him, all our days. And you, child, shall be called the prophet of the Most High; for you will walk before the Lord to prepare his ways, in order to give the knowledge of salvation to his people together with forgiveness of their sins, through

the mercy of our God, in which the dawn from on high
has graciously visited us, to shine upon those who sit in
darkness and in the shadow of death, and to direct our
feet in the way of peace.'

And the child grew and was strengthened by the
Spirit; and he lived in the desert places until the day
when he was displayed to Israel.

ZACHARIAS had a great vision for his son. He thought of him
as the prophet and the forerunner who would prepare the way
of the Lord. All devout Jews hoped and longed for the day
when the Messiah, God's anointed king, would come. Most
of them believed that, before he came, a forerunner would
announce his coming and prepare his way. The usual belief
was that Elijah would return to do so (Malachi 4:5). Zacharias
saw in his son the one who would prepare the way for the
coming of God's king.

Verses 75-7 give a great picture of the steps of the Christian
way.

(1) There is *preparation.* All life is a preparation to lead
us to Christ. When Sir Walter Scott was young his aim was to
be a soldier. An accident made him slightly lame and that
dream had to be abandoned. He took to reading the old
Scottish histories and romances and so became the master
novelist. An old man said of him, 'He was makin' himsell a'
the time; but he didna ken maybe what he was about till years
had passed.' In life God is working all things together to bring
us to Christ.

(2) There is *knowledge.* It is the simple fact that there
was no real understanding of what God was like until Jesus
came. The Greeks thought of a passionless God, beyond
all joy and sorrow, looking on humanity in calm unmoved
detachment – no help there. Jews thought of a demanding
God, whose name was law and whose function was that of

judge – nothing but fear there. Jesus came to tell that God was love, and in staggered amazement people said, 'We never knew that God was like that.' One of the great functions of the incarnation was to bring to men and women the knowledge of God.

(3) There is *forgiveness*. We must be clear about one thing regarding forgiveness. It is not so much the remission of penalty as the restoration of a relationship. Nothing can deliver us from certain consequences of our sins; the clock cannot be put back; but estrangement from God is turned to friendship, the distant God has become near and the God we feared has become the lover of human souls.

(4) There is *walking* in the ways of peace. *Peace* in Hebrew does not mean merely freedom from trouble; it means all that makes for our highest good; and through Christ we are enabled to walk in the ways that lead to everything that means life, and no longer to all that means death.

JOURNEY TO BETHLEHEM

Luke 2:1–7

In these days a decree went out from Caesar Augustus that a census should be taken of all the world. The census first took place when Quirinius was governor of Syria; and everyone went to enrol himself, each man to his own town. So Joseph went up from Galilee, from the town of Nazareth, to Judaea, to David's town, which is called Bethlehem, because he belonged to the house and the line of David, to enrol himself with Mary who was betrothed to him and she was with child. When they arrived there her time to bear the child was completed; and she bore her first-born son and wrapped him in swaddling clothes and laid him in a manger

because there was no room for them in the place where
they had meant to lodge.

I<small>N</small> the Roman Empire periodical censuses were taken with
the double object of assessing taxation and of discovering
those who were liable for compulsory military service. The
Jews were exempt from military service, and, therefore, in
Palestine a census would be predominantly for taxation
purposes. Regarding these censuses, we have definite information as to what happened in Egypt; and almost certainly
what happened in Egypt happened in Syria, too, and Judaea
was part of the province of Syria. The information we have
comes from actual census documents written on papyrus and
then discovered in the dust-heaps of Egyptian towns and
villages and in the sands of the desert.

Such censuses were taken every fourteen years. And from
A<small>D</small> 20 until about A<small>D</small> 270 we possess actual documents from
every census taken. If the fourteen-year cycle held good in
Syria this census must have been in 8 B<small>C</small> and that was the
year in which Jesus was born. It may be that Luke has
made one slight mistake. Quirinius did not actually become
governor of Syria until A<small>D</small> 6; but he held an official post
previously in those regions from 10 B<small>C</small> until 7 B<small>C</small> and it was
during that first period that this census must have been taken.

Critics used to question the fact that every man had to go
to his own city to be enrolled; but here is an actual government
edict from Egypt:

> Gaius Vibius Maximus, Prefect of Egypt orders: 'Seeing
> that the time has come for the house-to-house census, it
> is necessary to compel all those who for any cause what-
> soever are residing outside their districts to return to
> their own homes, that they may both carry out the
> regular order of the census, and may also diligently
> attend to the cultivation of their allotments.'

If that was the case in Egypt, it may well be that in Judaea, where the old tribal ancestries still held good, men had to go to the headquarters of their tribe. Here is an instance where further knowledge has shown the accuracy of the New Testament.

The journey from Nazareth to Bethlehem was eighty miles. The accommodation for travellers was most primitive. The eastern khan was like a series of stalls opening off a common courtyard. Travellers brought their own food; all that the innkeeper provided was fodder for the animals and a fire to cook. The town was crowded and there was no room for Joseph and Mary. So it was in the common courtyard that Mary's child was born. Swaddling clothes consisted of a square of cloth with a long bandage-like strip coming diagonally off from one corner. The child was first wrapped in the square of cloth and then the long strip was wound round and round about him. The word translated *manger* means a place where animals feed; and therefore it can be either the stable or the manger which is meant.

That there was no room in the inn was symbolic of what was to happen to Jesus. The only place where there was room for him was on a cross. He sought an entry to the overcrowded hearts of those around him; he could not find it; and still his search – and his rejection – go on.

SHEPHERDS AND ANGELS

Luke 2:8–20

> In this country there were shepherds who were in the fields, keeping watch over their flock by night. An angel of the Lord appeared to them and the glory of the Lord shone round about them and they were much afraid.

The angel said to them, 'Do not be afraid; for – look you – I am bringing you good news of great joy, which will be to every people, for today a Saviour has been born for you, in David's town, who is Christ the Lord. You will recognize him by this sign. You will find the babe wrapped in swaddling clothes and laid in a manger.' And suddenly with the angel there was a crowd of heaven's host, praising God and saying, 'In the highest heights glory to God; and on earth peace to the men whose welfare he ever seeks.' When the angels had left them and gone away to heaven, the shepherds said to each other, 'Come! Let us go across to Bethlehem and let us see this thing which has happened which the Lord has made known to us.' So they hurried on and they discovered Mary and Joseph, and the babe lying in a manger. When they had seen him they told everyone about the word which had been spoken to them about this child; and all who heard were amazed at what was told them by the shepherds. But Mary stored up these things in her memory and in her heart kept wondering what they meant. So the shepherds returned glorifying and praising God for all that they had seen, just as it had been told to them.

It is a wonderful thing that the story should tell that the first announcement of God came to some shepherds. Shepherds were despised by the orthodox good people of the day. They were quite unable to keep the details of the ceremonial law; they could not observe all the meticulous handwashings and rules and regulations. Their flocks made constant demands on them; and so the orthodox looked down on them. It was to simple men of the fields that God's message first came.

But these were in all likelihood very special shepherds. We have already seen how in the Temple, morning and evening, an unblemished lamb was offered as a sacrifice to

God. To see that the supply of perfect offerings was always available the Temple authorities had their own private sheep flocks; and we know that these flocks were pastured near Bethlehem. It is most likely that these shepherds were in charge of the flocks from which the Temple offerings were chosen. It is a lovely thought that the shepherds who looked after the Temple lambs were the first to see the Lamb of God who takes away the sin of the world.

We have already seen that when a boy was born, the local musicians congregated at the house to greet him with simple music. Jesus was born in a stable in Bethlehem and therefore that ceremony could not be carried out. It is lovely to think that the minstrelsy of heaven took the place of the minstrelsy of earth, and angels sang the songs for Jesus that the earthly singers could not sing.

All through these readings we must have been thinking of the rough simplicity of the birth of the Son of God. We might have expected that, if he had to be born into this world at all, it would be in a palace or a mansion. There was a European monarch who worried his court by often disappearing and walking incognito among his people. When he was asked not to do so for security's sake, he answered, 'I cannot rule my people unless I know how they live.' It is the great thought of the Christian faith that we have a God who knows the life we live because he too lived it and claimed no special advantage over ordinary people.

THE ANCIENT CEREMONIES ARE OBSERVED

Luke 2:21–4

When the eight days necessarily prior to circumcision had elapsed, he was called by the name of Jesus, the

name by which he had been called by the angel before
he had been conceived in the womb. When the time
which, according to the law of Moses, must precede
the ceremony of purification had elapsed, they brought
him up to Jerusalem to present him to the Lord (in
accordance with the regulation in the Lord's law, 'Every
male that opens the womb shall be called holy to the
Lord') and to make the sacrifice which the regulation
in the Lord's law lays down, that is, a pair of doves or
two young pigeons.

In this passage we see Jesus undergoing three ancient ceremonies which every Jewish boy had to undergo.

(1) *Circumcision.* Every Jewish boy was circumcised on
the eighth day after his birth. So sacred was that ceremony
that it could be carried out even on a Sabbath when the law
forbade almost every other act which was not absolutely
essential; and on that day a boy received his name.

(2) *The Redemption of the First-born.* According to the
law (Exodus 13:2) every first-born male, both of human
beings and of cattle, was sacred to God. That law may have
been a recognition of the gracious power of God in giving
human life, or it may even have been a relic of the day when
children were sacrificed to the gods. Clearly if it had been
carried out literally, life would have been disrupted. There
was therefore a ceremony called the Redemption of the First-
born (Numbers 18:16). It is laid down that for the sum of five
shekels – almost a month's pay – parents could, as it were,
buy back their son from God. The sum had to be paid to the
priests. It could not be paid sooner than thirty-one days
after the birth of the child and it might not be long delayed
after that.

(3) *The Purification after Childbirth.* When a woman had
borne a child, if it was a boy, she was unclean for forty days,

if it was a girl, for eighty days. She could go about her household and her daily business but she could not enter the Temple
or share in any religious ceremony (Leviticus 12). At the end
of that time she had to bring to the Temple a lamb for a burnt
offering and a young pigeon for a sin offering. That was a
somewhat expensive sacrifice, and so the law laid it down
(Leviticus 12:8) that if she could not afford the lamb she
might bring another pigeon. The offering of the two pigeons
instead of the lamb and the pigeon was technically called *the
Offering of the Poor*. It was the offering of the poor which
Mary brought. Again we see that it was into an ordinary home
that Jesus was born, a home where there were no luxuries, a
home where the cost of everything had to be considered
carefully, a home where the members of the family knew all
about the difficulties of making a living and the haunting
insecurity of life. When life is worrying for us we must
remember that Jesus knew what the difficulties of making
ends meet can be.

These three ceremonies are strange old ceremonies; but
all three have at the back of them the conviction that a child
is a gift of God. The Stoics used to say that a child was not
given to a parent but only *lent*. Of all God's gifts there is
none for which we shall be so answerable as the gift of a
child.

A DREAM REALIZED

Luke 2:25–35

> Now – look you – there was a man in Jerusalem called
> Simeon. This man was good and pious. He was waiting
> for the comforting of Israel and the Holy Spirit was
> upon him. He had received a message from the Holy

Spirit that he would not see death until he had seen the
Lord's Anointed One. So he came in the Spirit to the
Temple precincts. When his parents brought in the child
Jesus, to do regarding him the customary ceremonies
laid down by the law, he took him into his arms and
blessed God and said, 'Now O Lord, as you said, let
your servant depart in peace, because my eyes have seen
your instrument of salvation, which you have prepared
before all the people, a light to bring your revelation to
the Gentiles, and the glory of your people Israel.' His
father and mother were amazed at what was said about
him. Simeon blessed them and said to Mary his mother,
'Look you, this child is appointed to be the cause
whereby many in Israel will fall and many rise and for
a sign which will meet with much opposition. As for
you – a sword will pierce your soul – and all this will
happen that the inner thoughts of many hearts may be
revealed.'

THE Jews regarded their own nation as the chosen people,
but they saw quite clearly that by human means their nation
could never attain to the supreme world greatness which they
believed their destiny involved. By far the greater number of
them believed that because the Jews were the chosen people
they were bound some day to become masters of the world
and lords of all the nations. To bring in that day some believed
that some great, celestial champion would descend upon
the earth; some believed that there would arise another king
of David's line and that all the old glories would revive; some
believed that God himself would break directly into history
by supernatural means. But in contrast to all that, there were
a few people who were known as *the Quiet in the Land.*
They had no dreams of violence and of power and of armies
with banners; they believed in a life of constant prayer and
quiet watchfulness until God should come. All their lives

they waited quietly and patiently upon God. Simeon was like that; in prayer, in worship, in humble and faithful expectation he was waiting for the day when God would comfort his people. God had promised him through the Holy Spirit that his life would not end before he had seen God's own anointed king. In the baby Jesus he recognized that king and was glad. Now he was ready to depart in peace and his words have become the *Nunc Dimittis,* another of the great and precious hymns of the Church.

In verse 34 Simeon gives a kind of summary of the work and fate of Jesus.

(1) He will be the cause whereby *many will fall.* This is a strange and a hard saying but it is true. It is not so much God who judges us; we judge ourselves; and our judgment is our reaction to Jesus Christ. If, when we are confronted with that goodness and that loveliness, our heart runs out in answering love, we are within the kingdom. If, when so confronted, we remain coldly unmoved or actively hostile, we are condemned. There is a great refusal just as there is a great acceptance.

(2) He will be the cause whereby *many will rise.* Long ago Seneca said that what people needed above all was a hand let down to lift them up. It is the hand of Jesus which lifts us out of the old life and into the new, out of the sin into the goodness, out of the shame into the glory.

(3) He will meet with *much opposition.* Towards Jesus Christ there can be no neutrality. We either surrender to him or are at war with him. And it is the tragedy of life that our pride often keeps us from making that surrender which leads to victory.

A LOVELY OLD AGE

Luke 2:36–40

There was a prophetess called Anna. She was the
daughter of Phanuel and she belonged to the tribe of
Asher. She was far advanced in years. She had lived
with her husband ever since seven years after she came
to womanhood; and now she was a widow of eighty-four
years of age. She never left the Temple and day and
night she worshipped with fastings and with prayers.
At that very time she came up and she began to give
thanks to God and she kept speaking about him to all
those who were waiting expectantly for the deliverance
of Jerusalem. When they had completed everything
which the Lord's law lays down they returned to Galilee
to their own town of Nazareth. And the child grew
bigger and stronger and he was filled with wisdom, and
God's grace was on him.

ANNA, too, was one of the Quiet in the Land. We know nothing
about her except what these verses tell, but even in this brief
compass Luke has drawn us a complete character sketch.

(1) Anna was a widow. *She had known sorrow and she had
not grown bitter.* Sorrow can do one of two things to us. It can
make us hard, bitter, resentful, rebellious against God. Or it
can make us kinder, softer, more sympathetic. It can rob us of
our faith; or it can root faith ever deeper. It all depends how
we think of God. If we think of him as a tyrant we will resent
him. If we think of him as Father we too will be sure that

> A Father's hand will never cause
> His child a needless tear.

(2) She was eighty-four years of age. *She was old and she
had never ceased to hope.* Age can take away the bloom and

33

the strength of our bodies; but age can do worse – the years can take away the life of our hearts until the hopes that once we cherished die and we become dully content and grimly resigned to things as they are. Again it all depends on how we think of God. If we think of him as distant and detached we may well despair; but if we think of him as intimately connected with life, as having his hand on the helm, we too will be sure that the best is yet to be and the years will never kill our hope.

How then did Anna come to be as she was?

(1) *She never ceased to worship.* She spent her life in God's house with God's people. God gave us his Church to be our mother in the faith. We rob ourselves of a priceless treasure when we neglect to be one with his worshipping people.

(2) *She never ceased to pray.* Public worship is great; but private worship is also great. As someone has truly said, 'They pray best together who first pray alone.' The years had left Anna without bitterness and in unshakable hope because day by day she kept her contact with him who is the source of strength and in whose strength our weakness is made perfect.

THE DAWNING REALIZATION

Luke 2:41–52

> Every year his parents used to go to Jerusalem for the feast of the Passover. When he was twelve years of age, they went up according to the custom of the feast, and when they had completed the days of the feast and returned home, the child Jesus stayed on in Jerusalem. His parents were not aware of this. They thought he was in the caravan and when they had gone a day's

journey they looked for him among their kinsfolk and acquaintances. When they did not find him they turned back to Jerusalem, looking for him all the time. After three days they found him in the Temple precincts, sitting in the middle of the Rabbis, listening to them and asking them questions. All who were listening were astonished at his understanding and at his answers. When they saw him they were amazed. His mother said to him, 'Child, why did you do this to us? Look you, your father and I have been looking for you and we have been very worried.' He said to them, 'Why were you looking for me? Did you not know that I was bound to be in my Father's house?' They did not understand the meaning of what he said to them. So he came home with them and went to Nazareth and he was obedient to them. His mother kept all these things in her heart. And Jesus grew wise and grew bigger and increased in favour with God and man.

THIS is a supremely important passage in the gospel story. It was laid down by law that every adult male Jew who lived within fifteen miles of Jerusalem must attend the Passover. In point of fact it was the aim of every Jew in all the world at least once in a lifetime to attend that feast.

A Jewish boy became a man when he was twelve years of age. Then he became *a son of the law* and had to take the obligations of the law upon him. So at twelve Jesus for the first time went to the Passover. We may well imagine how the holy city and the Temple and the sacred ritual fascinated him.

When his parents returned he lingered behind. It was not through carelessness that they did not miss him. Usually the women in a caravan started out much earlier than the men for they travelled more slowly. The men started later and travelled faster and the two sections would not meet until the evening encampment was reached. It was Jesus' first Passover. No doubt Joseph thought he was with Mary, Mary thought that he was with Joseph and not until the evening camp did they miss him.

They returned to Jerusalem to search for him. For the Passover season it was the custom for the Sanhedrin to meet in public in the Temple court to discuss, in the presence of all who would listen, religious and theological questions. It was there they found Jesus. We must not think of it as a scene where a precocious boy was dominating a crowd of his seniors. *Hearing and asking questions* is the regular Jewish phrase for a student learning from his teachers. Jesus was listening to the discussions and eagerly searching for knowledge like an avid student.

And now comes one of the key passages in the life of Jesus. '*Your father* and I,' said Mary, 'have been looking for you anxiously.' 'Did you not know,' said Jesus, 'that I must be in *my Father's* house?' See how very gently but very definitely Jesus takes the name *father* from Joseph and gives it to God. At some time Jesus must have discovered his own unique relationship to God. He cannot have known it when he was a child in the manger and a baby at his mother's breast or he would be a freak. As the years went on he must have had thoughts; and then at this first Passover, with manhood dawning, there came in a sudden blaze of realization the consciousness that he was in a unique sense the Son of God.

Here we have the story of the day when Jesus discovered who he was. And mark this – the discovery did not make him proud. It did not make him look down on his humble parents, the gentle Mary and the hard-working Joseph. He went home and *he was obedient to them*. The fact that he was God's Son made him the perfect son of his human parents. Truly godly people do not despise earthly ties; rather because they belong to God they discharge human duties with supreme fidelity.

THE COURIER OF THE KING

Luke 3:1-6

In the fifteenth year of the reign of Tiberius Caesar, when Pontius Pilate was governor of Judaea, and when Herod was tetrarch of Galilee, his brother Philip tetrarch of Ituraea and the district of Trachonitis, and Lysanias tetrarch of Abilene, in the high priesthood of Annas and Caiaphas, the word of God came to John, the son of Zacharias, when he was in the desert. So he came into the territory around Jordan, preaching a baptism of repentance whereby sins might be forgiven – as it stands written in the book of the words of Isaiah, the prophet. 'The voice of one crying in the wilderness, "Get ready the road of the Lord, make his paths straight; every ravine shall be filled up; every mountain and hill will be made low; the twisted places will be made into straight roads and the rough places into smooth; and all flesh shall see God's instrument of salvation."'

To Luke the emergence of John the Baptist was one of the hinges on which history turned. So much so is that the case that he dates it in no fewer than six different ways.

(1) Tiberius was the successor of Augustus and therefore the second of the Roman emperors. As early as AD 11 or 12 Augustus had made him his colleague in the imperial power but he did not become sole emperor until AD 14. The fifteenth year of his reign would therefore be AD 28-9. Luke begins by setting the emergence of John against a world background, the background of the Roman Empire.

(2) The next three dates Luke gives are connected with the political organization of Palestine. The title tetrarch literally means *governor of a fourth part*. In such provinces as Thessaly and Galatia, which were divided into four sections or areas, the governor of each part was known as a *tetrarch*; but later the word widened its meaning and came to mean the governor of any part. Herod the Great died in 4 BC after a reign of about forty years. He divided his kingdom between three of his sons and in the first instance the Romans approved the decision.

(a) To Herod Antipas were left Galilee and Peraea. He reigned from 4 BC to AD 39 and therefore Jesus' life was lived in Herod's reign and very largely in Herod's dominions in Galilee.

(b) To Herod Philip were left Ituraea and Trachonitis. He reigned from 4 BC to AD 33. Caesarea Philippi was called after him and was actually built by him.

(c) To Archelaus were left Judaea, Samaria and Edom. He was a thoroughly bad king. The Jews in the end actually petitioned Rome for his removal; and Rome, impatient of the continual troubles in Judaea, installed a procurator or governor. That is how the Romans came directly to rule Judaea. At this time Pilate, who was in power from AD 25 until AD 37, was the Roman governor. So in this one sentence Luke gives us a panoramic view of the division of the kingdom which had once belonged to Herod the Great.

(3) Of Lysanias we know practically nothing.

(4) Having dealt with the world situation and the Palestinian political situation, Luke turns to the religious situation and dates John's emergence as being in the priesthood of Annas and Caiaphas. There never at any time were two high priests at the one time. What then does Luke mean by giving these two names? The high priest was at one and

the same time the civil and the religious head of the community. In the old days the office of high priest had been hereditary and for life. But with the coming of the Romans the office was the object of all kinds of intrigue. The result was that between 37 BC and AD 26 there were no fewer than twenty-eight different high priests. Now Annas was actually high priest from AD 7 until AD 14. He was therefore at this time out of office; but he was succeeded by no fewer than four of his sons and Caiaphas was his son-in-law. Therefore, although Caiaphas was the reigning high priest, Annas was the power behind the throne. That is in fact why Jesus was brought first to him after his arrest (John 18:13) although at that time he was not in office. Luke associates his name with Caiaphas because, although Caiaphas was the actual high priest, Annas was still the most influential priestly figure in the land.

Verses 4-6 are a quotation from Isaiah 40:3-5. When a king proposed to tour a part of his dominions in this region, he sent a courier before him to tell the people to prepare the roads. So John is regarded as the courier of the King. But the preparation on which he insisted was a preparation of heart and of life. 'The King is coming,' he said. 'Mend, not your roads, but your lives.' There is laid on every one of us the duty to make life fit for the King to see.

JOHN'S SUMMONS TO REPENTANCE

Luke 3:7-18

> To the crowds who came out to be baptized by him, John used to say, 'You spawn of vipers, who put it into your heads to flee from the coming wrath? Produce fruits to match repentance. Do not begin to say among

39

yourselves, "We have Abraham as our father." I tell
you that God is able to raise up children to Abraham
from these stones. Even now the axe is laid at the root
of the trees. Every tree that does not bear good fruit is
cut down and thrown into the fire.' The crowds asked
him, 'What are we to do?' He answered them, 'Let him
who has two robes give one to one who has none and
let him who has food do likewise.' The tax-collectors
came to be baptized and said to him, 'Teacher, what are
we to do?' He said to them, 'Exact no more beyond
what your instructions lay down.' The soldiers, too,
asked him, 'What are we to do?' He said to them, 'Treat
no man with violence and do not play the false informer
and be content with your pay.'

When the people were in a state of expectancy and
when they were all wondering in their hearts about John,
as to whether he could be the Anointed One, John
answered them all, 'I baptize you with water, but the
One who is stronger than I is coming, the latchet of
whose sandals I am not worthy to unloose. He will
baptize you with the Holy Spirit and with fire. His
winnowing fan is in his hand to cleanse his threshing-
floor and he will gather the corn into his store but he
will burn the chaff with unquenchable fire.'

HERE we have the message of John to the people. Nowhere
does the difference between John and Jesus stand out so
clearly because, whatever the message of John was, it was
not a gospel. It was not good news; it was news of terror.

John had lived in the desert. The face of the desert was
covered with stubble and brushwood, as dry as tinder. Sometimes a spark set the face of the desert alight and out from
their crannies came the vipers, scurrying in terror from the
menacing flames. It was to them John likened the people who
came to be baptized.

The Jews had not the slightest doubt that in God's economy there was a favoured-nation clause. They held that God would judge other nations with one standard but the Jews with another. They, in fact, held that they were safe from judgment simply by virtue of the fact that they were Jewish. Children of Abraham were exempt from judgment. John told them that racial privilege meant nothing; that life not lineage was God's standard of judgment.

There are three outstanding things about John's message.

(1) It began by demanding that people should share with one another. It was a social gospel which laid it down that God will never absolve anyone who is content to have too much while others have too little.

(2) It ordered people, not to leave their jobs, but to work out their own salvation by doing those jobs as they should be done. Let the tax-collector be a good tax-collector; let the soldier be a good soldier. People had a duty to serve God where God had set them.

In the words of a spiritual:

> There's a king and captain high,
> And he's coming by and by,
> And he'll find me hoeing cotton when he comes,
> You can hear his legions charging in the regions of
>   the sky,
> And he'll find me hoeing cotton when he comes.
> There's a man they thrust aside,
> Who was tortured till he died,
> And he'll find me hoeing cotton when he comes.
>
> He was hated and rejected,
> He was scorned and crucified,
> And he'll find me hoeing cotton when he comes.
> When he comes! when he comes!
> He'll be crowned by saints and angels when he comes,

> They'll be shouting out Hosanna! to the man that
>   men denied,
> And I'll kneel among my cotton when he comes.

It was John's conviction that there is nowhere we can serve God better than in our daily work.

(3) John was quite sure that he himself was only the forerunner. The King was still to come and with him would come judgment. The winnowing fan was a great flat wooden shovel; with it the grain was tossed into the air, the heavy grain fell to the ground and the chaff was blown away. And just as the chaff was separated from the grain so the King would separate the good and bad.

So John painted a picture of judgment, but it was a judgment which could be met with confidence only by those who had discharged their duty to their neighbour and who had faithfully done their day's work.

John was one of the world's supremely effective preachers. Once, the great preacher Thomas Chalmers was congratulated on a sermon. 'Yes,' he said, *'but what did it do?'* It is clear that John preached for action and produced it. He did not deal in theological subtleties but in life.

THE ARREST OF JOHN

Luke 3:19–20

> So then, urging the people with many other pleas, John preached the gospel to them. But, when Herod the tetrarch was rebuked by him concerning the matter of Herodias, his brother's wife, and concerning all the other wicked things he had done, he added this also to them all – he shut up John in prison.

JOHN was so plain and blunt a preacher of righteousness that he was bound to run into trouble. In the end Herod arrested him. The Jewish historian Josephus says that the reason for the arrest was that Herod 'feared lest the great influence John had over the people might put it in his power and inclination to raise a rebellion; for they seemed ready to do anything he should advise'. That is no doubt true but the New Testament writers give a much more personal and immediate cause. Herod Antipas had married Herodias and John rebuked him for it.

The relationships involved in this marriage are extremely complicated. Herod the Great was a much-married man. Herod Antipas, who married Herodias and who arrested John, was the son of Herod the Great by a woman called Malthake. Herodias herself was the daughter of Aristobulus, who was the son of Herod the Great by Mariamne, commonly called the Hasmonean. As we have seen, Herod had divided up his realm between Archelaus, Herod Antipas and Herod Philip. He had another son, also called Herod, who was his son by another Mariamne, the daughter of a high priest. This Herod had no share in his father's realms, and lived as a private citizen in Rome; he married Herodias. He was in fact her half-uncle, because her father, Aristobulus, and he were both sons of Herod by different wives. Herod Antipas, on a visit to Rome, seduced her from his half-brother and married her. She was at one and the same time his sister-in-law, because she was married to his half-brother, and his niece because she was the daughter of Aristobulus, another half-brother.

The whole proceeding was utterly revolting to Jewish opinion and quite contrary to Jewish law, and indeed improper by any standards. It was a dangerous thing to rebuke a tyrant, but John did so. The result was that he was arrested and imprisoned in the dungeon castle of Machaerus on the shores of the Dead Sea. There could be no greater cruelty than to take this child of the desert and shut him up in a dungeon cell. Ultimately he was beheaded to gratify the resentment of Herodias (Matthew 14:5–12; Mark 6:17–29).

It is always dangerous to speak the truth; and yet although anyone who sides with the truth may be imprisoned or even executed, in the final count that person is the victor. Once the Earl of Morton, who was regent of Scotland, threatened Andrew Melville, the reformer. 'There will never,' he said menacingly, 'be quietness in this country till half a dozen of you be hanged or banished.' Melville answered him, 'Tush! sir, threaten not your courtiers in that fashion. It is the same to me whether I rot in the air or in the ground . . . God be glorified, it will not lie in your power to hang nor exile his truth.' Plato once said that the wise man will always choose to suffer wrong rather than to do wrong. We need only ask ourselves whether in the last analysis and at the final judgment we would prefer to be Herod Antipas or John the Baptist.

THE HOUR STRIKES FOR JESUS

Luke 3:21–2

> When all the people had been baptized and when Jesus too had been baptized, as he was praying, the heaven was opened and the Holy Spirit in bodily form like a dove came down upon him and there was a voice from heaven, 'You are my beloved son; in you I am well pleased.'

THE thinkers of the Church have always sought an answer to the problem, 'Why did Jesus go to John to be baptized?' The baptism of John was a baptism of repentance and it is our conviction that Jesus was without sin. Why then did he offer himself for this baptism? In the early Church it was sometimes suggested, with a homely touch, that he did it to please Mary, his mother, and in answer to her entreaties; but we need a better reason than that.

In the life of each of us there are certain definite stages, certain hinges on which our whole life turns. It was so with Jesus, and every now and again we must stop and try to see his life as a whole. The first great hinge was the visit to the Temple when he was twelve, when he discovered his unique relationship to God. By the time of the emergence of John, Jesus was about thirty (Luke 3:23). That is to say at least eighteen years had passed. All through these years he must have been realizing more and more his own uniqueness. But still he remained the village carpenter of Nazareth. He must have known that a day must come when he must say goodbye to Nazareth and go out upon his larger task. He must have waited for some sign.

When John emerged the people flocked out to hear him and to be baptized. Throughout the whole country there was an unprecedented *movement towards God.* And Jesus knew that *his hour had struck.* It was not that he was conscious of sin and of the need of repentance. It was that he knew that he too must identify himself with this movement towards God. For Jesus the emergence of John was God's call to action; and his first step was to identify himself with the people in their search for God.

But in Jesus' baptism something happened. Before he could take this tremendous step he had to be sure that he was right; and in the moment of baptism *God spoke to him.* Make no mistake, what happened in the baptism was an experience personal to Jesus. The voice of God came to him and told him that he had taken the right decision. But more – far more – that very same voice mapped out all his course for him.

God said to him, 'You are my beloved Son; with you I am well pleased.' That saying is composed of two texts. *You are my beloved Son* – that is from Psalm 2:7 and was always accepted as a description of the Messianic King. *In whom I am well pleased* – that is part of Isaiah 42:1 and is from a description of the servant of the Lord whose portrait culminates in the sufferings of Isaiah 53. Therefore in his baptism Jesus realized, first, that he was the Messiah, God's anointed king; and, second, that this involved not power and glory, but suffering and a cross. The cross did not come on Jesus unawares; from the first moment of realization he saw it ahead. The baptism shows us Jesus asking for God's approval and receiving the destiny of the cross.

THE LINEAGE OF JESUS

Luke 3:23–38

> When Jesus began his ministry he was about thirty years of age. He was the son (as it was supposed) of Joseph, the son of Heli, the son of Matthat, the son of Levi, the son of Melchi, the son of Jannai, the son of Joseph, the son of Mattathias, the son of Amos, the son of Nahum, the son of Esli, the son of Naggai, the son of Maath, the son of Mattathias, the son of Semein, the son of Josech, the son of Joda, the son of Joanan, the son of Rhesa, the son of Zerubbabel, the son of Shealtiel, the son of Neri, the son of Melchi, the son of Addi, the son of Cosam, the son of Elmadam, the son of Er, the son of Jesus, the son of Eliezer, the son of Jorim, the son of Matthat, the son of Levi, the son of Symeon, the son of Judas, the son of Joseph, the son of Jonam, the son of Eliakim, the son of Melea, the son of Menna, the son of Mattatha, the son of Nathan, the son of David, the son of Jesse,

the son of Obed, the son of Boaz, the son of Salmon,
the son of Nashon, the son of Amminadab, the son of
Arni, the son of Hezron, the son of Perez, the son of
Judah, the son of Jacob, the son of Isaac, the son
of Abraham, the son of Terah, the son of Nahor, the
son of Serug, the son of Reu, the son of Pelag, the son
of Eber, the son of Shelah, the son of Cainan, the son of
Arphaxad, the son of Shem, the son of Noah, the son of
Lamech, the son of Methuselah, the son of Enoch, the
son of Jared, the son of Mahalaleel, the son of Cainan,
the son of Enos, the son of Seth, the son of Adam, the
son of God.

THIS passage begins with the most suggestive statement. It
tells us that when Jesus began his ministry he was no less
than about thirty years of age. Why did he spend thirty years
in Nazareth when he had come to be the Saviour of the world?
It is commonly said that Joseph died fairly young and that
Jesus had to take upon himself the support of Mary and of
his younger brothers and sisters, and that not until they were
old enough to take the business on their own shoulders did
he feel free to leave Nazareth and go into the wider world.
Whether that is so or not, three things are true.

(1) It was essential that Jesus should carry out with the
utmost fidelity the more limited tasks of family duty before
he could take up the universal task of saving the world. It
was by his conscientiousness in the performance of the narrow
duties of home that Jesus fitted himself for the great task
he had to do. When he told the parable of the talents, the
word to the faithful servants was, 'Well done, good and
faithful servant; you have been faithful in a few things, I
will put you in charge of many things' (cf. Matthew 25:21,
23). Beyond a doubt he was putting his own experience into
words when he said that. When the writer J. M. Barrie's

mother died, he said, 'I can look back and I cannot see the smallest thing undone.' It was because Jesus faithfully performed the smallest duties that the greatest task in all the world was given him.

(2) It gave him the opportunity to live out his own teaching. Had he always been a homeless, wandering teacher with no human ties or obligations, people might have said to him, 'What right have you to talk about human duties and human relationships, you, who never fulfilled them?' But Jesus was able to say, not, 'Do as I say,' but, 'Do as I have done.' Leo Tolstoy was the man who always talked about living the way of love; but his wife wrote poignantly of him, 'There is so little genuine warmth about him; his kindness does not come from the heart, but merely from his principles. His biographies will tell of how he helped the labourers to carry buckets of water, but no one will ever know that he never gave his wife a rest and never – in all these thirty-two years – gave his child a drink of water or spent five minutes by his bedside to give me a chance to rest a little from all my labours.' No one could ever speak like that of Jesus. He lived at home what he preached abroad.

(3) If Jesus was to help people he had to know how they lived. And because he spent these thirty years in Nazareth, he knew the problems of making a living, the haunting insecurity of the life of the working man, the ill-natured customer, those who would not pay their debts. It is the glory of the incarnation that we face no problem of life and living which Jesus did not also face.

Here we have Luke's genealogy of Jesus. The Jews were interested in genealogies. Genealogies, especially of the priests, who had to prove unbroken descent from Aaron, were kept among the public records. In the time of Ezra and Nehemiah we read of priests who lost their office because they could not produce their genealogy (Ezra 2:61–3; Nehemiah 7:63–5).

But the problem of this genealogy is its relationship with that in Matthew 1:1–17. The facts are these – only Luke gives the section from Adam to Abraham; the section from Abraham to David is the same in both; but the section from David to Joseph is almost completely different. From the early days of New Testament study, an explanation has been sought for the differences.

(1) It is said that both genealogies are symbolic and that Matthew gives the *royal* descent of Jesus and Luke the *priestly* descent.

(2) One of the earliest suggestions was that Matthew in fact gives the genealogy of *Joseph* and Luke of *Mary*.

(3) The most ingenious explanation is as follows. In Matthew 1:16 Joseph's father is *Jacob*; in Luke 3:23 it is *Heli*. According to the Jewish law of levirate marriage (Deuteronomy 25:5f.) if a man died childless his brother must, if free to do so, marry the widow and ensure the continuance of the line. When that happened a son of such a marriage could be called the son either of the first or of the second husband. It is suggested that Joseph's mother married twice. Joseph was in actual fact the son of Heli, the second husband, but he was in the eyes of the law the son of Jacob, the first husband who had died. It is then suggested that while Heli and Jacob had the same mother they had different fathers and that Jacob's father was descended from David through Solomon and Heli's father was descended from David through Nathan. This ingenious theory would mean that both genealogies are correct. In fact, all we can say is that we do not know.

Two things, however, are to be noted about the genealogy of Jesus which Luke gives.

(1) It stresses the real humanity of Jesus. It stresses the fact that he was truly one of us. He was no phantom or demigod. To save humanity he became in the most real sense a human.

(2) Matthew stops at Abraham; Luke goes right back to Adam. To Matthew, Jesus was the possession of the Jews; to Luke, he was the possession of all peoples, because his line is traced back not to the founder of the Jewish nation but to the founder of the human race. Luke removes the national and racial boundaries even from the ancestry of Jesus.

THE BATTLE WITH TEMPTATION

Luke 4:1–13

> Jesus came back from the Jordan full of the Holy Spirit. He was led by the Spirit into the wilderness, and for forty days he was tempted by the devil; and in those days he ate nothing, and when they were completed he was hungry. The devil said to him, 'If you really are the Son of God, tell these stones to become bread.' Jesus answered him, 'It stands written, "Man shall not live by bread alone."' He took him up and showed him in an instant of time all the kingdoms of the inhabited world. The devil said to him, 'I will give you all this power and the glory of them, because it has been handed over to me, and I can give it to whomsoever I wish. If then you worship me all of it will be yours.' Jesus answered him, 'It stands written, "You must worship the Lord God and him only must you serve."' He brought him to Jerusalem and set him on a pinnacle of the Temple, and said to him, 'If you really are the Son of God throw yourself down from here, for it stands written, "He has given his angels instructions

concerning you, to take care of you, and they will bear
you up in their hands lest you dash your foot against
a stone."' Jesus answered him, 'It has been said, "You
must not try to test the Lord your God."' So when he
had gone through the whole gamut of temptation, the
devil left him for a time.

WE have already seen how there were certain great milestones
in the life of Jesus, and here is one of the greatest. In the
Temple when he was twelve there had come the realization
that God was his Father in a unique way. In the emergence of
John, the hour had struck and in his baptism God's approval
had come. At this time Jesus was just about to begin his
campaign. Before beginning a campaign a leader must choose
the methods to be employed. The temptation story shows
us Jesus choosing once and for all the method by which
he proposed to win men and women to God. It shows him
rejecting the way of power and glory and accepting the way
of suffering and the cross.

Before we go on to think of this story in detail there are
two general points we must note.

(1) This is the most sacred of stories, for it can have come
from no other source than Jesus' own lips. At some time he
must have himself told his disciples about this most intimate
experience of his soul.

(2) Even at this time Jesus must have been conscious of
quite exceptional powers. The whole point of the temptations is that they could have come only to a man who could
do astonishing things. It is no temptation to us to turn stones
into bread or leap from a Temple pinnacle, for the simple
reason that it is impossible for us to do such things. These
are temptations which could have come only to a man whose
powers were unique and who had to decide how to use
them.

First of all let us think of the scene, namely, the wilderness. The inhabited part of Judaea stood on the central plateau which was the backbone of southern Palestine. Between it and the Dead Sea stretched a terrible wilderness, thirty-five by fifteen miles. It was called Jeshimmon, which means 'the Devastation'. The hills were like dust-heaps; the limestone looked blistered and peeling; the rocks were bare and jagged; the ground sounded hollow to the horses' hooves; it glowed with heat like a vast furnace and ran out to the precipices, 1,200 feet high, which plunged down to the Dead Sea. It was in that awesome devastation that Jesus was tempted.

We must not think that the three temptations came and went like scenes in a play. We must rather think of Jesus deliberately retiring to this lonely place and for forty days wrestling with the problem of how he could win people over. It was a long battle which never ceased until the cross, and the story ends by saying that the tempter left Jesus – *for a season.*

(1) The first temptation was to turn stones into bread. This wilderness was not a wilderness of sand. It was covered by little bits of limestone exactly like loaves. The tempter said to Jesus, 'If you want people to follow you, use your wonderful powers to give them material things.' He was suggesting that Jesus should *bribe people* into following him. Back came Jesus' answer in a quotation of Deuteronomy 8:3. 'No one', he said, 'will ever find life in material things.'

The task of Christianity is not to produce new conditions, although the weight and voice of the Church must be behind all efforts to make life better. Its real task is to produce *new men and women*; and given the new men and women, the new conditions will follow.

(2) In the second temptation Jesus in imagination stood upon a mountain from which the whole civilized world could be seen. The tempter said, 'Worship me, and all will be yours.'

This is the temptation to compromise. The devil said, 'I have got people in my grip. Don't set your standards so high. Strike a bargain with me. Just compromise a little with evil and people will follow you.' Back came Jesus' answer, 'God is God, right is right and wrong is wrong. There can be no compromise in the war on evil.' Once again Jesus quotes Scripture (Deuteronomy 6:13, 10, 20).

It is a constant temptation to seek to win people over by compromising with the standards of the world. G. K. Chesterton said that the tendency of the world is to see things in terms of an indeterminate grey; but the duty of the Christian is to see things in terms of black and white. As Thomas Carlyle said, 'The Christian must be consumed by the conviction of the infinite beauty of holiness and the infinite damnability of sin.'

(3) In the third temptation Jesus in imagination saw himself on the pinnacle of the Temple where Solomon's Porch and the Royal Porch met. There was a sheer drop of 450 feet into the Kedron Valley below. This was the temptation *to do something sensational for the people.* 'No,' said Jesus, 'you must not make senseless experiments with the power of God' (Deuteronomy 6:16). Jesus saw quite clearly that a sensational action would cause amazement for a short time; but he also saw that sensationalism would never last.

The hard way of service and of suffering leads to the cross, but after the cross to the crown.

THE GALILAEAN SPRINGTIME

Luke 4:14–15

So Jesus returned in the power of the Spirit to Galilee; and the story of him spread throughout the whole

> countryside. He kept on teaching in their synagogues;
> and he was held in high reputation by all.

No sooner had Jesus left the wilderness than he was faced with another decision. He knew that for him the hour had struck; he had settled once and for all the method he was going to take. Now he had to decide where he would start.

(1) He began in *Galilee*. Galilee was an area in the north of Palestine about fifty miles from north to south and twenty-five miles from east to west. The name itself means a circle and comes from the Hebrew word *Galil*. It was so called because it was encircled by non-Jewish nations. Because of that, new influences had always played upon Galilee and it was the most forward-looking and least conservative part of Palestine. It was extraordinarily densely populated. Josephus, who was himself at one time governor of the area, says that it had 204 villages or towns, none with a population less than 15,000. It seems incredible that there could be some 3,000,000 people congregated in Galilee.

It was a land of extraordinary fertility. There was a proverb which said that 'it is easier to raise a legion of olive trees in Galilee than to bring up one child in Judaea'. The wonderful climate and the superb water supply made it the garden of Palestine. The very list of trees which grew there shows how amazingly fertile it was – the vine, the olive, the fig, the oak, the walnut, the terebinth, the palm, the cedar, the cypress, the balsam, the fir tree, the pine, the sycamore, the bay tree, the myrtle, the almond, the pomegranate, the citron and the oleander.

The Galilaeans themselves were the highlanders of Palestine. Josephus says of them, 'They were ever fond of innovations and by nature disposed to changes, and delighted in seditions. They were ever ready to follow a leader who would begin an insurrection. They were quick in temper and given to quarrelling.' 'The Galilaeans', it was said, 'have never been destitute of courage.' 'They were ever more anxious for honour than for gain.'

That is the land in which Jesus began. It was his own land; and it would give him, at least at the beginning, an audience who would listen and be stirred into life by his message.

(2) *He began in the synagogue.* The synagogue was the real centre of religious life in Palestine. There was only one Temple; but the law said that wherever there were ten Jewish families there must be a synagogue; and so in every town and village it was in the synagogue that the people met to worship. There were no sacrifices in the synagogue. The Temple was designed for sacrifice; the synagogue was for teaching. But how could Jesus gain an entry into the synagogue and how could he, a layman, the carpenter from Nazareth, deliver his message there?

In the synagogue service there were three parts.

(a) The worship part in which prayer was offered.

(b) The reading of the Scriptures. Seven people from the congregation read. As they read, the ancient Hebrew, which was no longer widely understood, was translated by the Targumist into Aramaic or Greek, in the case of the law, one verse at a time, in the case of the prophets, three verses at a time.

(c) The teaching part. In the synagogue there was no professional ministry nor any one person to give the address; the president would invite any distinguished person present to speak, and discussion and talk would follow. That is how Jesus got his chance. The synagogue and its platform were open to him at this stage.

(3) The passage ends by saying that he was held in high reputation by all. This period of Jesus' ministry has been called the Galilaean springtime. He had come like a breath of

the very wind of God. The opposition had not yet crystallized. Human hearts were hungry for the word of life, and they had not yet realized what a blow he was to strike at the orthodoxy of his time. The person who has a message will always command an audience.

WITHOUT HONOUR IN HIS OWN COUNTRY

Luke 4:16–30

So Jesus came to Nazareth where he had been brought up; and, as was his habit, he went into the synagogue on the Sabbath day, and he stood up to read the lesson. The roll of the prophet Isaiah was given to him. He opened the roll and found the passage where it is written, 'The Spirit of the Lord is upon me because he has anointed me to bring the good news to the poor. He has sent me to announce release to the captives, and recovering of sight to the blind, to set at liberty those who have been bruised, to proclaim that the year which everyone is waiting for has come.' And he folded up the roll and handed it back to the officer and sat down; and the eyes of all in the synagogue were fixed intently on him. He began to say to them, 'Today this scripture has been fulfilled in your ears.' And all witnessed to him and were amazed at the words of grace that came from his mouth. And they said, 'Is this not the son of Joseph?' He said to them, 'You are bound to quote the proverb to me, "Physician, heal yourself; we have heard about all that happened in Capernaum; do the same kind of things in your own home country."' He said, 'This is the truth that I tell you. No prophet is accepted in his own home country. In truth I tell you there were many widows in Israel in the days of Elijah, when the heaven was shut up for three years and six months and when

there was a great famine all over the earth. And to none
of them was Elijah sent but he was sent to Zarephath, to
a widow of Sidon. There were many lepers in Israel in
the times of Elisha the prophet; and none of them was
healed; but Naaman the Syrian was.' And the people in
the synagogue were filled with anger as they listened to
these things; and they rose up and hustled him out of
the town. They took him to the brow of the hill on which
their town is built, to throw him down; but he passed
through the midst of them and went upon his way.

ONE of Jesus' very early visits was to Nazareth, his home
town. Nazareth was not a village. It is called a *polis* which
means a town or city; and it may well have had as many as
20,000 inhabitants. It stood in a little hollow in the hills on
the lower slopes of Galilee near the Plain of Jezreel. But a
boy had only to climb to the hilltop above the town and he
could see an amazing panorama for miles around.

The biblical scholar Sir George Adam Smith vividly
described the scene from the hilltop. The history of Israel
stretched out before the watcher's eye. There was the plain
of Esdraelon where Deborah and Barak had fought; where
Gideon had won his victories; where Saul had crashed to
disaster and Josiah had been killed in battle; there was
Naboth's vineyard and the place where Jehu slaughtered
Jezebel; there was Shunem where Elisha had lived; there was
Carmel where Elijah had fought his epic battle with the
prophets of Baal, and, blue in the distance, there was the
Mediterranean and the isles of the sea.

Not only the history of Israel was there; the world unfolded
itself from the hilltop above Nazareth. Three great roads
skirted it. There was the road from the south carrying pilgrims
to Jerusalem. There was the great Way of the Sea which led
from Egypt to Damascus with laden caravans moving along

it. There was the great road to the east bearing caravans from Arabia and Roman legions marching out to the eastern frontiers of the Empire. It is wrong to think of Jesus as being brought up in a backwater; he was brought up in a town in sight of history and with the traffic of the world almost at its doors.

We have already described the synagogue service, and this passage gives us a vivid picture of it in action. It was not a book that Jesus took, for at this time everything was written on rolls. It was from Isaiah 61 that he read. In verse 20 the Authorized Version speaks misleadingly of *the minister.* The official in question was the *Chazzan.* He had many duties. He had to take out and put back the sacred rolls of Scripture; he had to keep the synagogue clean; he had to announce the coming of the Sabbath with three blasts of the silver trumpet from the synagogue roof; and he was also the teacher in the village school. Verse 20 says that Jesus sat down. That gives us the impression that he was finished. In point of fact it means that he was about to start, because the speaker gave the address seated and Rabbis taught sitting down (cf. our own phrase, a professor's *chair*).

What angered the people was the apparent compliment that Jesus paid to Gentiles. The Jews were so sure that they were God's people that they tended to look down on all others. Some believed that 'God had created the Gentiles to be fuel for the fires of hell.' And here was this young Jesus, whom they all knew, preaching as if the *Gentiles* were specially favoured by God. It was beginning to dawn upon them that there were things in this new message the like of which they had never dreamed.

We must note two other things.

(1) It was Jesus' habit to go to the synagogue on the Sabbath. There must have been many things with which he

radically disagreed and which grated on him – *yet he went.*
The worship of the synagogue might be far from perfect; yet
Jesus never omitted to join himself to God's worshipping
people on God's day.

(2) We have only to read the passage of Isaiah that Jesus
read to see the difference between Jesus and John the Baptist.
John was the preacher of doom and those who heard his
message must have shuddered with terror. It was a *gospel* –
good news – which Jesus brought. Jesus, too, knew the wrath
of God but it was always the wrath of love.

THE SPIRIT OF AN UNCLEAN DEVIL

Luke 4:31-7

> Jesus came down to Capernaum, a town in Galilee, and
> he was teaching them on the Sabbath day; and they
> were astonished at his teaching because his speech was
> with authority. There was in the synagogue a man
> who had a spirit of an unclean demon and he cried out
> with a loud voice, 'What have we to do with you, Jesus
> of Nazareth? Have you come to destroy us? I know
> who you are – the Holy One of God.' So Jesus rebuked
> it. 'Be muzzled,' he said, 'and come out of him.' And
> after the demon had thrown him into the midst of them,
> it came out of him and it did him no harm. Astonishment
> fell on them all and they kept saying to each other,
> 'What word is this? because he gives orders to unclean
> spirits with authority and with power and they come
> out.' And the story of him went out to every place in
> the surrounding district.

WE would have liked to know as much about Capernaum as
we do about Nazareth, but the strange fact is that there is

even doubt as to the site of this lakeside town where so much of Jesus' mighty work was done.

This passage is specially interesting because it is the first in Luke where we encounter demon-possession. The ancient world believed that the air was thickly populated with evil spirits which sought entry into people. Often they entered through food or drink. All illness was caused by them. The Egyptians believed there were thirty-six different parts of the human body and any of them could be entered and controlled by one of these evil spirits. There were spirits of deafness, of dumbness, of fever; spirits which took a person's sanity and wits away; spirits of lying and of deceit and of uncleanness. It was such a spirit that Jesus exorcised here.

To many people this is a problem. On the whole, we regard belief in spirits as something primitive and superstitious which we have outgrown. Yet Jesus seemed to believe in them. There are three possibilities.

(1) Jesus actually did believe in them. If that is so, as far as scientific knowledge went he was not in advance of his own age but under all the limitations of contemporary medical thought. There is no need to refuse such a conclusion for, if Jesus was really human, in scientific things he must have had the knowledge available at that time.

(2) Jesus did not believe in them. But the sufferer did believe intensely and Jesus could cure people only by assuming their beliefs about themselves to be true. Saying to someone who is ill, 'There's nothing wrong with you', is no help. The reality of the pain has to be admitted before a cure can follow. The people believed they were possessed by devils and Jesus, like a wise doctor, knew he could not heal them unless he assumed that their view of their trouble was real.

(3) Increasingly people are prepared to admit that perhaps there is something in demons after all. There are certain

troubles which have no bodily cause as far as can be discovered. There is no reason for the illness, but the person is
ill. Since there is no physical explanation some people now
think there must be a spiritual one and that demons may not
be so unreal after all.

The people were astonished at Jesus' power – and no
wonder. The middle east was full of people who could exorcise
demons. But their methods were weird and wonderful. An
exorcist would put a ring under the afflicted person's nose;
he would recite a long spell; and then all of a sudden there
would be a splash in a basin of water which he had put near
to hand – and the demon was out! A magical root called
Baaras was specially effective. When anyone approached it,
it shrank into the ground unless gripped, and to grip it was
certain death. So the ground round it was dug away; a dog
was tied to it; the struggles of the dog tore up the root; and
when the root was torn up the dog died, as a substitute for
the one who was possessed. What a difference between all
this hysterical paraphernalia and the calm single word of
command of Jesus! It was his sheer authority which staggered
them.

Jesus' authority was something quite new. When the
Rabbis taught they supported every statement with quotations.
They always said, 'There is a saying that . . .' 'Rabbi so and
so said that . . .' They always appealed to authority. When the
prophets spoke, they said, 'Thus saith the Lord.' Theirs was a
delegated authority. When Jesus spoke, he said, '*I* say to you.'
He needed no authorities to buttress him; his was not a
delegated authority; he was authority incarnate. Here was a
man who spoke as one who knew.

In every sphere of life the expert bears an air of authority.
A musician tells how when Toscanini mounted the rostrum
authority flowed from him and the orchestra felt it. When we

need technical advice we call in the expert. *Jesus is the expert in life.* He speaks and we know that this is beyond human argument – this is God.

A MIRACLE IN A COTTAGE

Luke 4:38-9

> Jesus left the synagogue and came into Simon's house; and Simon's mother-in-law was in the grip of a major fever. They asked him to do something for her. He stood over her and rebuked the fever and it left her. Immediately she got up and began to serve them.

HERE Luke the doctor writes. *In the grip of a major fever* – every word is a medical term. *In the grip of* is the medical Greek for someone definitely laid up with an illness. The Greek medical writers divided fevers into two classes – major and minor. Luke knew just how to describe this illness.

There are three great truths in this short incident.

(1) Jesus was always ready to serve. He had just left the synagogue. Preachers know what it is like after a service. They have given of themselves and need rest. The last thing they want is a crowd of people and a fresh call upon their energy. But no sooner had Jesus left the synagogue and entered Peter's house than the insistent cry of human need was at him. He did not claim that he was tired and must rest. He answered it without complaint.

Members of the Salvation Army tell of a Mrs Berwick in the days of the London blitzes of the Second World War. She had been in charge of the Army's social work in Liverpool and had retired to London. People had strange ideas during the blitzes and they had the idea that somehow Mrs Berwick's house was safe; and so they gathered there. Though she had

retired, the instinct to help was still with her. She got together
a simple first-aid box and then put a notice in her window, 'If
you need help, knock here.' Always Jesus was ready to help;
his followers must be the same.

(2) Jesus did not need a crowd to work a miracle. So often
we will make an effort in company that we will not make
among our own private circle. So often we are at our best in
society and at our worst at home. All too commonly we are
gracious, courteous, obliging to strangers and the very
opposite when there is no one but our own family or friends
to see. But Jesus was prepared to put out all his power in a
village cottage in Capernaum when the crowds were gone.

(3) When Peter's mother-in-law was cured, *immediately
she began to serve them.* She realized that she had been
given back her health to spend it in the service of others. She
wanted no fussing and no petting; she wanted to get on with
cooking and serving her family and Jesus. Mothers are like
that. We would do well to remember that if God gave us the
priceless gift of health and strength, he gave it that we might
use it always in the service of others.

THE INSISTENT CROWDS

Luke 4:40–4

> When the sun was setting all who had friends who were
> ill with all kinds of sicknesses brought them to Jesus;
> and he laid his hands upon each one of them and cured
> them. Out of many there came demons, shouting out
> and saying, 'You are the Son of God.' And he rebuked
> them and would not allow them to speak, because they
> knew that he was the Anointed One. When day came,
> he went out and went to a desert place; and the crowds

kept looking for him and they tried to restrain him so
that he would not go away from them; but he said to
them, 'I must tell the good news of the kingdom of God
to other towns too, because that is what I was sent to
do.'

(1) Early in the morning Jesus went out to be alone. He
was able to meet the insistent needs of others only because
he first made time to be with God. Once, in the First World
War, a staff conference was due to begin. All were present
except Marshal Foch, the commander-in-chief. An officer
who knew him well said, 'I think I know where we may find
him.' He led them round to a ruined chapel close beside
General Headquarters and there, before the shattered altar,
the great soldier was kneeling in prayer. Before he met his
men he must first meet God.

(2) There is no word of complaint or resentment when
Jesus' privacy was invaded by the crowds. Prayer is great but
in the last analysis human need is greater. Florence Allshorn,
the great missionary teacher, used to run a training college
for missionaries. She knew human nature and she had little
time for people who suddenly discovered that their quiet
hour was due just when the dishes were to be washed! Pray
we must; but prayer must never be an escape from reality.
Prayer cannot preserve us from the insistent cry of human
need. It must prepare us for it; and sometimes we will need
to rise from our knees too soon and get to work – even when
we do not want to.

(3) Jesus would not let the demons speak. Over and over
again we get on Jesus' lips this injunction to silence. Why?
For this very good reason – the Jews had their own popular
ideas of the Messiah. To many of them the Messiah was to be
a conquering king who would set his foot upon the eagle's
neck and sweep the Romans from Palestine. Palestine was in

a volatile state. Rebellion was always just below the surface and often broke out. Jesus knew that if the report went out that he was the Messiah the revolutionaries would be ready to flare up. Before people could call him Messiah, he had to teach them that Messiah meant not a conquering king but a suffering servant. His injunctions to silence were given because people did not yet know what Messiahship meant, and if they started out with the wrong ideas death and destruction would surely follow.

(4) Here is the first mention of the kingdom of God in Luke's gospel. Jesus came preaching the kingdom of God (Mark 1:15). That was the essence of his message. What did he mean by the kingdom of God? For Jesus the kingdom was three things at the same time.

(a) It was *past*. Abraham, Isaac and Jacob were in the kingdom and they had lived centuries ago (Luke 13:28).

(b) It was *present*. 'The kingdom', he said, 'is within you, or among you' (Luke 17:21).

(c) It was *future*. It was something which God was still to give and which must be constantly prayed for.

How can the kingdom be all these things at the same time? Turn to the Lord's Prayer. There are two petitions in it side by side. Your kingdom come; Your will be done in earth as it is in heaven (Matthew 6:10). Now, as any verse of the Psalms will show, the Hebrew language has a way of saying things twice; and always the second way explains, or develops, or amplifies the first way. Put these two phrases together – Your kingdom come; Your will be done in earth as it is in heaven. The second explains the first; therefore, *the kingdom of God is a society upon earth where God's will is as perfectly done as it is in heaven.* If anyone in the past has perfectly done God's will, that person is in the kingdom; if anyone does it now, that person is in the kingdom; but the day when everyone will do that will is still far distant, therefore the consummation is still to come; and so the kingdom is past and present and future all at the same time.

We do that will spasmodically, sometimes obeying, sometimes disobeying. Only Jesus always did it perfectly. That is why he is the foundation and the incarnation of the kingdom. He came to make it possible for us all to do the same. To do God's will is to be a citizen of the kingdom of God. We may well pray – 'Lord, bring in your kingdom, beginning with me.'

THE CONDITIONS OF A MIRACLE

Luke 5:1-11

Jesus was standing on the shore of the Lake of Gennesaret while the crowds pressed in upon him to listen to the word of God. He saw two boats riding close to the shore. The fishermen had disembarked from them and were washing their nets. He embarked on one of the boats, which belonged to Simon, and asked him to push out a little from the land. He sat down and continued to teach the crowds from the boat. When he stopped speaking, he said to Simon, 'Push out into the deep water and let down your nets for a catch.' Simon answered, 'Master, we have toiled all night long and we caught nothing; but, if you say so, I will let down the nets.' When they had done so they enclosed a great crowd of fishes; their nets were torn with the numbers; so they signalled to their partners in the other boat to come and help them. They came and they filled both the boats so that they began to sink. When Simon Peter saw this he fell at Jesus' knees. 'Leave me, Lord,' he said, 'because I am a sinful man.' Wonder gripped him

and all who were with him at the number of fishes
they had caught. It was the same with James and John,
Zebedee's sons, who were partners with Simon. Jesus
said to Simon, 'From now on you will be catching men.'
So they brought the boats to land and they left everything and followed him.

THE famous sheet of water in Galilee is called by three names
– the Sea of Galilee, the Sea of Tiberias and the Lake of
Gennesaret. It is thirteen miles long by eight miles wide. It
lies in a dip in the earth's surface and is 680 feet below sea
level. That fact gives it an almost tropical climate. Nowadays
it is not very populous but in the days of Jesus it had nine
townships clustered round its shores, none of fewer than
15,000 people.

Gennesaret is really the name of the lovely plain on the
west side of the lake, a most fertile piece of land. The Jews
loved to play with derivations, and they had three derivations
for Gennesaret all of which show how beautiful it was.

(1) From *kinnor*, which means a harp, either because 'its
fruit is as sweet as the sound of a harp' or because 'the voice
of its waves is pleasant as the voice of the harp'.

(2) From *gan*, a garden, and *sar*, a prince – hence 'the
prince of gardens'.

(3) From *gan*, a garden, and *asher*, riches – hence 'the
garden of riches'.

We are here confronted with a turning point in the career
of Jesus. Last time we heard him preach he was in the
synagogue; now he is at the lakeside. True, he will be back in
the synagogue again; but the time is coming when the door
of the synagogue will be shut to him and his church will be
the lakeside and the open road, and his pulpit a boat. He
would go anywhere where people would listen to him. 'Our
societies', said John Wesley, 'were formed from those who

were wandering upon the dark mountains, that belonged to no Christian church; but were awakened by the preaching of the Methodists, who had pursued them through the wilderness of this world to the High-ways and the Hedges – to the Markets and the Fairs – to the Hills and the Dales – who set up the Standard of the Cross in the Streets and Lanes of the Cities, in the Villages, in the Barns, and Farmers' Kitchens, etc. – and all this done in such a way, and to such an extent, as never had been done before since the Apostolic age.' 'I love a commodious room,' said Wesley, 'a soft cushion and a handsome pulpit, but field preaching saves souls.' When the synagogue was shut Jesus took to the open road.

There is in this story what we might call a list of the conditions of a miracle.

(1) There is the eye that sees. There is no need to think that Jesus *created* a shoal of fishes for the occasion. In the Sea of Galilee there were phenomenal shoals which covered the sea as if it was solid for as much as an acre. Most likely Jesus' discerning eye saw just such a shoal and his keen sight made it look like a miracle. We need the eye that really sees. Many people saw steam raise the lid of a kettle; only James Watt went on to think of a steam engine. Many people saw an apple fall; only Isaac Newton went on to think out the law of gravity. The earth is full of miracles for the eye that sees.

(2) There is the spirit that will make an effort. If Jesus said it, tired as he was Peter was prepared to try again. For most people the disaster of life is that they give up just one effort too soon.

(3) There is the spirit which will attempt what seems hopeless. The night was past and that was the time for fishing. All the circumstances were unfavourable, but Peter said, 'Let circumstances be what they may, if you say so, we will try again.' Too often we wait because the time is not opportune.

If we wait for a perfect set of circumstances, we will never begin at all. If we want a miracle, we must take Jesus at his word when he bids us attempt the impossible.

TOUCHING THE UNTOUCHABLE

Luke 5:12-15

> While Jesus was in one of the towns – look you – a man who was a severe case of leprosy saw him. He fell before him and besought him, 'Lord, if you are willing to do so you are able to cleanse me.' Jesus stretched out his hand and touched him. 'I am willing,' he said. 'Be cleansed.' Immediately the leprosy left him. Jesus enjoined him to tell no one. 'But,' he said, 'go and show yourself to the priest, and bring the offering for cleansing, as Moses's law laid it down, to prove to them that you are cured.' Talk about him spread all the more; and many crowds assembled to listen to him and to be cured of their illnesses.

In Palestine there were two kinds of leprosy. There was one which was rather like a very bad skin disease, and it was the less serious of the two. There was one in which the disease, starting from a small spot, ate away the flesh until the wretched sufferer was left with only the stump of a hand or a leg. It was literally a living death.

The regulations concerning leprosy are in Leviticus, chapters 13 and 14. The most terrible thing about it was the isolation it brought. Lepers were to cry 'Unclean! unclean!' wherever they went and were condemned to live alone in a dwelling 'outside the camp' (Leviticus 13:45-6), banished from society and exiled from home. The result was, and still is, that the psychological consequences of leprosy were as serious as the physical.

Dr A. B. MacDonald, in an article on the leper colony in Itu, of which he was in charge, wrote, 'The leper is sick in mind as well as body. For some reason there is an attitude to leprosy different from the attitude to any other disfiguring disease. It is associated with shame and horror, and carries, in some mysterious way, a sense of guilt, although innocently acquired like most contagious troubles. Shunned and despised, frequently do lepers consider taking their own lives and some do.'

Lepers were hated by others until they came to hate themselves. The leper came to Jesus; he was unclean; *and Jesus touched him.*

(1) *Jesus touched the untouchable.* His hand went out to the man from whom everyone else would have shrunk away. Two things emerge. First, when we despise ourselves, when our hearts are filled with bitter shame, let us remember that, in spite of all, Christ's hand is still stretched out. The writer Mark Rutherford wished to add a new beatitude: 'Blessed are those who heal us of our self-despisings.' That is what Jesus did and does. Second, it is of the very essence of Christianity to touch the untouchable, to love the unlovable, to forgive the unforgivable. Jesus did – and so must we.

(2) Jesus sent the man to carry out the normal, prescribed routine for cleansing. The regulations are described in Leviticus 14. That is to say a miracle did not dispense with what medical science of the time could do. It did not absolve the man from carrying out the prescribed rules. We will never get miracles by neglecting the gifts and the wisdom God has given us. It is when human skill combines with God's grace that wonder happens.

(3) Verse 15 tells us of the popularity Jesus enjoyed. But it was only because people wanted something out of him.

Many desire the gifts of God but repudiate the demands of God – and, there can be nothing more dishonourable.

THE OPPOSITION INTENSIFIES

Luke 5:16–17

> Jesus withdrew into the desert places and he continued in prayer. On a certain day he was teaching and, sitting listening, there were Pharisees and experts in the law who had come from every village in Galilee and from Judaea and Jerusalem. And the power of the Lord was there to enable him to heal.

THERE are only two verses here; but as we read them we must pause, for this indeed is a milestone. The scribes and the Pharisees had arrived on the scene. The opposition which would never be satisfied until it had killed Jesus had emerged into the open.

If we are to understand what happened to Jesus we must understand something about the law, and the relationship of the scribes and the Pharisees to it. When the Jews returned from Babylon about 440 BC they knew well that, humanly speaking, their hopes of national greatness were gone. They therefore deliberately decided that they would find their greatness in being a people of the law. They would bend all their energies to knowing and keeping God's law.

The basis of the law was the Ten Commandments. These commandments are principles for life. They are not rules and regulations; they do not legislate for each event and for every circumstance. For a certain section of the Jews that was not enough. They desired not great principles but a rule to cover every conceivable situation. From the Ten Commandments they proceeded to develop and elaborate these rules.

Let us take an example. The commandment says,
'Remember the sabbath day and keep it holy'; and then goes
on to lay it down that on the Sabbath no work must be done
(Exodus 20:8–11). But the Jews asked, 'What is work?' and
went on to define it under thirty-nine different headings which
they called 'Fathers of Work'. Even that was not enough.
Each of these headings was greatly subdivided. Thousands
of rules and regulations began to emerge. These were called
the oral law, and they began to be set even above the Ten
Commandments.

Again, let us take an actual example. One of the works
forbidden on the Sabbath was carrying a burden. Jeremiah
17:21–4 says, 'For the sake of your lives, take care that you
do not bear a burden on the sabbath day.' But, the legalists
insisted, a burden must be defined. So definition was given.
A burden is 'food equal in weight to a dried fig, enough wine
for mixing in a goblet, milk enough for one swallow, oil
enough to anoint a small member, water enough to moisten
an eye-salve, paper enough to write a custom-house notice
upon, ink enough to write two letters of the alphabet, reed
enough to make a pen' . . . and so on endlessly. So for a tailor
to leave a pin or needle in his robe on the Sabbath was to
break the law and to sin; to pick up a stone big enough to
fling at a bird on the Sabbath was to sin. Goodness became
identified with these endless rules and regulations.

Let us take another example. To heal on the Sabbath was
to work. It was laid down that only if life was in actual danger
could healing be done; and then steps could be taken only to
keep the sufferer from getting worse, not to improve their
condition. A plain bandage could be put on a wound, but not
any ointment; plain wadding could be put into a sore ear, but
not medicated. It is easy to see that there could be no limit to
this.

The scribes were the experts in the law who knew all these rules and regulations, and who deduced them from the law. The name Pharisee means 'the separated one'; and the Pharisees were those who had separated themselves from ordinary people and ordinary life in order to keep these rules and regulations.

Note two things. First, for the scribes and Pharisees these rules were a matter of life and death; to break one of them was deadly sin. Second, only people desperately in earnest would ever have tried to keep them, for they must have made life supremely uncomfortable. It was only the best people who would even make the attempt.

Jesus had no use for rules and regulations like that. For him, the cry of human need superseded all such things. But to the scribes and Pharisees he was a law-breaker, a bad man who broke the law and taught others to do the same. That is why they set themselves against him and in the end brought about his death. The tragedy of the life of Jesus was that those who were most in earnest about their religion drove him to the cross. It was the irony of things that the best people of the day in the' end were responsible for his crucifixion.

From this time on there was to be no rest for him. Always he was to be under the scrutiny of hostile and critical eyes. The opposition had crystallized and there was but one end.

Jesus knew this and before he met the opposition he withdrew to pray. The love in the eyes of God compensated him for the hostility in people's eyes. God's approval nerved him to meet human criticism. He drew strength for the battle of life from the peace of God – and it is enough for his disciples that they should be as their Lord.

FORGIVEN AND HEALED

Luke 5:18–26

Now – look you – there came men bearing on a bed a
man who was paralysed, and they were trying to carry
him in and to lay him before Jesus. When they could
find no way to carry him in because of the crowd they
climbed up on to the roof and they let him down, bed
and all, through the tiles right into the middle of them
in front of Jesus. When Jesus saw their faith, he said,
'Man, your sins are forgiven you.' The scribes and
Pharisees began to raise questions. 'Who,' they said,
'is this who insults God? Who can forgive sins but
God alone?' Jesus was well aware of what they were
thinking. He answered, 'What are you thinking about
in your hearts? Which is easier – to say, "Your sins are
forgiven you," or to say, "Rise and walk"? But that
you may know that the Son of Man has authority on
earth to forgive sins (he said to the paralysed man), I
tell you rise, take up your bed, and go to your own
house.' And immediately he stood up in front of them
and lifted up the bedding on which he was lying and
went away to his house, glorifying God. Astonishment
gripped them all and they glorified God and were filled
with awe. 'Today,' they said, 'we have seen amazing
things.'

HERE we have a vivid story. Jesus was in a house teaching.
The Palestinian house was flat-roofed. The roof had only the
slightest tilt, sufficient to make the rain water run off. It was
composed of beams laid from wall to wall and quite a short
distance apart. The space between the beams was filled with
closely packed twigs, compacted together with mortar and
then marled over. It was the easiest thing in the world to take

out the packing between two beams. In fact coffins were very often taken in and out of a house via the roof.

What does the passage about forgiving sins mean? We must remember that sin and suffering were in Palestine inextricably connected. It was implicitly believed that suffering was the consequence of sin. And therefore the sufferer very often had an even morbid sense of sin. That is why Jesus began by telling the man that his sins were forgiven. Without that the man would never believe that he could be cured. This shows how in debate the scribes and Pharisees were completely routed. They objected to Jesus claiming to extend forgiveness to the man. But on their own arguments and assumptions the man was ill because he had sinned; and if he was cured that was proof that his sins were forgiven. The complaint of the Pharisees recoiled on them and left them speechless.

The wonderful thing is that here is a man who was saved by the faith of his friends. *When Jesus saw their faith* – the eager faith of those who stopped at nothing to bring their friend to Jesus won his cure. It still happens.

(1) There are those who are saved by the faith of their parents. Thomas Carlyle used to say that still across the years there came his mother's voice to him, 'Trust in God and do the right.' When Augustine was living a reckless and immoral life his devout mother came to ask the help of a Christian bishop. 'It is impossible,' he said, 'that the child of such prayers and tears should perish.' Many of us would gladly witness that we owe all that we are and ever will be to the faith of godly parents.

(2) There are those who are daily saved by the faith of those who love them. When H. G. Wells was newly married and success was bringing new temptations to him, he said, 'It was as well for me that behind the folding doors at 12

Mornington Road there slept one so sweet and clean that it
was unthinkable that I should appear before her squalid or
drunken or base.' Many of us would do the shameful thing
but for the fact that we could not meet the pain and sorrow in
someone's eyes.

In the very structure of life and love – blessed be God –
there are precious influences which save human souls.

THE GUEST OF AN OUTCAST

Luke 5:27–32

> After that Jesus went out, and he saw a tax-collector,
> called Levi, sitting at his tax-collector's table. He said
> to him, 'Follow me!' He left everything and rose and
> followed him. And Levi made a great feast for him in
> his house; and a great crowd of tax-collectors and others
> who were their friends sat down at table with them.
> The Pharisees and scribes complained at this, and
> said to the disciples, 'Why do you eat and drink with
> tax-collectors and sinners?' Jesus answered, 'Those who
> are healthy have no need of a doctor but those who are
> ill have. I did not come to invite the righteous but sinners
> to repentance.'

HERE we have the call of Matthew (cf. Matthew 9:9–13). Of
all people in Palestine the tax-collectors were the most hated.
Palestine was a country subject to the Romans; tax-collectors
had taken service under the Roman government; therefore
they were regarded as renegades and traitors.

The taxation system lent itself to abuse. The Roman custom
had been to farm out the taxes. They assessed a district at a
certain figure and then sold the right to collect that figure to
the highest bidder. As long as the buyer handed over the

assessed figure at the end of the year he was entitled to retain whatever else he could extract from the people; and since there were no newspapers, radio or television, and no ways of making public announcements that would reach everyone, the ordinary people had no real idea of what they had to pay.

This particular system had led to such gross abuses that by New Testament times it had been discontinued. There were, however, still taxes to be paid, still despised tax-collectors working for the Romans, and still abuses and exploitation.

There were two types of taxes. First, there were stated taxes. There was a poll tax which all men aged between fourteen and sixty-five, and all women aged between twelve and sixty-five, had to pay simply for the privilege of existing. There was a ground tax which consisted of one-tenth of all grain grown, and one-fifth of wine and oil. This could be paid in kind or commuted into money. There was income tax, which was one per cent of a person's income. In these taxes there was not a great deal of room for extortion.

Second, there were all kinds of duties. A tax was payable for using the main roads, the harbours, the markets. A tax was payable on a cart, on each wheel of it, and on the animal which pulled it. There was purchase tax on certain articles, and there were import and export duties. A tax-collector could bid a man stop on the road and unpack his bundles and charge him well-nigh what he liked. If a man could not pay, sometimes the tax-collector would offer to lend him money at an exorbitant rate of interest and so get him further into his clutches.

Robbers, murderers and tax-collectors were classed together. A tax-collector was barred from the synagogue. A Roman writer tells us that he once saw a monument to an honest tax-collector. An honest specimen of this renegade profession was so rare that he received a monument.

Yet Jesus chose Matthew the tax-collector to be an apostle.

(1) The first thing Matthew did was to invite Jesus to a feast – he could well afford it – and to invite his fellow tax-collectors and their outcast friends to meet him. Matthew's first instinct was to share the wonder he had found. John Wesley once said, 'No man ever went to Heaven alone; he must either find friends or make them.' It is a Christian duty to share the blessedness that we have found.

(2) The scribes and Pharisees objected. The Pharisees – the separated ones – would not even let the skirt of their robe touch the likes of Matthew. Jesus gave the perfect answer. Once the Greek philosopher Epictetus called his teaching 'the medicine of salvation'. Jesus pointed out that it is only sick people who need doctors; and people like Matthew and his friends were the very people who needed him most. It would be well if we were to regard the sinner not as a criminal but as someone who is ill; and if we were to look on the person who has made a mistake not as someone deserving contempt and condemnation but as someone needing love and help to find the right way.

THE HAPPY COMPANY

Luke 5:33–5

> They said to him, 'John's disciples fast frequently and pray. So do the disciples of the Pharisees; but your disciples eat and drink.' Jesus said to them, 'You cannot make the children of the bridechamber fast while the bridegroom is with them. But the days will come – and when the bridegroom is taken away from them in those days they will fast.'

WHAT amazed and shocked the scribes and the Pharisees was the normality of the followers of Jesus. Collie Knox tells how once a well-loved chaplain said to him, 'Young Knox, don't make an agony of your religion.' It was said of Robert Burns that he was haunted rather than helped by his religion. The orthodox Jews had an idea that people were not being religious unless they were uncomfortable.

They had systematized their religious observances. They fasted on Mondays and Thursdays; and often they whitened their faces so that no one could fail to see that they were fasting. True, fasting was not so very serious because it lasted only from sunrise to sunset and after that ordinary food could be taken. The idea was to call God's attention to the faster. Sometimes they even thought of it in terms of sacrifice. By fasting people were in essence offering nothing less than their own flesh to God. Even prayer was systematized. It was to be offered two or three times daily, at morning and evening and sometimes at noon.

Jesus was opposed radically to religion by rule. He used a vivid picture. When two young people married in Palestine they did not go away for a honeymoon; they stayed at home, and for a week kept open house. They dressed in their best; sometimes they even wore crowns; for that week they were king and queen and their word was law. The daily routine of life was hard and they would never again have a week like that. And the favoured guests who shared this festive week were called the children of the bridechamber.

(1) It is extremely significant that more than once Jesus likened the Christian life to a wedding feast. Joy is a primary Christian characteristic. It was said of a famous American teacher by one of her students, 'She made me feel as if I was bathed in sunshine.' Far too many people think of Christianity as something which compels them to do all the things they

do not want to do and hinders them from doing all the things they do want to do. Laughter has become a sin, instead of – as a famous philosopher called it – 'a sudden glory'. Robert Louis Stevenson was right, when he wrote in 'The Celestial Surgeon':

> If I have faltered more or less
> In my great task of happiness;
> If I have moved among my race
> And shown no glorious morning face;
> If beams from happy human eyes
> Have moved me not; if morning skies,
> Books, and my food, and summer rain
> Knocked on my sullen heart in vain:
> Lord, thy most pointed pleasure take
> And stab my spirit broad awake;
> Or, Lord, if too obdurate I,
> Choose thou, before that spirit die,
> A piercing pain, a killing sin,
> And to my dead heart run them in!

(2) At the same time Jesus knew there would come a day when the bridegroom would be taken away. He was not caught unawares by death. Ahead he saw the cross; but even on the way to the cross he knew the joy that no one can take away, because it is the joy of the presence of God.

THE NEW IDEA

Luke 5:36–9

> He spoke a parable to them like this: 'Nobody puts a patch from a new garment on an old garment. If he does the new will tear it and the patch from the new will not match the old. No one puts new wine into old skins. If he does the new wine will burst the skins and it will be

spilled and the skins will be ruined. But new wine must
be put into new skins, and no one who drinks old wine
wishes for new for he says, "The old is good."'

THERE is in religious people a kind of passion for the old.
Nothing moves more slowly than a church. The trouble with
the Pharisees was that the whole religious outlook of Jesus
was so startlingly new they simply could not adjust to it.

The mind soon loses the quality of elasticity and will not
accept new ideas. Jesus used two illustrations. 'You cannot
put a new patch on an old garment,' he said. 'The strong new
cloth will only rip the rent in the old cloth wider.' Bottles in
Palestine were made of skin. When new wine was put into
them it fermented and gave off gas. If the bottle was new,
there was a certain elasticity in the skin and it gave with the
pressure; but if it was old, the skin was dry and hard and it
would burst. 'Don't', says Jesus, 'let your mind become like
an old wine skin. People say of wine, "The old is better." It
may be at the moment, but they forget that it is a mistake to
despise the new wine, for the day will come when it has
matured and it will be best of all.'

The whole passage is Jesus' condemnation of the shut mind
and a plea that new ideas should not be rejected.

(1) We should never be afraid of adventurous thought. If
there is such a person as the Holy Spirit, God must always be
leading us into new truth. The American Baptist, Harry
Emerson Fosdick, somewhere asks, 'How would medicine
fare if doctors were restricted to drugs and methods and
techniques 300 years old?' And yet our standards of orthodoxy
are far older than that. The person with something new has
always to fight. Galileo was branded a heretic when he held
that the earth moved round the sun. Joseph Lister had to fight
for antiseptic technique in surgical operations. Sir James

Simpson had to battle against opposition in the merciful use of chloroform. Let us take care that when we resent new ideas we are not simply demonstrating that our minds have grown old and inelastic; and let us never shirk the adventure of thought.

(2) We should never be afraid of new methods. That a thing has *always* been done may very well be the best reason for stopping doing it. That a thing has *never* been done may very well be the best reason for trying it. No business could exist on outworn methods – and yet the Church tries to. Any business which had lost as many customers as the Church has would have tried new ways long ago – but the Church tends to resent all that is new.

Once on a world tour Rudyard Kipling saw General William Booth come aboard the ship. He came aboard to the beating of tambourines which the more conventional Kipling resented. Kipling got to know the General and told him how he disliked tambourines and all such things. Booth looked at him. 'Young man,' he said, 'if I thought I could win one more soul for Christ by standing on my head and beating a tambourine with my feet I would learn how to do it.'

There is a wise and an unwise conservatism. Let us take care that in thought and in action we are not hidebound reactionaries when we ought, as Christians, to be gallant adventurers.

THE INCREASING OPPOSITION

Luke 6:1–5

> One Sabbath day, Jesus happened to be going through the corn fields, and his disciples were plucking the ears of corn and rubbing them in their hands and eating them.

Some of the Pharisees said, 'Why are you doing what it
is illegal to do on the Sabbath?' Jesus answered, 'Have
you not read what David did when he and his comrades
were hungry? – how he went into the house of God and
took the loaves of the presence and ate them and gave
them to his comrades, although it is not legal for any
but the priests to eat them. The Son of Man', he said to
them, 'is the Lord of the Sabbath.'

THIS is the first of two incidents which show the opposition
to Jesus rapidly coming out into the open and which make it
clear that the immediate charge against him was that he was
a breaker of the Sabbath law. He and his disciples were
passing along one of the paths which intersected the corn
fields. The fact that the disciples plucked the ears of corn
was in itself no crime. One of the merciful laws of the Old
Testament laid it down that anyone passing through a corn
field was free to pluck the corn as long as a sickle was not
put into it (Deuteronomy 23:25). On any other day there
would have been no complaint; but this was the Sabbath.
Four of the forbidden kinds of work were reaping, threshing,
winnowing and preparing food; and technically the disciples
had broken every one of them. By plucking the corn they
were guilty of reaping; by rubbing it in their hands of threshing; by flinging away the husks of winnowing; and the very
fact that they ate it showed that they had prepared food on
the Sabbath. To us the whole thing seems fantastic; but we
must remember that to a strict Pharisee this was deadly sin;
rules and regulations had been broken; this was a matter of
life and death.

They made their accusation and Jesus quoted the Old
Testament to them. He quoted the incident in I Samuel 21:1-
6 when David and his comrades, when they were very hungry,
ate the shewbread of the Tabernacle. A better name for it is

the Bread of the Presence. Every Sabbath morning there were laid before God twelve wheaten loaves baked of flour sieved no fewer than eleven times. There was one loaf for every tribe. In the time of Jesus these loaves were laid on a table of solid gold, three feet long, one and a half feet broad, and nine inches high. The table stood lengthwise along the northern side of the Holy Place. The bread stood for the very presence of God and none but the priests might eat of it (Leviticus 24:5–9). But David's need had taken precedence over rules and regulations.

The Rabbis themselves said, 'The Sabbath is made for you and not you for the Sabbath.' That is to say at their highest and their best the Rabbis admitted that human need repealed ritual law. If that is so, how much more is the Son of Man, with his heart of love and mercy, Lord of the Sabbath? How much more can he use it for his purposes of love? But the Pharisees had forgotten the claims of mercy because they were immersed in their rules and regulations. It is most significant that they were watching Jesus and his disciples as they passed through the corn fields. Clearly they were spying; from now on every act of Jesus' life was to be scrutinized by those bleak and critical and hostile eyes.

This passage contains a great general truth. Jesus said to the Pharisees, 'Have you not read what David did?' The answer of course was, 'Yes' – but they had never seen what it meant. It is possible to read Scripture meticulously, to know the Bible inside out from cover to cover, to be able to quote it verbatim and to pass any examination on it – and yet completely miss its real meaning. Why did the Pharisees miss the meaning – and why do we so often miss it?

(1) They did not bring to Scripture *an open mind.* They came to Scripture not to learn God's will but to find proof texts to buttress up their own ideas. Far too often people take

their theology to the Bible instead of finding their theology in the Bible. When we read Scripture we must say, not, 'Listen, Lord, for your servant is speaking,' but, 'Speak, Lord, for your servant is listening.'

(2) They did not bring *a needy heart*. The person who comes with no sense of need always misses the deepest meaning of Scripture. When need awakens, the Bible is a new book. When Bishop Butler was dying he was troubled. 'Have you forgotten, my lord,' said his chaplain, 'that Jesus Christ is a Saviour?' 'But,' said the dying bishop, 'how can I know that he is a Saviour for me?' 'It is written,' said the chaplain, 'him that cometh unto me I will in nowise cast out.' And Butler answered, 'I have read these words a thousand times and I never saw their meaning until now. Now I die in peace.' The sense of need unlocked for him the treasury of Scripture.

When we read God's book we must bring to it the open mind and the needy heart – and then to us also it will be the greatest book in the world.

THE DEFIANCE OF JESUS

Luke 6:6–11

> On another Sabbath Jesus went into the synagogue and was teaching, and there was a man there whose right hand was withered. The scribes and the Pharisees watched him to see if he would heal on the Sabbath day in order to find a charge against him. He knew well what they were thinking. He said to the man with the withered hand, 'Rise, and stand in the midst.' He rose and stood. Jesus said to them, 'Here is a question for you – is it legal to do good on the Sabbath day or to do

> evil? To save a life or to destroy it?' He looked round
> on them and said to him, 'Stretch out your hand.' He
> did so and his hand was restored. They were filled with
> insane anger, and they discussed with each other what
> they could do to Jesus.

BY this time the opposition to Jesus was quite open. He was teaching in the synagogue on the Sabbath day and the scribes and Pharisees were there with the set purpose of watching him so that, if he healed, they could charge him with breaking the Sabbath. There is this interesting touch. If we compare the story in Matthew 12:10–13 and Mark 3:1–6 with Luke's version, we find that only Luke tells us that it was the man's *right* hand which was withered. There speaks the doctor, interested in the details of the case.

In this incident Jesus openly broke the law. To heal was to work and work was prohibited on the Sabbath day. True, if there was any danger to life, steps might be taken to help a sufferer. For instance, it was always legal to treat diseases of the eye or throat. But this man was in no danger of his life; he might have safely waited until the next day. But Jesus laid down the great principle that, whatever the rules and regulations may say, it is always right to do a good thing on the Sabbath day. He asked the piercing questions, 'Is it legal to save life or to destroy it on the Sabbath?' That must have struck home, for while he was seeking to help the life of the man, they were doing all they could to destroy *him*. It was he who was seeking to save and they who were seeking to destroy.

In this story there are three characters.

(1) There is *the man with the withered hand*. We can tell two things about him.

(a) One of the apocryphal gospels, that is, one which never gained admission into the New Testament, tells us that he

was a stone mason and he came to Jesus, begging his help
and saying, 'I was a stone mason earning my living with my
hand; I beseech you, Jesus, give me back my health that I
may not have to beg my bread with shame.' *He was a man
who wanted to work.* God always looks with approval on
anyone who wants to do an honest day's work.

(b) *He was a man who was prepared to attempt the
impossible.* He did not argue when Jesus told him to stretch
out his useless hand; he tried and, in the strength Jesus gave
him, he succeeded. *Impossible* is a word which should be
banished from the vocabulary of the Christian. As a famous
scientist said, 'The difference between the difficult and the
impossible is only that the impossible takes a little longer to
do.'

(2) There is *Jesus.* There is in this story a glorious atmosphere of defiance. Jesus knew that he was being watched but
without hesitation he healed. He asked the man to stand
out in front of everybody. This thing was not going to be
done in a corner. There is a story of one of John Wesley's
preachers who proposed to preach in a hostile town. He hired
the town-crier to announce the meeting and the town-crier
announced it in a terrified whisper. The preacher took the
bell from him and rang it and thundered out, 'Mr So and So
will preach in such and such a place and at such and such a
time tonight – *and I am the man.*' Real Christians display
with pride the banner of their faith and bid the opposition do
its worst.

(3) There are *the Pharisees.* Here were men who took the
quite extraordinary course of hating a man who had just cured
a sufferer. They are the outstanding example of men who
loved their rules and regulations more than they loved God.
We see this happen in churches over and over again. Disputes
are not about the great matters of the faith but about matters

of church government and the like. Robert Leighton, the seventeenth-century Bishop of Glasgow, once said, 'The mode of church government is unconstrained; but peace and concord, kindness and goodwill are indispensable.' There is an ever-present danger of setting loyalty to a system above loyalty to God.

JESUS CHOOSES THE TWELVE

Luke 6:12–19

> In these days Jesus went away into a mountain to pray; and he spent the whole night in prayer to God. When day came he called his disciples. From them he chose twelve, whom he also called apostles – Simon, whom he named Peter, and Andrew his brother, and James, and John, and Philip, and Bartholomew, and Matthew, and Thomas, and James the son of Alphaeus, and Simon who was called the Zealot, and Judas the son of James, and Judas Iscariot, who became a traitor. He came down with them and took his stand with them on a place in the plain; and there was a great crowd of his disciples there, and a great crowd of people from all Judaea and Jerusalem and from the coastal district of Tyre and Sidon, who had come to listen to him and to be healed from their diseases; and those who were distressed by unclean spirits were healed and the whole crowd sought to touch him because power went out from him, and he healed all.

HERE we see Jesus choosing the Twelve. It is interesting and salutary to see why he chose them, because it is for the same reasons that he still wants and needs men and women.

(1) Mark 3:14 tells us that he chose them *that they might be with him*. That means two things.

(a) He chose them to be his friends. It is amazing that Jesus needed human friendship. It is of the very essence of the Christian faith that we can say in all reverence and humility that God cannot be happy without men and women. Just because God is Father there is a blank in his heart until the last person comes home.

(b) Jesus knew that the end was coming. Had he lived in a later age he might have written a book which would have carried his teaching all over the world. But, living when he did, Jesus chose these men that he might write his message upon them. They were to be his living books. They were to share his company so that they might some day take his message to all people.

(2) Jesus chose them *to be his disciples*. The word disciple means *a learner*. They were to be those who were always learning more and more about him. Christians spend their whole lives learning about that Lord whom they will some day meet face to face and will then know even as they are known.

(3) Jesus chose them to be *his apostles*. The Greek word *apostolos* means *someone who is sent out*. It can be used for an envoy or an ambassador. They were to be his ambassadors to men and women. A little girl received in the Sunday School a lesson on the disciples. She did not get the word quite right because she was very young; and she came home and told her parents that she had been learning about Jesus' *samples*. Ambassadors are those who in a foreign land represent their own country, becoming supremely the samples of that country. Christians are sent to be ambassadors for Christ, not only by their words but by their lives and deeds.

About the Twelve themselves we may note two things.

(1) They were very *ordinary men*. There was not a wealthy, nor a famous, nor an influential man among them;

they had no special education; they were men of the common people. It is as if Jesus said, 'Give me twelve ordinary men and I will change the world.' The work of Jesus is not in the hands of those whom the world calls great, but in the hands of ordinary people like ourselves.

(2) They were *a strange mixture*. To take but two of them – Matthew was a tax-collector, and, therefore, a traitor and a renegade. Simon was a Zealot, and the Zealots were fanatical nationalists, who were sworn to assassinate every traitor and every Roman they could. It is one of the miracles of the power of Christ that Matthew the tax-collector and Simon the Zealot could live at peace in the close company of the apostolic band. When people are really Christian the most diverse and divergent types can live at peace together. It was said of the writer G. K. Chesterton and his brother Cecil, 'They always argued, they never quarrelled.' It is only in Christ that we can solve the problem of living together; because even people who are complete opposites may be united in their love for him. If we really love him, we will also love each other.

THE END OF THE WORLD'S VALUES

Luke 6:20–6

> Jesus lifted up his eyes upon his disciples and said, 'Happy are you poor, because yours is the kingdom of God. Happy are you who are hungry now because you will be filled. Happy are you who weep now because you will laugh. Happy are you when men will hate you and shut you off from their company and insult you and cast out your name as an evil name, for the sake of the Son of Man; for – look you – your reward in heaven will be great. Their fathers used to treat the prophets in the same way. But woe to you who are rich because

you have all the comfort you are going to get. Woe to
you who are filled because you will be hungry. Woe
to you who laugh now because you will grieve and
weep. Woe to you when all men speak well of you, for
that is what your fathers use to do to the false prophets.'

LUKE'S Sermon on the Plain and Matthew's Sermon on the
Mount (Matthew, chapters 5–7) closely correspond. Both start
with a series of beatitudes. There are differences between the
versions of Matthew and Luke, but this one thing is clear –
they are a series of bombshells. It may well be that we have
read them so often that we have forgotten how revolutionary
they are. They are quite unlike the laws which a philosopher
or a typical wise man might lay down. Each one is a challenge.

As the scholar Adolf Deissmann said, 'They are spoken in
an electric atmosphere. They are not quiet stars but flashes of
lightning followed by a thunder of surprise and amazement.'
They take the accepted standards and turn them upside down.
The people whom Jesus called happy the world would call
wretched; and the people Jesus called wretched the world
would call happy. Just imagine anyone saying, 'Happy are
the poor, and, Woe to the rich!' To talk like that is to put an
end to the world's values altogether.

Where then is the key to this? It comes in verse 24. There
Jesus says, 'Woe to you who are rich because you have all
the comfort you are going to get.' The word Jesus uses for
have is the word used for receiving payment in full of an
account. What Jesus is saying is this, 'If you set your heart
and bend your whole energies to obtain the things which the
world values, you will get them – but that is all you will ever
get.' In the expressive phrase, literally, you have had it! But
if on the other hand you set your heart and bend all your
energies to be utterly loyal to God and true to Christ, you
will run into all kinds of trouble; you may by the world's

standards look unhappy, but much of your payment is still to come; and it will be joy eternal.

We are here face to face with an eternal choice which begins in childhood and never ends till life ends. Will you take the easy way which yields immediate pleasure and profit? or, Will you take the hard way which yields immediate toil and sometimes suffering? Will you seize on the pleasure and the profit of the moment? or, Are you willing to look ahead and sacrifice them for the greater good? Will you concentrate on the world's rewards? or, Will you concentrate on Christ? If you take the world's way, you must abandon the values of Christ. If you take Christ's way, you must abandon the values of the world.

Jesus had no doubt which way in the end brought happiness. It has been said that Jesus promised his disciples three things – that they would be completely fearless, absurdly happy and in constant trouble. G. K. Chesterton, whose principles constantly got him into trouble, once said, 'I like getting into hot water. It keeps you clean!' It is Jesus' teaching that the joy of heaven will amply compensate for the trouble of earth. As Paul said, 'This slight momentary affliction is preparing us for an eternal weight of glory beyond all measure' (2 Corinthians 4:17). The challenge of the beatitudes is, 'Will you be happy in the world's way, or in Christ's way?'

THE GOLDEN RULE

Luke 6:27–38

> Jesus said, 'But to you who are listening I say, Love your enemies, do good to those who hate you, bless those who curse you, pray for those who ill-use you. To

him who strikes you on one cheek offer the other cheek also. If anyone takes away your cloak, do not stop him taking your tunic, too. Give to everyone who asks you; if anyone takes away your belongings, do not demand them back again. As you would like men to act towards you, so do you act towards them. If you love those who love you, what special grace is there in that? Even sinners love those who love them. If you are kind to those who are kind to you, what special grace is there in that? Even sinners do that. If you lend to those from whom you wish to get, what special grace is in that? Even sinners lend to sinners in order to get as much back again. But you must love your enemies; and do good to them; and lend with no hope of getting anything in return. Your reward will be great and you will be the sons of the Most High, because he is kind both to the thankless and to the wicked. Be merciful as your Father in heaven is merciful; do not judge and you will not be judged; do not condemn and you will not be condemned; forgive and you will be forgiven. Give and it will be given to you. People will give into your bosom, good measure pressed together, shaken down, running over; for with what measure you measure it will be measured to you back again.'

THERE is no commandment of Jesus which has caused so much discussion and debate as the commandment to love our enemies. Before we can obey it we must discover what it means. In Greek there are three words for 'to love'. There is *eran*, which describes passionate love, the love between the sexes. There is *philein*, which describes our love for our nearest and dearest, the warm affection of the heart. Neither of these two words is used here; the word used here is *agapan*, which needs a whole paragraph to translate it.

Agapan describes an active feeling of benevolence towards other people; it means that no matter what others do to us we will never allow ourselves to desire anything but their highest good; and we will deliberately and of set purpose go out of our way to be good and kind to them. This is most suggestive. We cannot love our enemies as we love our nearest and dearest. To do so would be unnatural, impossible and even wrong. But we can see to it that, no matter what others do to us, even if they insult, ill-treat and injure us, we will seek nothing but their highest good.

One thing emerges from this. The love we bear to our dear ones is something we cannot help. We speak of *falling* in love; it is something which happens to us. But this love towards our enemies is not only something of the heart; it is something of the will. It is something which by the grace of Christ we may will ourselves to do.

This passage has in it two great facts about the Christian ethic.

(1) The Christian ethic is *positive*. It does not consist in *not doing* things but in *doing* them. Jesus gave us the Golden Rule which bids us do to others as we would have them do to us. That rule exists in many writers of many creeds in its *negative* form. Hillel, one of the great Jewish Rabbis, was asked by a man to teach him the whole law while he stood on one leg. He answered, 'What is hateful to thee, do not to another. That is the whole law and all else is explanation.' Philo, the great Jew of Alexandria, said, 'What you hate to suffer, do not do to anyone else.' Isocrates, the Greek orator, said, 'What things make you angry when you suffer them at the hands of others, do not you do to other people.' The Stoics had as one of their basic rules, 'What you do not wish to be done to yourself, do not you do to any other.' When Confucius was asked, 'Is there one word which may serve as a rule of

practice for all one's life?' he answered, 'Is not reciprocity such a word? What you do not want done to yourself, do not do to others.'

Every one of these forms is negative. It is not unduly difficult to keep yourself from such action; but it is a very different thing to go out of your way to do to others what you would want them to do to you. The very essence of Christian conduct is that it consists, not in refraining from bad things, but in actively doing good things.

(2) The Christian ethic is based on *the extra thing.* Jesus described the common ways of sensible conduct and then dismissed them with the question, 'What special grace is in that?' So often people claim to be just as good as their neighbours. Very likely they are. But the question of Jesus is, 'How much *better* are you than the ordinary person?' It is not our neighbour with whom we must compare ourselves; we may well stand that comparison very adequately; it is *God* with whom we must compare ourselves; and in that comparison we are all in default.

(3) What is the reason for this Christian conduct? The reason is that it makes us like God, for that is the way he acts. God sends his rain on the just and the unjust. He is kind to the person who brings him joy and equally kind to the person who grieves his heart. God's love embraces saint and sinner alike. It is that love we must copy; if we, too, seek even our enemy's highest good we will in truth be the children of God.

Verse 38 has the strange phrase, 'People will give into your bosom.' It was customary for a Jew to wear a long loose robe down to the feet, and round the waist a girdle. The robe could be pulled up so that the bosom of the robe above the girdle formed a kind of outsize pocket in which things could be carried. So another way of saying this would be, 'People will fill your pocket.'

RULES FOR LIFE AND LIVING

Luke 6:39–46

> Jesus spoke a parable to them: 'Surely a blind man
> cannot lead a blind man? If he tries to do so will not
> both fall into the ditch? The disciple cannot advance
> beyond his teacher, but every disciple will be equipped
> as his teacher is. Why do you look at the speck of dust
> that is in your brother's eye and never notice the plank
> that is in your own eye? Or, how can you say to your
> brother, "Brother, let me take out the speck of dust that
> is in your eye," when you yourself do not notice the
> plank in your own eye? You hypocrite! First put the
> plank out of your own eye and then you will see clearly
> to put out the speck of dust that is in your brother's eye.
> There is no good tree which produces rotten fruit; nor
> again, is there a rotten tree which produces good fruit.
> Each tree is recognized by its own fruit. People do not
> gather figs from thistles nor do they gather grapes from
> a bramble bush. The good man produces good from the
> treasure of his heart. The evil man produces evil from
> the evil. The mouth speaks out of whatever abounds in
> the heart.'

THIS reads like a disconnected series of separate sayings. Two
things are possible. It may well be that Luke is collecting
together here sayings of Jesus which were spoken on different
occasions and so giving us a kind of compendium of rules
for life and living. Or, this may be an instance of the Jewish
method of preaching. The Jews called preaching *Charaz*,
which means *stringing beads*. The Rabbis held that the
preacher must never linger more than a few moments on any
topic but, in order to maintain interest, must move quickly
from one topic to another. Such preaching, therefore, often
gives us the impression of being disconnected.

The passage falls into four sections.

(1) Verses 39 and 40. Jesus warned that teachers cannot lead pupils beyond their own level of achievement. That is a double warning to us. In our learning we must seek only the best teacher for only the most knowledgeable can lead us farthest on; in our teaching we must remember that we cannot teach what we do not know.

(2) Verses 41 and 42. Here is an example of the humour of Jesus. It must have been with a smile that Jesus drew the picture of a man with a plank in his own eye trying to extract a speck of dust from someone else's eye. He taught that we have no right to criticize unless we ourselves are free of faults. That simply means that we have no right to criticize at all, because 'there is so much bad in the best of us and so much good in the worst of us that it ill becomes any of us to find fault with the rest of us'.

(3) Verses 43 and 44 remind us that people cannot be judged in any other way than by their deeds. It was said to a teacher, 'I cannot hear what you say for listening to what you are.' Teaching and preaching are both 'truth through personality'. Fine words will never take the place of fine deeds. That is very relevant today. We fear the growth of secularism within society. We will never overcome this by writing books and pamphlets and holding discussion groups. The only way to prove the superiority of Christianity is to show by our lives that it produces better men and women.

(4) Verse 45. In this verse Jesus offers a reminder that the words of our lips are in the last analysis the product of our hearts. We cannot speak of God with our mouths unless God's Spirit is in our hearts. Nothing shows the state of our hearts so well as words spoken without careful consideration, when talking freely and saying, as we put it, the first thing which comes into our heads. If you ask directions to a certain place,

one person may tell you it is near such and such a *church*; another, that it is near such and such a *cinema*; another, that it is near such and such a *football ground*; another, that it is near such and such a *bar*. The very words of the answer to a chance question often show where our thoughts most naturally turn and where the interests of our hearts lie. Always our speech betrays us.

THE ONLY SURE FOUNDATION

Luke 6:47–9

> Jesus said, 'Why do you call me, Lord, Lord, and do not what I say? I will show you what everyone who comes to me and listens to my words and does them is like. He is like a man building a house, who dug deep down into the earth and laid the foundation on a rock. When the flood rose the river dashed against that house but it could not shake it because it was well founded. But he who has listened to me and has not done what I say is like a man who built his house on the top of earth without any foundation. The river dashed against it and immediately it collapsed, and great was the fall of it.'

To get the real picture behind this parable we have to read Matthew's version of it as well (Matthew 7:24–7). In Luke's version the river does not seem to make sense; that is because Luke was not a native of Palestine and did not have a clear picture of the circumstances in his own mind; whereas Matthew did belong to Palestine and knew just what the picture was. In summer many of the rivers dried up altogether and left a sandy bed empty of water. But in winter, after the September rains had come, the empty river bed became a raging torrent. Many a man, looking for a site for a house, found an inviting stretch of sand and built there, only to discover when the winter came, that he had built his house in the middle of a raging river which swept it away. The wise man searched for rock, where it was much more difficult to build and where it was hard labour to cut out the foundations. When the wild winter weather came, his toil was amply repaid, for his house stood strong and firm and secure. In either form the parable teaches the importance of laying the right foundation for life; the only true foundation is obedience to the teaching of Jesus.

What made the foolish builder choose so unwisely?

(1) He wanted *to avoid toil*. He could not be bothered to dig into the rock. The sand was much more attractive and much less trouble. It may be easier to take our way than it is to take Jesus' way but the end is ruin; Jesus' way is the way to security here and hereafter.

(2) He was *short-sighted*. He never troubled to think what his chosen site would be like six months afterwards. In every decision in life there is a short view and a long view. Happy is the person who never barters future good for present pleasure. Happy is the person who sees things, not in the light of the moment, but in the light of eternity.

When we learn that the hard way is often the best way, and that the long view is always the right view, we will found our lives upon the teaching of Jesus and no storms will ever shake them.

A SOLDIER'S FAITH

Luke 7:1-10

> When Jesus had completed all his words in the hearing of the people, he went into Capernaum. The servant of

a certain centurion was so ill that he was going to die, and he was very dear to him. When he heard about Jesus he sent some Jewish elders to him and asked him to come and save his servant's life. They came to Jesus and strenuously urged him to come. 'He is', they said, 'a man who deserves that you should do this for him, for he loves our nation and has himself built us our synagogue.' So Jesus went with them. When he was now quite near the house the centurion sent friends to him. 'Sir,' he said, 'do not trouble yourself. I am not worthy that you should come under my roof; nor do I count myself fit to come to you; but just speak a word and my servant will be cured. For I myself am a man under orders, and I have soldiers under me, and I say to one, "Go," and he goes; and to another, "Come," and he comes; and I say to my servant, "Do this," and he does it.' When Jesus heard this he was amazed at him. He turned to the crowd who were following him and said, 'I tell you I have not found such great faith not even in Israel.' And those who had been sent returned to the house and found the servant completely cured.

THE central character is a Roman centurion; and he was no ordinary man.

(1) The mere fact that *he was a centurion* meant he was no ordinary man. A centurion was the equivalent of a regimental sergeant-major; and the centurions were the backbone of the Roman army. Wherever they are spoken of in the New Testament they are spoken of well (cf. Luke 23:47; Acts 10:22; 22:26; 23:17, 23, 24; 24:23; 27:43). Polybius, the historian, describes their qualifications. They must be not so much 'seekers after danger as men who can command, steady in action, and reliable; they ought not to be over-anxious to rush into the fight; but when hard pressed they must be ready to hold their ground and die at their posts'.

The centurion must have had the respect of his men or he would never have held the post which was his.

(2) *He had a completely unusual attitude to his slave.* He loved this slave and would go to any trouble to save him. In Roman law a slave was defined as a living tool; he had no rights; a master could ill-treat him and even kill him if he chose. A Roman writer on estate management recommends the farmer to examine his implements every year and to throw out those which are old and broken, and to do the same with his slaves. Normally when a slave was past his work he was thrown out to die. The attitude of this centurion to his slave was quite unusual.

(3) *He was clearly a deeply religious man.* A man would need to be more than superficially interested before he would go to the lengths of building a synagogue. It is true that the Romans encouraged religion from the cynical motive that it kept people in order. They regarded it as the opiate of the people. Augustus recommended the building of synagogues for that very reason. As Edward Gibbon, the author of *The Decline and Fall of the Roman Empire*, said in a famous sentence, 'The various modes of religion which prevailed in the Roman world were all considered by the people as equally true; by the philosopher as equally false; *and by the magistrate as equally useful.*' But this centurion was no administrative cynic; he was a sincerely religious man.

(4) *He had an extremely unusual attitude to the Jews.* If the Jews despised the Gentiles, the Gentiles hated the Jews. Anti-semitism is not a new thing. The Romans called the Jews a filthy race; they spoke of Judaism as a barbarous superstition; they spoke of the Jewish hatred of humankind; they accused the Jews of worshipping an ass's head and annually sacrificing a Gentile stranger to their God. True, many of the Gentiles, weary of the many gods and loose morals of

paganism, had accepted the Jewish doctrine of the one God and the austere Jewish ethic. But the whole atmosphere of this story implies a close bond of friendship between this centurion and the Jews.

(5) *He was a humble man.* He knew quite well that a strict Jew was forbidden by the law to enter the house of a Gentile (Acts 10:28); just as he was forbidden to allow a Gentile into his house or have any communication with him. He would not even come to Jesus himself. He persuaded his Jewish friends to approach him. This man who was accustomed to command had an amazing humility in the presence of true greatness.

(6) *He was a man of faith.* His faith is based on the soundest argument. He argued from the here and now to the there and then. He argued from his own experience to an understanding of God. If his authority produced the results it did, how much more must that of Jesus? He came with that perfect confidence which looks up and says, 'Lord, I *know* you can do this.' If only we had a faith like that, for us too the miracle would happen and life become new.

THE COMPASSION OF CHRIST

Luke 7:11–17

> Next, after that, Jesus was on his way to a town called Nain; and his disciples and a great crowd accompanied him on the journey. When he came near the gate of the town – look you – a man who had died was being carried out to burial. He was his mother's only son, and she was a widow. There was a great crowd of townspeople with her. When the Lord saw her he was moved to the depths of his heart for her and said to her, 'Don't go on weeping!' He went up and touched the bier. Those who

were carrying it stood still. 'Young man,' he said, 'I tell you, rise!' And the dead man sat up and began to speak. And he gave him back to his mother. And awe gripped them all. They glorified God saying, 'A great prophet has been raised up among us,' and, 'God has graciously visited his people.' This story about him went out in all Judaea and all the surrounding countryside.

In this passage, as in the one immediately preceding, once again Luke the doctor speaks. In verse 10 the word we translated *completely cured is* the technical medical term for *sound in wind and limb.* In verse 15 the word used for *sitting up* is the technical term for a patient *sitting up in bed.*

Nain was a day's journey from Capernaum and lay between Endor and Shunem, where Elisha, as the old story runs, raised another mother's son (2 Kings 4:18–37). To this day, ten minutes' walk from Nain on the road to Endor there is a cemetery of rock tombs in which the dead are laid.

In many ways this is the loveliest story in all the gospels.

(1) It tells of *the pathos and the poignancy of human life.* The funeral procession would be headed by the band of professional mourners with their flutes and their cymbals, uttering in a kind of frenzy their shrill cries of grief. There is all the ageless sorrow of the world in the austere and simple sentence, 'He was his mother's only son, and she was a widow.'

> Never morning wore to evening
> But some heart did break.

In Shelley's *Adonais*, his lament for Keats, he writes:

> As long as skies are blue, and fields are green,
> Evening must usher night, night urge the morrow,
> Month follow month with woe, and year wake
>   year to sorrow.

Virgil, the Roman poet, in an immortal phrase spoke about 'The tears of things' – *sunt lacrimae rerum.* In the nature of things we live in a world of broken hearts.

(2) To the pathos of human life, Luke adds *the compassion of Christ.* Jesus was moved to the depths of his heart. There is no stronger word in the Greek language for sympathy and again and again in the gospel story it is used of Jesus (Matthew 14:14, 15:32, 20:34; Mark 1:41, 8:2).

To the ancient world this must have been a staggering thing. The noblest faith in antiquity was Stoicism. The Stoics believed that the primary characteristic of God was *apathy, incapability of feeling.* This was their argument. If someone can make another sad or sorry, glad or joyful, it means that, at least for the moment, he can influence that other person. If he can influence him that means that, at least for the moment, he is greater than the other person. Now, no one can be greater than God; therefore, no one can influence God; therefore, in the nature of things, God must be incapable of feeling.

Here we are presented with the amazing conception of one who was the Son of God being moved to the depths of his being. As Michael Bruce wrote:

> In ev'ry pang that rends the heart,
> The Man of sorrows has a part.

For many that is the most precious thing about the God and Father of our Lord Jesus Christ.

(3) To the compassion of Jesus, Luke adds *the power of Jesus.* He went up and touched the bier. It was not a coffin, for coffins were not used in the middle east. Very often long wickerwork baskets were used for carrying the body to the grave. It was a dramatic moment. In the words of one great commentator, 'Jesus claimed as his own what death had seized as his prey.'

It may well be that here we have a miracle of diagnosis; that Jesus with those keen eyes of his saw that the young man was in a cataleptic trance and saved him from being buried alive, as so many were in Palestine. It does not matter; the fact remains that Jesus claimed for life a young man who had been marked for death. Jesus is not only the Lord of life; he is the Lord of death who himself triumphed over the grave and who has promised that, because he lives, we shall live also (John 14:19).

THE FINAL PROOF

Luke 7:18–29

> John's disciples told him about all these things; so John called two of his disciples and sent them to the Lord saying, 'Are you he who is to come, or, are we to look for another?' When they arrived, the men said to him, 'John, the Baptizer, has sent us to you. Are you the One who is to come,' he asks, 'or are we to look for another?' At that time he cured many of their diseases and afflictions and of evil spirits, and to many blind people he gave the gift of sight. 'Go,' he answered them, 'and tell John what you have seen and heard. The blind recover their sight; the lame walk; the lepers are cleansed; the deaf hear; the dead are raised up; the poor have the good news told to them; and blessed is he who does not find a stumbling-block in me.'
>
> When John's messengers had gone away, Jesus began to say to the crowds concerning John, 'What did you go out into the desert to see? A reed shaken by the wind? But what did you go out to see? A man dressed in soft clothes? Look you – those who wear expensive clothes and live in luxury are in royal palaces. But what did

you go out to see? A prophet? Yes, I say to you, and something more than a prophet. This is he of whom it stands written – "Look you, I send my messenger before you to prepare your way before you." I tell you there is no one greater among those born of women than John. But he who is least in the kingdom of God is greater than he.' When the people and the tax-collectors heard this they called God righteous for they had been baptized with John's baptism.

JOHN sent emissaries to Jesus to ask if he really was the Messiah or if they must look for someone else.

(1) This incident has worried many because they have been surprised at the apparent doubt in the mind of John. Various explanations have been advanced.

(a) It is suggested that John took this step, not for his own sake, but *for the sake of his disciples*. He was sure enough; but they had their qualms and he desired that they should be confronted with proof unanswerable.

(b) It is suggested that John wished to hurry Jesus on because he thought it was time Jesus moved towards decisive action.

(c) The simplest explanation is the best. Think what was happening to John. John, the child of the desert and of the wide-open spaces, was confined in a dungeon cell in the castle of Machaerus. Once, one of the MacDonalds, a highland chieftain, was confined in a little cell in Carlisle Castle. In his cell was one little window. To this day you may see in the sandstone the marks of the feet and hands of the highlander as he lifted himself up and clung to the window ledge day by day to gaze with infinite longing upon the border hills and valleys he would never walk again. Shut in his cell, choked by the narrow walls, John asked his question because his cruel captivity had put tremors in his heart.

(2) Note the proof that Jesus offered. He pointed at the facts. The sick and the suffering and the humble poor were experiencing the power and hearing the word of the good news. Here is a point which is seldom realized – *this is not the answer John expected.* If Jesus was God's Anointed One, John would have expected him to say, 'My armies are massing. Caesarea, the headquarters of the Roman government, is about to fall. The sinners are being obliterated. And judgment has begun.' He would have expected Jesus to say, 'The wrath of God is on the march,' but Jesus said, 'The mercy of God is here.' Let us remember that where pain is soothed and sorrow turned to joy, where suffering and death are vanquished, there is the kingdom of God. Jesus' answer was, 'Go back and tell John that the love of God is here.'

(3) After John's emissaries had gone, Jesus paid his own tribute to him. People had crowded out into the desert to see and hear John and they had not gone to see a reed shaken by the wind. That may mean one of two things.

(a) Nothing was more familiar by Jordan's banks than a reed shaken by the wind. It was in fact a proverbial phrase for the commonest of sights. It may then mean that the crowds went out to see no ordinary sight.

(b) It may stand for fickleness. It was no vacillating, swaying character that people went out to see like a swaying reed, but a man immovable as a mighty tree.

They had not gone out to see someone like the soft, silk-clad courtiers of the royal palace.

What then had they gone to see?

(1) Jesus pays John a great tribute. The expectation was that before God's anointed king arrived upon the earth, Elijah would return to prepare the way and act as his herald (Malachi 4:5). John was the herald of the Highest.

(2) Jesus states quite clearly the limitations of John. The least in the kingdom of heaven was greater than he. Why? Some have said that it was because John had wavered, if but for a moment, in his faith. It was not that. It was because John marked a dividing line in history. Since John's proclamation had been made, Jesus had come; eternity had invaded time; heaven had invaded earth; God had arrived in Jesus; life could never be the same again. We date all time as before Christ and after Christ – BC and AD. Jesus is the dividing line. Therefore, all who come after him and who receive him are of necessity granted a greater blessing than all who went before. The entry of Jesus into the world divided all time into two; and it divided all life in two. If we are in Christ, we become a new creation (cf. 2 Corinthians 5:17).

As the sixteenth-century Protestant martyr, Thomas Bilney, said, 'When I read that Christ Jesus came into the world to save sinners, it was as if day suddenly broke on a dark night.'

HUMAN PERVERSITY

Luke 7:30–5

> But the Pharisees and the scribes frustrated God's purpose for themselves because they were not baptized by him. 'To whom', asked Jesus, 'will I compare the men of this generation? And to whom are they like? They are like children seated in the market place who call to one another, "We have piped to you, and you did not dance. We have sung you a dirge and you did not weep." John the Baptizer came neither eating bread nor drinking wine, and you say, "He has a demon." The Son of Man came eating and drinking and you say, "Look! a gluttonous man and a wine-drinker, the friend

of tax-collectors and sinners." But wisdom is justified
by her children.'

THIS passage has two great warnings in it.

(1) It tells of the perils of free will. The scribes and the
Pharisees had succeeded in frustrating God's purpose for
themselves. The tremendous truth of Christianity is that the
coercion of God is not of force but of love. It is precisely
there that we can glimpse the sorrow of God. It is always
love's greatest tragedy to look upon some loved one who has
taken the wrong way and to see what might have been, what
could have been and what was meant to have been. That is
life's greatest heartbreak.

Sir William Watson wrote a poem entitled *Lux Perdita*,
the 'Lost Light'.

> These were the weak, slight hands
> That might have taken this strong soul, and bent
> Its stubborn substance to thy soft intent,
> And bound it unresisting with such bands
> As not the arm of envious heaven had rent.
>
> These were the calming eyes
> That round my pinnace could have stilled the sea,
> And drawn thy voyager home, and bid him be
> Pure with their pureness, with their wisdom wise,
> Merged in their light, and greatly lost in thee.
>
> But thou – thou passedst on,
> With whiteness clothed of dedicated days,
> Cold, like a star; and me in alien ways
> Thou leftest, following life's chance lure, where shone
> The wandering gleam that beckons and betrays.

The words of John Whittier are certainly true:

> Of all sad words of tongue and pen
> The saddest are those, 'It might have been.'

God's tragedy, too, is the 'might have been' of life. As G. K. Chesterton said, 'God had written not so much a poem, but rather a play; a play he had planned as perfect, but which had necessarily been left to human actors and stage managers, who had since made a great mess of it.' God save us from making shipwreck of life and bringing heartbreak to himself by using our free will to frustrate his purposes.

(2) It tells of human perversity. John had come, living with a hermit's austerity, and the scribes and Pharisees had said that he was a mad eccentric and that some demon had taken his wits away. Jesus had come, living life to the full and entering into every kind of activity, and they had taunted him with loving earth's pleasures far too much. We all know the days when a child will complain at anything and the moods when nothing will please us. The human heart can be lost in a perversity in which any appeal God may make will be met with wilful and childish discontent.

(3) But there are the few who answer; and God's wisdom is in the end justified by those who are his children. We may misuse our free will to frustrate God's purposes; in our perversity we may be blind and deaf to all his appeal. Had God used the force of coercion and laid on us the iron bonds of a will that could not be denied, there would have been a world of automata and a world without trouble. But God chose the dangerous way of love, and love in the end will triumph.

A SINNER'S LOVE

Luke 7:36–50

> One of the Pharisees invited Jesus to eat with him. He went into the Pharisee's house and reclined at table; and – look you – there was a woman in the town, a bad

woman. She knew that he was at table in the Pharisee's house, so she took an alabaster phial of perfume and stood behind him, beside his feet, weeping. She began to wash his feet with tears, and she wiped them with the hairs of her head; and she kept kissing his feet and anointing them with the perfume. When the Pharisee, who had invited him, saw this, he said to himself, 'If this fellow was a prophet, he would have known who and what kind of a person this woman is who keeps touching him, for she is a bad woman.' Jesus answered him. 'Simon, I have something to say to you.' He said, 'Master, say it.' Jesus said, 'There were two men who were in debt to a certain lender. The one owed him 500 denarii, the other 50 denarii. Since they were unable to pay he cancelled the debt to both. Who then will love him the more?' Simon answered, 'I presume, he to whom the greater favour was shown.' He said to him, 'Your judgment is correct.' He turned to the woman and said to Simon, 'Do you see this woman? I came into your house – you gave me no water for my feet. She has washed my feet with her tears, and wiped them with the hairs of her head. You did not give me any kiss. But she, from the time I came in, has not ceased to kiss my feet. You did not anoint my head with oil. She has anointed my feet with perfume. Wherefore, I tell you, her sins – her many sins – are forgiven for she loved much. He to whom little is forgiven loves little.' He said to her, 'Your sins are forgiven.' Those who were at table with him began to say to themselves, 'Who is this who forgives even sins?' He said to the woman, 'Your faith has saved you. Go in peace.'

THIS story is so vivid that it makes one believe that Luke may well have been an artist.

(1) The scene is the courtyard of the house of Simon the Pharisee. The houses of well-to-do people were built round

an open courtyard in the form of a hollow square. Often in the courtyard there would be a garden and a fountain; and there in the warm weather meals were eaten. It was the custom that when a Rabbi was at a meal in such a house, all kinds of people came in – they were quite free to do so – to listen to the pearls of wisdom which fell from his lips. That explains the presence of the woman.

When a guest entered such a house three things were always done. The host placed his hand on the guest's shoulder and gave him the kiss of peace. That was a mark of respect which was never omitted in the case of a distinguished Rabbi. The roads were only dust tracks, and shoes were merely soles held in place by straps across the foot. So always cool water was poured over the guest's feet to cleanse and comfort them. Either a pinch of sweet-smelling incense was burned or a drop of attar of roses was placed on the guest's head. These things good manners demanded, and in this case not one of them was done.

In the middle east the guests did not sit, but reclined, at table. They lay on low couches, resting on the left elbow, leaving the right arm free, with the feet stretched out behind; and during the meal the sandals were taken off. That explains how the woman was standing beside Jesus' feet.

(2) Simon was a Pharisee, one of the separated ones. Why should such a man invite Jesus to his house at all? There are three possible reasons.

(a) It is just possible that he was an admirer and a sympathizer, for not all the Pharisees were Jesus' enemies (cf. Luke 13:31). But the whole atmosphere of discourtesy makes that unlikely.

(b) It could be that Simon had invited Jesus with the deliberate intention of enticing him into some word or action which might have been made the basis of a charge against him.

Simon may have been an *agent provocateur*. Again it is not likely, because in verse 40 Simon gives Jesus the title, Rabbi.

(c) Most likely, Simon was a collector of celebrities; and with a half-patronizing contempt he had invited this startling young Galilaean to have a meal with him. That would best explain the strange combination of a certain respect with the omission of the usual courtesies. Simon was a man who tried to patronize Jesus.

(3) The woman was a bad woman, and a notoriously bad woman, a prostitute. No doubt she had listened to Jesus speak from the edge of the crowd and had glimpsed in him the hand which could lift her from the mire of her ways. Round her neck she wore, like all Jewish women, a little phial of concentrated perfume; these were called alabasters, and they were very costly. She wished to pour it on his feet, for it was all she had to offer. But as she saw him the tears came and fell upon his feet. For a Jewish woman to appear with hair unbound was an act of the gravest immodesty. On her wedding day a girl bound up her hair and never would she appear with it unbound again. The fact that this woman loosed her long hair in public showed how she had forgotten everyone except Jesus.

The story demonstrates a contrast between two attitudes of mind and heart.

(1) Simon was conscious of no need and therefore felt no love, and so received no forgiveness. Simon's impression of himself was that he was a good man in the sight of others and of God.

(2) The woman was conscious of nothing else than a burning need, and therefore was overwhelmed with love for him who could supply it, and so received forgiveness.

The one thing which shuts us off from God is self-sufficiency. And the strange thing is that the better we are, the more keenly we feel our sin. Paul could speak of sinners 'of whom I am the foremost' (1 Timothy 1:15). Francis of Assisi could say, 'There is nowhere a more wretched and a more miserable sinner than I.' It is true to say that the greatest of sins is to be conscious of no sin; but a sense of need will open the door to the forgiveness of God, because God is love, and love's greatest glory is to be needed.

ON THE ROAD

Luke 8:1–3

> After that, Jesus travelled through the country, town by town, and village by village, preaching the good news of the kingdom of God. The Twelve were with him, as were certain women, who had been cured from evil spirits and from illnesses. There was Mary, who is called Mary Magdalene, out of whom there went seven devils, and Joanna, the wife of Chuza, who was Herod's agent, and Susanna and many others. It was their habit to minister to their needs out of their resources.

THE time we saw coming had now come. Jesus was on the road. The synagogues were not now open to him, as once they had been. He had begun, as it were, in the church, where anyone with a message from God might expect to find a responsive and receptive audience. Instead of a welcome he had found opposition; instead of eager listeners he had found the scribes and Pharisees bleakly waiting to catch him out; so now he took to the open road and the hillside and the lake shore.

(1) Once more we are confronted with a fact which we have already noted. This passage lists a little group of women who served him out of their resources. It was always con-

sidered to be a pious act to support a Rabbi, and the fact that
the devoted followers of Jesus helped him in this way was in
direct line with ordinary practice. But, as with the disciples,
so with these women, we cannot fail to see how mixed a
company they were. There was Mary Magdalene, that is Mary
from the town of Magdala, out of whom he had cast seven
devils. Clearly she had a dark and terrible past. There was
Joanna. She was the wife of Chuza, Herod's *epitropos*. A
king had many entitlements and much private property; his
epitropos was the official who looked after the king's financial
interests. In the Roman Empire, even in provinces which were
governed by proconsuls appointed by the senate, the emperor
still had his *epitropos* to safeguard his interests. There could
be no more trusted and important official. It is an amazing
thing to find Mary Magdalene, with the dark past, and Joanna,
the lady of the court, in the one company.

It is one of the supreme achievements of Jesus that he can
enable the most diverse people to live together without in
the least losing their own personalities or qualities. G. K.
Chesterton writes about the text which says that the lion
will lie down with the lamb. 'But remember that this text is
too lightly interpreted. It is constantly assumed . . . that when
the lion lies down with the lamb the lion becomes lamb-like.
But that is brutal annexation and imperialism on the part of
the lamb. That is simply the lamb absorbing the lion instead
of the lion eating the lamb. The real problem is – Can the
lion lie down with the lamb and still retain his royal ferocity?
That is the problem the Church attempted; *that* is the miracle
she achieved.' There is nothing which the Church needs
more than to learn how to yoke in common harness the diverse
temperaments and qualities of different people. If we are
failing it is our own fault, for, in Christ, it can be done – and
has been done.

(2) In this list of women we have a group whose help was practical. Being women, they would not be allowed to preach; but they gave the gifts they had. There was an old shoemaker who once had wished to become a minister but the way had never opened up. He was the friend of a young divinity student; and when the young man one day was called to his first church the old man asked him for a favour. He asked to be allowed always to make his shoes so that he might feel the preacher was wearing his shoes in that pulpit into which he could never go himself.

It is not always the person in the foreground who is doing the greatest work. Many who occupy public positions could not sustain their place for one week without support from home! There is no gift which cannot be used in the service of Christ. Many of his greatest servants are in the background, unseen but essential to his cause.

THE SOWER AND THE SEED

Luke 8:4–15

> When a great crowd had gathered, and when they came to him from every city, Jesus spoke to them by means of a parable. The sower went out to sow his seed. As he sowed, some seed fell by the wayside. It was trampled upon and the birds of the heaven devoured it. Other seed fell on rocky ground where it grew up and withered because there was no moisture. Other seed fell in the middle of thorns and the thorns grew up along with it and choked the life out of it. Other seed fell into good ground and it produced a crop a hundredfold. As he told the story he said, 'He that has an ear to hear let him hear.'

The disciples asked him what the parable meant. He said, 'It is given to you to know the secrets of the kingdom of God. To the others it is presented in parables, so that they may see, and yet not see, and so that they may hear and yet not understand.'

The meaning of the parable is this. The seed is the word of God. Those by the wayside stand for those who have heard, and then the devil comes and takes the word from their hearts so that they may not believe and be saved. Those on the rocky ground stand for those, who, whenever they hear the word, gladly receive it; but they have no root; they believe for a time; but when a time of trial comes they fall away. The seed that falls among thorns stands for those, who, when they have heard, go their way and are suffocated by the cares, the wealth and the pleasures of this life, and so never complete their crop. The seed that is in the good ground stands for those who have heard the word and keep hold of it in a heart that is fine and good, and bear fruit with fortitude.

In this parable Jesus used a picture that all his hearers would recognize. It is in fact quite likely that he was looking at some sower sowing his seed as he spoke.

The parable speaks of four kinds of ground.

(1) The common ground in Palestine was split into long narrow strips; between the strips there were paths which were rights of way; when the seed fell on these paths, which were beaten as hard as the road, it had no chance of getting in.

(2) There was the rocky ground. This does not mean ground that was full of stones but ground which was only a thin skin of earth over a shelf of limestone rock. In such ground there was no moisture or nourishment, and the growing plant was bound to wither and die.

(3) The ground which was full of thorns was ground which at the moment looked clean enough. It is possible to make

any bit of ground *look* clean simply by turning it over. But the seeds of the weeds and the fibrous roots of the wild grasses had been left in it. The good seed and the weeds grew together, but the weeds grew more strongly; and so the life was choked out of the good seed.

(4) The good ground was ground that was deep and clean and well prepared.

Verses 9 and 10 have always been puzzling. It sounds as if Jesus is saying that he spoke in parables so that people would not be able to understand; but we cannot believe he would deliberately cloak his meaning from his listeners. Various explanations have been suggested.

(1) Matthew 13:13 puts it slightly differently. He says that Jesus spoke in parables *because* people could not rightly see and understand. Matthew seems to say that it was not to hinder people from seeing and understanding but to help them that Jesus so spoke.

(2) Matthew quotes immediately after this a saying of Isaiah 6:9, 10, which in effect says, 'I have spoken to them the word of God and the only result is that they have not understood a word of it.' So then the saying of Jesus may indicate not the object of his teaching in parables but the result of it.

(3) What Jesus really meant is this – people can become so dull and heavy and blunted in mind that when God's truth comes to them they cannot see it. It is not God's fault. They have become so mentally lazy, so blinded by prejudice, so unwilling to see anything they do not want to see, that they have become incapable of assimilating God's truth.

There are two interpretations of this parable.

(1) It is suggested that it means that the fate of the word of God depends on the heart into which it is sown.

(a) The hard path represents the shut mind, the mind which refuses to take it in.

(b) The shallow ground represents those who accept the word but who never think it out and never realize its consequences and who therefore collapse when the strain comes.

(c) The thorny ground stands for those whose lives are so busy that the things of God get crowded out. We must always remember that the things which crowd out the highest need not necessarily be bad. The worst enemy of the best is the second best.

(d) The good ground stands for the good hearer. Good hearers do three things. First, they listen attentively. Second, they keep what they hear in their minds and hearts and think over it until they discover its meaning for themselves. Third, they act upon it. They translate what they have heard into action.

(2) It is suggested that the parable is really a counsel against despair. Think of the situation. Jesus has been banished from the synagogues. The scribes and the Pharisees and the religious leaders are up against him. Inevitably the disciples would be disheartened. It is to them Jesus speaks this parable and in it he is saying, 'Every farmer knows that some of his seed will be lost; it cannot all grow. But that does not discourage him or make him stop sowing because he knows that, in spite of all, the harvest is sure. I know we have our setbacks and our discouragements; I know we have our enemies and our opponents; but, never despair, in the end the harvest is sure.'

This parable can be both a warning as to how we hear and receive the word of God and an encouragement to banish all despair in the certainty that not all the setbacks can defeat the ultimate harvest of God.

LAWS FOR LIFE

Luke 8:16–18

No one lights a lamp and then hides it under a vessel or puts it under a bed. No! he puts it on a lamp-stand so that those who come in may see the light. There is nothing hidden which will not be made manifest; there is nothing secret which will not be known and brought into the open. Take care, then, how you listen; for to him who has it will be given; and from him who has not there shall be taken away even what he thinks he has.

HERE we have three sayings, each with its own warning for life.

(1) Verse 16 stresses the essential conspicuousness of the Christian life. Christianity is in its very nature something which must be seen. It is easy to find convenient reasons why we should not flaunt our Christianity in the world's face. In almost every person there is an instinctive fear of being different; and the world is always likely to persecute those who do not conform to pattern.

A writer tells how he kept hens. In the hen-run all the hens were precisely the same in marking except one. The one different hen was pecked to death by the other occupants of the hen-run. Even in the animal world to be different is a crime.

Hard as it may be, the duty is laid upon us of never being ashamed to show whose we are and whom we serve; and if we regard the matter in the right way it will be, not a duty, but a privilege.

A short time before the coronation of Queen Elizabeth II in 1953 most houses and shops were displaying flags. I was out on a country road at that time; and in a little copse by the roadside I came upon a traveller's camp. It consisted of only one little tent, and beside the tent there fluttered on a pole a Union Jack nearly as big as the tent itself. It was as if that traveller said, 'I haven't got much in this world; but I am going to attach my colours to what I have.'

All Christians, however humble their position and their sphere, must never be ashamed to show their colours.

(2) Verse 17 stresses the impossibility of secrecy. There are three people from whom we try to hide things.

(a) Sometimes we try to hide things from ourselves. We shut our eyes to the consequences of certain actions and habits, consequences of which we are well aware. It is like deliberately shutting our eyes to symptoms of an illness which we know that we have. We have only to state that to see its incredible folly.

(b) Sometimes we try to hide things from one another. Things have a way of coming out. The person with a secret is ill at ease. The contented person has nothing to hide. It is told that once an architect offered to build for Plato a house in which every room would be hidden from the public eye. 'I will give you twice the money,' said Plato, 'if you build me a house into every room of which all men's eyes can see.' If only we could have the confidence to speak like that.

(c) Sometimes we try to hide things from God. No one ever attempted a more impossible task. We would do well to have before our eyes forever the text which in the Revised Standard Version says, 'Thou art a God of seeing' (Genesis 16:13).

(3) Verse 18 lays down the universal law that those who have will get more; and that those who have not will lose what they have. Those who are physically fit and keep themselves so will be ready for even greater efforts; if they

let themselves go flabby, they will lose even the abilities they have. The more we learn, the more we can learn; but if we refuse to go on learning, we will lose the knowledge we have. This is just another way of saying that there is no standing still in life. All the time we are either going forward or going back. Those who seek will always find; but those who stop seeking will lose even what they have.

TRUE KINSHIP

Luke 8:19-21

> Jesus' mother and brothers came to him, and they could not get at him because of the crowd. He was given a message. 'Your mother and your brothers are standing outside and they want to see you.' 'My mother and my brothers', he answered them, 'are those who hear the word of God and do it.'

IT is not difficult to see that, at least during his lifetime, Jesus' family were not in sympathy with him. Mark 3:21 tells us how his relatives came and tried to restrain him because they believed him to be mad. In Matthew 10:36 Jesus warns his followers that opposition may well come from those within the home – and he was speaking out of hard and bitter experience.

There is in this passage a great and practical truth. It may very well be that we find ourselves closer to people who are not related to us than to our own flesh and blood. The deepest relationship of life is not merely a blood relationship; it is the relationship of mind to mind and heart to heart. True kinship develops when people have common aims, common principles, common interests and a common goal.

Let us remember that definition of the kingdom which we already worked out. The kingdom of God is a society upon earth where God's will is as perfectly done as it is in heaven. It was Jesus' supreme quality that he alone succeeded in fully achieving the identity of his will and the will of God. Therefore, all whose one aim in life is to make God's will their will are the true kindred of Jesus. We speak of all people being children of God; and in a very real and precious sense that is true, because God loves saint and sinner; but the deepest form of this relationship is ethically conditioned. It is when we put our wills in line with God's will by the help of the Holy Spirit that real kinship begins.

The Stoics declared that that was the only way to happiness in this life. They had the conviction that everything that happens – joy and sorrow, triumph and disaster, gain and loss, sunshine and shadow – was the will of God. Those who refused to accept it were banging their heads against the walls of the universe and could bring themselves nothing but pain and trouble of heart.

When we look up to God and say, 'Do with me as you wish,' we have found the way to joy.

Two things emerge.

(1) There is a loyalty which surpasses all earthly loyalties; there is something which takes precedence of the dearest things on earth. In that sense Jesus Christ is a demanding master, for he will share the heart of any one of us with nothing and with no one. Love is necessarily exclusive. We can love only one person at a time and serve only one master at a time.

(2) That is hard; but there is this great wonder – that when we give ourselves absolutely to Christ we become members of a family whose boundaries are the earth. Whatever loss we may experience is counterbalanced by what we gain. As John Oxenham wrote:

In Christ there is no East or West,
   In him no South or North,
But one great fellowship of love
   Throughout the whole wide earth.

In him shall true hearts everywhere
   Their high communion find,
His service is the golden cord
   Close-binding all mankind.

Join hands, then, brother of the faith,
   Whate'er your race may be!
Who serves my Father as a son
   Is surely kin to me.

In Christ now meet both East and West,
   In him meet South and North,
All Christly souls are one in him,
   Throughout the whole wide earth.

Those who, through Jesus Christ, seek the will of God have entered into a family which includes all the saints in earth and in heaven.

CALM AMID THE STORM

Luke 8:22–5

One day Jesus and his disciples embarked upon a ship. 'Let us go over,' he said to them, 'to the other side of the lake.' So they set sail. As they sailed he fell asleep. A violent squall of wind came down upon the lake; and the boat began to fill with water; and they were in peril. They came to him and woke him. 'Master, Master,' they said, 'we are perishing.' When he awoke, he rebuked the wind and the surf of the water. They ceased their raging, and there was a calm. 'Where is your faith?,' he

said to them. But they were awe-stricken and amazed.
'Who can this be,' they said to each other, 'because he
gives his orders even to the winds and the water, and
they obey him?'

LUKE tells this story with an extraordinary economy of words,
and yet with extraordinary vividness. It was no doubt for
much-needed rest and quiet that Jesus decided to cross the
lake. As they sailed, he fell asleep.

It is a lovely thing to think of the sleeping Jesus. He was
tired, just as we become tired. He, too, could reach the point
of exhaustion when the claim of sleep is imperative. He
trusted his disciples; they were the fishermen of the lake and
he was content to leave things to their skill and seamanship,
and to relax. He trusted God; he knew that he was as near to
God by sea as ever he was by land.

Then the storm came down. The Sea of Galilee is famous
for its sudden squalls. A traveller says, 'The sun had scarcely
set when the wind began to rush down towards the lake, and
it continued all night long with increasing violence, so that
when we reached the shore next morning the face of the
lake was like a huge boiling caldron.' The reason is this.
The Sea of Galilee is more than 600 feet below sea level. It is
surrounded by table lands beyond which the great mountains
rise. The rivers have cut deep ravines through the table lands
down into the sea. These ravines act like great funnels to
draw down the cold winds from the mountains; and thus the
storms arise. The same traveller tells how they tried to pitch
their tents in such a gale. 'We had to double-pin all the tent-
ropes, and frequently were obliged to hang on with our whole
weight upon them to keep the quivering tabernacle from being
carried up bodily into the air.'

It was just such a sudden storm that struck the boat that
day, and Jesus and his disciples were in peril of their lives.

The disciples woke Jesus and with a word he calmed the storm.

Everything that Jesus did had more than a merely temporal significance. And the real meaning of this incident is that, *wherever Jesus is, the storm becomes a calm.*

(1) Jesus comes, calms *the storms of temptation.* Sometimes temptation comes with almost overwhelming force. As Robert Louis Stevenson once said, 'You know the Caledonian Railway Station in Edinburgh? One cold bleak morning I met Satan there.' It comes to us all to meet Satan. If we meet the tempest of temptation alone we will perish; but Christ brings the calm in which temptations lose their power.

(2) Jesus calms *the storms of passion.* Life is doubly difficult for the hot-headed person who has a blazing temper. A friend met someone just like that. 'I see', he said, 'that you have succeeded in conquering your temper.' 'No,' said the man, 'I didn't conquer it. Jesus conquered it for me.'

> When deep within our swelling hearts
>   The thoughts of pride and anger rise,
> When bitter words are on our tongues
>   And tears of passion in our eyes,
> Then we may stay the angry blow,
>   Then we may check the hasty word,
> Give gentle answers back again,
>   And fight a battle for our Lord.

It is a losing battle unless Jesus gives us the calm of victory.

(3) Jesus *calms the storms of sorrow.* Into every life some day the tempest of sorrow must come, for sorrow is so often the penalty of love and if we love we will also know sorrow. When the nineteenth-century theologian E. B. Pusey's wife died, he said, 'It was as if there was a hand beneath my chin

to hold me up.' In that day, in the presence of Jesus, the tears
are wiped away and the wounded heart is soothed.

THE DEFEAT OF THE DEMONS

Luke 8:26–39

They came in their voyage to the district of the
Gerasenes, which is across the lake from Galilee. When
Jesus had disembarked on the land there met him a man
from the town who had demons. For a long time he had
gone unclothed, and he did not stay in a house but
among the tombs. When he saw Jesus he uttered a great
cry and fell down before him and shouted, 'What have
you and I to do with each other, Jesus, you Son of the
Most High God? I beseech you – don't torture me!' –
for Jesus had commanded the unclean spirit to come
out of the man. For many a time it had snatched at him,
and he was kept bound with chains and fetters, but when
he was driven into the deserted places by the demons,
he would burst the fetters. Jesus answered, 'What is
your name?' He said, 'A regiment' – because many
demons had entered into him, and they begged him not
to order them to depart to the abyss. There was a herd
of many pigs there, feeding on the mountainside. The
demons asked him to allow them to go into them. He
did so. So the demons came out of the man and into the
pigs, and the herd rushed down the precipice into the
lake and were drowned. When those who were in charge
of them saw what had happened, they fled and brought
the story to the town and to the countryside round about.
They came out to see what had happened. They came
to Jesus and found the man from whom the demons had
gone out sitting there at Jesus' feet, clothed and in his
senses – and they were afraid. Those who had seen what

had happened told them how the demon-possessed man had been cured; and the whole crowd from the Gerasene countryside asked him to go away from them, because they were in the grip of a great fear. So he embarked on the ship and went away. The man from whom the demons had gone out begged to be allowed to go with him; but he sent him away. 'Go back,' he said, 'to your home and tell the story of all that God did for you.' So he went away and proclaimed throughout the whole town all that God had done for him.

WE will never even begin to understand this story unless we realize that, whatever we think about the demons, they were intensely real to the people of Gerasa and to the man whose mind was deranged. This man was a case of violent insanity. He was too dangerous to live in the community and he lived amid the tombs, which were believed to be the home and the haunt of demons. We may well note the sheer courage of Jesus in dealing with him. The man had a maniacal strength which enabled him to snap his fetters. People were so terrified of him that they would never try to do anything for him; but Jesus faced him calm and unafraid.

When Jesus asked the man his name, he answered, 'Legion.' A Roman legion was a regiment of 6,000 soldiers. Doubtless this man had seen a Roman legion on the march, and his poor, afflicted mind felt that there was not one demon but a whole regiment inside him. It may well be that the word haunted him because he had seen atrocities carried out by a Roman legion when he was a child. It is possible that it was the sight of such atrocities which left a scar upon his mind and ultimately caused his mental illness.

Far too much difficulty has been made out of the pigs. Jesus has been condemned for sending the demons into the innocent swine. That has been characterized as a cruel and

immoral action. Again we must remember the intensity of
the belief in demons. The man, thinking the demons were
speaking through him, pleaded with Jesus not to send them
into the abyss of hell to which they would be consigned in
the final judgment. He would never have believed that he
was cured unless he had visible demonstration. Nothing less
than the visible departure of the demons would have convinced him.

Surely what happened was this. The herd of swine was
feeding there on the mountainside. Jesus was exerting his
power to cure what was a very stubborn case. Suddenly the
man's wild shouts and screams disturbed the swine and they
went dashing down the steep place into the sea in blind terror.
'Look!' said Jesus, 'Look! Your demons are gone!' Jesus *had*
to find a way to get into the mind of this poor man; and in
that way he found it.

In any event, can we compare the value of a herd of swine
with the value of a man's immortal soul? If it cost the lives of
these swine to save that soul, are we to complain? Is it not
perverse fastidiousness which complains that swine were
killed in order to heal a man? Surely we ought to preserve a
sense of proportion. If the only way to convince this man of
his cure was that the swine should perish, it seems quite
extraordinarily blind to object that they did.

We must look at the reaction of two sets of people.

(1) There were *the Gerasenes*. They asked Jesus to go
away.

(a) They hated having the routine of life disturbed. Life
went peacefully on till there arrived this disturbing Jesus;
and they hated him. More people hate Jesus because he
disturbs them than for any other reason. If he says to someone,
'You must give up this habit, you must change your life'; if
he says to an employer, 'You can't be a Christian and make

people work under conditions like that'; if he says to a landlord, 'You can't take money for slums like that' – one and all are liable to say to him, 'Go away and let me be in peace.'

(b) They loved their swine more than they valued a human soul. One of life's supreme dangers is to value things more than persons. That is what created slums and vicious working conditions. Nearer home, that is what makes us selfishly demand our ease and comfort even if it means that someone who is tired has to slave for us. No thing in this world can ever be as important as a person.

(2) There was *the man who was cured.* Very naturally he wanted to come with Jesus but Jesus sent him home. Christian witness, like Christian charity, begins at home. It would be so much easier to live and speak for Christ among people who do not know us. But it is our duty, where Christ has set us, there to witness for him. And if it should happen that we are the only Christian in the shop, the office, the school, the factory, the circle in which we live or work, that is not a matter for lamentation. It is a challenge in which God says, 'Go and tell the people you meet every day what I have done for you.'

AN ONLY CHILD IS HEALED

Luke 8:40–2 and 49–56

> When Jesus came back the crowd welcomed him for they were all waiting for him. A man called Jairus came to him. He was the president of the synagogue. He threw himself at Jesus' feet and asked him to come to his house, because he had an only daughter who was about twelve years of age and she was dying. As he

went the crowd pressed round him . . . While he was still speaking someone came from the president's house. 'Your daughter is dead,' he said. 'Don't bother the Master any more.' Jesus heard this. 'Don't be afraid,' he said. 'Just have faith and she will be cured.' When he had come to the house he allowed no one to come in with him, except Peter and John and James, and the girl's father and mother. They were all weeping and wailing for her. 'Stop weeping,' he said, 'for she is not dead but sleeping.' They laughed him down because they were sure she was dead. He took hold of her hand and said to her, 'Child, rise!' Her breath came back to her and immediately she rose. He told them to give her something to eat. Her parents were out of themselves with amazement; but he enjoined them to tell no one what had happened.

HERE is the pathos of life suddenly turned to gladness. Very keenly Luke felt the tragedy of this girl's death. There were three things which made it so poignant.

(a) She was an only child. Only Luke tells us that. The light of her parents' life had gone out.

(b) She was about twelve years of age. That is to say she was just at the dawn of womanhood. What should have been the morning of life had become the night.

(c) Jairus was the president of the synagogue. That is to say, he was the man who was responsible for the administration of the synagogue and the ordering of public worship. He had reached the highest post that life could give him in the respect of his community. No doubt he was well to do; no doubt he had climbed the ladder of earthly ambition and prestige. It seemed as if life – as it sometimes does – had given lavishly of many things but was about to take the most precious thing away. All the pathos of life is in the background of this story.

The wailing women had already come. To hire these wailing women was a token of respect to the dead that was never omitted. They were sure she was dead, but Jesus said she was asleep. It is perfectly possible that Jesus meant this literally. It may well be that here we have a real miracle of diagnosis; that Jesus saw the girl was in a deep trance and that she was on the point of being buried alive. From the evidence of the tombs in Palestine it is clear that many were buried alive. It could happen the more easily because climatic conditions in Palestine made burial within a matter of hours a sheer necessity. However that may be, Jesus gave her back her life.

We must note one very practical touch. Jesus ordered that the girl should be given something to eat. Is it possible that he was thinking just as much of the mother as of the girl? The mother, with the pain of grief and the sudden shock of joy, must have been almost on the point of collapse. At such a time to do some practical thing with one's hands is a life-saver. And it may well be that Jesus, in his kindly wisdom which knew human nature so well, was giving the over-wrought mother a job to do to calm her nerves.

But by far the most interesting character in this story is Jairus.

(1) He was clearly *a man who could swallow his pride*. He was the president of the synagogue. By this time the synagogue doors were rapidly closing on Jesus, if indeed they had not already closed. He could have had no love for Jesus and he must have regarded Jesus as a breaker of the law. But in his hour of need, he swallowed his pride and asked for help.

There is a famous story of Roland, the paladin of Charlemagne. He was in charge of the rearguard of the army and he was suddenly caught by the Saracens at Roncesvalles.

The battle raged fiercely against terrible odds. Now Roland had a horn called Olivant which he had taken from the giant Jatmund and its blast could be heard thirty miles away. So mighty was it that, so they said, the birds fell dead when its blast tore through the air. Oliver, his friend, begged him to blow the horn so that Charlemagne would hear and come back to help. But Roland was too proud to ask for help. One by one his men fell fighting till only he was left. Then at last with his dying breath he blew the horn, and Charlemagne came hastening back. But it was too late, for Roland was dead – because he was too proud to ask for help.

It is easy to think that we can handle life ourselves. But the way to find the miracles of the grace of God is to swallow our pride and humbly to confess our need and ask. Ask, and you will receive – but there is no receiving without asking

(2) Jairus was clearly *a man of a stubborn faith.* Whatever he felt, he did not wholly accept the verdict of the wailing women; for with his wife he went into the room where the girl lay. He hoped against hope. No doubt in his heart there was the feeling, 'You never know what this Jesus can do.' And none of us knows all that Jesus can do. In the darkest day we can still hope in the unsearchable riches and the all-sufficient grace and the unconquerable power of God.

NOT LOST IN THE CROWD

Luke 8:43–8

There was a woman who had had a flow of blood for twelve years. She had spent all her living on doctors and she could not be cured by any of them. She came up behind Jesus and she touched the tassel of his robe; and immediately her flow of blood was stayed. Jesus

said, 'Who touched me?' When they were all denying
that they had done so, Peter and his companions said,
'Master, the crowds are all round you and press in upon
you.' Jesus said, 'Someone has touched me, for I know
that power has gone out of me.' The woman saw that
she could not hide. She came all trembling; she threw
herself at his feet; and in front of everyone she had told
him why she had touched him, and that she had been
cured there and then. 'Daughter,' he said to her, 'your
faith has cured you. Go in peace.'

THIS story laid hold on the heart and the imagination of the
early Church. It was believed that the woman was a Gentile
from Caesarea Philippi. Eusebius, the great church historian
(AD 300), relates how it was said that the woman had at her
own cost erected a statue commemorating her cure in her
native city. It was said that that statue remained there until
Julian, the Roman emperor who tried to bring back the pagan
gods, destroyed it, and erected his own in place of it, only to
see his own statue blasted by a thunderbolt from God.

The shame of the woman was that ceremonially she was
unclean (Leviticus 15:19–33). Her issue of blood had cut
her off from life. That was why she did not come openly
to Jesus but crept up in the crowd; and that was why at
first she was so embarrassed when Jesus asked who touched
him.

All devout Jews wore robes with fringes on them (Numbers
15:37–41; Deuteronomy 22:12). The fringes ended in four
tassels of white thread with a blue thread woven through them.
They were to remind a Jew every time he dressed that he was
a man of God and committed to the keeping of God's laws.
Later, when it was dangerous to be a Jew, these tassels were
worn on the undergarments. Nowadays they still exist on the
talith or shawl that Jews wear round their heads and shoulders

when they are at prayer. But in the time of Jesus they were worn on the outer garment, and it was one of these the woman touched.

Luke the doctor is here in evidence again. Mark says of the woman that she had spent all she had on the doctors and was no better *but rather grew worse* (Mark 5:26). Luke misses out the final phrase, because he did not like this gibe against the doctors!

The lovely thing about this story is that from the moment Jesus was face to face with the woman, there seemed to be nobody there but the two of them. It happened in the middle of a crowd, but the crowd was forgotten and Jesus spoke to that woman as if she was the only person in the world. She was a poor, unimportant sufferer, with a trouble that made her unclean, and yet to that one unimportant person Jesus gave all of himself.

We are very apt to attach labels to people and to treat them according to their relative importance. To Jesus a person had none of these labels. He or she was simply a human soul in need. Love never thinks of people in terms of human importances.

A distinguished visitor once came to call on Thomas Carlyle. He was working and could not be disturbed, but Jane, his wife, agreed to take this visitor up and open the door just a chink that he might at least see the sage. She did so, and as they looked in at Carlyle, immersed in his work and oblivious of all else, penning the books that made him famous, she said, 'That's Tammas Carlyle about whom all the world is talking – *and he's my man.*' It was not in terms of the world's labels Jane thought, but in terms of love.

A traveller tells how she was travelling in the southern Russian state of Georgia in the days before the Second World War. She was taken to see a very humble old woman in a little cottage. The old peasant woman asked her if she was going to Moscow. The traveller said she was. 'Then,' asked the woman, 'would you mind delivering a parcel of home-made toffee to my son? He cannot get anything like it in Moscow.' Her son's name was Josef Stalin. We do not normally think of the man who was once dictator of Soviet Russia as a man who liked toffee – but his mother did! For her the labels did not matter.

Almost everybody would have regarded the woman in the crowd as totally unimportant. For Jesus she was someone in need, and therefore he, as it were, withdrew from the crowd and gave himself to her. 'God loves each one of us as if there was only one of us to love.'

EMISSARIES OF THE KING

Luke 9:1-9

Jesus called the Twelve together and gave them power and authority over all demons, and to cure diseases. He sent them out to proclaim the kingdom of God, and to cure those who were ill. He said to them, 'Take nothing for the road, neither a staff nor a wallet, nor bread nor money, nor two tunics. Whatever house you go into, stay there, and leave from there. As for whoever do not receive you – when you leave that town shake off the dust from your feet as evidence against them.' So they went out, and they went through the villages, preaching and healing everywhere.

Herod, the tetrarch, heard about the things which were going on. He did not know what to make of them, because it was said by some, 'John is risen from the dead'; and by some, 'Elijah has appeared'; and by others, 'One of the prophets of the ancient days has

risen again.' But Herod said, 'John I myself beheaded.
Who is this about whom I hear such reports?' And he
tried to see him.

IN the time of Jesus there was in effect only one way of
spreading a message abroad and that was by word of mouth.
Newspapers did not exist; books had to be handwritten, and
a book the size of Luke–Acts would have cost a great deal to
produce. Radio and television had not even been dreamed of.
That is why Jesus sent out the Twelve on this mission. He
was under the limitations of time and space, his helpers had
to be mouths to speak for him.

They were to travel light. That was simply because those
who travel light travel far and fast. The more we are cluttered
up with material things the more we are shackled to one place.
God needs a settled ministry; but he also needs those who
will abandon earthly things to adventure for him.

If they were not received they were to shake off the dust
from their feet when they left the town. When Rabbis entered
Palestine after some journey in a Gentile land, they shook off
the last particle of heathen dust from their feet. A village or
town which would not receive them was to be treated as a
strict Jew would treat a heathen country. It had refused its
opportunity and had condemned itself.

That this ministry was mightily effective is plain from
Herod's reaction. Things were happening. Perhaps Elijah, the
forerunner, had at last come. Perhaps even the great promised
prophet had arrived (Deuteronomy 18:15). But as Hamlet said,
'conscience doth make cowards of us all', and there was a
lingering fear in Herod's mind that John the Baptizer, whom
he thought he had eliminated, had come back to haunt him.

One thing which stands out about the ministry which Jesus
laid upon the Twelve is this – over and over again in this
short passage *it joins preaching and healing.* It joins concern

for physical and spiritual wellbeing. It was something which was not to deal only in words, however comforting; but also in deeds. It was a message which was not confined to news of eternity; it proposed to change conditions on earth. It was the reverse of a religion of 'pie in the sky'. It insisted that physical health was as integral a part of God's purpose as spiritual health.

Nothing has done the Church more harm than the repeated statement that the things of this world do not matter. In the 1930s unemployment invaded many respectable and decent homes. The father's skill was rusting in idleness; the mother was trying to make a shilling do what a pound ought to do; children could not understand what was going on except that they were hungry. People grew bitter or broken. To go and tell them that material things make no difference was unforgivable, especially if the teller lived in reasonable comfort. General William Booth of the Salvation Army was once blamed for offering food and meals to poor people instead of the simple gospel. The old warrior flashed back, 'It is impossible to comfort men's hearts with the love of God when their feet are perishing with cold.'

Of course, it is possible to overstress material things. But it is equally possible to neglect them. The Church will forget only at her peril that Jesus first sent out his followers *to preach the kingdom and to heal*, to save men and women in body and in soul.

FOOD FOR THE HUNGRY

Luke 9:10–17

When the apostles returned they told Jesus all that they had done. So he took them and withdrew privately to a place called Bethsaida. When the crowds found out where he was they followed him; and he welcomed them, and talked to them about the kingdom of God, and healed those who had need of healing. The day began to draw to a close. The Twelve came to him. 'Send the crowd away,' they said, 'that they may go to the surrounding villages and countryside and find some place to stay and get food because here we are in a desert place.' He said to them, 'Do you give them food to eat.' They said, 'All we have is five loaves and two fishes – unless we go and buy food for all this people.' For there were about 5,000 men. He said to his disciples, 'Make them sit down in companies of fifty.' They did so, and they got them all seated. He took the five loaves and the two fishes and looked up into heaven and blessed them and broke them and gave them to his disciples to set before the crowd. And all of them ate and were satisfied; and what they had left over was taken up and there were twelve baskets of the fragments.

THIS is the only miracle of Jesus related in all the four gospels (cf. Matthew 14:13; Mark 6:30; John 6:1). It begins with a lovely thing. The Twelve had come back from their tour. Never was there a time when Jesus needed more to be alone with them, so he took them to the neighbourhood of Bethsaida, a village on the far side of the Jordan to the north of the Sea of Galilee. When the people discovered where he had gone they followed him in hordes – *and he welcomed them.*

There is all the divine compassion here. Most people would have resented the invasion of their hard-won privacy. How would we feel if we had sought out some lonely place to be with our most intimate friends and suddenly a clamorous throng of people turned up with their insistent demands? Sometimes we are too busy to be disturbed, but to Jesus human need took precedence over everything.

The evening came; home was far away; and the people were tired and hungry. Jesus, astonishingly, ordered his disciples to give them a meal. There are two ways in which we can quite honestly look at this miracle. First, we can see in it simply a miracle in which Jesus created food for this vast multitude. Second, some people think that this is what happened. The people were hungry – *and they were utterly selfish.* They all had something with them, but they would not even produce it for themselves in case they had to share it with others. The Twelve laid before the multitude their little store and thereupon others were moved to produce theirs; and in the end there was more than enough for everyone. So it may be regarded as a miracle which turned selfish, suspicious folk into generous people, a miracle of Christ's changing determined self-interest into a willingness to share.

Before Jesus distributed the food he blessed it; he said grace. There was a Jewish saying that 'he who enjoys anything without thanksgiving is as though he robbed God'. The blessing said in every home in Palestine before every meal ran, 'Blessed art thou, Yahweh, our God, King of the world, who causest bread to come forth from the earth.' Jesus would not eat without giving thanks to the giver of all good gifts.

This is a story which tells us many things.

(1) *Jesus was concerned that people were hungry.* It would be most interesting to work out how much time Jesus spent, not talking, but easing human pain and satisfying hunger. He still needs the service of human hands. The mother who has spent a lifetime cooking meals for a hungry family; the nurse, the doctor, the friend, relation or parent, who has sacrificed life and time to ease another's pain; social reformers who have burned themselves out to seek better conditions for men and women – they have all preached far more effective sermons than the eloquent orator.

(2) *Jesus' help was generous.* There was enough, and more than enough. In love there is no nice calculation of the less and more. God is like that. When we sow a packet of seeds we usually have to thin the plants out and throw away far more than we can keep. God has created a world where there is more than enough for all if we will share it.

(3) As always there is permanent truth in an action in time. *In Jesus all our needs are supplied.* There is a hunger of the soul; there is in each of us, sometimes at least, a longing to find something in which we may invest our lives. Our hearts are restless until they rest in him. 'My God will fully satisfy every need of yours,' said Paul (Philippians 4:19) – even in the desert places of this life.

THE GREAT DISCOVERY

Luke 9:18–22

It happened that when Jesus was praying alone his disciples were with him. He asked them, 'Who do the crowds say that I am?' They answered, 'Some say that you are John the Baptizer; others that you are Elijah; others that one of the prophets of the ancient days has risen again.' He said to them, 'But *you* – who do you say that I am?' Peter answered, 'The Anointed One of God.' Jesus warned and enjoined them to tell this to no one. 'The Son of Man', he said, 'must suffer many things, and must be rejected by the elders and chief priests and scribes, and must be killed, and must be raised again on the third day.'

THIS is one of the most crucial moments in the life of Jesus. He asked this question when he was already turning his face to go to Jerusalem (Luke 9:51). He well knew what awaited him there, and the answer to his question was of supreme importance. He *knew* that he was going to a cross to die; he *wanted to know* before he went, if there was anyone who had really discovered who he was. The right answer would make all the difference. If instead there was dull incomprehension, all his work would have gone for nothing. If there was any realization, however incomplete, it meant that he had lit such a flame in human hearts as time would never put out. How Jesus' heart must have lifted when Peter's sudden discovery rushed to his lips – 'You are the Anointed One of God!' When Jesus heard that, he knew he had not failed.

Not only had the Twelve to discover the fact; they had also to discover what the fact meant. They had grown up against a background of thought which expected from God a conquering king who would lead them to world dominion. Peter's eyes would blaze with excitement when he said this. But Jesus had to teach them that God's Anointed One had come to die upon a cross. He had to take their ideas of God and of God's purposes and turn them upside down; and from this time that is what he set himself to do. They had discovered who he was; now they had to learn what that discovery meant.

There are two great general truths in this passage.

(1) Jesus began by asking what people were saying about him; and then, suddenly, he flashes the question at the Twelve, 'Who do *you* say that I am?' It is never enough to know what other people have said about Jesus. It might be possible to pass any examination on what has been said and thought about Jesus, or to read every book about christology written in every language upon earth, and still not be a Christian. Jesus must always be our own personal discovery. Our religion can never simply be a matter of rumour or report. To each of us Jesus comes asking, not, 'Can you tell me what others have said and written about me?' but, 'Who do *you* say that I am?' Paul did

not say, 'I know *what* I have believed'; he said, 'I know the one in whom I have put my trust' (2 Timothy 1:12). Christianity does not mean reciting a creed; it means knowing a person.

(2) Jesus said, 'I must go to Jerusalem and die.' It is of the greatest interest to look at the times in Luke's gospel when Jesus said *must*. 'I *must* be in my Father's house' (2:49). 'I *must* proclaim the good news of the kingdom' (4:43). 'Yet today, tomorrow, and the next day I *must* be on my way' (13:33). Over and over again he told his disciples he *must* go to his cross (9:22, 17:25, 24:7). Jesus knew he had a destiny to fulfil. God's will was his will. He had no other object but to do upon earth what God had sent him to do. Christians, like their Lord, are people under orders.

THE CONDITIONS OF SERVICE

Luke 9:23–7

> Jesus said to them all, 'If any man wishes to come after me, let him deny himself, and day by day let him take up his cross and follow me. Whoever wishes to save his life will lose it. Whoever loses his life for my sake will save it. What profit is it to a man if he gains the whole world and loses himself or has himself confiscated? Whoever is ashamed of me and of my words, of him shall the Son of Man be ashamed when he shall come in his own glory, and in the glory of his Father and of the holy angels. I tell you truly that there are some of these who are standing here who will not taste death until they see the kingdom of God.'

HERE Jesus lays down the conditions of service for those who would follow him.

(1) They are called to self-denial. What does that mean? One scholar comes at the meaning in this way. Peter once

denied his Lord. That is to say, he said of Jesus, 'I do not
know the man.' To deny ourselves is to say, 'I do not
know myself.' It is to ignore the very existence of oneself.
It is to treat the self as if it did not exist. Usually we treat
ourselves as if our self was by far the most important thing in
the world. If we are to follow Jesus, we must forget that self
exists.

(2) They are called to take up a cross. Jesus knew what
crucifixion meant. When he was a young boy of about eleven
years of age, Judas the Galilaean had led a rebellion against
Rome. He had raided the royal armoury at Sepphoris, which
was only four miles from Nazareth. The Roman vengeance
was swift and sudden. Sepphoris was burned to the ground;
its inhabitants were sold into slavery; and 2,000 of the rebels
were crucified on crosses which were set in lines along the
roadside that they might be a dreadful warning to others
tempted to rebel. To take up our cross means to be prepared
to face things like that for loyalty to Jesus; it means to be
ready to endure the worst that anyone can do to us for the
sake of being true to him.

(3) They are called to spend life, not hoard it. The whole
gamut of the world's standards must be changed. The questions are not, 'How much can I *get*?' but, 'How much can I
give?' Not, 'What is the *safe* thing to do?' but, 'What is the
right thing to do?' Not, 'What is the minimum permissible in
the way of work?' but, 'What is the maximum possible?'
Christians must realize that life is given, not to keep for
themselves but to spend for others; not to nurture its flame
but to burn it out for Christ and for others.

(4) Loyalty to Jesus will have its reward, and disloyalty
its punishment. If we are true to him in time, he will be true to
us in eternity. If we seek to follow him in this world, in the
next he will point to us as one of his people. But if by our lives

we disown him, even though with our lips we confess him, the day must come when he cannot do other than disown us.

(5) In the last verse of this passage Jesus says that some standing there will see the kingdom of God before they die. Some people maintain that Jesus was looking forward to his return in glory, that he was declaring that this would happen within the lifetime of some of those present; and that therefore he was completely mistaken. That is not so.

What Jesus was saying is this, 'Before this generation has passed away you will see signs that the kingdom of God is on the way.' Beyond a doubt that came to pass. Something came into the world which, like leaven in dough, began to change it. It would be well if, sometimes, we turned from our pessimism and thought rather of the light that has been slowly breaking on the world.

As A. H. Clough wrote:

> Say not the struggle naught availeth,
>   The labour and the wounds are vain,
> The enemy faints not, nor faileth,
>   And as things have been they remain.
>
> If hopes were dupes, fears may be liars;
>   It may be, in yon smoke conceal'd,
> Your comrades chase e'en now the fliers,
>   And, but for you, possess the field.
>
> For while the tired waves, vainly breaking,
>   Seem here no painful inch to gain,
> Far back, through creeks and inlets making,
>   Comes silent, flooding in, the main.
>
> And not by eastern windows only,
>   When daylight comes, comes in the light.
> In front the sun climbs slow, how slowly!
>   But westward, look, the land is bright!

Be of good cheer – the kingdom is on the way – and we do
well to thank God for every sign of its dawning.

THE MOUNTAIN TOP OF GLORY

Luke 9:28–36

> About eight days after these words, Jesus took Peter
> and John and James and went up into a mountain to
> pray. While he was praying the appearance of his face
> became different and his clothing became white as the
> lightning's flash. And – look you – two men were
> talking with him, who were Moses and Elijah. They
> appeared in glory, and they talked about the departure
> which he was going to accomplish in Jerusalem. Peter
> and his friends were heavy with sleep. When they were
> fully awake they saw his glory, and the two men
> standing with him. And when they were going to leave
> him, Peter said, 'Master, it is good for us to be here. So
> let us make three booths, one for you and one for Moses
> and one for Elijah,' for he did not know what he was
> saying. As he was saying this a cloud came and
> overshadowed them and they feared as they entered into
> the cloud. A voice came from the cloud saying, 'This is
> my beloved Son, my chosen one! Hear him!' And when
> the voice had passed, Jesus was found alone. They kept
> silent in those days and did not tell anyone anything
> about what they had seen.

HERE we have another of the great hinges in Jesus' life upon
earth. We must remember that he was just about to set out to
Jerusalem and to the cross. We have already looked at one
great moment when he asked his disciples who they believed
him to be, in order that he might discover if anyone had
realized who he was. But there was one thing Jesus would

never do – he would never take any step without the approval of God. In this scene that is what we see him seeking and receiving.

What happened on the Mount of Transfiguration we can never know, but we do know that something tremendous did happen. Jesus had gone there to seek the approval of God for the decisive step he was about to take. There Moses and Elijah appeared to him. Moses was the great law-giver of the people of Israel; Elijah was the greatest of the prophets. It was as if the princes of Israel's life and thought and religion told Jesus to go on.

Jesus could set out to Jerusalem now, certain that at least one little group of men knew who he was, certain that what he was doing was the consummation of all the life and thought and work of his nation, and certain that God approved of the step that he was taking.

There is a vivid sentence here. It says of the three apostles, 'When they were fully awake they saw his glory.'

(1) In life we miss so much because our minds are asleep. There are certain things which are liable to keep our minds asleep.

(a) There is *prejudice*. We may be so set in our ideas that our minds are shut. A new idea knocks at the door but we are like sleepers who will not awake.

(b) There is mental *lethargy*. There are so many who refuse the strenuous struggle of thought. 'The unexamined life', said Socrates, 'is the life not worth living.' How many of us have really thought things out and thought them through? It was said of someone that he had skirted the howling deserts of infidelity and a wiser man said that he would have been better to have fought his way through them. Sometimes we are so lethargic that we will not even face our questions and our doubts.

(c) There is *the love of ease*. There is a kind of defence mechanism in us that makes us automatically shut the door against any disturbing thought.

We can drug ourselves mentally until our minds are sound asleep.

(2) But life is full of things designed to waken us.

(a) There is *sorrow*. Once, the English composer Sir Edward Elgar said of a young singer, who was technically perfect, but quite without feeling and expression, 'She will be great when something breaks her heart.' Often sorrow can rudely awaken us, but in that moment, through the tears, we will see the glory.

(b) There is *love*. Robert Browning tells of two people who fell in love. She looked at him; he looked at her – 'and suddenly life awoke'. Real love is an awakening to horizons we never dreamed were there.

(c) There is *the sense of need*. It is easy enough to live the routine of life half-asleep; then all of a sudden there comes some completely insoluble problem, some quite unanswerable question, some overwhelming temptation, some summons to an effort which we feel is beyond our strength. In that day there is nothing left to do but to 'cry, clinging heaven by the hems'. And that sense of need awakens us to God.

We would do well to pray, 'Lord, keep me always awake to you.'

COMING DOWN FROM THE MOUNT

Luke 9:37–45

> On the next day, when they had come down from the mountain, a great crowd of people met him. And – look you – a man shouted from the crowd, 'Teacher, I beg

you to look with pity upon my son, because he is my
only child. And – look you – a spirit seizes him and he
suddenly shouts out; he convulses him until he foams
at the mouth; he shatters him and will hardly leave him.
I begged your disciples to cast out the spirit but they
could not do it.' Jesus answered, 'O faithless and twisted
generation! How long will I be with you? How long
will I bear you? Bring your son here.' While he was
coming the demon dashed him down and convulsed
him. Jesus rebuked the unclean spirit and healed the
boy, and gave him back to his father; and everyone was
astonished at the majesty of God.

While they were all wondering at the things which
he kept doing, he said to his disciples, 'Let these words
sink into your ears – the Son of Man is going to be
delivered into the hands of men.' They did not know
what this word meant; and its meaning was concealed
from them so that they did not perceive it; and they
were afraid to ask him about this word.

No sooner had Jesus descended from the mountain top than
the demands and disappointments of life were upon him. A
man had come to the disciples seeking their help, for his only
son was an epileptic. Of course his epilepsy was attributed to
the malign activity of a demon. The word used in verse 42 is
very vivid. As he was coming to Jesus, the demon *dashed
him down*. It is the word used of a boxer dealing a knock-out
blow to his opponent or of a wrestler throwing someone. It
must have been a pitiful sight to see the boy convulsed; and
the disciples were quite helpless to cure him. But when Jesus
came he dealt with the situation with calm mastery and gave
the boy back to his father cured.

Two things stand out.

(1) The moment on the mount was absolutely necessary,
but it could not be prolonged beyond its own time. Peter, not

really knowing what he was saying, would have liked to linger on the mountain top. He wished to build three tabernacles so that they might stay there in all the glory; but they had to descend again. Often there come to us moments that we would like to prolong indefinitely. But after the time on the mountain top we must come back to the battle and the routine of life; that time is meant to give us strength for life's everyday struggles.

After the great struggle at Mount Carmel with the prophets of Baal, Elijah, in reaction, ran away. Out into the desert he went and there, as he lay under a juniper tree asleep, an angel twice prepared a meal for him. Then comes the sentence, 'He got up, and ate and drank; then he went in the strength of that food forty days and forty nights' (1 Kings 19:1–8). To the mountain top of the presence of God we must go, not to remain there but to go in the strength of that time for many days. It was said of Captain Robert Scott, the great explorer, that he was 'a strange mixture of the dreamy and the practical, and never more practical than immediately after he had been dreamy'. We cannot live forever in the moment on the mountain but we cannot live at all without it.

(2) In no incident is the sheer competence of Jesus so clearly shown. When he came down from the mountain the situation was out of hand. The whole impression is that of people running about not knowing what to do. The disciples were helplessly baffled; the boy's father was bitterly disappointed and upset. Into this scene of disorder came Jesus. He gripped the situation in a flash and in his mastery the disorder became a calm. So often we feel that life is out of control; that we have lost our grip on things. Only the Master of life can deal with life with the calm competence that brings everything under control.

(3) Once again the incident finished with Jesus pointing at the cross. Here was triumph; here Jesus had mastered the demons and astonished the people. And in that very moment when they were ready to acclaim him, Jesus told them he was on the way to die. It would have been so easy to take the way of popular success; it was Jesus' greatness that he rejected it and chose the cross. He would not himself shirk that cross to which he called others.

TRUE GREATNESS

Luke 9:46-8

> There arose an argument among them as to which of them should be the greatest. But when Jesus knew the thoughts of their hearts he took a child and set him beside him. 'Whoever', he said to them, 'receives this child in my name, receives me; and whoever receives me, receives him that sent me. He who is least among you, he it is who is the greatest.'

So long as the Twelve thought of Jesus' kingdom as an earthly kingdom it was inevitable that they should be in competition for the highest places in it. In the eighth century the Venerable Bede suggested that this particular quarrel arose because Jesus had taken Peter, John and James up into the mountain top with him and the others were jealous.

Jesus knew what was going on in their hearts. He brought a child to sit beside him; that would be the seat of highest honour. He went on to say that whoever received a little child, received him; and whoever received him, received God. What did he mean? The Twelve were the chosen lieutenants of Jesus; but this child occupied no place of honour and held no official position. Jesus was saying, 'If you are prepared to spend your lives serving, helping, loving people who, in the eyes of the world, do not matter at all, you are serving me and serving God. If you are prepared to spend your life doing these apparently unimportant things and never trying to be what the world calls great, you will be great in the eyes of God.'

There are so many wrong motives for service.

(1) There is the desire for *prestige.* The author A. J. Cronin tells of a district nurse he knew when he was in practice as a doctor. For twenty years, single-handed, she had served a ten-mile district. 'I marvelled', he says, 'at her patience, her fortitude and her cheerfulness. She was never too tired at night to rise for an urgent call. Her salary was most inadequate, and late one night, after a particularly strenuous day, I ventured to protest to her, "Nurse, why don't you make them pay you more? God knows you are worth it." "If God knows I'm worth it," she answered, "that's all that matters to me." ' She was working, not for human recognition, but for God. And when we work for God, prestige will be the last thing that enters into our mind, for we will know that even our best is not good enough for him.

(2) There is the desire for *place.* If we are given a task or a position or an office in the Church, we should regard it not as an honour but as a responsibility. There are those who serve within the Church, not thinking really of those they serve, but thinking of themselves. A certain English Prime Minister was offered congratulations on attaining to that office. 'I do not want your congratulations,' he said, 'but I do want your prayers.' To be chosen for office is to be set apart for service, not elevated to honour.

(3) There is the desire for *prominence.* Many people will serve or give so long as their service and their generosity are known and they are thanked and praised. It is Jesus' own

instruction that we should not let our left hand know what our right hand is doing. If we give only to gain something out of the giving for ourselves, we have undone much of its good.

TWO LESSONS IN TOLERANCE

Luke 9:49–56

> John said to Jesus, 'Master, we saw a man casting out demons in your name; and we stopped him because he does not follow with us.' Jesus said to him, 'Don't try to stop him, for he who is not against us is for us.'
>
> When the days that he should be received up were on their way to being completed he fixed his face firmly to go to Jerusalem. He sent messengers on ahead. When they had gone on they went into a village of the Samaritans to make ready for him; and they refused to receive them because his face was set in the direction of Jerusalem. When his disciples, James and John, learned of this they said, 'Lord, would you like us to order fire to come down from heaven and destroy them?' He turned to them and rebuked them; and they went on to another village.

HERE we have two lessons in tolerance.

There were many exorcists in Palestine, all claiming to be able to cast out demons; and no doubt John regarded this man as a competitor and wished to eliminate him. But Jesus would not permit him.

The direct way from Galilee to Jerusalem led through Samaria; but most Jews avoided it. There was a centuries-old quarrel between the Jews and the Samaritans (John 4:9). The Samaritans in fact did everything they could to hinder and even to injure any bands of pilgrims who attempted to pass through their territory. For Jesus to take that way to Jerusalem was unusual; and to attempt to find hospitality in a Samaritan village was still more unusual. When he did this he was extending a hand of friendship to a people who were enemies. In this case not only was hospitality refused but the offer of friendship was spurned. No doubt, therefore, James and John believed they were doing a praiseworthy thing when they offered to call in divine aid to blot out the village. But Jesus would not permit them.

There is no passage in which Jesus so directly teaches the duty of tolerance as in this. In many ways tolerance is a lost virtue, and often, where it does exist, it exists from the wrong cause. Of all the greatest religious leaders none was such a model of tolerance as John Wesley. 'I have no more right', he said, 'to object to a man for holding a different opinion from mine than I have to differ with a man because he wears a wig and I wear my own hair; but if he takes his wig off and shakes the powder in my face, I shall consider it my duty to get quit of him as soon as possible . . . The thing which I resolved to use every possible method of preventing was a narrowness of spirit, a party zeal, a being straitened in our own bowels – that miserable bigotry which makes many so unready to believe that there is any work of God but among themselves . . . We think and let think.' When his nephew, Samuel, the son of his brother Charles, entered the Roman Catholic Church, he wrote to him, 'Whether in this Church or that I care not. You may be saved in either or damned in either; but I fear you are not born again.' The Methodist invitation to the sacrament is simply, 'Let all who love the Lord come here.'

The conviction that our beliefs and our methods alone are correct has been the cause of more tragedy and distress in the Church than almost any other thing. Oliver Cromwell wrote once to the intransigent Scots, 'I beseech you by the bowels of Christ, think it possible that you may be mistaken.' And we do well to note another saying, 'Remember that whatever your hand finds to do, someone thinks differently!'

There are many ways to God. He has his own secret stairway into every heart. He fulfils himself in many ways; and no individual or church has a monopoly of his truth.

But – and this is intensely important – our tolerance must be based not on indifference but on love. We ought to be tolerant not because we could not care less; but because we look at the other person with eyes of love. When Abraham Lincoln was criticized for being too courteous to his enemies and reminded that it was his duty to destroy them, he gave the great answer, 'Do I not destroy my enemies when I make them my friends?' Even if someone is utterly mistaken, that person must never be regarded as an enemy to be destroyed but as a strayed friend to be recovered by love.

THE HONESTY OF JESUS

Luke 9:57–62

> As they were journeying along the road, a man said to Jesus, 'I will follow you wherever you go.' Jesus said to him, 'The foxes have dens; the birds of the air have places to roost; but the Son of Man has nowhere to lay his head.'
>
> He said to another man, 'Follow Me!' 'Lord,' he said, 'let me go first and bury my father.' He said to him, 'Let the dead bury their dead; but do you go and tell abroad the news of the kingdom of God.'
>
> Another man said to him, 'Lord, I will follow you; but let me first say goodbye to the folk at home.' Jesus

said to him, 'No man who puts his hand to the plough
and looks back is the right kind of man for the kingdom
of God.'

HERE we have the words of Jesus to three would-be followers.

(1) To the first man, his advice was, 'Before you follow
me, count the cost.' No one can ever claim to have been
induced to follow Jesus under false pretences. Jesus has paid
us the compliment of pitching his demands so high that they
cannot be higher. It may well be that we have done great hurt
to the Church by letting people think that church membership
need not make so very much difference. We ought to tell
them that it should make all the difference in the world. We
might have fewer people; but those we had would be really
pledged to Christ.

(2) Jesus' words to the second man sound harsh, but they
need not be so. In all probability the man's father was not
dead, and not even nearly dead. His saying most likely meant,
'I will follow you after my father has died.' The story is told
of a very brilliant young Arab who was offered a scholarship
to Oxford or Cambridge. His answer was, 'I will take it after
I have buried my father.' At the time his father was not much
more than forty years of age.

The point Jesus was making is that in everything there is a
crucial moment; if that moment is missed the thing most likely
will never be done at all. The man in the story had stirrings in
his heart to get out of his spiritually dead surroundings; if he
missed that moment he would never get out.

Psychologists tell us that every time we have a fine feeling,
and do not act on it, the less likely we are to act on it at all.
The emotion becomes a substitute for the action. Take one
example – sometimes we feel that we would like to write a
letter, perhaps of sympathy, perhaps of thanks, perhaps of
congratulations. If we put it off until tomorrow, it will in all

likelihood never be written. Jesus urges us to act at once when our hearts are stirred.

(3) His words to the third man state a truth which no one can deny. No ploughman ever ploughed a straight furrow looking back over his shoulder. There are some whose hearts are in the past. They walk forever looking backwards and thinking wistfully of the good old days. The story is told of a certain famous preacher who, when visiting the seaside with his little grandson, met an old minister. The old man was very disgruntled and, to add to all his troubles, he had a slight touch of sunstroke. The little boy had been listening but had not picked it up quite correctly; and when they left the grumbling complaints of the old man, he turned and said, 'Grandad, I hope *you* never suffer from a *sunset*!'

The Christian advances, not to the sunset, but to the dawn. The watchword of the kingdom is not 'Backwards!' but 'Forwards!' To this man Jesus did not say either 'Follow!' or 'Return!' He said, 'I accept no lukewarm service,' and left the man to make his own decision.

LABOURERS FOR THE HARVEST

Luke 10:1-16

> After these things the Lord appointed other seventy men and sent them out in twos ahead of him into every town and place where he intended to go. 'The harvest is great,' he said to them, 'but the workers are few. Pray then the Lord of the harvest to send out workers for the harvest. Go! Look you – I am sending you out as sheep in the midst of wolves. Do not take a purse or a wallet or sandals. Greet no one on the road. Into whatever house you go, say first of all, "Peace to this house!" If it is a

son of peace who lives there your peace will remain
upon it; but if not it will return to you. Remain in the
same house eating and drinking whatever they give you;
for the workman deserves his pay. Do not go from house
to house. If you go into any town and they receive you,
eat what is put before you. Heal those in it who are ill,
and keep saying to them, "The kingdom of God has
come near you!" If you go into any town and they do
not receive you, go out into its streets and say, "The
very dust which clings to our feet from this town, we
wipe off against you. But realize this – the kingdom of
God has come near you!" I tell you, things will be easier
for Sodom in that day than for that town. Woe to you
Chorazin! Woe to you Bethsaida! For if the mighty
works which have been done in you had been done in
Tyre and Sidon, they would long ago have sat in dust
and ashes and repented. But at the judgment things will
be easier for Tyre and Sidon than for you. And you
Capernaum – will you be exalted to heaven? You will
be cast down to hell. He who listens to you, listens to
me; and he who sets no value on you, sets no value on
me; and he who sets no value on me, sets no value on
him that sent me.'

THIS passage describes a wider mission than the first mission
of the Twelve.

The number seventy was to the Jews symbolic.

(a) It was the number of the elders who were chosen to
help Moses with the task of leading and directing the people
in the wilderness (Numbers 11:16–17, 24–5).

(b) It was the number of the Sanhedrin, the supreme
council of the Jews. If we relate the Seventy to either of these
bodies, they will be the helpers of Jesus.

(c) It was held to be the number of nations in the world.
Luke was the writer with the universalist view and it may

well be that he was thinking of the day when every nation in the world would know and love his Lord.

There is an interesting sidelight here. One of the towns on which woe is pronounced is Chorazin. It is implied that Jesus did many mighty works there. In the gospel history as we have it Chorazin is never even mentioned, and we do not know one thing that Jesus did or one word that he spoke there. Nothing could show so vividly how much we do not know about the life of Jesus. The gospels are not biographies; they are only sketches of his life (cf. John 21:25).

This passage tells us certain supremely important things about both the preacher and the hearer.

(1) The preacher is not to be cluttered up with material things, but must travel light. It is easy to get entangled in the things of this life. Once Dr Johnson, the great eighteenth-century man of letters, after viewing a great castle and its policies, remarked grimly, 'These are the things which make it difficult to die.' Earth must never blot out heaven.

(2) The preacher is to concentrate on the task in hand and greet no one on the way. This goes back to Elisha's instruction to Gehazi in 2 Kings 4:29. It is not an instruction to discourtesy; but means that those who serve God must not turn aside or linger on the lesser things while the great things call them.

(3) The preacher must not be in the work for what can be got out of it, but eat whatever is offered and not think to move from house to house in search of better and more comfortable quarters. It was not long before the Church had its spongers. There is a work called *The Teaching of the Twelve Apostles*. It was written about AD 100, and is the Church's first book of order. In those days there were prophets who wandered from town to town. It is laid down that if a

prophet wishes to stay in a place for more than three days without working, that prophet is false; and if a prophet in the Spirit asks for money or a meal, that prophet is false! Labourers are worthy of their hire, but the servants of a crucified Master cannot be seekers after luxury.

(4) To have heard God's word is a great responsibility. We will be judged according to what we have had the chance to know. We allow things in a child that we condemn in an adult. Responsibility is the other side of privilege.

(5) It is a terrible thing to reject God's invitation. There is a sense in which every promise of God that we have ever heard can become our condemnation. If we receive these promises they are our greatest glory, but each one that we have rejected will some day be a witness against us.

TRUE GLORY

Luke 10:17–20

> The Seventy returned with joy. 'Lord,' they said, 'at your name the demons are subject to us.' He said to them, 'I saw Satan fall like lightning from heaven. Look you – I have given you authority to walk upon snakes and scorpions and over all the power of the Enemy. Nothing will hurt you. But do not rejoice in this – that the spirits are subject to you; but rejoice that your names are written in heaven.'

WHEN the Seventy returned they were radiant with the triumphs which they had achieved in the name of Jesus. Jesus said to them, 'I saw Satan fall like lightning from heaven.' That is a difficult phrase to understand. It can have two meanings.

(1) It may mean, 'I saw the forces of darkness and evil defeated; the citadel of Satan is stormed and the kingdom of God is on the way.' It may mean that Jesus knew that the death-blow to Satan and all his powers had been struck, however long his final conquest might be delayed.

(2) Equally well it may be a warning against pride. The legend was that it was for a pride which rebelled against God that Satan was cast out of heaven where once he had been the chief of the angels. It may be that Jesus was saying to the Seventy, 'You have had your triumphs; keep yourselves from pride, for once the chief of all the angels fell to pride and was cast from heaven.'

Certainly Jesus went on to warn his disciples against pride and overconfidence. It was true that they were given all power, but their greatest glory was that their names were written in heaven.

It will always remain true that our greatest glory is not what we have done but what God has done for us. It might well be claimed that the discovery of the use of chloroform saved the world more pain than any other single medical discovery. Once someone asked Sir James Simpson, who pioneered its use, 'What do you regard as your greatest discovery?' expecting the answer, 'Chloroform'. But Simpson answered, 'My greatest discovery was that Jesus Christ is my Saviour.'

Even the greatest among us can say in the presence of God only, using words from A. M. Toplady's great hymn 'Rock of Ages':

> Nothing in my hand I bring,
> Simply to thy cross I cling;
> Naked, come to thee for dress;
> Helpless, look to thee for grace;
> Foul, I to the fountain fly;
> Wash me, Saviour, or I die.

Pride bars from heaven; humility is the passport to the presence of God.

THE UNSURPASSABLE CLAIM

Luke 10:21–4

> At that time Jesus rejoiced in the Holy Spirit. 'I thank you, O Father, Lord of heaven and earth,' he said, 'that you have hidden these things from the wise and clever and that you have revealed them to babes. Yes, O Father, for so it was your good pleasure in your sight. All things have been handed over to me by my Father. No one knows who the Son is except the Father; and no one knows who the Father is except the Son, and he to whom the Son wishes to reveal him.' He turned to his disciples when they were in private and said, 'Happy are the eyes which see the things which you are seeing for I tell you that many prophets and kings desired to see the things that you are seeing and did not see them, and to hear the things that you are hearing and did not hear them.'

THERE are three great thoughts in this passage:

(1) Verse 21 tells us of the wisdom of simplicity. The simple mind could receive truths that learned minds could not take in. The author Arnold Bennett once said, 'The only way to write a great book is to write it with the eyes of a child who sees things for the first time.' It is possible to be too clever. It is possible to be so learned that in the end we cannot see the wood for the trees. Someone has said that the test of a really great scholar is how much he or she is able to forget. After all, Christianity does not mean knowing

all the theories about the New Testament; still less does it mean knowing all the theologies and the christologies. Christianity does not mean *knowing about Christ*, it means *knowing Christ*; and to do that requires not earthly wisdom but heavenly grace.

(2) Verse 22 tells of the unique relationship between Jesus and God. This is what the Fourth Gospel means when it says, 'The Word became flesh' (John 1:14), or when it makes Jesus say, 'The Father and I are one,' or, 'Whoever has seen me has seen the Father' (John 10:30, 14:9). To the Greeks God was unknowable. There was a great gulf fixed between matter and spirit, humanity and God. 'It is very difficult', they said, 'to know God, and when you do know him it is impossible to tell anyone else about him.' But when Jesus came he said, 'If you want to know what God is like, look at me.' Jesus did not so much tell people about God as show them God, because in himself were God's mind and heart.

(3) Verses 23 and 24 tell us that Jesus is the consummation of all history. In these verses Jesus said, 'I am the one to whom all the prophets and the saints and the kings looked forward and for whom they longed.' This is what Matthew means when over and over again in his gospel he wrote, 'This was done that it might be fulfilled which was spoken by the prophet saying . . .' (cf. Matthew 2:15, 17, 23). Jesus was the peak to which history had been climbing, the goal to which it had been advancing, the dream which had always haunted men and women of God. To express this another way: we believe in evolution, the slow climb upwards of human beings from the level of the beasts. Jesus is the end and climax of the evolutionary process because in him men and women meet God; and he is at once the perfection of humanity and the fullness of godhead.

WHO IS MY NEIGHBOUR?

Luke 10:25–37

Look you – an expert in the law stood up and asked
Jesus a test question. 'Teacher,' he said, 'what is it I
am to do to become the possessor of eternal life?' He
said to him, 'What stands written in the law? How do
you read?' He answered, 'You must love the Lord your
God with your whole heart, and with your whole mind,
and your neighbour as yourself.' 'Your answer is
correct,' said Jesus. But he, wishing to put himself in
the right, said to Jesus, 'And who is my neighbour?'
Jesus answered, 'There was a man who went down from
Jerusalem to Jericho. He fell among brigands who
stripped him and laid blows upon him, and went away
and left him half-dead. Now, by chance, a priest came
down by that road. He looked at him and passed by on
the other side. In the same way when a Levite came to
the place he looked at him and passed by on the other
side. A Samaritan who was on the road came to where
he was. He looked at him and was moved to the depths
of his being with pity. So he came up to him and bound
up his wounds, pouring in wine and oil; and he put him
on his own beast and brought him to an inn and cared
for him. On the next day he put down two denarii and
gave it to the innkeeper. "Look after him," he said, "and
whatever more you are out of pocket, when I come back
this way, I'll square up with you in full." Which of these
three, do you think, was neighbour to the man who fell
into the hands of brigands?' He said, 'He who showed
mercy on him.' 'Go,' said Jesus to him, 'and do
likewise.'

FIRST, let us look at *the scene* of this story. The road from
Jerusalem to Jericho was a notoriously dangerous road.

Jerusalem is 2,300 feet above sea level; the Dead Sea, near which Jericho stood, is 1,300 feet below sea level. So then, in somewhat less than twenty miles, this road dropped 3,600 feet. It was a road of narrow, rocky passages, and of sudden turnings which made it the happy hunting-ground of brigands. In the fifth century Jerome tells us that it was still called 'The Red, or Bloody Way'. In the nineteenth century it was still necessary to pay safety money to the local Sheiks before one could travel on it. As late as the early 1930s the travel writer H. V. Morton tells us that he was warned to get home before dark, if he intended to use the road, because a certain Abu Jildah was an adept at holding up cars and robbing travellers and tourists, and escaping to the hills before the police could arrive. When Jesus told this story, he was telling about the kind of thing that was constantly happening on the Jerusalem to Jericho road.

Second, let us look at the *characters.*

(a) There was *the traveller.* He was obviously a reckless and foolhardy character. People seldom attempted the Jerusalem to Jericho road alone if they were carrying goods or valuables. Seeking safety in numbers, they travelled in convoys or caravans. This man had no one but himself to blame for the plight in which he found himself.

(b) There was *the priest.* He hastened past. No doubt he was remembering that anyone who touched a dead man was unclean for seven days (Numbers 19:11). He could not be sure but he feared that the man was dead; to touch him would mean losing his turn of duty in the Temple; and he refused to risk that. He set the claims of ceremonial above those of charity. The Temple and its liturgy meant more to him than human suffering.

(c) There was *the Levite.* He seems to have gone nearer to the man before he passed on. The bandits were in the habit of using decoys. One of their number would act the part of a wounded man; and when some unsuspecting traveller stopped over him, the others would rush upon him and overpower him. The Levite was a man whose motto was, 'Safety first'. He would take no risks to help anyone else.

(d) There was *the Samaritan.* The listeners would obviously expect that with his arrival the villain had arrived. He may not have been *racially* a Samaritan at all. The Jews had no dealings with the Samaritans and yet this man seems to have been a kind of commercial traveller who was a regular visitor to the inn. In John 8:48 the Jews call Jesus a Samaritan. The name was sometimes used to describe someone who was considered a heretic and a breaker of the ceremonial law. Perhaps this man was a Samaritan in the sense of being one whom orthodox good people despised.

We note two things about him.

(1) His credit was good! Clearly the innkeeper was prepared to trust him. He may have been theologically unsound, but he was an honest man.

(2) He alone was prepared to help. A heretic he may have been, but the love of God was in his heart. It is not uncommon to find the orthodox more interested in dogmas than in help and to find those whom the orthodox despise to be the ones who show the greatest love for others. In the end we will be judged not by the creed we hold but by the life we live.

Third, let us look at *the teaching* of the parable. The scribe who asked this question was in earnest. Jesus asked him what was written in the law, and then said, 'How do you read?' Strict orthodox Jews wore round their wrists little leather boxes called phylacteries, which contained certain passages of Scripture – Exodus 13:1–10, 11–16; Deuteronomy 6:4–9, 11:13–20. 'You shall love the Lord your God' is from Deuteronomy 6:4 and 11:13. So Jesus said to the scribe, 'Look at the phylactery on your own wrist and it will answer your question.' To that the scribes added Leviticus 19:18, which has the bidding 'love your neighbour as yourself'; but with their passion for definition the Rabbis sought to define who a person's neighbour was; and at their worst and their narrowest they confined the word *neighbour* to their *fellow Jews*. For instance, some of them said that it was illegal to help a Gentile woman in her sorest time, the time of childbirth, for that would only have been to bring another Gentile into the world. So then the scribe's question, 'Who is my neighbour?' was genuine.

Jesus' answer involves three things.

(1) We must be prepared to help others even when they have brought their trouble on themselves, as the traveller had done.

(2) Anyone from any nation who is in need is our neighbour. Our help must be as wide as the love of God.

(3) The help must be practical and not consist merely in *feeling* sorry. No doubt the priest and the Levite felt a pang of pity for the wounded man, but they *did* nothing. Compassion, to be real, must issue in deeds.

What Jesus said to the scribe, he says to us – 'Go *you* and do the same.'

THE CLASH OF TEMPERAMENTS

Luke 10:38–42

> As they journeyed, Jesus entered into a village. A woman called Martha received him into her house. She had a sister called Mary, and she sat at Jesus' feet and kept listening to his word. Martha was worried about much serving. She stood over them and said, 'Lord,

> don't you care that my sister has left me alone to do the
> serving? Tell her to give me a hand.' 'Martha, Martha,'
> the Lord answered her, 'you are worried and troubled
> about many things. Only one thing is necessary. Mary
> has chosen the better part, and it is not going to be taken
> away from her.'

IT would be hard to find more vivid character drawing in
greater economy of words than we find in these verses.

(1) They show us *the clash of temperaments*. We have
never allowed enough for the place of temperament in
religion. Some people are naturally dynamos of activity;
others are naturally quiet. It is hard for the active person to
understand the person who sits and contemplates. And the
person who is devoted to quiet times and meditation is apt to
look down on the person who would rather be active.

There is no right or wrong in this. God did not make
everyone alike. One person may pray using Fay Inchfawn's
words:

> Lord of all pots and pans and things.
>   Since I've no time to be
> A saint by doing lovely things,
>   Or watching late with thee,
> Or dreaming in the dawnlight,
>   Or storming heaven's gates,
> Make me a saint by getting meals
>   And washing up the plates.

Another may sit with folded hands and mind intense to think
and pray. Both are serving God. God needs his Marys and his
Marthas, too.

(2) These verses show us something more – they show us
the wrong type of kindness. Think where Jesus was going
when this happened. He was on his way to Jerusalem – to

die. His whole being was taken up with the intensity of the inner battle to bend his will to the will of God. When Jesus came to that home in Bethany it was a great day; and Martha was eager to celebrate it by laying on the best the house could give. So she rushed and fussed and cooked; *and that was precisely what Jesus did not want.* All he wanted was quiet. With the cross before him and with the inner tension in his heart, he had turned aside to Bethany to find an oasis of calm away from the demanding crowds if only for an hour or two; and that is what Mary gave him and what Martha, in her kindness, did her best to destroy. 'One thing is necessary' – quite possibly this means, 'I don't want a big spread; one course, the simplest meal is all I want.' It was simply that Mary understood and that Martha did not.

Here is one of the great difficulties in life. So often we want to be kind to people – but we want to be kind to them *in our way*; and should it happen that our way is not the necessary way, we sometimes take offence and think that we are not appreciated. If we are trying to be kind the first necessity is to try to see into the heart of the person we desire to help – and then to forget all our own plans and to think only of what he or she needs. Jesus loved Martha and Martha loved him, but when Martha set out to be kind, it had to be her way of being kind which was really being unkind to him whose heart cried out for quiet. Jesus loved Mary and Mary loved him, and Mary understood.

TEACH US TO PRAY

Luke 11:1-4

Jesus was praying in a certain place, and when he stopped, one of his disciples said to him, 'Lord, teach

us to pray, as John taught his disciples.' He said to them,
'When you pray, say,

> O Father, let your name be held in reverence.
> Let your kingdom come.
> Give to us each day our bread for the day.
> And forgive us our sins as we too forgive everyone
>   who is in debt to us.
> And lead us not into temptation.'

It was the regular custom for a Rabbi to teach his disciples a simple prayer which they might habitually use. John had done that for his disciples, and now Jesus' disciples came asking him to do the same for them. This is Luke's version of the Lord's Prayer. It is shorter than Matthew's, but it will teach us all we need to know about how to pray and what to pray for.

(1) It begins by calling God *Father.* That was the characteristic Christian address to God (cf. Galatians 4:6; Romans 8:15; 1 Peter 1:17). The very first word tells us that in prayer we are not coming to someone out of whom gifts have to be unwillingly extracted, but to a father who delights to supply his children's needs.

(2) In Hebrew *the name* means much more than merely the name by which a person is called. *The name* means the whole character of the person as it is revealed and known to us. Psalm 9:10 says, 'Those who know your name put their trust in you.' That means far more than knowing that God's name is Yahweh. It means that those who know the whole character and mind and heart of God will gladly put their trust in him.

(3) We must note particularly the order of the Lord's Prayer. Before anything is asked for ourselves, God and his glory, and the reverence due to him, come first. Only when we give God his place will other things take their proper place.

(4) The prayer covers all life.

(a) It covers *present need*. It tells us to pray for our daily bread; but it is bread *for the day* for which we pray. This goes back to the old story of the manna in the wilderness (Exodus 16:11–21). Only enough for the needs of the day might be gathered. We are not to worry about the unknown future, but to live a day at a time. As Cardinal Newman wrote in that well-loved hymn 'Lead Kindly Light':

> I do not ask to see
> The distant scene – one step enough for me.

(b) It covers *past sin*. When we pray we cannot do other than pray for forgiveness, for even the best of us is a sinner coming before the purity of God.

(c) It covers *future trials*. *Temptation* means any testing situation. It includes far more than the mere seduction to sin; it covers every situation which is a challenge to and a test of a person's humanity and integrity and fidelity. We cannot escape it, but we can meet it with God.

Someone has said that the Lord's Prayer has two great uses in our private prayers. If we use it at the beginning of our devotions it awakens all kinds of holy desires which lead us on into the right pathways of prayer. If we use it at the end of our devotions it sums up all we ought to pray for in the presence of God.

ASK AND YOU WILL RECEIVE

Luke 11:5–13

> Jesus said to them, 'Suppose one of you has a friend and goes to him towards midnight and says to him, "Friend, lend me three loaves because a friend of mine

has arrived at my house from a journey and I have
nothing to set before him"; and suppose his friend
answers from within, "Don't bother me; the door has
already been shut and my children are in bed with me; I
can't get up and supply you" – I tell you, if he will not
rise and supply him because he is his friend, he will
rise and give him as much as he needs because of his
shameless persistence. For I say to you, "Ask and it
will be given to you; seek and you will find; knock and
it will be opened to you. For everyone who asks
receives; and he who seeks finds; and to him who knocks
it will be opened. If a son asks any father among you
for bread, will he give him a stone? Or, if he asks a fish,
will he, instead of a fish, give him a serpent? Or if he
asks an egg, will he give him a scorpion? If you then,
who are evil, know to give good gifts to your children,
how much more will your Father who is in heaven give
the Holy Spirit to those who ask him?"'

TRAVELLERS often journeyed late in the evening to avoid the
heat of the midday sun. In Jesus' story just such a traveller
had arrived towards midnight at this friend's house. In the
middle east hospitality is a sacred duty; it was not enough to
set before a visitor a bare sufficiency; the guest had to be
confronted with an ample abundance. In the villages bread
was baked at home. Only enough for the day's needs was
baked because if it was kept and became stale, no one would
wish to eat it.

The late arrival of the traveller confronted the householder
with an embarrassing situation, because his larder was empty
and he could not fulfil the sacred obligations of hospitality.
Late as it was, he went out to borrow from a friend. The
friend's door was shut. In this part of the world no one would
knock on a shut door unless the need was imperative. In the
morning the door was opened and remained open all day, for

there was little privacy; but if the door was shut, that was a definite sign that the householder did not wish to be disturbed. But the seeking householder was not deterred. He knocked, and kept on knocking.

The poorer Palestinian house consisted of one room with only one little window. The floor was simply of beaten earth covered with dried reeds and rushes. The room was divided into two parts, not by a partition but by a low platform. Two-thirds of it were on ground level. The other third was slightly raised. On the raised part the charcoal stove burned all night, and round it the whole family slept, not on raised beds but on sleeping mats. Families were large and they slept close together for warmth. For one to rise was inevitably to disturb the whole family. Further, in the villages it was the custom to bring the livestock, the hens and the cocks and the goats, into the house at night.

Is there any wonder that the man who was in bed did not want to rise? But the determined borrower knocked on with shameless persistence – that is what the Greek word means – until at last the householder, knowing that by this time the whole family was disturbed anyway, arose and gave him what he needed.

'That story', said Jesus, 'will tell you about prayer.' The lesson of this parable is not that we must persist in prayer; it is not that we must batter at God's door until we finally compel him for very weariness to give us what we want, until we coerce an unwilling God to answer.

A parable literally means *something laid alongside*. If we lay something beside another thing to teach a lesson, that lesson may be drawn from the fact that the things are like each other or from the fact that the things are a contrast to each other. The point here is based, not on likeness, but on *contrast*. What Jesus says is, 'If a churlish and unwilling householder can in the end be coerced by a friend's shameless persistence into giving him what he needs, *how much more* will God who is a loving Father supply all his children's needs?' 'If you,' he says, 'who are evil, know that you are bound to supply your children's needs, *how much more* will God?'

This does not absolve us from intensity in prayer. After all, we can guarantee the reality and sincerity of our desire only by the passion with which we pray. But it does mean this, that we are not wringing gifts from an unwilling God, but going to one who knows our needs better than we know them ourselves and whose heart towards us is the heart of generous love. If we do not receive what we pray for, it is not because God grudgingly refuses to give it but because he has some better thing for us. There is no such thing as unanswered prayer. The answer given may not be the answer we desired or expected; but even when it is a refusal it is the answer of the love and the wisdom of God.

A MALICIOUS SLANDER

Luke 11:14-23

> Jesus was casting out a dumb demon. When the demon came out the dumb man spoke and the crowds were amazed. Some of them said, 'He casts out demons by the help of Beelzebul, who is the prince of demons.' Others, trying to put him to the test, sought a sign from heaven from him. He knew what they were thinking. 'Every kingdom', he said, 'that is divided against itself is devastated; and every house that is divided against itself falls; so if Satan is divided against himself how will his kingdom stand? You must answer that question

because you say that I cast out demons by the help of
Beelzebul. If I cast out demons by the power of
Beelzebul, by whose power do your sons cast them out?
You have become your own judges. But if it is by the
finger of God that I cast out the demons, then the
kingdom of God has come upon you. When a strong
man in full panoply guards his own homestead, his
goods are in peace. But when a stronger man than he
comes and conquers him, he will take away the armour
in which he trusted, and will divide his spoil. He who is
not with me is against me; and he who does not gather
with me scatters.'

WHEN Jesus' enemies were helpless to oppose him by fair
means they resorted to slander. They declared that his power
over the demons was due to the fact that he was in league
with the prince of demons. They attributed his power not to
God but to the devil. Jesus gave them a double and a crushing
answer.

First, he struck them a shrewd blow. There were many
exorcists in Jesus' time in Palestine. Josephus traces this
power back to Solomon. Part of Solomon's wisdom was
that he was skilful with herbs and had invented incantations
which drove out demons in such a way that they never
came back; and Josephus states that he had seen Solomon's
methods used with success even in his own day (Josephus,
Antiquities of the Jews, 8:5:2). So Jesus delivers a home-
thrust. 'If I', he said, 'cast out devils because I am in league
with the prince of devils, what of your own people who do
the same thing? If you condemn me, you are only condemning
yourselves.'

Second, he used a really unanswerable argument. No
kingdom in which there is a civil war can survive. If the prince
of devils is lending his power to defeat his own emissaries he

is finished. There is only one way for a strong man to be defeated and that is for a still stronger man to master him. 'Therefore,' said Jesus, 'if I cast out devils, so far from that proving that I am in league with the prince of devils, it proves that the devil's citadel is breached, the strong man of evil is overcome, and the kingdom of God is here.'

Out of this passage emerge certain permanent truths.

(1) It is by no means uncommon for people to resort to slander when honest opposition is helpless. The British Prime Minister Gladstone was interested in the reformation of the prostitutes of the streets of London. His enemies suggested that he was interested in them for very different and very inferior reasons. There is nothing so cruel as slander, for it is apt to stick because the human mind always tends to think the worst and very often the human ear prefers to hear the derogatory rather than the complimentary tale. We need not think that we are free of that particular sin. How often do *we* tend to think the worst of other people? How often do we deliberately impute low motives to someone whom we dislike? How often do we repeat the slanderous and the malicious tale and murder reputations in idle chatter? To think of this will not cause complacency but call for self-examination.

(2) Once again we must note that Jesus' proof that the kingdom had come was the fact that sufferers were healed and health walked where disease had been. Jesus' aim was not only *soul* salvation; it was also *whole* salvation.

(3) Luke finishes this section with the saying of Jesus that he who was not with him was against him and that he who did not help to gather the flock helped to scatter it abroad. There is no place for neutrality in the Christian life. If we stand aloof from the good cause we automatically help the evil one. We are either on the way or in the way.

THE PERIL OF THE EMPTY SOUL

Luke 11:24–8

> When the unclean spirit goes out of a man, it goes
> through waterless places seeking for rest. And when it
> does not find it, it says, 'I will go back to my house
> from which I came out.' So it comes and finds the house
> swept and in order. Then it goes and gets in addition
> seven spirits worse than itself, and they enter in and
> settle there; and the last state of that man is worse than
> the first.
>
> When he was speaking a woman lifted up her voice
> from the crowd and said, 'Happy is the womb that bore
> you and the breasts at which you sucked.' 'But,' he
> said, 'rather, happy are those who hear the word of God
> and keep it.'

HERE is a grim and terrible story. There was a man from whom
an unclean spirit was expelled. The spirit wandered seeking
rest and found none. It determined to return to the man. It
found his soul swept and garnished – but empty. So the spirit
went and collected seven spirits worse than itself and came
back and entered in; and the man's last state was worse than
his first.

(1) Here is the fundamental truth that you cannot leave a
person's soul empty. It is not enough to banish the evil
thoughts and the evil habits and the old ways and leave the
soul empty. An empty soul is a soul in peril. A certain preacher
liked to take the text, 'Do not get drunk with wine, for that is
debauchery; but be filled with the Spirit' (Ephesians 5:18).
When he did so his opening sentence was, 'You've got to fill
a man with something.' It is not enough to drive out evil;
good must come in.

(2) That means we can never erect a real religion on negatives. Take a very clear example – the question of Sunday observance still raises difficulties in the Church today. Too often it is approached with a tirade against the things which people allow themselves to do on Sunday and a catalogue of forbidden things. But those to whom we speak have a perfect right to ask, 'Well, what *may* I do?' And unless we tell them, their last state is worse than their first, for we have simply condemned them to idleness, and Satan is adept at finding mischief for idle hands to do. It is always the peril of religion that it may present itself in a series of negatives. Cleansing is necessary; but after the rooting out of evil, there must come the filling with good.

(3) The best way to avoid evil is to do good. The loveliest garden I ever saw was so full of flowers that there was scarcely room for a weed to grow. In no garden is it enough to uproot weeds; flowers must be sown and planted until the space is filled. Nowhere is this truer than in the world of thoughts. Often we may be troubled with wrong thoughts. If we go no further than to say to ourselves, 'I will not think about that,' all we do is fix our thoughts upon it more and more. The cure is to think of something else, to banish the evil thought by thinking a good thought. We never become good by *not* doing things, but by filling life with lovely things.

Verses 27 and 28 show Jesus speaking sternly but truly. The woman who spoke was carried away by a moment of emotion. Jesus pulled her back to reality. The moment of emotion is a fine thing; but the greatest thing is a life of obedience in everyday routine things. No amount of fine feeling can take the place of faithful doing.

THE RESPONSIBILITY OF PRIVILEGE

Luke 11:29–32

When the crowds were thronging upon him, he began to say, 'This generation is a wicked generation. It seeks a sign, and no sign will be given to it except the sign of Jonah; for just as Jonah was a sign to the people of Nineveh so the Son of Man will be to this generation. The queen of the south will rise up in judgment with the men of this generation and will condemn them, because she came from the ends of the earth to hear the wisdom of Solomon, and – look you – something greater than Solomon is here. The men of Nineveh will rise up in judgment with this generation and will condemn it, because they repented at the preaching of Jonah, and – look you – something greater than Jonah is here.'

THE Jews wanted Jesus to do something sensational to prove that he really was the Anointed One of God. Later than this, about the year AD 45, a man called Theudas arose claiming to be the Messiah. He persuaded the people to follow him out to the Jordan with the promise that he would cleave the river in two and give them a pathway through it to the other side. Needless to say he failed, and the Romans dealt summarily with his rising; but that is the kind of thing the people wanted Jesus to do to prove his claims. They could not see that the greatest sign that God could ever send was Jesus himself.

Just as once long ago Jonah had been God's sign to Nineveh, so now Jesus was God's sign to them – and they failed to recognize him. When Solomon was king the Queen of Sheba recognized his wisdom and came from far to benefit from it; when Jonah preached the people of Nineveh recognized the authentic voice of God and responded to it. In the day of judgment these people would rise up and condemn the Jews of Jesus' time, because these Jews had had an opportunity and a privilege far beyond anything they had ever had and had refused to accept it. The condemnation of the Jews would be all the more complete because their privileges were so great.

Privilege and responsibility always go hand in hand. Think of two of our greatest privileges and how we use them.

(1) Available to everyone is the Bible, the word of God. It did *not* cost nothing. There was a time when it was death to teach the English Bible. When John Wyclif wrote to a certain scholar, about the year 1350, asking him to teach the common people the gospel stories in the English tongue, he answered, 'I know well that I am holden by Christ's law to perform thy asking, but, natheless, we are now so far fallen away from Christ's law, that if I would answer to thy askings *I must in case undergo the death*; and thou wottest well that a man is beholden to keep his life as long as he may.' Later on, we learn from Foxe's *Book of Martyrs* that in those days some sat up all night to read and hear the word of God in English. 'Some gave five marks (equal to £40 or $60 of our money), some more, some less for a book; some gave a load of hay for a few chapters of St James or St Paul in English.' It was William Tyndale who gave England its first printed Bible. To do so, as he said himself, he suffered, 'poverty, exile, bitter absence from friends, hunger and thirst and cold, great dangers and innumerable other hard and sharp fightings'. In 1536 he was martyred. When, some years before, the authorities had burned the book, he said, 'They did none other thing than I looked for; no more shall they do if they burn me also.'

There is no book which cost so much as the Bible. Today it is in serious danger of deserving the cynical definition of a classic – a book of which everyone has heard and which no one reads. We have the privilege of possessing the Bible and that privilege is a responsibility for which we shall answer.

(2) We have freedom to worship as we think right; and that, too, is a privilege which cost lives. The tragedy is that so many people have used that freedom in order not to worship at all. That privilege, too, is a responsibility for which we shall answer.

Those who possess Christ, and Christ's book, and Christ's Church, are the heirs of all the privileges of God; and if they neglect them or refuse them, they, like the Jews in the time of Jesus, are under condemnation.

THE DARKENED HEART

Luke 11:33-6

> No one lights a lamp and puts it in a cellar or under a bushel, but upon a lamp-stand, so that those who come in may see the light. The lamp of the body is your eye. When your eye is sound your whole body is full of light; but if the eye is diseased the whole body is full of darkness. Take care, then, lest the light that is in you is darkness. If, then, your whole body is full of light, without any part of darkness, it will be altogether bright as when the lamp with its ray gives you light.

THE meaning is not easy to grasp, but probably it is this. The light of the body depends on the eye; if the eye is healthy the body receives all the light it needs; if the eye is diseased the light turns to darkness. Just so, *the light of life depends on the heart*; if the heart is right the whole life is irradiated with light; if the heart is wrong all life is darkened. Jesus urges us to see that the inner lamp is always burning.

What is it that darkens the inner light? What is it that can go wrong with our hearts?

(1) Our hearts may become *hard*. Sometimes, if we have to do something unaccustomed with our hands, the skin is irritated and we have pain; but if we repeat the action often enough the skin becomes hardened and we can do what once hurt us without any trouble. It is so with our hearts. The first time we do a wrong thing we do it with a tremor and sometimes with a sore heart. Each time we repeat it the tremor grows less, until in the end we can do it without a qualm. There is a terrible hardening power in sin. None of us ever took the first step to sin without the warnings sounding in our hearts; but if we sin often enough the time comes when we cease to care. What we were once afraid and reluctant to do becomes a habit. We have nobody but ourselves to blame if we allow ourselves to reach that stage.

(2) Our hearts may become *dull*. It is tragically easy to accept things. In the beginning our hearts may be sore at the sight of the world's suffering and pain; but in the end most people become so used to it that they accept it and feel nothing at all.

It is all too true that for most people the feelings of youth are far more intense than those of age. That is specially true of the cross of Jesus Christ. Florence Barclay tells how when she was a little girl she was taken to church for the first time. It was Good Friday, and the long story of the crucifixion was read and beautifully read. She heard Peter deny and Judas betray; she heard Pilate's bullying cross-examination; she saw the crown of thorns, the buffeting of the soldiers; she heard of Jesus being delivered to be crucified, and then there came the words with their terrible finality, 'and there they crucified him'. No one in the church seemed to care; but suddenly the little girl's face was buried in her mother's coat, and she was sobbing her heart out, and her little voice rang through the silent church, 'Why did they do it? Why did they do it?'

That is how we all ought to feel about the cross, but we have heard the story so often that we can listen to it with no reaction at all. God keep us from the heart which has lost the power to feel the agony of the cross – borne for us.

(3) Our hearts may be actively *rebellious*. It is quite possible to know the right way and deliberately to take the wrong way, to feel God's hand upon our shoulder and twitch that shoulder away. With open eyes we may take the way to the far country when God is calling us home.

God save us from the darkened heart.

THE WORSHIP OF DETAILS AND THE NEGLECT OF THE THINGS THAT MATTER

Luke 11:37-44

> After Jesus had spoken a Pharisee asked him to dine with him. He came in and reclined at the table. The Pharisee was surprised when he saw that he did not dip his hands in water before he ate. The Lord said to him, 'You Pharisees cleanse the outside of the cup and the dish, but inside you are full of grasping and wickedness. Fools! Did he who made the outside not make the inside also? But cleanse the things that are within – and look you – all things will be pure for you.
>
> 'But woe to you Pharisees! because you give tithes of mint and rue and every herb and pass by justice and the love of God. These you ought to have done without omitting the others. Woe to you Pharisees! because you love the chief seats in the synagogues and greetings in the market places. Woe to you! because you are like

tombs which are not seen, and the men who walk over
them do not know that they are doing it.'

THE Pharisee was surprised that Jesus did not wash his hands
before eating. This was not a matter of cleanliness but of
the ceremonial law. The law laid it down that the hands must
be washed in a certain way before eating and that this handwashing must be repeated between the courses. As usual every
littlest detail was worked out. Large stone vessels of water
were specially kept for the purpose because ordinary water
might be unclean; the amount of water used must be at
least a quarter of a log, that is, enough to fill one and a half
eggshells. First the water must be poured over the hands
beginning at the tips of the fingers and running right up to the
wrist. Then the palm of each hand must be cleansed by
rubbing the fist of the other into it. Finally, water must again
be poured over the hand, this time beginning at the wrist and
running down to the fingertips. To the Pharisee, to omit the
slightest detail of this was to sin. Jesus' comment was that if
they were as particular about cleansing their hearts as they
were about washing their hands, they would be better people.

There were certain dues which the meticulously orthodox
would never omit to pay.

(a) *The first fruits of the soil.* The first fruits of the seven
kinds – wheat, barley, vines, fig trees, pomegranates, olives
and honey – were offered in the Temple.

(b) There was *the Terumah.* The first fruits were given to
God, but the Terumah was a contribution to the upkeep of the
priests. It was the presentation of the first fruits of every
growing thing. The amount to be given was one-fiftieth of
the total yield.

(c) There was *the tithe.* The tithe was paid directly to the
Levites, who, in turn, paid a tithe of what they received to the

priests. It was one-tenth of 'everything that can be used as food and is cultivated and grows out of the earth'. The meticulousness of the Pharisees in tithing is shown by the fact that even the law said it was not necessary to tithe rue. No matter what their inner hearts and feelings were like, however much they neglected justice and forgot love, they never omitted the tithe.

The chief seats at the synagogue were the seats out in front facing the audience. In the congregation itself the best seats were at the front and they decreased in honour the further back they got. The advantage of these seats was that they could be seen by all!

The more exaggerated the respect of the greetings the Pharisees received in the streets the better they were pleased.

The point of verse 44 is this. Numbers 19:16 lays it down that 'whoever in the open field touches a grave shall be unclean seven days'. To be unclean was to be debarred from all religious worship. Now, it might be that someone might touch a grave without realizing. That did not matter; its touch made the person unclean. Jesus said that the Pharisees were exactly like that. Although people might not know it their influence could do nothing but harm. All unawares, those who came in contact with them were being touched for evil. They might not suspect the corruption but it was there; all the time they were being infected with wrong ideas of God and of his demands.

Two things stand out about the Pharisees and for these two things Jesus condemned them.

(1) They concentrated on *externals*. As long as the externals of religion were carried out that was all that mattered. They might be utterly lacking in charity and even in justice; but as long as they went through the correct motions at the

correct time they considered themselves good in the eyes of God.

People may be regular in their church attendance; they may be diligent students of the Bible; they may be generous givers to the Church; but if in their hearts there are thoughts of pride and of contempt, if they have no charity in their dealings with others in everyday life, if they are unjust to their subordinates or dishonest to their employer, they are not Christians. No one who meticulously observes the conventions of religion and forgets the realities is a Christian.

(2) They concentrated on *details*. Compared with love and kindness, justice and generosity, the washing of hands and the giving of tithes with mathematical accuracy were unimportant details. Once a man came to Dr Johnson with a tale of woe. He worked in a paper factory; he had taken for his own purposes a very little piece of paper and a very little bit of string, and he had convinced himself that he had committed a deadly sin and would not stop talking about it. At last Johnson broke out, 'Sir, stop bothering about paper and packthread when we are all living together in a world that is bursting with sin and sorrow.' How often church authorities and church people get lost in totally unimportant details of church government and administration, and even argue and fight about them, and forget the great realities of the Christian life!

THE SINS OF THE LEGALISTS

Luke 11:45-54

> A scribe answered, 'Teacher, when you talk like that you are insulting us.' Jesus said, 'Woe to you scribes too! because you bind burdens upon men that are hard

to bear and you yourselves do not lay a finger on the burdens. Woe to you! because you build the tombs of the prophets whom your fathers killed! So you are witnesses that you agree with the deeds of your fathers, because they killed them and you build them tombs. Because of this God in his wisdom said, "I will send prophets and apostles to them, some of whom they will slay and persecute, so that the blood of all the prophets, shed from the foundation of the world, will be required from this generation, from the blood of Abel to the blood of Zacharias who perished between the altar and the Temple." Yes, I tell you, it will be required from this generation. Woe to you scribes! You did not enter in yourselves and you hindered those who were trying to enter.'

As Jesus went away from them, the scribes and Pharisees began to watch him intensely, and to try to provoke him to discuss on many subjects, for they were laying traps for him, to hunt for something out of his mouth which they could use as a charge against him.

THREE charges are levelled against the scribes.

(1) They were experts in the law; they laid upon people the thousand and one burdens of the ceremonial law; but they did not keep them themselves, because they were experts in evasion. Here are some of their evasions.

The limit of a Sabbath day's journey was 2,000 cubits (1,000 yards) from a man's residence. But if a rope was tied across the end of the street, the end of the street became his residence and he could go 1,000 yards beyond that; if on the Friday evening he left at any given point enough food for two meals that point technically became his residence and he could go 1,000 yards beyond that!

One of the forbidden works on the Sabbath was the tying of knots, sailors' or camel-drivers' knots and knots in ropes.

But a woman might tie the knot in her girdle. Therefore, if a bucket of water had to be raised from a well a rope could not be knotted to it, but a woman's girdle could, and it could be raised with that!

To carry a burden was forbidden, but the codified written law laid it down, 'he who carries anything, whether it be in his right hand, or in his left hand, or in his bosom, or on his shoulder is guilty; but he who carries anything on the back of his hand, with his foot, or with his mouth, or with his elbow, or with his ear, or with his hair, or with his money bag turned upside down, or between his money bag and his shirt, or in the fold of his shirt or in his shoe, or in his sandal is guiltless, because he does not carry it in the usual way of carrying it out'.

It is incredible that anyone should ever have thought that God could have laid down laws like that, and that the working out of such details was a religious service and the keeping of them a matter of life and death. But that was scribal religion. Little wonder that Jesus turned on the scribes, and that the scribes regarded him as an irreligious heretic.

(2) The attitude of the scribes to the prophets was paradoxical. They professed a deep admiration for the prophets. But the only prophets they admired were dead; when they met a living one they tried to kill him. They honoured the dead prophets with tombs and memorials, but they dishonoured the living ones with persecution and death.

'Your new moons,' said Isaiah, 'and your appointed festivals my soul hates' (Isaiah 1:14). 'He has told you, O mortal, what is good,' said Micah; 'and what does the Lord require of you but to do justice, and to love kindness, and to walk humbly with your God?' (Micah 6:8). That was the essence of the prophetic message; and it was the very antithesis of scribal teaching. No wonder the scribes, with their external details, hated the prophets, and Jesus walked in the prophetic line. The murder of Zacharias is described in 2 Chronicles 24:20–1.

(3) The scribes shut the people off from Scripture. Their interpretation of Scripture was so fantastic that it was impossible for ordinary people to understand it. In their hands Scripture became a book of riddles. In their mistaken ingenuity they refused to see its plain meaning themselves, and they would not let anyone else see it either. The Scriptures had become the property of the expert and a dark mystery to ordinary people.

None of this is so very out of date. There are still those who demand from others standards which they themselves refuse to satisfy. There are still those whose religion is nothing other than legalism. There are still those who make the word of God so difficult that many who are genuinely seeking after truth become bewildered and do not know what to believe or to whom to listen.

THE CREED OF COURAGE AND OF TRUST

Luke 12:1–12

In the meantime, when the people had been gathered together in their thousands, so that they trampled on each other, Jesus began to say first of all to his disciples, 'Be on your guard against the leaven of the Pharisees, which is hypocrisy. There is nothing covered up which will not be unveiled, and there is nothing secret which shall not be known. All, therefore, that you have spoken in the dark shall be heard in the light; and what you have spoken into someone's ear in the inner room will be proclaimed on the housetops. I tell you, my friends, do not be afraid of those who kill the body and who after that are not able to do anything further. I will warn you whom you are to fear – fear him who after he has killed you has authority to cast you into hell. Yes, I tell you, fear him! Are not five sparrows sold for two pennies? And yet not one of them is forgotten before God. But as for you – even the hairs of your head are all numbered. Do not be afraid. You are of more value than many sparrows. I tell you, everyone who acknowledges me before men, him will the Son of Man acknowledge before the angels of God; but he who denies me before men will be denied before the angels of God. If anyone speaks a word against the Son of Man it will be forgiven him; but he who speaks irreverently of the Holy Spirit will not be forgiven. When they bring you before synagogues and rulers and those set in authority, do not worry how you will defend yourself or about what defence you will make, or about what you will say, for the Holy Spirit will teach you in that same hour what you ought to say.'

WHEN we read this passage we are reminded again of the Jewish definition of preaching – Charaz, which means *stringing pearls*. This passage, too, is a collection of pearls strung together without the close connection which modern preaching demands. But in it there are certain dominant ideas.

(1) It tells us of the *forbidden sin*, which is *hypocrisy*. The word *hypocrite* began by meaning *someone who answers*; and *hypocrisy* originally meant *answering*. First the words were used of the ordinary flow of question and answer in any talk or in any dialogue; then they began to be connected with question and answer *in a play*. From that they went on to be connected with *acting a part*. The hypocrite is never genuine but is always play-acting. The basis of hypocrisy is insincerity. God would rather have a blunt, honest sinner, than someone who puts on an act of goodness.

(2) It tells of the *correct attitude to life*, which is an attitude of *fearlessness*. There are two reasons for fearlessness.

(a) One person's power over another is strictly limited to this life. It is possible to destroy someone else's life *but not* that person's soul. In the First World War *Punch* had a famous cartoon in which it showed the German emperor saying to King Albert of Belgium, 'So now you have lost everything'; and back came Albert's answer, 'But not my soul!' On the other hand, God's power is such that it can blot out a person's very soul. It is, therefore, only reasonable to fear God rather than to fear other people. It was said of John Knox, as his body was being lowered into the grave, 'Here lies one who feared God so much that he never feared the face of man.'

(b) God's care is the most detailed of all. To God we are never lost in the crowd. Matthew says, 'Are not two sparrows sold for a penny?' (Matthew 10:29). Here Luke says, 'Are not *five* sparrows sold for two pennies?' If you were prepared to pay the extra penny you got not four, but five sparrows. One was flung into the bargain as having no value at all. Not even the sparrow thrown into the bargain without real value is forgotten before God. The very hairs of our head are numbered. It has been computed that a blond person has about 145,000 hairs; a dark-haired person, 120,000; and a person with red hair, 90,000! The Jews were so impressed with the individual care of God that they said that every blade of grass had its guardian angel. None of us needs to fear for each can say, 'God cares for *me*.'

(3) It tells us of *the unforgivable sin*, which is the sin against the Holy Spirit. Both Matthew and Mark record that Jesus spoke about this sin immediately after the scribes and Pharisees had attributed his cures to the prince of devils instead of to God (Matthew 12:31-2; Mark 3:28-9). These men could look at the very grace and power of God and call

it the work of the devil. To understand this we must remember that Jesus was talking about the Holy Spirit as *the Jews* understood that conception, not in the full Christian sense, about which his audience at that time obviously knew nothing.

To a Jew, God's Spirit had two great functions. Through the Spirit he told his truth to men and women, and it was by the action of the Spirit in human minds and hearts that he could recognize and grasp God's truth. Now, if we for long enough refuse to use a faculty we will lose it. If we refuse to use any part of the body long enough it atrophies. Charles Darwin tells how when he was a young man he loved poetry and music; but he so devoted himself to biology that he completely neglected them. The consequence was that in later life poetry meant nothing to him and music was only a noise, and he said that if he had his life to live over again he would see to it that he would read poetry and listen to music so that he would not lose the faculty of enjoying them.

Just so, we can lose the faculty of recognizing God. By repeatedly refusing God's word, by repeatedly taking our own way, by repeatedly shutting our eyes to God and closing our ears to him, we can come to a stage when we do not recognize him when we see him, when to us evil becomes good and good becomes evil. That is what happened to the scribes and Pharisees. They had so blinded and deafened themselves to God that when he came they called him the devil.

Why is that the unforgivable sin? Because in such a state *repentance is impossible.* If people do not even realize that they are sinning, if goodness no longer makes any appeal to them, they cannot repent. God has not shut them out; by their repeated refusals they have shut themselves out. That means that the very people who can never have committed un-forgivable sins are those who fear that they have, for once people have committed it, they are so dead to God that they are conscious of no sin at all.

(4) It tells us of *the rewarded loyalty*. The reward of loyalty is no material thing. It is that in heaven Jesus will say of us, 'You stood by me. Well done!'

(5) It tells us of *the help of the Holy Spirit*. In the Fourth Gospel the favourite title of the Holy Spirit is the *Paraclete*. *Parakletos* means *someone who stands by to help*. It can be used of a witness, or an advocate to plead our cause. In the day of trouble there need be no fear, for no less a person than the Holy Spirit of God stands by to help.

THE PLACE OF MATERIAL POSSESSIONS IN LIFE

Luke 12:13–34

One of the crowd said to Jesus, 'Teacher, tell my brother to divide the inheritance with me.' He said to him, 'Man, who appointed me a judge or an arbitrator over you?' He said to them, 'Watch and guard yourself against the spirit which is always wanting more; for even if a man has an abundance his life does not come from his possessions.' He spoke a parable to them. 'The land', he said, 'of a rich man bore good crops. He kept thinking what he would do. "What will I do," he said, "because I have no room to gather in my crops?" So he said, "This is what I will do. I will pull down my barns and I will build bigger ones, and I will gather there all my corn and all my good things; and I will say to my soul, Soul, you have many good things laid up for many years. Take your rest, eat, drink and enjoy yourself." But God said to him, "Fool! This night your soul is demanded from you; and, the things you prepared – who will get

them all?" So is he who heaps up treasure for himself
and is not rich towards God.'

Jesus said to his disciples, 'I therefore tell you, do
not worry about your life – about what you are to eat;
nor about your body – about what you are to wear. For
your life is something more than food, and your body
than clothing. Look at the ravens. See how they do not
sow or reap; they have no storehouse or barn; but God
feeds them. How much more valuable are you than the
birds? Which of you, by worrying about it, can add a
few days to his span of life? If, then, you cannot do the
littlest thing why worry about the other things? Look at
the lilies. See how they grow. They do not work; they
do not spin; but, I tell you, not even Solomon in all his
glory was clothed like one of these. If God so clothe
the grass in the field, which is there today and which
tomorrow is cast into the oven, how much more will he
clothe you, O you of little faith? Do not seek what you
are to eat and what you are to drink; do not be tossed
about in a storm of anxiety. The peoples of the world
seek for all these things. Your Father knows that you
need them. But seek his kingdom and all these things
will be added to you. Do not fear, little flock, because it
is your Father's will to give you the kingdom. Sell your
possessions and give alms. Make yourselves purses
which never grow old, a treasure in the heavens that
does not fail, where a thief does not come near and a
moth does not destroy. For where your treasure is there
your heart will also be.'

IT was not uncommon for people in Palestine to take their
unsettled disputes to respected Rabbis; but Jesus refused to
be mixed up in anyone's disputes about money. But out of
that request there came to Jesus an opportunity to lay down
what his followers' attitude to material things should be. He

had something to say both to those who had an abundant supply of material possessions and to those who had not.

(1) To those who had an abundant supply of possessions Jesus spoke this parable of the rich fool. Two things stand out about this man.

(a) *He never saw beyond himself.* There is no parable which is so full of the words, I, me, my and mine. A schoolboy was once asked what parts of speech *my* and *mine* are. He answered, 'Aggressive pronouns'. The rich fool was aggressively self-centred. It was said of a self-centred young lady, 'Edith lived in a little world, bounded on the north, south, east and west by Edith.' The famous criticism was made of a self-centred person, 'There is too much ego in his cosmos.' When this man had a superfluity of goods the one thing that never entered his head was to give any away. His whole attitude was the very reverse of Christianity. Instead of denying himself he aggressively affirmed himself; instead of finding his happiness in giving he tried to conserve it by keeping.

John Wesley's rule of life was to *save* all he could and *give* all he could. When he was at Oxford he had an income of £30 a year. He lived on £28 and gave £2 away. When his income increased to £60, £90 and £120 a year, he still lived on £28 and gave the balance away. The Accountant-General for Household Plate demanded a return from him. His reply was, 'I have two silver tea spoons at London and two at Bristol. This is all the plate which I have at present; and I shall not buy any more, while so many around me want bread.'

The Romans had a proverb which said that money was like sea water; the more you drink the thirstier you become. Similarly, as long as our attitude is that of the rich fool our desire will always be to get more – and that is the reverse of the Christian way.

(b) *He never saw beyond this world.* All his plans were made on the basis of life here. There is a story of a conversation between an ambitious youth and an older man who knew life. Said the young man, 'I will learn my trade.' 'And then?' said the older man. 'I will set up in business.' 'And then?' 'I will make my fortune.' 'And then?' 'I suppose that I shall grow old and retire and live on my money.' 'And then?' 'Well, I suppose that some day I will die.' '*And then?*' came the last stabbing question.

Those who never remember that there is another world are destined some day for the grimmest of grim shocks.

(2) But Jesus had something to say to those who had few possessions. In all this passage the thought which Jesus forbids is *anxious thought* or *worry.* Jesus never ordered anyone to live in a shiftless, thriftless, reckless way. What he did tell people was to do their best and then leave the rest to God. The lilies Jesus spoke of were the scarlet anemones. After one of the infrequent showers of summer rain, the mountainside would be scarlet with them; they bloomed one day and died. Wood was scarce in Palestine, and it was the dried grasses and wild flowers that were used to feed the oven fire. 'If', said Jesus, 'God looks after the birds and the flowers, how much more will he care for you?'

Jesus said, 'Seek first the kingdom of God.' We saw that God's kingdom was a state on earth in which his will was as perfectly done as it is in heaven. So Jesus is saying, 'Bend all your life to obeying God's will and rest content with that. So many people give all their effort to heap up things which in their very nature cannot last. Work for the things which last forever, things which you need not leave behind when you leave this earth, but which you can take with you.'

In Palestine wealth was often in the form of costly raiment; the moths could get at the fine clothes and leave them ruined.

But if people clothe their souls with the garments of honour and purity and goodness, nothing on earth can injure them. If they seek the treasures of heaven, their hearts will be fixed on heaven; but if they seek the treasures of earth, their hearts will be bound to earth – and some day they must say goodbye to those things that were so precious, for, as the grim Spanish proverb has it, 'There are no pockets in a shroud.'

BE PREPARED

Luke 12:35–48

'Let your loins be girt and your lamps burning. Be like men who are waiting for their master to come home from the wedding feast, so that, when he comes and knocks, they will open to him immediately. Happy are those servants whom the master will come and find awake. This is the truth that I tell you – he will gird himself; he will make them recline at table; and he will come and serve them. Happy are they if he finds them so, even if he comes in the second or third watch. Know this – that if the householder knew at what time the thief would come he would have been awake and he would not have allowed his home to be broken into. So you must show yourselves ready, for the Son of Man comes at an hour you do not expect.'

Peter said, 'Lord, are you speaking this parable to us or to everyone?' The Lord said, 'Who, then, is the faithful and wise steward, whom the master will set over the administration of his house to give them their ration of food at the right time? Happy is that servant whom the master will come and find acting like this. I tell you truly that he will put him in charge of all his possessions. But if that servant says in his heart, "My master is delayed in coming," and if he begins to beat the men servants and the maid servants, and to eat and drink and get drunk, the master of that servant will arrive on a day on which he is not expecting him and at an hour which he does not know, and he will cut him in pieces and he will place his part with the unfaithful. That servant who knew the will of his master, and who failed to have things ready, and to act in accordance with that will, will be beaten with many stripes. But he who did not know, even if he did things that deserved stripes, will be beaten with few stripes. To whom much is given, from him much will be required; and men will demand much from him to whom much was entrusted.'

THIS passage has two senses. In its narrower sense it refers to the second coming of Jesus Christ; in its wider sense it refers to the time when God's summons enters a person's life, a call to prepare to meet our God.

There is praise for the servant who is ready. The long flowing robes of the middle east were a hindrance to work; and when a man prepared to work he gathered up his robes under his girdle to leave himself free for activity. The type of lamp used was like a cotton wick floating in a sauce-boat of oil. Always the wick had to be kept trimmed and the lamp replenished or the light would go out.

No one can tell the day or the hour when eternity will invade time and summons will come. How, then, would we like God to find us?

(1) We would like him to find us *with our work completed.* Life for so many of us is filled with loose ends. There are things undone and things half-done; things put off and things not even attempted. Great men and women have always the sense of a task that must be finished. Keats wrote:

When I have fears that I may cease to be
Before my pen has glean'd my teeming brain.

Robert Louis Stevenson wrote:

The morning drum-call on my eager ear
Thrills unforgotten yet; the morning dew
Lies yet undried along my field of noon.

But now I pause at whiles in what I do,
And count the bell, and tremble lest I hear
(My work untrimmed) the sunset gun too soon.

Jesus himself said, 'I glorified you on earth by finishing the work that you gave me to do' (John 17:4). No one should ever lightly leave undone a task that ought to have been finished, before night falls.

(2) We would like God to find us *at peace with one another*. It would be a haunting thing to pass from this world in bitterness with a neighbour. We should never let the sun go down on our anger (Ephesians 4:26), least of all the last sun of all and we never know which sun that will be.

(3) We should like God to find us *at peace with him*. It will make all the difference at the last whether we feel that we are going out to a stranger or an enemy, or going to fall asleep in the arms of God.

In the second section of this passage Jesus draws a picture of the wise and the unwise steward. In the middle east the steward had almost unlimited power. He was himself a slave, yet he had control of all the other slaves. A trusted steward ran his master's house for him and administered his estate. The unwise steward made two mistakes.

(1) He said, *I will do what I like while my master is away*; he forgot that the day of reckoning must come. We have a habit of dividing life into compartments. There is a part in

which we remember that God is present; and there is a part in which we never think of him at all. We tend to draw a line between sacred and secular; but if we really know what Christianity means we will know that there is no part of life when the master is away. We are working and living forever in our great taskmaster's eye.

(2) He said, *I have plenty of time to put things right before the master comes*; there is nothing so fatal as to feel that we have plenty of time. Jesus said, 'We must work the works of him who sent me while it is day; night is coming when no one can work' (John 9:4). It is told that when the writer J. M. Barrie was old, he would never make arrangements or give invitations for a distant date. 'Short notice now!' he would say. One of the most dangerous days of our life is when we discover the word 'tomorrow'.

The passage finishes with the warning that knowledge and privilege always bring responsibility. Sin is doubly sinful to those who knew better; failure is doubly blameworthy in those who had every chance to do well.

THE COMING OF THE SWORD

Luke 12:49–53

Jesus said, 'I came to cast fire upon the earth. And what do I wish? Would that it were already kindled! There is an experience through which I must pass; and now I am under tension until it is accomplished! Do you think I came to give peace in the earth? Not that, I tell you, but division! From now on in one house there will be five people divided – three against two, and two against three. They will be divided, father against son, and son against father, mother against daughter, and

daughter against mother, mother-in-law against her
daughter-in-law, and daughter-in-law against her
mother-in-law.'

To those who were learning to regard Jesus as the Messiah,
the Anointed One of God, these words would come as a bleak
shock. They regarded the Messiah as conqueror and king,
and the Messianic age as a golden time.

(1) In Jewish thought fire is almost always the symbol of
judgment. So, then, Jesus regarded the coming of his kingdom
as a time of judgment. The Jews firmly believed that God
would judge other nations by one standard and themselves
by another; that the very fact they were Jewish would be
enough to absolve them. However much we may wish to
eliminate the element of judgment from the message of Jesus
it remains stubbornly and unalterably there.

(2) The Authorized Version and the Revised Standard
Version translate verse 50, 'I have a baptism to be baptized
with.' The Greek verb *baptizein* means *to dip*. In the passive
it means to be submerged. Often it is used metaphorically.
For instance, it is used of a ship sunk beneath the waves. It
can be used of someone submerged in drink and therefore
dead-drunk. It can be used of a scholar submerged (or *sunk*,
as we say) by an examiner's questions. Above all it is used
of the person who is submerged in some grim and terrible
experience – someone who can say, 'All the waves and
billows are gone over me.'

That is the way in which Jesus uses it here. 'I have,' he
said, 'a terrible experience through which I must pass; and
life is full of tension until I pass through it and emerge
triumphantly from it.' The cross was constantly before his
eyes. How different from the Jewish idea of God's King!
Jesus came not with avenging armies and flying banners, but
to give his life as ransom for many.

(3) His coming would inevitably mean division; in point of fact it did. That was one of the great reasons why the Romans hated Christianity – it tore families in two. Over and over again people had to decide whether they loved better their families or Christ. The essence of Christianity is that loyalty to Christ has to take precedence over the dearest loyalties of this earth. We must be prepared to count all things but loss for the excellence of Jesus Christ.

WHILE THERE IS STILL TIME

Luke 12:54-9

> Jesus said to the crowds, 'When you see a cloud rising in the west, immediately you say, "Rain is coming." And so it happens. When you feel the south wind blowing, you say, "There will be scorching heat." And so it happens. Hypocrites! you can read the signs of the face of the earth and the sky. How can you not read the signs of this time? Why do you not for yourselves judge what is right? When you are going with your adversary to the magistrate, make an effort to come to an agreement with him on the way, lest he drag you to the judge, and the judge will hand you over to the officer, and the officer will throw you into prison. I tell you, you will not come out from there until you have paid the last penny.'

THE Jews of Palestine were weatherwise. When they saw the clouds forming in the west, over the Mediterranean Sea, they knew rain was on the way. When the south wind blew from the desert they knew the sirocco-like wind was coming. But those who were so wise to read the signs of the sky could not, or would not, read the signs of the times. If they had,

they would have seen that the kingdom of God was on the
way.

Jesus used a very vivid illustration. He said, 'When you
are threatened with a lawsuit, come to an agreement with your
adversary before the matter comes to court, for if you do not
you will have imprisonment to endure and a fine to pay.' The
assumption is that the defendant has a bad case which will
inevitably go against him. 'Everyone', Jesus implied, 'has a
bad case in the presence of God; and if we are wise, we will
make our peace with God while there is still time.'

Jesus and all his great servants have always been obsessed
with the urgency of time. The seventeenth-century poet
Andrew Marvell spoke of hearing 'time's winged chariot
hurrying near'. There are some things we cannot afford to
put off; above all, making our peace with God.

We read in the last verse of paying to the last *penny*. We
have already come across several references to money; and it
will be useful if we collect the information about Jewish
coinage in the time of Jesus. In order of value the principal
coins were as follows:

The *lepton*; *lepton* means the *thin one*; it was the smallest
coin, and had the least value. It was the widow's mite (Mark
12:42) and is the coin mentioned here.

The *quadrans* was worth two lepta. It is mentioned in
Matthew 5:26.

The *assarion* is mentioned in Matthew 10:29 and Luke
12:6. It was worth about four times the value of the quadrans.

The *denarius* was a day's pay for a working man (Matthew
20:2) and was the coin that the Good Samaritan left with the
innkeeper (Luke 10:25).

The *drachma* was a silver coin worth slightly more than a
denarius. It was the coin which the woman lost and searched
for (Luke 15:8).

The *didrachma* or *half-shekel* was worth about two days'
pay. It was the amount of the Temple tax which everyone had
to pay. It was for thirty didrachmae – about two months'
wages – that Judas betrayed Jesus.

The *shekel* was equal to about four days' wages, and was
the coin found in the fish's mouth (Matthew 17:27).

The *mina is* the coin mentioned in the parable of the pounds
(Luke 19:11–27). It was equal to 100 drachmae; and was,
therefore, the equivalent of about three months' wages.

The *talent* was not so much a coin but a weight of silver. It
would take about fifteen years to earn such a sum. It is
mentioned in Matthew 18:24 and in the parable of the talents
(Matthew 25:14–30).

SUFFERING AND SIN

Luke 13:1–5

> At this time some men came and told Jesus about the
> Galilaeans whose blood Pilate had mingled with their
> sacrifices. 'Do you think,' he answered, 'that these
> Galilaeans were sinners above all the Galilaeans because
> this happened to them? I tell you, No! But unless you
> repent you will all perish in like manner. Or, as for the
> eighteen on whom the tower in Siloam fell – do you
> think they were debtors to God beyond all those who
> dwell in Jerusalem? I tell you, No! But unless you repent
> you will perish in the same way.'

WE have here references to two disasters about which we
have no definite information and can only speculate.

First, there is the reference to the Galilaeans whom Pilate
murdered in the middle of their sacrifices. As we have seen,
Galilaeans were always liable to get involved in political

trouble because they were a highly inflammable people. Just about this time Pilate had been involved in serious trouble. He had decided rightly that Jerusalem needed a new and improved water supply. He proposed to build it and to finance it with certain Temple monies. It was a laudable object and a more than justifiable expenditure. But at the very idea of spending Temple monies like that, the Jews were up in arms. When the mobs gathered, Pilate instructed his soldiers to mingle with them, wearing cloaks over their battle dress for disguise. They were instructed to carry cudgels rather than swords. At a given signal they were to fall on the mob and disperse them. This was done, but the soldiers dealt with the mob with a violence far beyond their instructions and a considerable number of people lost their lives. Almost certainly Galilaeans would be involved in that. We know that Pilate and Herod were at enmity, and only became reconciled after Pilate had sent Jesus to Herod for trial (Luke 23:6-12). It may well be that it was this very incident which provoked that enmity.

As for the eighteen on whom the tower in Siloam fell, they are still more obscure. The Authorized Version uses the word *sinners* of them also; but, as the margin shows, it should be not *sinners* but debtors. Maybe we have a clue here. It has been suggested that they had actually taken work on Pilate's hated aqueducts. If so, any money they earned was due to God and should have been voluntarily handed over, because it had already been stolen from him; and it may well be that popular talk had declared that the tower had fallen on them because of the work they had consented to do.

But there is far more than a historical problem in this passage. The Jews rigidly connected sin and suffering. Eliphaz had long ago said to Job, 'Who that was innocent ever perished?' (Job 4:7). This was a cruel and a heartbreaking doctrine, as Job knew well, And Jesus utterly denied it in the case of the individual. As we all know very well, it is often the greatest saints who have to suffer most.

But Jesus went on to say that if his hearers did not repent they too would perish. What did he mean? One thing is clear – he foresaw and foretold the destruction of Jerusalem, which happened in AD 70 (cf. Luke 21:21-4). He knew well that if the Jews went on with their intrigues, their rebellions, their plottings and their political ambitions, they were simply going to commit national suicide; he knew that in the end Rome would step in and obliterate the nation; and that is precisely what happened. So what Jesus meant was that if the Jewish nation kept on seeking an earthly kingdom and rejecting the kingdom of God they could come to only one end.

To put the matter like that leaves, at first sight, a paradoxical situation. It means that we cannot say that individual suffering and sin are inevitably connected but we can say that national sin and suffering are so connected. The nation which chooses the wrong ways will in the end suffer for it. But the individual is in a very different position. An individual is not an isolated unit, but is bound up in the bundle of life. Often he or she may object, and object violently, to the course the nation is taking; but when the consequence of that course comes, it is not possible to escape being involved in it. Individuals are often caught up in situations which are not of their making, suffering often through no fault of their own; but the nation is a unit and chooses its own policy and reaps the fruit of it. It is always dangerous to attribute human suffering to human sin; but always safe to say that the nation which rebels against God is on the way to disaster.

THE GOSPEL OF THE OTHER CHANCE
AND THE THREAT OF THE LAST CHANCE

Luke 13:6–9

> Jesus spoke this parable, 'A man had a fig tree planted
> in his vineyard. He came looking for fruit on it and did
> not find it. He said to the keeper of the vineyard, "Look
> you – for the last three years I have been coming and
> looking for fruit on this fig tree, and I still am not finding
> any. Cut it down! Why should it use up the ground?"
> "Lord," he answered him, "let it be this year too, until I
> dig round about it and manure it, and if it bears fruit in
> the coming year, well and good; but if not, you will cut
> it down."'

HERE is a parable at one and the same time lit by grace and
closely packed with warnings.

(1) The fig tree occupied *a specially favoured position.* It
was not unusual to see fig trees, thorn trees and apple trees in
vineyards. The soil was so shallow and poor that trees were
grown wherever there was soil to grow them; but the fig tree
had a more than average chance, and it had not proved worthy
of it. Repeatedly, directly and by implication, Jesus reminded
people that they would be judged according to the opportunities they had. The philosopher C. E. M. Joad once said,
'We have the powers of gods and we use them like irrespon-
sible schoolboys.' Never was a generation entrusted with so
much as ours and, therefore, never was a generation so
answerable to God.

(2) The parable teaches that *uselessness invites disaster.*
It has been claimed that the whole process of evolution in
this world is to produce useful things, and that what is useful
will go on from strength to strength, while what is useless

will be eliminated. The most searching question we can be asked is: 'Of what use were you in this world?'

(3) Further, the parable teaches that *nothing which only takes out can survive*. The fig tree was drawing strength and sustenance from the soil; and in return was producing nothing. That was precisely its sin. In the last analysis, there are two kinds of people in this world – those who take out more than they put in, and those who put in more than they take out.

In one sense we are all in debt to life. We came into it at the peril of someone else's life; and we would never have survived without the care of those who loved us. We have inherited a Christian civilization and a freedom which we did not create. There is laid on us the duty of handing things on better than we found them.

'Die when I may,' said Abraham Lincoln, 'I want it said of me that I plucked a weed and planted a flower wherever I thought a flower would grow.' Once a student was being shown bacteria under the microscope. He could actually see one generation of these microscopic living things being born and dying and another being born to take its place. He saw, as he had never seen before, how one generation succeeds another. 'After what I have seen,' he said, 'I pledge myself never to be a weak link.'

If we take that pledge we will fulfil the obligation of putting into life at least as much as we take out.

(4) The parable tells us of *the gospel of the second chance*. A fig tree normally takes three years to reach maturity. If it is not fruiting by that time it is not likely to fruit at all. But this fig tree was given another chance.

It is always Jesus' way to give us chance after chance. Peter and Mark and Paul would all gladly have witnessed to that. God is infinitely kind to those who fall and rise again.

(5) But the parable also makes it quite clear that *there is a final chance*. If we refuse chance after chance, if God's appeal and challenge come again and again in vain, the day finally comes, not when God has shut us out, but when we by deliberate choice have shut ourselves out. God save us from that!

MERCY MORE THAN LAW

Luke 13:10–17

> Jesus was teaching in one of the synagogues on the Sabbath; and – look you – there was a woman there who had had a spirit of weakness for eighteen years. She was bent together and could not straighten up properly. When Jesus saw her he called her to him. 'Woman,' he said, 'you are set free from your weakness'; and he laid his hands upon her; and immediately she was straightened. The president of the synagogue was vexed that Jesus had healed on the Sabbath. 'Are there not six days', he said to the crowd, 'in which work ought to be done? Come and be healed on them and not on the Sabbath day.' 'Hypocrites!' the Lord answered. 'Does each one of you not loose his ox or his ass from the manger on the Sabbath, and lead him out and give him drink? And as for this woman, a daughter of Abraham, whom – look you – Satan bound for eighteen years, should she not have been loosed from this bond on the Sabbath day?' And, as he said this, his opponents were put to shame, and all the crowd rejoiced at the glorious things that were done by him.

THIS is the last time we ever hear of Jesus being in a synagogue. It is clear that by this time the authorities were watching his every action and waiting to pounce upon him whenever they got the chance. Jesus healed a woman who for eighteen years had not been able to straighten her bent body; and then the president of the synagogue intervened. He had not even the courage to speak directly to Jesus. He addressed his protest to the waiting people, although it was meant for Jesus. Jesus had healed on the Sabbath; technically healing was work; and, therefore he had broken the Sabbath. But he answered his opponents out of their own law. The Rabbis abhorred cruelty to animals and, even on the Sabbath, it was perfectly legal to loose animals from their stalls and water them. Jesus demanded, 'If you can loose an animal from a stall and water it on the Sabbath day, surely it is right in the sight of God to loose this poor woman from her infirmity.'

(1) The president of the synagogue and those like him were *people who loved systems more than people.* They were more concerned that their own petty little laws should be observed than that a woman should be helped.

One of the great problems of a developed civilization is the relationship of the individual to the system. In times of war the individual vanishes. Men and women cease to be individuals and become members of such and such an age group or the like. They are lumped together, not as individuals, but as living ammunition that is, in that terrible word, expendable. They become little more than statistics. Sidney and Beatrice Webb, afterwards Lord and Lady Passfield, were two great economists and statistical experts; but H. G. Wells said of Beatrice Webb that her trouble was that 'she saw men as specimens walking'.

In Christianity the individual comes before the system. It is true to say that without Christianity there can be no such thing as democracy, because Christianity alone guarantees and defends the value of the ordinary, individual man or woman. If ever Christian principles are banished from political and economic life there is nothing left to keep at bay the totalitarian state where individuals are lost in the system, and exist, not for their own sake, but only for the sake of that system.

Strangely enough, this worship of systems commonly invades the Church. There are many church people – it would be a mistake to call them Christian people – who are more concerned with the method of church government than they are with the worship of God and the service of others. It is all too tragically true that more trouble and strife arise in churches over legalistic details of procedure than over any other thing.

In the world and in the Church we are constantly in peril of loving systems more than we love God and more than we love one another.

(2) Jesus' action in this matter makes it clear that it is not God's will that any human being should suffer one moment longer than is absolutely necessary. The Jewish law was that it was perfectly legal to help someone on the Sabbath who was in actual mortal danger. If Jesus had postponed the healing of this woman until the next day no one could have criticized him; but he insisted that suffering must not be allowed to continue until tomorrow if it could be helped today. Over and over again in life some good and kindly scheme is held up until this or that regulation is satisfied, or this or that technical detail worked out. The one who gives twice gives quickly, as the Latin proverb has it. No helpful deed that we can do today should be postponed until tomorrow.

THE EMPIRE OF CHRIST

Luke 13:18–19

> So Jesus said to them, 'To what is the kingdom of God
> like, and to what will I compare it? It is like a grain of
> mustard seed, which a man took and cast into his garden;
> and it grew until it became a tree, and the birds of the
> air found a lodging in its branches.'

THIS is an illustration which Jesus used more than once, and
for different purposes. In the middle east mustard is not a
garden herb but a field plant. It does literally grow to be a
tree. A height of seven or eight feet is common, and a traveller
tells how once he came across a mustard plant which was
twelve feet high, and which was higher than a horse and its
rider. It is common to see a cloud of birds around such trees,
for they love the little black mustard seeds.

Matthew (13:31, 32) also relates this parable but with a
different emphasis. His version is,

> Jesus put another parable before them, saying. 'The
> kingdom of heaven is like a grain of mustard seed, which
> a man took and sowed in his field. It is the smallest of
> all seeds, but, when it has grown, it is the greatest of
> shrubs, and becomes a tree, so that the birds of the air
> come and make nests in its branches.'

The point of the parable in Matthew and in Luke is quite
different. Matthew stresses *the smallness of the seed* which
Luke never even mentions; and Matthew's point is that the
greatest things can start from the smallest beginnings and so
does the kingdom of heaven. Luke's version leads up to the
birds making nests in the branches. In the east the regular
symbol of a great empire was a mighty tree; and the subject

nations who found shelter and protection within it were typified by birds in the branches (cf. Ezekiel 31:6, 17:23). As we have seen more than once, Luke is the universalist who dreamed of a world for Christ; and his point is that the kingdom of God will grow into a vast empire in which all kinds of people and nations will come together and will find the shelter and the protection of God. There is much in Luke's conception that we would do well to learn.

(1) There is room in the kingdom for *a wide variety* of *beliefs*. No individual and no church has a monopoly of all truth. To think ourselves right and everyone else wrong can lead to nothing but trouble and bitterness and strife. So long as beliefs are stemmed in Christ they are all facets of God's truth.

(2) There is room in the kingdom for *a wide variety of experiences*. We do infinite harm when we try to standardize Christian experience and insist that everyone must come to Christ in the same way. One person may have a sudden shattering experience and be able to point to the day and the hour, even the very minute, when God invaded his or her life. Another's heart may open to Christ naturally and without crisis, as the petals of a flower open to the sun. Both experiences come from God and both these people belong to God.

(3) There is room in the kingdom for *a wide variety of ways of worship*. One person finds contact with God in an elaborate ritual and a splendid liturgy; another finds him in the bare simplicities. There is no right or wrong here. It is the glory of the Church that within its fellowship somewhere each of us will find the worship that brings us to God. Let each of us discover it for ourselves, but let us not think our way the only way and criticize another's.

(4) There is room in the kingdom for *all kinds of people*. The world has its labels and its distinctions and its barriers.

But in the kingdom there is no distinction between rich and poor, small and great, famous and unknown. The Church is the one place where distinctions have no legitimate place.

(5) There is room in the kingdom *for all nations*. In the world today are many national barriers; but none of them has any standing with God. In Revelation 21:16 we are given the dimensions of the holy city. It is a square each of whose sides is 12,000 furlongs. 12,000 furlongs is 1,500 miles; and the area of a square whose sides are 1,500 miles is 2,250,000 square miles! There is room in the city of God for all the world and more.

THE LEAVEN OF THE KINGDOM

Luke 13:20–1

> Again Jesus said, 'To what will I liken the kingdom of God? It is like leaven, which a woman took and hid in three measures of meal, until the whole was leavened.'

THIS is an illustration which Jesus took from his own home. In those days bread was baked at home. Leaven was a little piece of dough which had been kept over from the last baking and had fermented in the keeping. Leaven is regularly used in Jewish thought for influence, usually for bad influence, because the Jews identified fermentation with putrefaction. Jesus had seen Mary put a little bit of leaven in the dough and had seen the whole character of the dough changed because of it. 'That,' he said, 'is how my kingdom comes.'

There are two interpretations of this parable. From the first the following points emerge.

(1) The kingdom of heaven starts *from the smallest beginnings*. The leaven was very small but it changed the

214

whole character of the dough. We well know how in any court, or committee, or board, one person can be a focus of trouble or a centre of peace. The kingdom of heaven starts from the dedicated lives of individual men and women. In the place where we work or live we may be the only professing Christians; if that is so, it is our task to be the leaven of the kingdom there.

(2) The kingdom of heaven *works unseen*. We do not see the leaven working but all the time it is fulfilling its function. The kingdom is on the way. Anyone who knows a little history will be bound to see that. Seneca, the greatest of all Roman thinkers, could write, 'We strangle a mad dog; we slaughter a fierce ox; we plunge the knife into sickly cattle lest they taint the herd; children who are born weakly and deformed we drown.' In AD 60 that was the normal thing. Things like that cannot happen today because slowly, but inevitably, the kingdom is on the way.

(3) The kingdom of heaven *works from inside*. As long as the leaven was outside the dough it was powerless to help; it had to get right inside. We will never change people from the outside. New houses, new conditions, better material things change only the surface. It is the task of Christianity to make new people; and once the new people are created a new world will surely follow. That is why the Church is the most important institution in the world; it is the factory where *men and women* are produced.

(4) The power of the kingdom *comes from outside*. The dough had no power to change itself. Neither have we. We have tried and failed. To change life we need a power outside and beyond us. We need the Master of life, and he is forever waiting to give us the secret of victorious living.

The second interpretation of this parable insists that far from working unseen the work of the leaven is manifest to all because it turns the dough into a bubbling, seething mass. On this basis, the leaven stands for the disturbing power of Christianity. In Thessalonica it was said of the Christians, 'These people who have been turning the world upside down have come here also' (Acts 17:6). True religion is never dope, never sends people comfortably to sleep, never makes them placidly accept the evils that should be striven against. Real Christianity is the most revolutionary thing in the world; it works revolution in the individual life and in society. 'May God', said Unamuno the great Spanish mystic, 'deny you peace and give you glory.' The kingdom of heaven is the leaven which fills each of us at one and the same time with the peace of God and with the divine discontent which will not rest until the evils of earth are swept away by the changing, revolutionizing power of God.

THE RISK OF BEING SHUT OUT

Luke 13:22–30

Jesus continued to go through towns and villages, teaching and making his way to Jerusalem. 'Lord,' someone said to him, 'are those who are to be saved few in number?' He said to them, 'Keep on striving to enter through the narrow door, because many, I tell you, will seek to enter in and will not be able to. Once the master of the house has risen and shut the door, and when you begin to stand outside and knock, saying, "Lord, open to us," he will answer you, "I do not know where you come from." Then you will begin to say, "We have eaten and drunk in your presence and you taught in our streets." He will say, "I tell you, I do not know where you come from. Depart from me all you who are workers of iniquity." There will be weeping

and gnashing of teeth there, when you will see Abraham
and Isaac and Jacob in the kingdom of God and
yourselves cast out. And they will come from the east
and from the west, and from the north and from the
south, and take their places at table in the kingdom of
God. And – look you – there are those who are last who
will be first, and there are those first who will be last.'

WHEN this questioner asked his question it would certainly
be on the assumption that the kingdom of God was for the
Jews and that Gentiles would all be shut out. Jesus' answer
must have come as a shock to him.

(1) He declared that entry to the kingdom can never be
automatic but is the result and the reward of a struggle. 'Keep
on striving to enter,' he said. The word for *striving* is the
word from which the English word *agony* is derived. The
struggle to enter in must be so intense that it can be described
as an agony of soul and spirit.

We run a certain danger. It is easy to think that, once we
have made a commitment of ourselves to Jesus Christ, we
have reached the end of the road and can, as it were, sit back
as if we had achieved our goal. There is no such finality in
the Christian life. We must always be going forward or
necessarily we go backwards.

The Christian way is like a climb up a mountain pathway
towards a peak which will never be reached in this world. It
was said of two gallant climbers who died on Mount Everest,
'When last seen they were going strong for the top.' It was
inscribed on the grave of an Alpine guide who had died on
the mountainside, 'He died climbing.' For the Christian, life
is constantly an upward and an onward way.

(2) The defence of these people was, 'We ate and drank
in your presence, and you taught in our streets.' There are
those who think that just because they are members of a

society based on Christian principles all is well. But those who live in such a society are not necessarily Christian. They may be enjoying all its benefits and are certainly living on the Christian capital which others before them have built up; but that is no reason for sitting back content that all is well. Rather it challenges us, 'What did you do to initiate all this? What have you done to preserve and develop it?' We cannot live on borrowed goodness.

(3) There will be surprises in the kingdom of God. Those who are very prominent in this world may have to be very humble in the next; those whom no one notices here may have real significance in the world to come. There is a story of a woman who had been used to every luxury and to all respect. She died, and when she arrived in heaven, an angel was sent to conduct her to her house. They passed many lovely mansions and the woman thought that each one, as they came to it, must be the one allotted to her. When they had passed through the main streets they came to the outskirts where the houses were much smaller; and on the very fringe they came to a house which was little more than a hut. 'That is your house,' said the conducting angel. 'What,' said the woman, 'that! I cannot live in that.' 'I am sorry,' said the angel, 'but that is all we could build for you with the materials you sent up.'

The standards of heaven are not the standards of earth. Earth's first will often be last, and its last will often be first.

COURAGE AND TENDERNESS

Luke 13:31-5

> At that hour some Pharisees came to Jesus. 'Depart,' they said to him, 'and get on your way from this place,

because Herod is out to kill you.' 'Go,' he said, 'and
tell that fox, look you, I cast out demons and I work
cures today and tomorrow, and on the third day my work
is perfected. I must be on my way today, and tomorrow
and the next day, because it is not possible for a prophet
to perish out of Jerusalem. Jerusalem! Jerusalem! Killer
of the prophets! Stoner of those who were sent to you!
How often I wanted to gather together your children as
a hen gathers her brood under her wings – and you
would not! Look you, your house is desolate. I tell you,
you will not see me until you shall say, "Blessed is he
who comes in the name of the Lord."'

BECAUSE of the behind-the-scenes insight that it gives into
the life of Jesus, this is one of the most interesting passages
in Luke's gospel.

(1) It gives us the, at first sight, surprising information
that not all the Pharisees were hostile to Jesus. Here we
have some of them actually warning him that he was in
danger, and advising him to seek safety. It is true that from
the gospels we do get a one-sided picture of the Pharisees.
The Jews themselves knew very well that there were good
and bad Pharisees. They divided them into seven different
classes.

(a) *The Shoulder Pharisees.* These wore their good deeds
on their shoulder and performed them to be seen by others.

(b) *The Wait-a-little Pharisees.* They could always find a
good excuse for putting off a good deed until tomorrow.

(c) *The Bruised or Bleeding Pharisees.* No Jewish Rabbi
could be seen talking to any woman on the street, not even
his wife or mother or sister. But certain of the Pharisees
went further. They would not even look at a woman on the
street; they even shut their eyes to avoid seeing a woman;
they, therefore, knocked into walls and houses and bruised

themselves; and then exhibited their bruises as special badges of extraordinary piety.

(d) *The Pestle-and-Mortar or Hump-backed Pharisees.* They walked bent double in a false and cringing humility; their fawning ways were full of insincerity.

(e) *The Ever-reckoning Pharisees.* They were always reckoning up their good deeds and, as it were, striking a balance sheet of profit and loss with God.

(f) *The Timid or Fearing Pharisees.* They went about in constant fear of the wrath of God. They were, as it was said of Robert Burns, not helped but haunted by their religion.

(g) *The God-loving Pharisees.* They were copies of Abraham and lived in faith and charity.

There may have been six bad Pharisees for every good one; but this passage shows that even among the Pharisees there were those who admired and respected Jesus.

(2) This passage shows us Jesus addressing Herod Antipas king of Galilee, who was out to stop him. To Jews the fox was a symbol of three things. First, it was regarded as the slyest of animals. Second, it was regarded as the most destructive of animals. Third, it was the symbol of a worthless and insignificant man.

It takes a brave person to call the reigning king a fox. Bishop Latimer was once preaching in Westminster Abbey when Henry VIII himself was one of the congregation. In the pulpit he soliloquized, 'Latimer! Latimer! Latimer! Be careful what you say. The king of England is here!' Then he went on, 'Latimer! Latimer! Latimer! Be careful what you say. The King of Kings is here.'

Jesus took his orders from God, and he would not shorten his work by one day to please or to escape any earthly king.

(3) The lament over Jerusalem is most important, because it is another of the passages which shows how little we really

know of Jesus' life. It is quite clear that Jesus could never have spoken like this, unless he had more than once gone with his offer of love to Jerusalem, but in the first three gospels there is no indication of any such visits. Once again it is made plain that in the gospels we have the merest sketch of Jesus' life.

Nothing hurts so much as to go to someone and offer love and have that offer spurned. It is life's bitterest tragedy to give one's heart to someone only to have it broken. That is what happened to Jesus in Jerusalem; and still he comes to us, and still we reject him. But the fact remains that to reject God's love is in the end to be in peril of his wrath.

UNDER HOSTILE SCRUTINY

Luke 14:1-6

> On the Sabbath day Jesus had gone into the house of one of the rulers who belonged to the Pharisees to eat bread; and they were watching him. And – look you – there was a man before him who had dropsy. Jesus said to the scribes and Pharisees, 'Is it lawful to heal on the Sabbath? Or, is it not?' They kept silent. So he took him and healed him and sent him away. He said to them, 'Suppose one of you has an ass or an ox, and it falls into a well, will he not immediately pull it out, even if it is on the Sabbath day?' And they had no answer to these things.

IN the gospel story there are seven incidents in which Jesus healed on the Sabbath day. In Luke we have already studied the story of the healing of Simon's mother-in-law (4:38); of the man with the withered hand (6:6); and of the woman who was bent for eighteen years (13:13). To these John adds the story of the healing of the paralytic at the pool of Bethesda (John 5:9); and of the man born blind (John 9:14). Mark adds one more – the healing of the demon-possessed man in the synagogue at Capernaum (Mark 1:21).

Anyone would think that a record like that would have made a man beloved of all; but it is the tragic fact that every miracle of healing that Jesus performed on the Sabbath day only made the scribes and Pharisees more certain that he was dangerous and irreligious and must at all costs be stopped. If we are to understand what happened to Jesus it is essential to remember that the orthodox Jews of his day regarded him as a law-breaker. He healed on the Sabbath; therefore he worked on the Sabbath; therefore he broke the law.

On this occasion a Pharisee invited him to a meal on the Sabbath. The law had its meticulous regulations about Sabbath meals. Of course no food could be cooked on the Sabbath; that would have been to work. All food had to be cooked on the Friday; and, if it was necessary to keep it hot, it must be kept hot in such a way that it was not cooked any more! So it is laid down that food to be kept warm for the Sabbath must not be put into 'oil dregs, manure, salt, chalk or sand, whether moist or dry, nor into straw, grape-skins, flock or vegetables, if these are damp, though it may be if they are dry. It may be, however, put into clothes, amid fruits, pigeons' feathers and flax tow.' It was the observance of regulations like this that the Pharisees and scribes regarded as religion. No wonder they could not understand Jesus!

It is by no means impossible that the Pharisees 'planted' the man with the dropsy in this house to see what Jesus would do. They were watching him; and the word used for *watching* is the word used for 'interested and sinister espionage'. Jesus was under scrutiny.

Without hesitation Jesus healed the man. He knew perfectly well what they were thinking; and he quoted their own law and practice to them. Open wells were quite common in Palestine, and were not infrequently the cause of accidents (cf. Exodus 21:33). It was perfectly allowable to rescue an animal which had fallen in. Jesus, with searing contempt, demands how, if it is right to help an animal on the Sabbath, it can be wrong to help a human being.

This passage tells us certain things about Jesus and his enemies.

(1) It shows us the serenity with which Jesus met life. There is nothing more trying than to be under constant and critical scrutiny. When that happens to most people they lose their nerve and, even more often, lose their temper. They become irritable; and while there may be greater sins than irritability there is none that causes more pain and heartbreak. But even in things which would have broken most people's spirit, Jesus remained serene. If we live with him, he can make us like himself.

(2) It is to be noted that Jesus never refused anyone's invitation of hospitality. To the end he never gave up on people. To hope to change them or even to appeal to them might be the forlornest of forlorn hopes, but he would never let a chance go. He would not refuse even an enemy's invitation. It is as clear as daylight that we will never make our enemies our friends if we refuse to meet them and talk with them.

(3) The most amazing thing about the scribes and Pharisees is their staggering lack of a sense of proportion. They would go to endless trouble to formulate and to obey their petty rules and regulations; and yet they counted it a sin to ease a sufferer's pain on the Sabbath day.

If we had only one prayer to pray we might well ask to be given a sense of proportion. The things which disturb the peace of congregations are often trifles. The things which come between individuals and which destroy friendships are often little things to which sensible people, in their saner moments, would never allow any importance. The little things can bulk so large that they can fill the whole horizon. Only if we put first things first will all things take their proper place – and love comes first.

THE NECESSITY OF HUMILITY

Luke 14:7–11

> Jesus spoke a parable to the invited guests, for he noticed how they chose the first places at the table. 'When you are bidden by someone to a marriage feast,' he said, 'do not take your place at table in the first seat, in case someone more distinguished than you has been invited, for in that case the man who invited you will come and say to you, "Give place to this man." And then, with shame, you will begin to take the lowest place. But, when you have been invited, go and sit down in the lowest place, so that, when the man who has invited you comes, he will say to you, "Friend, come up higher." Then you will gain honour in front of all who sit at table with you. For he who exalts himself will be humbled, and he who humbles himself will be exalted.'

JESUS chose a homely illustration to point an eternal truth. If a quite undistinguished guest arrived early at a feast and annexed the top place, and if a more distinguished person then arrived, and the man who had usurped the first place was told to step down, a most embarrassing situation resulted. If, on the other hand, a man deliberately slipped into the bottom place, and was then asked to occupy a more distinguished place, his humility gained him all the more honour.

Humility has always been one of the characteristics of the truly great. When Thomas Hardy was so famous that any newspaper would gladly have paid enormous sums for his work, he used sometimes to submit a poem, and always with it a stamped and addressed envelope for the return of his manuscript should it be rejected. Even in his greatness he was humble enough to think that his work might be turned down.

There are many stories and legends of the humility of John Cairns, Principal of the United Presbyterian Divinity Hall, Edinburgh. He would never enter a room first. He always said, 'You first, I follow.' Once, as he came on to a platform, there was a great burst of applause in welcome. He stood aside and let the person behind him come first and began himself to applaud. He never dreamed that the applause could possibly be for him; he thought it must be for someone else. Men and women of real stature know nothing of self-importance.

How can we retain our humility?

(1) We can retain it by realizing the facts. However much we know, we still know very little compared with the sum total of knowledge. However much we have achieved, we still have achieved very little in the end. However important we may believe ourselves to be, when death removes us or when we retire from our position, life and work will go on just the same.

(2) We can retain it by comparison with the perfect. It is when we see or hear the expert that we realize how poor our own performance is. Many golfers have decided to burn their clubs after a day watching the professionals at golf's Open Championship. Many musicians have decided never to appear in public again after hearing a truly great performance. Many preachers have been humbled almost to despair when they

have heard a real saint of God speak. And if we set our lives
beside the life of the Lord of all good life, if we see our un-
worthiness in comparison with the radiance of his stainless
purity, pride will die and self-satisfaction will be shrivelled
up.

DISINTERESTED CHARITY

Luke 14:12-14

> Jesus said to the man who had invited him, 'Whenever
> you give a dinner or a banquet, do not call your friends,
> or your brothers, or your kinsfolk or your rich neigh-
> bours, in case they invite you back again in return and
> you receive a repayment. But when you give a feast,
> invite the poor, the maimed, the lame and the blind.
> Then you will be happy, because they cannot repay you.
> You will receive your repayment at the resurrection of
> the righteous.'

HERE is a searching passage, because it demands that we
should examine the motives behind all our generosity.

(1) Some people may give from a sense of duty.

> He dropped a penny in the plate
> And meekly raised his eyes,
> Glad the week's rent was duly paid
> For mansions in the skies.

We may give to God and to others much in the same way as
we pay our income tax – as the satisfaction of a grim duty
which we cannot escape.

(2) Some people may give purely from motives of self-
interest. Consciously or unconsciously they may regard their
giving as an investment. They may regard each gift as an

entry on the credit side of their account in the ledger of God. Such giving, so far from being generosity, is rationalized selfishness.

(3) Some people may give in order to feel superior. Such giving can be a cruel thing. It can hurt the recipient much more than a blunt refusal. To give like that is to look down on others. Some people may even throw in a short and smug lecture. It would be better not to give at all than to give merely to gratify one's own vanity and one's own desire for power. The Rabbis had a saying that the best kind of giving was when the giver did not know to whom he was giving, and when the receiver did not know from whom he was receiving.

(4) Some people may give because they cannot help it. That is the only real way to give. The law of the kingdom is this – that if we give to gain reward we will receive no reward; but if we give with no thought of reward our reward is certain. The only real giving is that which is the uncontrollable outflow of love. Once Dr Johnson cynically described gratitude as 'a lively sense of favours to come'. The same definition could equally apply to certain forms of giving. God gave because he so loved the world – and so must we.

THE KING'S BANQUET
AND THE KING'S GUESTS

Luke 14:15–24

> When one of those who were sitting at table with Jesus heard this, he said, 'Happy is the man who eats bread in the kingdom of God.' Jesus said to him, 'There was a man who made a great banquet, and who invited many people to it. At the time of the banquet he sent his servants to say to those who had been invited, "Come,

because everything is now ready." With one accord they all began to make excuses. The first said to him, "I have bought a field, and I must go out and see it. Please have me excused." Another said, "I have bought five yoke of oxen, and I am on my way to try them out. Please have me excused." Another said, "I have married a wife, and, therefore, I cannot come." So the servant came and told his master these things. The master of the house was enraged, and said to his servant, "Go out quickly to the streets and lanes of the town and bring here the poor, and the maimed, and the blind and the lame." The servant said, "Sir, your orders have been carried out and there is still room." So the master said to his servant, "Go out to the roads and to the hedges, and compel them to come in, so that my house may be filled. For I tell you that none of these men who were invited shall taste of my banquet.'"

THE Jews had a series of constantly recurring conventional pictures of what would happen when God broke into history and when the golden days of the new age arrived. One of these was the picture of the Messianic banquet. On that day God would give a great feast to his own people at which Leviathan, the sea monster, would be part of the food. It is of this banquet that the man who spoke to Jesus was thinking. When he spoke of the happiness of those who would be guests at that banquet he was thinking of Jews, and of Jews only, for the average, orthodox Jew would never have dreamed that Gentiles and sinners would find a place at the feast of God. That is why Jesus spoke this parable.

In Palestine, when anyone made a feast, the day was announced long beforehand and the invitations were sent out and accepted; but the exact time was not announced; and when the day came and all things were ready, servants were sent out to summon the already invited guests. To accept the invitation beforehand and then to refuse it when the day came was a grave insult.

In the parable the master stands for God. The originally invited guests stand for the Jews. Throughout all their history they had looked forward to the day when God would break in; and when he did, they tragically refused his invitation. The poor people from the streets and lanes stand for the tax-gatherers and sinners who welcomed Jesus in a way in which the orthodox never did. Those gathered in from the roads and the hedges stand for the Gentiles for whom there was still ample room at the feast of God. As Johannes Bengel, the great eighteenth-century commentator, put it, 'both nature and grace abhor a vacuum', and when the Jews refused God's invitation and left his table empty, the invitation went out to the Gentiles.

There is one sentence in this parable which has been sadly misused. 'Go out,' said the master, 'and compel them to come in.' Long ago Augustine used that text as a justification for religious persecution. It was taken as a command to coerce people into the Christian faith. It was used as a defence of the Inquisition, the thumb-screw, the rack, the threat of death and imprisonment, the campaigns against the heretics, all those things which are the shame of Christianity. Beside it we should always set another text – 'the love of Christ urges us on' (2 Corinthians 5:14). In the kingdom of God there is only one compulsion – the compulsion of love.

But though this parable spoke with a threat to the Jews who had refused God's invitation, and with an undreamed-of glory to the sinners and the outcasts and the Gentiles who had never dreamed of receiving it, there are in it truths which are forever permanent and as new as today. In the parable the invited guests made their excuses, and people's excuses do not differ so very much today.

(1) The first man said that he had bought a field and was going to see it. He allowed the claims of business to usurp the claims of God. It is still possible to be so immersed in this world that we have no time to worship, and even no time to pray.

(2) The second man said that he had bought five yoke of oxen and that he was going to try them out. He let the claims of novelty usurp the claims of Christ. It often happens that when people enter into new possessions they become so taken up with them that the claims of worship and of God get crowded out. It is perilously easy for a new game, a new hobby, even a new friendship, to take up the time that should be kept for God.

(3) The third man said, with even more finality than the others, 'I have married a wife, and I cannot come.' One of the wonderful merciful laws of the Old Testament laid it down, 'when a man is newly married, he shall not go out with the army or be charged with any related duty. He shall be free at home one year, to be happy with his wife whom he has married' (Deuteronomy 24:5). No doubt that very law was in this man's mind. It is one of the tragedies of life when good things crowd out the claims of God. There is no lovelier thing than a home and yet a home was never meant to be used selfishly. They live best together who live with God; they serve each other best who also serve their neighbours; the atmosphere of a home is most lovely when those who dwell within it remember that they are also members of the great family and household of God.

The Banquet of the Kingdom

Before we leave this passage we must note that verses 1 to 24 have all to do with feasts and banquets. It is most significant that Jesus thought of his kingdom and his service in terms of a feast. The symbol of the kingdom was the happiest thing that human life could know. Surely this is the final condemnation of Christians who are afraid to enjoy themselves.

There has always been a type of Christianity which has taken all the colour out of life. The Roman Emperor Julian spoke of those pale-faced, flat-breasted Christians for whom the sun shone and they never saw it. In his 'Hymn to Prosperine' Swinburne slandered Christ by saying:

> Thou hast conquered, O pale Galilaean,
> The world has grown gray from thy breath.

John Ruskin, who was brought up in a rigid and narrow home, tells how he was given a jumping-jack as a present and a pious aunt took it away from him, saying that toys were no things for a Christian child. Even so great and sane and healthy a scholar as A. B. Bruce of Glasgow's Free Church College said that you could not conceive of the child Jesus playing games when he was a boy, or smiling when he was a man. The Principal of Trinity College, Glasgow, W. M. Macgregor, in his Warrack Lectures, speaks with the scorn of which he was such a master, about one of John Wesley's few mistakes. He founded a school at Kingswood, near Bristol. He laid it down that no games were to be allowed in the school or in the grounds, because 'he who plays when he is a child will play when he is a man'. There were no holidays. The children rose at 4 am and spent the first hour of the day in prayer and meditation, and on Friday they fasted until three in the afternoon. W. M. Macgregor characterizes the whole set-up as 'nature-defying foolishness'.

We must always remember that Jesus thought of the kingdom in terms of a feast. A gloomy Christian is a contradiction in terms. John Locke, the great philosopher, defined laughter as 'a sudden glory'. There is no healthy pleasure which is forbidden to a Christian, for a Christian is like someone who is forever at a wedding feast.

ON COUNTING THE COST

Luke 14:25–33

Great crowds were on the way with Jesus. He turned and said to them, 'If any man comes to me and does not hate his father and mother, and wife and children, and brothers and sisters, and even his own life too, he cannot be my disciple. Whoever does not carry his cross and come after me cannot be my disciple. Which of you, if he wishes to build a tower, does not first sit down and reckon up the expense, to see whether he has enough to finish it? This he does lest, when he has laid the foundation and is unable to complete the work, all who see him begin to mock him, saying, "This man began to build and was unable to finish the job." Or, what king when he is going to engage in battle with another king, does not first sit down and take counsel, whether he is able with 10,000 men to meet him who comes against him with 20,000? If he finds he cannot, while he is still distant, he sends an embassy and asks for terms of peace. So, therefore, everyone of you who does not bid farewell to all his possessions cannot be my disciple.'

WHEN Jesus said this he was on the road to Jerusalem. He knew that he was on his way to the cross; the crowds who were with him thought that he was on his way to an empire. That is why he spoke to them like this. In the most vivid way possible he told them that those who followed him were not

on the way to worldly power and glory, but must be ready for
a loyalty which would sacrifice the dearest things in life and
for a suffering which would be like the agony of a man upon
a cross.

We must not take his words with cold and unimaginative
literalness. The language of the middle east is always as vivid
as the human mind can make it. When Jesus tells us to hate
our nearest and dearest, he does not mean that literally. He
means that no love in life can compare with the love we must
bear to him.

There are two suggestive truths within this passage.

(1) It is possible to be a follower of Jesus without being a
disciple; to be a camp-follower without being a soldier of the
king; to be a hanger-on in some great work without pulling
one's weight. Once someone was talking to a great scholar
about a younger man. He said, 'So and so tells me that he
was one of your students.' The teacher answered devastat-
ingly, 'He may have attended my lectures, but he was not
one of my students.' It is one of the supreme handicaps of the
Church that in it there are so many distant followers of Jesus
and so few real disciples.

(2) It is a Christian's first duty to count the cost of
following Christ. The tower which the man was going to
build was probably a vineyard tower. Vineyards were often
equipped with towers from which watch was kept against
thieves who might steal the harvest. An unfinished building
is always a humiliating thing. In Scotland, we may, for
instance, think of that weird structure called 'McCaig's Folly'
which stands behind Oban.

In every sphere of life each of us is called upon to count
the cost. In the introduction to the marriage ceremony according to the forms of the Church of Scotland, the minister says,
'Marriage is not to be entered upon lightly or unadvisedly,

but thoughtfully, reverently, and in the fear of God.' A man and woman must count the cost.

It is so with the Christian way. But if we are daunted by the high demands of Christ let us remember that we are not left to fulfil them alone. He who called us to the steep road will walk with us every step of the way and be there at the end to meet us.

THE INSIPID SALT

Luke 14:34-5

> Jesus said, 'Salt is a fine thing; but if salt has become insipid, by what means shall its taste be restored? It is fit neither for the land nor the dunghill. Men throw it out. He who has an ear to hear, let him hear.'

JUST sometimes Jesus speaks with a threat in his voice. When a person is always carping and criticizing and complaining, the repeated irritable anger ceases to have any significance or any effect. But when someone whose accent is the accent of love suddenly speaks with a threat we are bound to listen. What Jesus is saying is this – when a thing loses its essential quality and fails to perform its essential duty, it is fit for nothing but to be thrown away.

Jesus uses salt as a symbol of the Christian life. What, then, are its essential qualities? In Palestine it had three characteristic uses.

(1) Salt was used as *a preservative*. It is the earliest of all preservatives. The Greeks used to say that salt could put a new soul into dead things. Without salt a thing putrefied and went bad; with it its freshness was preserved. That means that true Christianity must act as a preservative

against the corruption of the world. As individual Christians we must be the conscience of our fellows; and the Church must be the conscience of the nation. As Christians we must be such that in our presence no doubtful language will be used, no questionable stories told, no dishonourable action suggested. We must be like a cleansing antiseptic in the circle in which we move. The Church must fearlessly speak against all evils and support all good causes. It must never hold its peace through fear or favour of anyone.

(2) Salt was used as *a flavouring*. Food, without salt, can be revoltingly insipid. Christians, then, must be the ones who bring flavour into life. The Christianity which acts like a shadow of gloom and a wet blanket is no true Christianity. Christians are the people who, by their courage, their hope, their cheerfulness and their kindness bring a new flavour into life.

(3) Salt was used *on the land*. It was used to make it easier for all good things to grow. It is the Christian's role to make it easier for people to be good and harder to be bad. We all know people in whose company there are certain things we would not and could not do; and equally we all know people in whose company we might well stoop to things which by ourselves we would not do. There are fine people in whose company it is easier to be brave and cheerful and good. As Christians we must carry with us a breath of heaven in which the fine things flourish and the evil things shrivel up.

That is the function of the Christian; failure to fulfil this function means that there is no good reason for existence; and we have already seen that in the economy of God uselessness invites disaster. Those who have ears to hear, let them hear.

THE SHEPHERD'S JOY

Luke 15:1-7

> The tax-collectors and sinners were all coming near to
> Jesus to hear him, and the Pharisees and scribes were
> murmuring, saying, 'This man welcomes sinners and
> eats with them.'
>
> He spoke this parable to them. 'What man of you,'
> he said, 'who has a hundred sheep, and who has lost
> one of them, does not leave the ninety-nine in the
> wilderness and go after the one that is lost until he finds
> it? And when he finds it, rejoicing he lays it on his
> shoulders; and when he comes home he calls together
> his friends and neighbours, saying to them, "Rejoice
> with me because I have found my sheep which was
> lost." I tell you that just so there will be joy in heaven
> over one sinner who repents more than over ninety-nine
> just people who have no need of repentance.'

THERE is no chapter of the New Testament so well known and
so dearly loved as the fifteenth chapter of Luke's gospel. It
has been called 'the gospel in the gospel', as if it contained
the very distilled essence of the good news which Jesus came
to tell.

These parables arose out of definite situations. It was an
offence to the scribes and Pharisees that Jesus associated with
men and women who, by the orthodox, were labelled as
sinners. The Pharisees gave to people who did not keep the
law a general classification. They called them *the People of
the Land*; and there was a complete barrier between the
Pharisees and the People of the Land. The Pharisaic regulations laid it down, 'When a man is one of the People of the
Land, entrust no money to him, take no testimony from him,
trust him with no secret, do not appoint him guardian of an

orphan, do not make him the custodian of charitable funds, do not accompany him on a journey.' A Pharisee was forbidden to be the guest of any such man or to have him as his guest. He was even forbidden, so far as it was possible, to have any business dealings with him. It was the deliberate Pharisaic aim to avoid every contact with the people who did not observe the petty details of the law. Obviously, they would be shocked to the core at the way in which Jesus kept company with people who were not only rank outsiders but sinners, contact with whom would necessarily defile. We will understand these parables more fully if we remember that the strict Jews said, not 'There will be joy in heaven over one sinner who repents', but, 'There will be joy in heaven over one sinner who is obliterated before God.' They looked forward not to the saving but to the destruction of the sinner.

So Jesus told them the parable of the lost sheep and the shepherd's joy. The shepherd in Judaea had a hard and dangerous task. Pasture was scarce. The narrow central plateau was only a few miles wide, and then it plunged down to the wild cliffs and the terrible devastation of the desert. There were no restraining walls and the sheep would wander. George Adam Smith, an Old Testament scholar who travelled extensively in Palestine, wrote of the shepherd, 'On some high moor across which at night the hyaenas howl, when you meet him, sleepless, far-sighted, weather-beaten, armed, leaning on his staff and looking out over his scattered sheep, every one of them on his heart, you understand why the shepherd of Judaea sprang to the front in his people's history; why they gave his name to the king and made him the symbol of providence; why Christ took him as the type of self-sacrifice.'

The shepherd was personally responsible for the sheep. If a sheep was lost the shepherd must at least bring home the

fleece to show how it had died. These shepherds were
experts at tracking and could follow the straying sheep's
footprints for miles across the hills. There was not a shepherd
for whom it was not all in the day's work to risk his life for
his sheep.

Many of the flocks were communal flocks, belonging, not
to individuals, but to villages. There would be two or three
shepherds in charge. Those whose flocks were safe would
arrive home on time and bring news that one shepherd was
still out on the mountainside searching for a sheep which
was lost. The whole village would be upon the watch, and
when, in the distance, they saw the shepherd striding home
with the lost sheep across his shoulders, there would rise from
the whole community a shout of joy and of thanksgiving.

That is the picture Jesus drew of God; that, said Jesus, is
what God is like. God is as glad when a lost sinner is found
as a shepherd is when a strayed sheep is brought home. As a
great saint said, 'God, too, knows the joy of finding things
that have gone lost.'

There is a wondrous thought here. It is the truly tremendous
truth that God is kinder than men and women. The orthodox
would write off the tax-collectors and the sinners as beyond
the pale and as deserving of nothing but destruction; not so
God. We may give up hope of a sinner; not so God. God
loves those who never stray away; but in his heart there is the
joy of joys when a lost one is found and comes home. It is
1,000 times easier to come back to God than to come home
to the bleak criticism of our fellow human beings. F. W.
Faber's hymn expresses this admirably:

> Souls of men! why will ye scatter
>   Like a crowd of frightened sheep?
> Foolish hearts! why will ye wander
>   From a love so true and deep?

Was there ever kindest shepherd
　　Half so gentle, half so sweet,
As the Saviour who would have us
　　Come and gather round his feet?

For the love of God is broader
　　Than the measure of man's mind;
And the heart of the Eternal
　　Is most wonderfully kind.

THE COIN A WOMAN LOST AND FOUND

Luke 15:8–10

'Or, what woman who has ten silver pieces, if she loses
one piece, does not light a lamp and sweep the house
and search carefully until she finds it? And when she
has found it she calls together her friends and neighbours, saying, "Rejoice with me because I have found
the silver piece which I lost." Even so, I tell you, there
is joy in the presence of the angels of God over one
sinner who repents.'

THE coin in question in this parable was a silver drachma. It
would not be difficult to lose a coin in a Palestinian peasant's
house and it might take a long search to find it. The houses
were very dark, for they were lit by one little circular window
not much more than about eighteen inches across. The floor
was beaten earth covered with dried reeds and rushes; and to
look for a coin on a floor like that was very much like looking
for a needle in a haystack. The woman swept the floor in the
hope that she might see the coin glint or hear it tinkle as it
moved.

There are two reasons why the woman may have been so
eager to find the coin.

(1) It may have been a matter of sheer necessity. It was only one coin but it would have been worth more than a whole day's wage for a working man in Palestine. These people lived always on the edge of things and very little stood between them and real hunger. The woman may well have searched with intensity because if she did not find the coin, the family would not eat.

(2) There may have been a much more romantic reason. The mark of a married woman was a head-dress made of ten silver coins linked together by a silver chain. For years maybe a girl would scrape and save to amass her ten coins, for the head-dress was almost the equivalent of her wedding ring. When she had it, it was so inalienably hers that it could not even be taken from her for debt. It may well be that it was one of these coins that the woman had lost, and so she searched for it as any woman would search if she lost her marriage ring.

In either case it is easy to think of the joy of the woman when at last she saw the glint of the elusive coin and when she held it in her hand again. God, said Jesus, is like that. The joy of God, and of all the angels, when one sinner comes home, is like the joy of a home when a coin which has stood between them and starvation has been lost and is found; it is like the joy of a woman who loses her most precious possession, with a value far beyond money, and then finds it again.

No Pharisee had ever dreamed of a God like that. A great Jewish scholar has admitted that this is the one absolutely new thing which Jesus taught about God – that he actually searched for us. A Jew might have agreed that those who came crawling home to God in self-abasement and prayed for pity might find it; but he would never have conceived of a God who went out to search for sinners. We believe in the seeking love of God, because we see that love incarnate in Jesus Christ, the Son of God, who came to seek and to save that which was lost.

THE STORY OF THE LOVING FATHER

Luke 15:11-32

Jesus said, 'There was a man who had two sons. The younger of them said to his father, "Father, give me the part of the estate which falls to me." So his father divided his living between them. Not many days after, the son realized it all and went away to a far country, and there in wanton recklessness scattered his substance. When he had spent everything a mighty famine arose throughout that country and he began to be in want. He went and attached himself to a citizen of that country, and he sent him into his fields to feed pigs; and he had a great desire to fill himself with the husks the pigs were eating; and no one gave anything to him. When he had come to himself, he said, "How many of my father's hired servants have more than enough bread, and I – I am perishing here with hunger. I will get up and I will go to my father, and I will say to him, 'Father, I have sinned against heaven and before you. I am no longer fit to be called your son. Make me as one of your hired servants.'" So he got up and went to his father. While he was still a long way away his father saw him, and was moved to the depths of his being and ran and flung his arms round his neck and kissed him tenderly. The son said to him, "Father, I have sinned against heaven and before you. I am no longer fit to be called your son." But the father said to his servants, "Quick! Bring out the best robe and put it on him; put a ring on his finger; put shoes on his feet; and bring the fatted calf and kill it and let us eat and rejoice, for this my son was dead and has come back to life again; he was lost and has been found." And they began to rejoice.

'Now the elder son was in the field. When he came near the house he heard the sound of music and dancing. He called one of the slaves and asked what these things could mean. He said to him, "Your brother has come, and your father has killed the fatted calf because he has got him back safe and sound." He was enraged and refused to come in. His father went out and urged him to come in. He answered his father, "Look you, I have served you so many years and I never transgressed your order, and to me you never gave a kid that I might have a good time with my friends. But when this son of yours – this fellow who consumed your living with harlots – came, you killed the fatted calf for him." "Child," he said to him, "you are always with me. Everything that is mine is yours. But we had to rejoice and be glad, for your brother was dead and has come back to life again; he was lost and has been found."'

NOT without reason this has been called the greatest short story in the world. Under Jewish law a father was not free to leave his property as he liked. The elder son must get two-thirds and the younger one-third (Deuteronomy 21:17). It was by no means unusual for a father to distribute his estate before he died, if he wished to retire from the actual management of affairs. But there is a certain heartless callousness in the request of the younger son. He said in effect, 'Give me now the part of the estate I will get anyway when you are dead, and let me get out of this.' The father did not argue. He knew that if the son was ever to learn he must learn the hard way; and he granted his request. Without delay the son realized his share of the property and left home.

He soon ran through the money; and he finished up feeding pigs, a task that was forbidden to a Jew because the law said, 'Cursed is he who feeds swine.' Then Jesus paid sinning humanity the greatest compliment it has ever been paid. *'When he came to himself'*, he said. Jesus believed that being away from God prevented people from being truly themselves. That was only possible once they were on their way home. Beyond a doubt Jesus did not believe in total depravity. He never believed that you could glorify God by denigrating human beings; he believed that we are never essentially ourselves until we come home to God.

So the son decided to come home and plead to be taken back not as a son but in the lowest rank of slaves, the hired servants, the men who were only day labourers. The ordinary slave was in some sense a member of the family, but the hired servant could be dismissed at a day's notice. He was not one of the family at all. He came home; and, according to the best Greek text, his father never gave him the chance to ask to be a servant. He broke in before that. The robe stands for honour; the ring for authority, for if a man gave to another his signet ring it was the same as giving him the power of attorney; the shoes for a son as opposed to a slave, for children of the family wore shoes and slaves did not. (The slave's dream in the words of the spiritual is of the time when 'all God's chillun got shoes', for shoes were the sign of freedom.) And a feast was made that all might rejoice at the wanderer's return.

Let us stop there and see the truth so far in this parable.

(1) It should never have been called the parable of the prodigal son, for the son is not the hero. It should be called the parable of the loving father, for it tells us rather about a father's love than a son's sin.

(2) It tells us much about the forgiveness of God. The father must have been waiting and watching for the son

to come home, for he saw him a long way off. When he came, he forgave him with no recriminations. There is a way of forgiving, when forgiveness is conferred as a favour. It is even worse, when someone is forgiven, but always by hint and by word and by threat the sin is held over them.

Once Abraham Lincoln was asked how he was going to treat the rebellious southerners when they had finally been defeated and had returned to the Union of the United States. The questioner expected that Lincoln would take a dire vengeance, but he answered, 'I will treat them as if they had never been away.'

It is the wonder of the love of God that he treats us like that.

That is not the end of the story. There enters the elder brother who was actually sorry that his brother had come home. He stands for the self-righteous Pharisees who would rather see a sinner destroyed than saved. Certain things stand out about him.

(1) His attitude shows that his years of obedience to his father had been years of grim duty and not of loving service.

(2) His attitude is one of utter lack of sympathy. He refers to the prodigal, not as *my brother* but as *your son.* He was the kind of self-righteous character who would cheerfully have kicked a man farther into the gutter when he was already down.

(3) He had a peculiarly nasty mind. There is no mention of harlots until he mentions them. He, no doubt, suspected his brother of the sins he himself would have liked to commit.

Once again we have the amazing truth that it is easier to confess to God than it is to another person; that God is more merciful in his judgments than many orthodox people; that God's love is far broader than human love; and that God can

forgive when we refuse to forgive. In face of a love like that
we cannot be other than lost in wonder, love and praise.

Three Lost Things

We must finally note that these three parables are not simply
three ways of stating the same thing. There is a difference.
The sheep went lost through *sheer foolishness*. It did not
think; and many of us would escape sin if we thought in
time. The coin was lost *through no fault of its own*. Many are
led astray; and God will not hold anyone guiltless who has
taught another to sin. The son *deliberately went lost*, callously
turning his back on his father.

The love of God can defeat human folly, the seduction of
the tempting voices, and even the deliberate rebellion of the
heart.

A BAD MAN'S GOOD EXAMPLE

Luke 16:1–13

> Jesus said to his disciples, 'There was a rich man who
> had a steward. He received information against the
> steward which alleged that he was dissipating his goods.
> He called him, and said to him, "What is this that I hear
> about you? Give an account of your stewardship, for
> you can no longer be steward." The steward said to
> himself, "What am I to do? I have not the strength to
> dig, and I am ashamed to beg. I know what I will do, so
> that, when I am removed from my stewardship, they
> will receive me into their houses." So he summoned
> each of the people who owed debts to his master. To
> the first he said, "How much do you owe my master?"
> He said, "900 gallons of oil." He said to him, "Take
> your account and sit down and write quickly, 450." Then

he said to another, "And you – how much do you owe?"
He said, "1,000 bushels of corn." He said to him, "Take
your accounts and write 800." And the master praised
the wicked steward because he acted shrewdly; for the
sons of this world are shrewder in their own generation
than the sons of light. And, I tell you, make for yourselves friends by means of your material possessions,
even if they have been unjustly acquired, so that when
your money has gone they will receive you into a
dwelling which lasts forever. He who is trustworthy in
a very little is also trustworthy in much; and he who is
dishonest in a very little is also dishonest in much. If
you have not shown yourself trustworthy in your
ordinary business dealings about material things, who
will trust you with the genuine wealth? If you have not
shown yourselves trustworthy in what belongs to someone else, who will give you what is your own? No
household slave can serve two masters, for either he
will hate the one and love the other, or he will hold to
the one and despise the other. You cannot be the slave
of God and of material things.'

THIS is a difficult parable to interpret. It is a story about as
choice a set of rogues as one could meet anywhere.

The steward was a rogue. He was a slave, but he was nonetheless in charge of the running of his master's estate. In
Palestine there were many absentee landlords. The master
may well have been one of these, and his business may well
have been entrusted to his steward's hands. The steward had
followed a career of embezzlement.

The debtors were also rogues. No doubt what they owed
was rent. Rent was often paid to a landlord, not in money, but
in kind. It was often an agreed proportion of the produce of
the part of the estate which had been rented. The steward
knew that he had lost his job. He, therefore, had a brilliant

idea. He falsified the entries in the books so that the debtors were debited with far less than they owed. This would have two effects. First, the debtors would be grateful to him; and second, and much more effective, he had involved the debtors in his own misdemeanours, and, if the worst came to the worst, he was now in a strong position to exercise a little judicious blackmail!

The master himself was something of a rogue, for, instead of being shocked at the whole proceeding, he appreciated the shrewd brain behind it and actually praised the steward for what he had done.

The difficulty of the parable is clearly seen from the fact that Luke attaches no fewer than four different lessons to it.

(1) In verse 8 the lesson is that the children of this world are wiser in their generation than the children of light. That means that, if only Christians were as eager and ingenious in their attempt to attain goodness as those with more worldly concerns are in their attempts to attain money and comfort, they would be much better people. If only people would give as much attention to the things which concern their souls as they do to the things which concern their business, they would be much better human beings. Over and over again people will expend twenty times the amount of time and money and effort on pleasure, on hobbies, gardening or sport as they do on their church. Our Christianity will begin to be real and effective only when we spend as much time and effort on it as we do on our worldly activities.

(2) In verse 9 the lesson is that material possessions should be used to cement the friendships wherein the real and permanent value of life lies. That could be done in two ways.

(a) It could be done as it affects eternity. The Rabbis had a saying, 'The rich help the poor in this world, but the poor help the rich in the world to come.' Ambrose, writing in the fourth century and commenting on the rich fool who built bigger barns to store his goods, said, 'The bosoms of the poor, the houses of widows, the mouths of children are the barns which last forever.' It was a Jewish belief that charity given to poor people would stand to a person's credit in the world to come. True wealth would consist not in what people kept, but in what they gave away.

(b) It could be done as it affects this world. Wealth can be used selfishly or to make life easier, not only for ourselves, but for ourselves, but for our friends and neighbours. Many a scholar is forever grateful to a wealthy benefactor who gave or left money to found bursaries and scholarships which made a university career possible! How many of us are grateful to a better-off friend who has seen us through some time of need in the most practical way? Possessions are not in themselves a sin, but they *are* a great responsibility, and those who use them to help their friends have gone far to discharge that responsibility.

(3) In verses 10 and 11 the lesson is that the way of fulfilling a small task is the best proof of fitness or unfitness to be entrusted with a bigger task. That is clearly true of earthly things. No one will be advanced to higher office until they have given proof of their honesty and ability in a smaller position. But Jesus extends the principle to eternity. He says, 'Upon earth you are in charge of things which are not really yours. You cannot take them with you when you die. They are only lent to you. You are only a steward over them. They cannot, in the nature of things, be permanently yours. On the other hand, in heaven you will get what is really and eternally yours. And what you get in heaven depends on how you use the things of earth. What you will be given as your very own will depend on how you use the things of which you are only steward.'

(4) Verse 13 lays down the rule that no slave can serve two masters. The master possessed the slave, and possessed him *exclusively*. Nowadays, it is quite easy to do two jobs and work for two people, for instance, working in an office by day and as a musician by night. Many people augment their income or find real interest in a spare-time occupation. But a slave had no spare time; every moment of his day, and every ounce of his energy, belonged to his master. He had no time which was his own. So, serving God can never be a part-time or a spare-time job. Once we choose to serve God every moment of our time and every atom of our energy belongs to God. God is the most exclusive of masters. We either belong to him totally or not at all.

THE LAW WHICH DOES NOT CHANGE

Luke 16:14–18

> When the Pharisees, who were characteristically fond of money, heard these things, they derided Jesus. So he said to them, 'You are those who make yourselves look righteous before men, but God knows your hearts, because that which is exalted among men is an abomination before God.
>
> 'The law and the prophets were until John; from then the good news of the kingdom of God is proclaimed; and everyone forces his way into it; but it is easier for heaven and earth to pass away than for one dot of the law to become invalid.
>
> 'Everyone who divorces his wife and marries another commits adultery, and he who marries a woman who has been divorced from her husband commits adultery.'

THIS passage falls into three sections.

(1) It begins with a rebuke to the Pharisees. It says that they *derided* Jesus. The word literally means that they turned up their noses at him. Jews tended to connect earthly prosperity with goodness; wealth was a sign that a person was good. The Pharisees put on a parade of goodness and they regarded material prosperity as a reward of that goodness; but the more they exalted themselves before others, the more they became an abomination to God. It is bad enough for people to think of themselves as good; it is worse when they point to material prosperity as an unanswerable proof of their goodness.

(2) Before Jesus the law and the prophets had been the final word of God; but Jesus came preaching the kingdom. When he did, the most unlikely people, the tax-collectors and the sinners, came storming their way into the kingdom even when the scribes and Pharisees would have set up barriers to keep them out. But Jesus emphasized that the kingdom was not the end of the law. True, the little details and regulations of the ceremonial law were wiped out. No one was to think that Christianity offered an easy way in which no laws remained. The great laws stood unaltered and unalterable. Certain Hebrew letters are very like each other and are distinguished only by the serif, the little line at the top or bottom. Not even a serif of the great laws would pass away.

(3) As an illustration of law that would never pass away Jesus took the law of chastity. This very definite statement of Jesus must be read against the contemporary background of Jewish life. Jews glorified fidelity and chastity. The Rabbis said, 'All things can God overlook except unchastity.' 'Unchastity causes the glory of God to depart.' A Jew must surrender his life rather than commit idolatry, murder or adultery.

But the tragedy was that at this time the marriage bond was on the way to being destroyed. In the eyes of Jewish law a woman was a thing. She could divorce her husband only if he became a leper or an apostate or if he sexually assaulted a virgin. Otherwise a woman had no rights whatever and no redress, other than that the marriage dowry must be repaid if she was divorced. The law said, 'A woman may be divorced with or without her will; a man only with his will.' The Mosaic law (Deuteronomy 24:1) said, 'Suppose a man enters into marriage with a woman but she does not please him because he finds something objectionable about her, and so he writes her a certificate of divorce.' The bill of divorce had to be signed before two witnesses and ran, 'Let this be from me thy writ of divorce and letter of dismissal and deed of liberation, that thou mayest marry whatsoever man thou wilt.' Divorce was as simple and easy as that.

The matter turned on the interpretation of the phrase *some indecency* in the Mosaic regulation. There were two schools of thought. The school of Shammai said that meant adultery and adultery alone. The school of Hillel said it could mean 'if she spoiled a dish of food; if she spun in the street; if she talked to a strange man; if she was guilty of speaking disrespectfully of her husband's relations in his hearing; if she was a brawling woman', which was defined as a woman whose voice could be heard in the next house. Rabbi Akiba went so far as to say that a man could divorce his wife if he found a woman who was fairer than she. Human nature being what it is, it was the school of Hillel which prevailed, so that in the time of Jesus things were so bad that women were refusing to marry at all and family life was in danger.

Jesus here lays down the sanctity of the marriage bond. The saying is repeated in Matthew 5:31–2 where adultery is made the sole exception to the universal rule. We sometimes think our own generation is bad, but Jesus lived in a generation where things were every bit as bad. If we destroy family life, we destroy the very basis of the Christian life, and Jesus here lays down a law which we relax only at our peril.

THE PUNISHMENT OF THE MAN
WHO NEVER NOTICED

Luke 16:19–31

There was a rich man who dressed habitually in purple and fine linen, and who feasted in luxury every day. A poor man, called Lazarus, was laid at his gate. He was full of ulcerated sores, and he desired to satisfy his hunger from the things which fell from the rich man's table; more, the dogs used to come and lick his sores. The poor man died, and he was carried by the angels to the bosom of Abraham. The rich man died and was buried. And in hell, being in torture, he lifted up his eyes, and from far away he saw Abraham, and Lazarus in his bosom. He called out, 'Father Abraham, have pity on me, and send Lazarus to me that he may dip the tip of his finger in water and cool my tongue, because I am in anguish in this fire.' Abraham said, 'Child, remember that you received in full your good things in your lifetime, just as Lazarus received evil things. Now he is comforted, and you are in anguish; and, besides all this, between you and us a great gulf is fixed, so that those who wish to pass from here to you cannot do so, nor can any cross from there to us.' He said, 'Well then, I ask you, father, to send him to my father's house, for I have five brothers, that he may warn them, so that they may not also come to this place of torture.' Abraham said, 'They have Moses and the prophets. Let them listen to them.' He said, 'No, father Abraham; but if

someone goes to them from the dead, they will repent.'
He said to them, 'If they will not listen to Moses and
the prophets, neither will they be convinced if someone
should rise from the dead.'

THIS is a parable constructed with such consummate skill that
not one phrase is wasted. Let us took at the two characters in
it.

(1) First, there is the rich man, usually called Dives, which
is the Latin for rich. Every phrase adds something to the
luxury in which he lived. He was clothed in purple and fine
linen. That is the description of the robes of the high priests,
and such robes were hugely expensive, costing many times
the value of a working man's daily wage. He feasted in luxury
every day. The word used for feasting is the word that is used
for a gourmet feeding on exotic and costly dishes. He did
this *every day.* In so doing he definitely and positively broke
the fourth commandment. That commandment not only
forbids work on the Sabbath; it also says *six days you shall
labour* (Exodus 20:9).

In a country where the people were fortunate if they ate
meat once in the week and where they toiled for six days of
the week, Dives is a figure of indolent self-indulgence.
Lazarus was waiting for the crumbs that fell from Dives' table.
In that time there were no knives, forks or napkins. Food was
eaten with the hands and, in very wealthy houses, the hands
were cleansed by wiping them on hunks of bread, which were
then thrown away. That was what Lazarus was waiting for.

(2) Second, there is Lazarus. Strangely enough Lazarus is
the only character in any of the parables who is given a name.
The name is the Latinized form of Eleazar and means *God is
my help.* He was a beggar; he was covered with ulcerated
sores; and so helpless that he could not even ward off the
street dogs, which pestered him.

Such is the scene in this world; then abruptly it changes to the next and there Lazarus is in glory and Dives is in torment. What was the sin of Dives? He had not ordered Lazarus to be removed from his gate. He had made no objections to his receiving the bread that was flung away from his table. He did not kick him in the passing. He was not deliberately cruel to him. The sin of Dives was that he never noticed Lazarus, that he accepted him as part of the landscape and simply thought it perfectly natural and inevitable that Lazarus should lie in pain and hunger while he wallowed in luxury. As someone said, 'It was not what Dives did that got him into jail; it was what he did not do that got him into hell.'

The sin of Dives was that he could look on the world's suffering and need and feel no answering sword of grief and pity pierce his heart; he looked at a fellow human being, hungry and in pain, and did nothing about it. His was the punishment of the man who never noticed.

It seems hard that his request that his brothers should be warned was refused. But it is the plain fact that if people possess the truth of God's word, and if, wherever they look, there is sorrow to be comforted, need to be supplied, pain to be relieved, and it moves them to no feeling and to no action, nothing will change them.

It is a terrible warning that the sin of Dives was not that he did wrong things, but that he did nothing.

LAWS OF THE CHRISTIAN LIFE

Luke 17:1–10

Jesus said to his disciples, 'It is impossible that snares to sin should not arise; but woe to him through whom they do arise! It would be better for him if a millstone

were hung around his neck and he were thrown into the
sea rather than that he should cause one of these little
ones to trip up.

'Take heed to yourselves. If your brother sins, rebuke
him; and if he repents, forgive him. Even if he sins
against you seven times in the day, and if seven times
he turns to you, saying, "I repent," you must forgive
him.'

The apostles said to the Lord, 'Give us also faith!'
The Lord said, 'If you have faith as a grain of mustard
seed, you would say to this sycamine tree, "Be rooted
up and be planted in the sea," and it would obey you.

'If any of you has a slave ploughing or watching the
flock, and the slave comes in from the field, will he say
to him, "Come at once and take your place at table"; or
rather, will he not say to him, "Get ready my evening
meal, and gird yourself and serve me, until I eat and
drink, and after that you shall eat and drink yourself"?
Does he thank a servant because he has done what he
was ordered to do? Even so, you too, when you have
done everything you were ordered to do, say, "We are
unworthy servants. We have done what it was our duty
to do."'

THIS passage falls into four definite and disconnected sections.

(1) Verses 1 and 2 condemn anyone who teaches others to
sin. The Revised Standard Version talks in these verses about
temptations to sin. The Greek word (*skandalon*) is exactly
the same word as the English *scandal*. It has two meanings.

(a) It originally meant the bait-stick in a trap.

(b) It then came to mean any stumbling-block placed in
the way to trip somebody up. Jesus said that it was impossible
to construct a world with no temptations; but woe betide the
person who taught another to sin or who took away another's
innocence.

Everyone must be given that first invitation to sin, that first push along the wrong way. The story is told of an old man who was dying. Something was obviously worrying him. He told them at last what it was. 'When I was a lad,' he said, 'I often played on a wide common. Near its centre two roads met and crossed, and, standing at the crossroads, was an old rickety signpost. I remember one day twisting it round in its socket, thus altering the arms and making them point in the wrong direction; and I've been wondering ever since how many travellers I sent on the wrong road.'

God will not hold anyone guiltless, who, on the road of life, sends a younger or a weaker person on the wrong way.

(2) Verses 3 and 4 speak of the necessity of forgiveness in the Christian life. They tell us to forgive seven times. The Rabbis had a saying that if one forgave another *three* times, one was perfect. The Christian standard takes the Rabbinic standard, doubles it and adds one; but it is not a matter of calculation. It simply means that the Christian standard of forgiveness must immeasurably exceed the best the world can achieve.

(3) Verses 5 and 6 tell us that faith is the greatest force in the world. We must again remember that it was the custom in this part of the world to use language in the most vivid way. This saying means that even that which looks completely impossible becomes possible, if it is approached with faith. We have only to think of the number of scientific marvels, of the number of surgical operations, of the feats of endurance which today have been achieved and which not so very long ago would have been regarded as utterly impossible. If we approach a thing saying, 'It can't be done,' it will not; if we approach it saying, 'It must be done,' the chances are that it will. We must always remember that we approach no task alone, but that with us there is God and all his power.

(4) Verses 7–10 tell us that we can never put God in our debt and can never have any claim on him. When we have done our best, we have done only our duty; and those who have done their duty have done only what, in any event, they could be compelled to do. As Isaac Watts wrote in that wonderful hymn, 'When I survey the wondrous cross':

> Were the whole realm of Nature mine,
>   That were an offering far too small;
> Love so amazing, so divine,
>   Demands my soul, my life, my all.

It may be possible to satisfy the claims of *law*; but every lover knows that nothing can ever satisfy the claims of *love*.

THE RARITY OF GRATITUDE

Luke 17:11–19

> When Jesus was on the way to Jerusalem, he was going along between Samaria and Galilee; and, as he entered a village, ten lepers, who stood far off, met him. They lifted up their voices and said, 'Jesus, Master, have pity upon us.' When he saw them, he said, 'Go, and show yourselves to the priests.' And as they went they were cleansed. One of them, when he saw that he was cured, turned back, glorifying God with a great voice. He fell on his face at Jesus' feet and kept on thanking him. And he was a Samaritan. Jesus said, 'Were the ten not cleansed? The nine – where are they? Were none found to turn back and give glory to God except this foreigner?' And he said to him, 'Rise and go! Your faith has made you well.'

Jesus was on the border between Galilee and Samaria and was met by a band of ten lepers. We know that the Jews had no dealings with the Samaritans; yet in this band there was at least one Samaritan. Here is an example of a great law of life. A common misfortune had broken down the racial and national barriers. In the common tragedy of their leprosy they had forgotten they were Jews and Samaritans and remembered only they were men in need. If a flood surges over a piece of country and the wild animals congregate for safety on some little bit of higher ground, you will find standing peacefully together animals that are natural enemies and at any other time would do their best to kill each other. Surely one of the things which should draw all people together is their common need of God.

The lepers stood far off (cf. Leviticus 13:45–6; Numbers 5:2). There was no specified distance at which they should stand, but we know that at least one authority laid it down that when to windward of a healthy person, the leper should stand at least fifty yards away. Nothing could better show the utter isolation in which lepers lived.

No story in all the gospels so poignantly shows human ingratitude. The lepers came to Jesus with desperate longing; he cured them; and nine never came back to give thanks. So often, once people have got what they want, they never come back.

(1) Often we are ungrateful to our parents. There was a time in our lives when a week's neglect would have killed us. Of all living creatures human beings take longest to become able to meet the needs essential for life. There were years when we were dependent on our parents for literally everything. Yet the day often comes when an aged parent is a nuisance; and many young people are unwilling to repay the debt they owe. As Shakespeare's King Lear said in the day of his own tragedy:

How sharper than a serpent's tooth it is
To have a thankless child!

(2) Often we are ungrateful to one another. Few of us have not at some time owed a great deal to another person. Few of us, at the moment, believed we could ever forget; but few of us in the end satisfy the debt of gratitude we owe. It often happens that a friend, a teacher, a doctor, a surgeon does something for us which it is impossible to repay; but the tragedy is that we often do not even try to repay it. As Shakespeare wrote:

Blow, blow, thou winter wind,
Thou art not so unkind
    As man's ingratitude.
(*As You Like It*, Act I, scene VI)

(3) Often we are ungrateful to God. In some time of bitter need we pray with desperate intensity; the time passes and we forget God. Many of us never even offer a grace before meals. God gave us his only Son and often we never give to him even a word of thanks. The best thanks we can give him is to try to deserve his goodness and his mercy a little better. 'Bless the Lord, O my soul, and *do not forget all his benefits*' (Psalm 103:2).

THE SIGNS OF HIS COMING

Luke 17:20–37

When Jesus was asked by the Pharisees when the kingdom of God was coming, he answered them, 'The kingdom of God does not come with signs that you can watch for; nor will they say, "Look here!" or "Look there!" For – look you – the kingdom of God is within you.'

He said to his disciples, 'Days will come when you will long to see one of the days of the Son of Man and you will not see it. And they will say to you, "Look there! Look here!" Do not depart, and do not follow them. For, as the flashing lightning lights up the sky from one side to another, so shall be the Son of Man in his day. But first he must suffer many things and be rejected by this generation. Even as it was in the days of Noah, so it will be in the days of the Son of Man. They were eating, they were drinking, they were marrying, they were being given in marriage, until the day on which Noah entered the ark and the flood came and wiped them all out. In the same way, so it was in the days of Lot. They were eating, they were drinking, they were buying, they were selling, they were planting, they were building, but, on the day on which Lot went out of Sodom, fire and brimstone rained from heaven and wiped them all out. It will be the same on the day on which the Son of Man is revealed. If, on that day, anyone is on the housetop, and his goods are in the house, let him not come down to take them. In the same way, if anyone is in the field, let him not turn back. Remember Lot's wife! Whoever seeks to gain his life will lose it, but whoever loses it will preserve it alive. This is the truth I tell you – on that night there will be two in one bed. One will be taken and the other will be left. Two women will be grinding corn together. One will be taken and the other left.' They said to him, 'Where, Lord?' He said to them, 'Where the body is, there the vultures will be gathered together.'

HERE are two very difficult passages.

In verses 20 and 21 Jesus answered the question of the Pharisees as to when the kingdom of God would come. He said that it would not come with signs that you can watch for. The word he used is the word used for a doctor watching a patient for symptoms of some suspected disease.

We are not quite sure what Jesus went on to say. The Greek may mean two things.

(a) It may mean, the kingdom of God is within you. That is to say, the kingdom of God works in human hearts; it is to produce not new things, but new people. It is not a revolution in material things that we are to look for, but a revolution in the hearts of men and women.

(b) It may mean, the kingdom of God is among you. That would refer to Jesus himself. He was the very embodiment of the kingdom, and they did not recognize him. It was as if he said, 'The whole offer and secret of God are here – and you will not accept them.'

Verses 22–37 speak of the second coming of Jesus. Out of this difficult passage we can pick only the things which are certain – and in truth they are enough.

(1) There will be times when Christians will long for the coming of Christ, and like the martyred saints, will cry out, 'How long?' (Revelation 6:10). But they will need to learn to light a candle of patience and wait. God takes his own time.

(2) The coming of Christ is certain, but its time is quite unknown. Speculation is vain. People will come with false prophecies and false predictions; but we must not leave our ordinary work to follow them. The best way that Christ can come upon any of us is when we are faithfully and humbly and watchfully doing our duty. As a great commentator said, 'No man will foresee it, and all men will see it.'

(3) When that day comes the judgments of God will operate, and of two people, who all their lives lived side by side, one will be taken and the other left. There is a warning here. Intimacy with a good person does not necessarily

guarantee our own salvation. 'No man can deliver his brother.' Is it not often true that a family is apt to leave the duties of church membership to one of its number? Is it not often true that a husband leaves the duties of the church to his wife? The judgment of God is an individual judgment. We cannot discharge our duty to God by proxy nor even by association. Often one will be taken and another left.

(4) When they asked Jesus when all this would happen, he answered by quoting a well-known proverb: 'Where the body is, there the vultures will be gathered together.' That simply meant that a thing would happen when the necessary conditions were fulfilled. That means for us that God will bring Jesus Christ again in his good time. We cannot know that time; we dare not speculate about it. We must live so that whenever he comes, at morning, at midday or at evening, he will find us ready.

UNWEARIED IN PRAYER

Luke 18:1–8

Jesus spoke a parable to them to show that it is necessary always to pray and not to lose heart. 'There was a judge', he said, 'in a town who neither feared God nor respected man. There was a widow in the same town who kept coming to him and saying, "Vindicate me against my adversary." For some time he refused. But afterwards he said to himself, "Even though I neither fear God nor respect man, because she bothers me, I will vindicate this widow, lest by her constant coming she exhausts me."' The Lord said, 'Listen to what the unjust judge says. And shall God not vindicate his own chosen ones who cry to him day and night, even though he seem to

wait for long? But when the Son of Man comes will he
find faith on earth?'

THIS parable tells of the kind of thing which could, and often
did, happen. There are two characters in it.

(1) The *judge* was clearly not a Jewish judge. All ordinary
Jewish disputes were taken before the elders, and not into the
public courts at all. If, under Jewish law, a matter was taken
to arbitration, one man could not constitute a court. There
were always three judges, one chosen by the plaintiff, one by
the defendant, and one independently appointed.

This judge was one of the paid magistrates appointed either
by Herod or by the Romans. Such judges were notorious.
Unless plaintiffs had influence and money to bribe their way
to a verdict they had no hope of ever getting a case settled.
These judges were said to pervert justice for a dish of meat.
People even punned on their title. Officially they were called
Dayyaneh Gezeroth, which means judges of prohibitions or
punishments. Popularly they were called *Dayyaneh Gezeloth*,
which means robber judges.

(2) The *widow* was the symbol of all who were poor and
defenceless. It was obvious that she, without resource of any
kind, had no hope of ever extracting justice from such a judge.
But she had one weapon – persistence. It is possible that what
the judge in the end feared was actual physical violence. The
word translated, lest she *exhausts* me, can mean, lest she *gives
me a black eye*. It is possible to close a person's eye in two
ways – either by sleep or by assault and battery! In either
event, in the end her persistence won the day.

This parable is like the parable of the friend at midnight.
It does not *liken* God to an unjust judge; it *contrasts* him to
such a person. Jesus was saying, 'If, in the end, an unjust and
rapacious judge can be wearied into giving a widow justice,

how much more will God, who is a loving father, give his children what they need?'

That is true, but it is no reason why we should expect to get whatever we pray for. Often a father has to refuse the request of a child, because he knows that what the child asks would hurt rather than help. God is like that. We do not know what is to happen in the next hour, let alone the next week, or month, or year. Only God sees time whole, and, therefore, only God knows what is good for us *in the long run*. That is why Jesus said we must never be discouraged in prayer. That is why he wondered if human faith would stand the long delays before the Son of Man should come. We will never grow weary in prayer and our faith will never falter if, after we have offered to God *our* prayers and requests, we add the perfect prayer, *Your* will be done.

THE SIN OF PRIDE

Luke 18:9–14

> Jesus spoke this parable to some who were self-confidently sure that they were righteous and who despised others. 'Two men went up to the Temple to pray. The one was a Pharisee, the other a tax-collector. The Pharisee stood and prayed thus with himself, "O God, I thank thee that I am not as the rest of men, thieves, unjust, adulterers, or even as this tax-collector. I fast twice a week. I give a tenth of all that I get." The tax-collector stood afar off, and would not lift even his eyes to heaven, and kept beating his breast and said, "O God, be merciful, to me – the sinner." I tell you, this man went down to his house accepted with God rather than the other, because everyone who exalts himself will be humbled, but he who humbles himself will be exalted.'

THE devout observed two or three prayer times daily – in the morning and the evening and sometimes also at noon. Prayer was held to be specially efficacious if it was offered in the Temple and so at these hours many went up to the Temple courts to pray. Jesus told of two men who went.

(1) There was a Pharisee. He did not really go to pray to God. He prayed *with himself.* True prayer is always offered to God and to God alone. A certain American cynically described a preacher's prayer as 'the most eloquent prayer ever offered to a Boston audience'. The Pharisee was really giving himself a testimonial before God.

The Jewish law prescribed only one absolutely obligatory fast – that on the Day of Atonement. But those who wished to gain special merit fasted also on Mondays and Thursdays. It is noteworthy that these were the market days when Jerusalem was full of country people. Those who fasted whitened their faces and appeared in dishevelled clothes, and those days gave their piety the biggest possible audience. The Levites were to receive a tithe of all a man's produce (Numbers 18:21; Deuteronomy 14:22). But this Pharisee tithed everything, even things which there was no obligation to tithe.

His whole attitude was not untypical of the worst in Pharisaism. There is a recorded prayer of a certain Rabbi which runs like this: 'I thank Thee, O Lord my God, that thou hast put my part with those who sit in the Academy, and not with those who sit at the street corners. For I rise early, and they rise early; I rise early to the words of the law, and they to vain things. I labour, and they labour; I labour and receive a reward, and they labour and receive no reward. I run, and they run; I run to the life of the world to come, and they to the pit of destruction.' It is on record that Rabbi Simeon ben Jocai once said, 'If there are only two righteous men in the world, I and my son are these two; if there is only one, I am he!'

The Pharisee did not really go to pray; he went to inform God how good he was.

(2) There was a tax-collector. He stood afar off, and would not even lift his eyes to God. The Authorized and Revised Standard Versions do not even do justice to his humility for he actually prayed, 'O God, be merciful to me – *the* sinner,' as if he was not merely *a* sinner, but *the* sinner *par excellence.* 'And,' said Jesus, 'it was that heartbroken, self-despising prayer which won him acceptance before God.'

This parable unmistakably tells us certain things about prayer.

(1) No one who is proud can pray. The gate of heaven is so low that none can enter it save upon their knees. Christina Rossetti's words express all that any of us can say:

> None other Lamb, none other Name,
>> None other Hope in heaven or earth or sea,
>> None other Hiding-place from guilt and shame,
>> None beside Thee.

(2) No one who despises others can pray. In prayer we do not lift ourselves above others. We remember that we are one of a great army of sinning, suffering, sorrowing humanity, all kneeling before the throne of God's mercy.

(3) True prayer comes from setting our lives beside the life of God. No doubt all that the Pharisee said was true. He did fast; he did meticulously give tithes; he was not like other people; still less was he like that tax-collector. But the question is not, 'Am I as good as my neighbour?' The question is, 'Am I as good as God?' Once I made a journey by train to England. As we passed through the Yorkshire moors I saw a little whitewashed cottage and it seemed to me to shine with

an almost radiant whiteness. Some days later I made the journey back to Scotland. The snow had fallen and was lying deep all around. We came again to the little white cottage, but this time its whiteness seemed drab and soiled and almost grey in comparison with the pure whiteness of the driven snow.

It all depends what we compare ourselves with. And when we set our lives beside the life of Jesus and beside the holiness of God, all that is left to say is, 'God be merciful to me – the sinner.'

THE MASTER AND THE CHILDREN

Luke 18:15-17

> People were bringing even their babies to Jesus that he might touch them. When the disciples saw it they rebuked them. But Jesus called them to him saying, 'Let the little children come to me, and don't stop them, for of such is the kingdom of God. This is the truth I tell you – whoever does not receive the kingdom of God as a little child shall not enter into it.'

IT was the custom for mothers to bring their children to some distinguished Rabbi on their first birthday that he might bless them. That is what the mothers wanted for their children from Jesus. We are not to think that the disciples were hard and cruel. It was kindness that made them act as they did. Remember where Jesus was going. He was on the way to Jerusalem to die upon a cross. The disciples could see upon his face the inner tension of his heart; and they did not want Jesus to be bothered. Often at home we may say to a little child, 'Don't bother your Daddy; he's tired and worried tonight.' That is exactly how the disciples felt about Jesus.

It is one of the loveliest things in all the gospel story that Jesus had time for the children even when he was on the way to Jerusalem to die.

When Jesus said that it was of the childlike that the kingdom of God was composed, what did he mean? What are the qualities of which he was thinking?

(1) Children still possess *the sense of wonder.* Tennyson tells of going early one morning into the bedroom of his little grandson and of seeing the child 'worshipping the sunbeam playing on the bedpost'. As we grow older we begin to live in a world which has grown grey and tired. Children live in a world with a sheen on it and in which God is always near.

(2) For children the whole of life is founded on *trust.* When we are young, we never doubt where the next meal is to come from or where our clothes will be found. We go to school certain that home will be there when we return, and all things ready for our comfort. When we go on a journey we never doubt that the fare will be paid or that our parents know the way and will take us safely there. The trust that children have in their parents is absolute, as ours should be in our Father – God.

(3) Children are naturally *obedient.* True, they often disobey and grumble at their parents' bidding. But their instinct is to obey. They know very well that they should obey and are not happy when they have been disobedient. In their heart of hearts their parents' word is law. So should it be with us and God.

(4) Children have an amazing faculty of *forgiveness.* Almost all parents are unjust to their children. We demand from them a standard of obedience, of good manners, of polite language, of diligence which we seldom satisfy ourselves. Time and again we scold them for doing the very things we do ourselves. If others treated us in the way we treat our

children in the matter of plain justice, we probably would never forgive. But children forgive and forget, and do not even realize it when they are very young. It would be so much lovelier a world if we could forgive as children forgive.

To keep alive the sense of wonder, to live in unquestioning trust, instinctively to obey, to forgive and to forget – that is the childlike spirit, and that is the passport to the kingdom of God.

THE MAN WHO WOULD NOT PAY THE PRICE

Luke 18:18–30

A ruler asked Jesus, 'Good teacher, what shall I do to inherit eternal life?' Jesus said to him, 'Why do you call me good? There is none good except one – God. You know the commandments – do not commit adultery, do not kill, do not steal, do not bear false witness, honour your father and your mother.' He said, 'From my youth I have kept all these.' When Jesus heard that, he said to him, 'You still lack one thing. Sell everything you have and distribute it to the poor, and you will have treasure in heaven. And come! Follow me!' When he heard these things he was very sad, because he was exceedingly rich. When Jesus saw him he said, 'How hard it is for those who have riches to enter into the kingdom of God! It is easier for a camel to go through the eye of a needle than for a rich man to enter the kingdom of God.' Those who heard him said, 'And who can be saved?' He said, 'The things which are impossible with men are possible with God.' Peter said, 'Look you – we have left our private possessions and have followed you.' He said to them, 'This is the truth I tell you – there is no one who has left house, or

> wife, or brother, or parents or children for the sake of
> the kingdom of God who will not get it all back many
> times over in this time, and, in the age that is coming,
> eternal life.'

THIS ruler addressed Jesus in a way which, for a Jew, was without parallel. In all the religious Jewish literature there is no record of any Rabbi being addressed as 'Good teacher'. The Rabbis always said 'there is nothing that is good but the law'. To address Jesus in such a way savoured of almost fulsome flattery. So Jesus began by driving him and his thoughts back to God. Jesus was always sure that his own power and his own message came to him from God. When the nine lepers failed to return, his grief was not that they had forgotten to come back to say thanks to him, but that they had not come back to glorify God (Luke 17:18).

It was indisputable that this ruler was a good man, but he felt within his heart and soul that in his life there was something lacking. Jesus' command to him was that if he wanted to find all that he was searching for in life he must sell all his possessions and distribute them to the poor and follow him. Why did Jesus make this demand specially from this man? When the man whom Jesus had cured in the country of the Gerasenes wished to follow him, he told him to stay at home (Luke 8:38–9). Why this very different advice to this ruler?

There is an apocryphal gospel called the *Gospel according to the Hebrews*, most of which is lost; in one of the fragments which remain there is an account of this incident which gives us a clue. 'The other rich man said to Jesus, "Master, what good thing must I do really to live?" Jesus said to him, "Man, obey the law and the prophets." He said, "I have done so."

Jesus said to him, "Go, sell all that you possess, distribute it among the poor, and come, follow me!" The rich man began to scratch his head because he did not like this command. The Lord said to him, "Why do you say that you have obeyed the law and the prophets? For it is written in the law, 'You must love your neighbour as yourself,' and look you – there are many brothers of yours, sons of Abraham, who are dying of hunger, and your house is full of many good things, and not one single thing goes out of it to them." And he turned and said to Simon, his disciple, who was sitting beside him, "Simon, son of Jonas, it is easier for a camel to go through the eye of a needle than for a rich man to enter the kingdom of heaven."'

There we have the secret and the tragedy of this rich ruler. He was living utterly selfishly. He was rich, and yet he gave nothing away. His real God was comfort, and what he really worshipped were his own possessions and his wealth. That is why Jesus told him to give it all away. Many people use such wealth as they possess to bring comfort and joy and good to others; but this man used it for nobody but himself. If a person's god is that to which he or she gives all time, thought, energy and devotion, then wealth was this man's god. If he was ever to find happiness he must be done with all that and live for others with the same intensity as that with which he had so long lived for himself.

Jesus went on to say that it was easier for a camel to go through the eye of a needle than for a rich man to enter the kingdom of God. Quite often the Rabbis talked of an elephant trying to get through the eye of a needle as a picture of something fantastically impossible. But Jesus' picture may have one of two origins.

(1) It is said that beside the great gate into Jerusalem through which traffic went, there was a little gate just wide

and high enough for a man to get through. It is said that that little gate was called the needle's eye, and that the picture is of a camel trying to struggle through it.

(2) The Greek word for a camel is *kamelos*. In this age of Greek there was a tendency for the vowel sounds to become very like each other, and there was another word which would sound almost exactly the same – the word *kamilos*, which means *a ship's hawser*, the thick cable used to secure it when docking. It may well be that what Jesus said was that it would be easier to thread a needle with a ship's hawser than for a rich man to enter the kingdom of God.

Why should it be so? The whole tendency of possessions is to shackle our thoughts to this world. Our stake in it becomes so big that we never want to leave it, and never think of anything else. It is not a sin to have much wealth – but it is a danger to the soul and a great responsibility.

Peter pointed out that he and his fellow disciples had left all to follow Jesus; and Jesus promised that no one would ever give up anything for the kingdom of God who would not be repaid many times over. It is the experience of all Christians that that is true. Once someone said to the explorer David Livingstone, thinking of the trials he had endured and the sorrows he had borne, of how he had lost his wife and ruined his health in Africa, 'What sacrifices you have made!' Livingstone answered, 'Sacrifices? I never made a sacrifice in all my life.'

For those who walk the Christian way there may be things the world calls hard, but, beyond them all and through them all, there is a peace which the world cannot give and cannot take away, and a joy that no one can take away.

THE WAITING CROSS

Luke 18:31-4

> Jesus took the Twelve and said to them, 'Look you –
> we are going up to Jerusalem, and everything that was
> written through the prophets about the Son of Man will
> be fulfilled. He will be handed over to the Gentiles; and
> he will be mocked and cruelly treated; and spat upon;
> and they will scourge him and kill him; and on the third
> day he will rise again.' But they did not understand these
> things; this word was hidden from them; and they did
> not grasp what was being said.

THERE are two kinds of courage. There is the courage found
in those who, suddenly and without warning, are confronted
with some emergency or some crisis, and who unhesitatingly
and even recklessly fling themselves into it. There is the
courage found in those who see a terrible situation looming
ahead and know that nothing short of flight can avoid it,
and who yet go steadfastly and inflexibly on. There is no
question which is the higher courage. Many of us are capable
of the heroic action on the spur of the moment; it takes
supreme courage to go on to face something which haunts
us for days ahead and which, by turning back, we could
escape.

In one novel the writer paints a picture of two children
walking along the road playing their children's games. One
says to the other, 'When you're walking along the road, do
you ever pretend that there is something terrible just around
the next corner waiting for you; and you've got to go and
face it? It makes it so exciting.' With Jesus it was no game of
let's pretend. It was the grim truth that there was something
terrible waiting for him. He knew what crucifixion was like;

he had seen it; and yet he went on. If Jesus was nothing else, he would still be one of the most heroic figures of all time.

In face of Jesus' frequent warning of what was to happen to him in Jerusalem, we sometimes wonder why, when the cross came, it was such a shock and such a shattering blow to his disciples. The truth is that they simply could not take in what he was saying to them. They were obsessed with the idea of a conquering king; they still clung to that hope that he would let loose his power in Jerusalem and blast his enemies off the face of the earth.

Here is a great warning to every listener. The human mind has a way of listening only to what it wants to hear. There are none so blind as those who refuse to see. There is a kind of wishful thinking which believes that the unpleasant truth cannot really be true, and that the thing it does not want to happen cannot happen. We must constantly struggle against the tendency to hear only what we want to hear.

One thing more we must note. Jesus never foretold the cross without foretelling the resurrection. He knew that shame lay before him, but he was equally certain that glory lay before him, too. He knew what human malice could do, but he knew also what God's power could do. It was in the certainty of ultimate victory that he faced the apparent defeat of the cross. He knew that without a cross there can never be any crown.

THE MAN WHO WOULD NOT BE SILENCED

Luke 18:35–43

> When Jesus was approaching Jericho, a blind man was sitting by the wayside begging. When he heard the crowd passing through he asked what it meant. They told him, 'Jesus of Nazareth is passing by.' He shouted,

'Jesus, Son of David, have pity on me!' Those who were going on in front rebuked him and told him to be quiet, but he cried all the more, 'Son of David, have pity on me.' Jesus stood, and ordered him to be brought to him. When he had come near he asked him, 'What do you want me to do for you?' He said, 'Lord, that I may receive my sight.' Jesus said to him, 'Receive your sight; your faith has made you well.' And immediately he received his sight and followed him glorifying God, and, when the people saw it, they all gave praise to God.

THE one thing which stands out in this story is the sheer, desperate persistence of the blind man. Jesus was on his way to Jerusalem to the Passover. At such a time pilgrims travelled in bands together. One of the commonest ways for a Rabbi to teach was to discourse as he walked. That was what Jesus was doing, and the rest of the pilgrim band were crowding close around him, not to miss anything that he might say. As such a pilgrim band passed through a village or a town those who themselves could not go to the feast lined the wayside to see the pilgrims pass and to bid them godspeed on the way.

It was among the wayside crowd that the blind man was sitting. When he heard the murmur of the approaching throng he asked what was happening and was told that Jesus was passing by. Immediately he cried out to Jesus for help and healing. Thereupon everyone tried to silence him. The people round Jesus were missing what he was saying because of the clamour of this blind man.

But the man would not be silenced. He shouted again. The word used for shout in verse 39 is quite different from that used in verse 38. In verse 38 it is an ordinary loud shout to attract attention. In verse 39 it is the instinctive shout of ungovernable emotion, a scream, almost an animal cry. The word well shows the utter desperation of the man.

So Jesus stopped, and the blind man found the healing he so passionately desired.

This story tells us two things.

(1) It tells us something about the blind man. He was determined to come face to face with Jesus. Nothing would stop him. He refused to be silent and he refused to be restrained. His sense of need drove him relentlessly into the presence of Jesus. Whoever wants a miracle must show that spirit. A gentle, sentimental longing never really taps the power of God; but the passionate, intense desire of the very depths of the human heart will never be disappointed.

(2) It tells us something about Jesus. At that moment he was discoursing to the crowd like any Rabbi. But at the blind man's cry of need he stopped, the discourse forgotten. For Jesus it was always more important to act than to talk. Words always took second place to deeds. Here was a human soul in need. Speech must end and action begin. Someone has said that many teachers are like those who throw chatty remarks to someone drowning in a tempestuous sea. Jesus was never like that; he leaped to the rescue of the man. There are many who cannot put two sentences together but they are loved because they are kind. An orator may command respect but the person who has helping hands inspires love. We admire a great mind but we love a big heart.

THE GUEST OF THE MAN
WHOM EVERYONE DESPISED

Luke 19:1–10

> Jesus entered Jericho and was passing through it. And
> – look you – there was a man called Zacchaeus by name,
> and he was commissioner of taxes, and he was rich. He

was seeking to see who Jesus was, and he could not for
the crowd, because he was short in height. So he ran on
ahead and climbed up into a sycamore tree, for he was
to pass that way. When Jesus came to the place he
looked up and said to him, 'Zacchaeus! Hurry and come
down! for this very day I must stay at your house.' So
he hurried and came down, and welcomed him gladly;
and when they saw it they all murmured, 'He has gone
in to be the guest of a man who is a sinner.' Zacchaeus
stood and said to the Lord, 'Look you – half of my
goods, Lord, I hereby give to the poor. If I have taken
anything from any man by fraud I give it back to him
four times over.' Jesus said to him, 'Today salvation
has come to this house, because he also is a son of
Abraham; for the Son of Man came to seek and to save
that which was lost.'

JERICHO was a very wealthy and very important town. It lay
in the Jordan valley and commanded both the approach to
Jerusalem and the crossings of the river which gave access to
the lands east of the Jordan. It had a great palm forest and
world-famous balsam groves which perfumed the air for miles
around. Its gardens of roses were known far and wide. It was
known as 'The City of Palms'. Josephus called it 'a divine
region', 'the fattest in Palestine'. The Romans carried its dates
and balsam to worldwide trade and fame.

All this combined to make Jericho one of the greatest
taxation centres in Palestine. We have already looked at the
taxes which the tax-collectors collected and the wealth they
rapaciously acquired (Luke 5:27-32). Zacchaeus was a man
who had reached the top of his profession; and he was the
most hated man in the district. There are three stages in his
story.

(1) Zacchaeus was wealthy but he was not happy.
Inevitably he was lonely, for he had chosen a way that made

him an outcast. He had heard of this Jesus who welcomed tax-collectors and sinners, and he wondered if he would have any word for him. Despised and hated by all, Zacchaeus was reaching after the love of God.

(2) Zacchaeus determined to see Jesus, and would let nothing stop him. For Zacchaeus to mingle with the crowd at all was a courageous thing to do, for many would take the chance to get a nudge, or kick, or push at the little tax-collector. It was an opportunity not to be missed. Zacchaeus would be black and blue with bruises that day. He could not see – the crowd took an ill delight in making sure of that. So he ran on ahead and climbed a fig-mulberry tree. A traveller describes the tree as being like 'the English oak, and its shade is most pleasing. It is consequently a favourite wayside tree ... It is very easy to climb, with its short trunk and its wide lateral branches forking out in all directions.' Things were not easy for Zacchaeus but the little man had the courage of desperation.

(3) Zacchaeus took steps to show all the community that he was a changed man. When Jesus announced that he would stay that day at his house, and when he discovered that he had found a new and wonderful friend, immediately Zacchaeus made a decision. He decided to give half of his goods to the poor; the other half he did not intend to keep to himself but to use to make restitution for the frauds of which he had been self-confessedly guilty.

In his restitution he went far beyond what was legally necessary. Only if robbery was a deliberate and violent act of destruction was a fourfold restitution necessary (Exodus 22:1). If it had been ordinary robbery and the original goods were not restorable, double the value had to be repaid (Exodus 22:4, 7). If voluntary confession was made and voluntary restitution offered, the value of the original goods had to be paid, plus one-fifth (Leviticus 6:5; Numbers 5:7). Zacchaeus was determined to do far more than the law demanded. He showed by his deeds that he was a changed man.

The point is brought home by a terrible story. There was a meeting in progress at which several women were giving their testimony. One woman kept grimly silent. She was asked to testify but refused. She was asked why and she answered, 'Four of these women who have just given their testimony owe me money, and I and my family are half-starved because we cannot buy food.'

A testimony is utterly worthless unless it is backed by deeds which guarantee its sincerity. It is not a mere change of words which Jesus Christ demands, but a change of life.

(4) The story ends with the great words, the Son of Man came to seek and to save that which was lost. We must always be careful how we take the meaning of this word *lost*. In the New Testament it does not mean damned or doomed. It simply means *in the wrong place*. A thing is lost when it has got out of its own place into the wrong place; and when we find such a thing, we return it to the place it ought to occupy. A person is lost when he or she has wandered away from God; and is found when once again that person occupies the rightful place as an obedient child in the household and the family of the Father.

THE KING'S TRUST IN HIS SERVANTS

Luke 19:11–27

As they were listening to these things, Jesus went on to tell them a parable because he was near Jerusalem, and they were thinking that the kingdom of God was going to appear immediately. So he said, 'There was a noble

man who went into a distant country to receive a kingdom for himself and then to return. He called ten of his
own servants and gave them £1 each and said to them,
"Trade with these until I come." His citizens hated him,
and they despatched an embassy after him, saying, "We
do not wish this man to be king over us." When he had
received the kingdom and had returned, he ordered the
servants to whom he had given the money to be called
to him, that he might know what they had made by
trading with it. The first came and said, "Sir, your £1
has produced £10." So he said to him, "Well done, good
servant! Because you have shown yourself faithful in a
little thing, you shall have authority over ten cities."
And the second came and said to him also, "Sir, your
£1 has made £5." He said to him also, "You, too, are
to be promoted over five cities." Another came to him
and said, "Sir, here is your £1, which I was keeping laid
away in a towel, for I was afraid of you, because I know
that you are a hard man. You take up what you did not
put down and you reap what you did not sow." He said
to him, "Out of your own mouth I judge you, wicked
servant. You knew that I am a hard man, taking up what
I did not put down, and reaping what I did not sow.
You ought, therefore, to have given my money to the
bankers, so that when I came, I would have received it
plus interest." He said to those standing by, "Take the
£1 from him and give it to him who has £10." They
said to him, "Sir, he has £10." I tell you, that to everyone
who has it will be given; but from him who has not,
even what he has will be taken away. But as for these
my enemies, who did not wish to have me as their king
– bring them here and hew them to pieces in my
presence.'

THIS is unique among the parables of Jesus, because it is the
only one whose story is in part based on an actual historical

event. It tells about a king who went away to receive a kingdom and whose subjects did their best to stop him receiving it. When Herod the Great died in 4 BC he left his kingdom divided between Herod Antipas, Herod Philip and Archelaus. That division had to be ratified by the Romans, who were the overlords of Palestine, before it became effective. Archelaus, to whom Judaea had been left, went to Rome to persuade Augustus to allow him to enter into his inheritance, whereupon the Jews sent a delegation of fifty men to Rome to inform Augustus that they did not wish to have him as king. In point of fact, Augustus confirmed him in his inheritance, though without the actual title of king. Anyone in Judaea, on hearing the parable, would immediately remember the historical circumstances on which it was based.

The parable of the king and his servants illustrates certain great facts of the Christian life.

(1) It tells of the king's *trust*. He gave his servants the money and then went away and left them to use it as they could and as they thought best. He did not in any way interfere with them, or stand over them. He left them entirely to their own devices. That is the way in which God trusts us. Someone once said, 'The nicest thing about God is that he trusts us to do so much by ourselves.'

(2) It tells of the king's *test*. As always, this trust was a test, of whether or not someone was faithful and reliable in little things. Sometimes a person justifies a certain large inefficiency in the ordinary routine affairs of life by claiming that he or she is above such trifles. God is not. It is precisely in these routine duties that God is testing us. There is no example of this like Jesus himself. Of his thirty-three years of life Jesus spent thirty in Nazareth. Had he not discharged with absolute fidelity the tasks of the

carpenter's shop in Nazareth and the obligation of being the breadwinner of the family, God could never have given him the supreme task of being the Saviour of the world.

(3) It tells us of the king's *reward*. The reward that the faithful servants received was not one which they could enjoy by sitting down and folding their hands and doing nothing. One was put over ten cities and the other over five. The reward of work well done was more work to do. The greatest compliment we can pay anyone is the offer of even greater and harder tasks to do. The great reward of God to the person who has satisfied the test is more trust.

(4) The parable concludes with one of the inexorable laws of life. To those who have more will be given; from those who have not what they have will be taken away. If we play a game and go on practising at it, we will play it with even greater efficiency; if we do not practise, we will lose much of whatever knack and ability we have. If we discipline and train our bodies, they will grow ever fitter and stronger; if we do not, they will grow flabby and lose much of the strength we have. If a schoolboy learns Latin, and goes on with his learning, the wealth of Latin literature will open wider and wider to him; if he does not go on learning, he will forget much of the Latin he knows. If we really strive after goodness and overcome this and that temptation, new vistas and new heights of goodness will open to us; if we give up the battle and take the easy way, much of the power to resist we once possessed will be lost and we will slip from whatever height we had attained.

There is no such thing as standing still in the Christian life. We either get more or lose what we have. We either advance to greater heights or slip back.

THE ENTRY OF THE KING

Luke 19:28–40

> When Jesus had said these things, he went on ahead on
> the way up to Jerusalem. When he had come near
> Bethphage and Bethany, which is near the mount called
> the Mount of Olives, he despatched two of his disciples.
> 'Go to the village opposite,' he said. 'As you come into
> it, you will find tethered a colt upon which no man has
> ever sat. Loose it and bring it here. And if anyone asks
> you, "Why are you loosing this colt?" you will say,
> "The Lord needs it."' Those who had been despatched
> went off, and found everything exactly as he had told
> them. And as they were loosing the colt, its owners said
> to them, 'Why are you loosing the colt?' They said,
> 'The Lord needs it'; and they brought it to Jesus. They
> flung their garments on the colt, and mounted Jesus on
> it. As he went they strewed their garments on the road.
> When he was now drawing near, at the descent from
> the Mount of Olives, the whole crowd of the disciples
> began to rejoice, and to praise God with shouts for all
> the deeds of power they had seen, saying, 'Blessed is
> the king who comes in the name of the Lord! Peace in
> heaven and glory in the heights!' Some of the Pharisees
> who were in the crowd said to him, 'Teacher, rebuke
> your disciples.' 'I tell you,' he answered, 'if these keep
> silent, the stones will cry out.'

FROM Jerusalem to Jericho was only seventeen miles, and
now Jesus had almost reached his goal. Jerusalem, journey's
end, lay just ahead. The prophets had a regular custom of
which they made use again and again. When words were of
no effect, when people refused to take in and understand the
spoken message, they resorted to some dramatic action which

put their message into a picture which none could fail to see. We get examples of such dramatic actions in 1 Kings 11:29-31; Jeremiah 13:1-11, 27:1-11; Ezekiel 4:1-3, 5:1-4. It was just such a dramatic action which Jesus planned now. He proposed to ride into Jerusalem in a way that would be an unmistakable claim to be the Messiah, God's anointed king. We have to note certain things about this entry into Jerusalem.

(1) It was carefully planned. It was no sudden, impulsive action. Jesus did not leave things until the last moment. He had his arrangement with the owners of the colt. *The Lord needs it* was a password chosen long ago.

(2) It was an act of glorious defiance and of superlative courage. By this time there was a price on Jesus' head (John 11:57). It would have been natural that, if he must go into Jerusalem at all, he should have slipped in unseen and hidden away in some secret place in the back streets. But he entered in such a way as to focus the whole limelight upon himself and to occupy the centre of the stage. It is a breathtaking thing to think of a man with a price upon his head, an outlaw, deliberately riding into a city in such a way that every eye was fixed upon him. It is impossible to exaggerate the sheer courage of Jesus.

(3) It was a deliberate claim to be king, a deliberate fulfilling of the picture in Zechariah 9:9. But even in this Jesus underlined the kind of kingship which he claimed. The donkey in Palestine was not the lowly beast that it is in this country. It was noble. Only in war did kings ride upon a horse; when they came in peace they came upon a donkey. So Jesus by this action came as a king of love and peace, and not as the conquering military hero whom the tumultuous crowds expected and awaited.

(4) It was one last appeal. In this action Jesus came, as it were, with pleading hands outstretched, saying, 'Even now,

will you not take me as your king?' Before human hatred
engulfed him, once again he confronted people with love's
invitation.

THE PITY AND THE ANGER OF JESUS

Luke 19:41–8

> When Jesus had come near, and when he saw the city,
> he wept over it. 'Would that, even today,' he said, 'you
> recognized the things which would give you peace! But
> as it is, they are hidden from your eyes; for days will
> come upon you when your enemies will cast a rampart
> around you, and will surround you, and will hem you in
> on every side, and they will dash you and your children
> within you to the ground, and they will not leave one
> stone upon another within you, because you did not
> recognize the day when God visited you.'
> And he entered into the Temple and began to cast
> out those who were selling. 'It is written,' he said to
> them, 'My house shall be a house of prayer, but you
> have made it a brigands' cave.'
> And he taught daily in the Temple. The chief priests
> and the scribes sought to kill him, as did the chief men
> of the nation; and they could not discover anything they
> could do to him, for all the people, as they listened to
> him, hung upon his words.

In this passage there are three separate incidents.

(1) There is Jesus' lament over Jerusalem. From the
descent of the Mount of Olives there is a magnificent view
of Jerusalem with the whole city fully displayed. As Jesus
came to a turn in the road he stopped and wept over Jerusalem.
He knew what was going to happen to the city. The Jews
were even then embarking upon that career of political

manoeuvre and intrigue which ended in the destruction of Jerusalem in AD 70, when the city was so devastated that a plough was drawn through the middle of it. The tragedy was that if only they had abandoned their dreams of political power and taken the way that Jesus offered it need never have happened.

The tears of Jesus are the tears of God when he sees the needless pain and suffering in which men and women involve themselves through foolish rebelling against his will.

(2) There is the cleansing of the Temple. Luke's account is very summary; Matthew's is a little fuller (Matthew 21:12, 13). Why did Jesus, who was the very incarnation of love, act with such violence to the money-changers and the sellers of animals in the Temple courts?

First, let us look at the money-changers. Every male Jew had to pay a Temple tax every year of half a shekel, and it must be remembered that a half-shekel was equal to nearly two days' pay for a working man. A month before the Passover, booths were set up in all the towns and villages and it could be paid there; but by far the greater part was actually paid by the pilgrims in Jerusalem when they came to the Passover Feast. In Palestine all kinds of currencies were in circulation, and, for ordinary purposes, they were all – Greek, Roman, Tyrian, Syrian, Egyptian – equally valid. But this tax had to be paid either in exact half-shekels of the sanctuary or in ordinary Galilaean shekels. That is where the money-changers came in. To change a coin of exact value they charged a commission. If a larger coin was tendered then commission was charged for the requisite half-shekel and again for the giving of change. By this means the money-changers made an annual profit equivalent to many thousands of pounds. It was a deliberate swindle, and an imposition on poor people, who could least of all afford it.

Second, let us look at the sellers of animals. Almost every visit to the Temple involved its sacrifice. Victims could be bought outside at very reasonable prices; but the Temple authorities had appointed inspectors, for a victim must be without spot or blemish. It was, therefore, far safer to buy victims from the booths officially set up in the Temple. But there were times when inside the Temple a pair of doves would cost as much as ten or fifteen times more than they would cost outside. Again it was a deliberately planned victimization of the poor pilgrims, nothing more or less than legalized robbery. Worse, these Temple shops were known as the Booths of Annas and were the property of the family of the high priest. That is why Jesus was brought first before Annas when he was arrested (John 18:13). Annas was delighted to gloat over this man who had struck such a blow at his evil monopoly. Jesus cleansed the Temple with such violence because its traffic was being used to exploit helpless men and women. It was not simply that the buying and selling interfered with the dignity and solemnity of worship; it was that the very worship of the house of God was being used to exploit the worshippers. It was the passion for social justice which burned in Jesus' heart when he took this drastic step.

(3) There is something almost incredibly audacious in the action of Jesus in teaching in the Temple courts when there was a price on his head. This was sheer defiance. At the moment the authorities could not arrest him, for the people hung upon his every word. But every time he spoke he took his life in his hands and he knew well that it was only a matter of time until the end should come. The courage of Christians should match the courage of their Lord. He left us an example that we should never be ashamed to show whose we are and whom we serve.

BY WHAT AUTHORITY?

Luke 20:1-8

> One day, while Jesus was teaching the people in the
> Temple and telling them the good news, the chief priests
> and scribes with the elders came up and said to him,
> 'Tell us, by what authority do you do these things? Or,
> who is it who gives you this authority?' He said to them,
> 'I, too, will ask you for a statement. Tell me, was the
> baptism of John from heaven or from men?' They
> discussed it with each other. 'If', they said to each other,
> 'we say, "From heaven," he will say, "Why did you not
> believe in him?" But, if we say, "From men," all the
> people will stone us, for they are convinced that John
> was a prophet.' So they answered that they did not know
> where it was from. Jesus said to them, 'Neither do I tell
> you by what authority I do these things.'

THIS chapter describes what is usually called *the Day of
Questions*. It was a day when the Jewish authorities, in all
their different sections, came to Jesus with question after
question designed to trap him, and when, in his wisdom, he
answered them in such a way as routed them and left them
speechless.

The first question was put by the chief priests, the scribes
and the elders. The chief priests were a body of men composed
of ex-high priests and of members of the families from which
the high priests were drawn. The phrase describes the
religious aristocracy of the Temple. The three sets of men –
chief priests, scribes and elders – were the component parts
of the Sanhedrin, the supreme council and governing body of
the Jews; and we may well take it that this was a question
concocted by the Sanhedrin with a view to formulating a
charge against Jesus.

No wonder they asked him by what authority he did these things! To ride into Jerusalem as he did and then to take the law into his own hands and cleanse the Temple required some explanation. To the orthodox Jews of the day, Jesus' calm assumption of authority was an amazing thing. No Rabbi ever delivered a judgment or made a statement without giving his authorities. He would say, 'There is a teaching that . . .' Or he would say, 'This was confirmed by Rabbi So and So when he said . . .' But none would have claimed the utterly independent authority with which Jesus moved among the people. What they wanted was that Jesus should say bluntly and directly that he was the Messiah and the Son of God. Then they would have a ready-made charge of blasphemy and could arrest him on the spot. But he would not give that answer, for his hour was not yet come.

The reply of Jesus is sometimes described as a clever debating answer, used simply to score a point. But it is far more than that. He asked them to answer the question, 'Was the authority of John the Baptist human or divine?' The point is that their answer to Jesus' question would answer their own question. Everyone knew how John had regarded Jesus and how he had considered himself only the forerunner of the one who was the Messiah. If they agreed that John's authority was divine then they had also to agree that Jesus was the Messiah, because John had said so. If they denied it, the people would rise against them. Jesus' answer in fact asks the question, 'Tell me – where do you yourself think I got my authority?' He did not need to answer their question if they answered his.

To face the truth may confront any one of us with a sore and difficult situation; but to refuse to face it confronts us with a tangle out of which there is no escape. The emissaries of the Pharisees refused to face the truth, and they had to withdraw frustrated and discredited with the crowd.

A PARABLE WHICH WAS A CONDEMNATION

Luke 20:9–18

> Jesus began to speak this parable to the people. 'A man planted a vineyard and let it out to tenants, and went away for a long time. At the proper time he despatched a servant to the tenants so that they might give him his share of the fruit of the vineyard. The tenants beat him and sent him away empty-handed. He went on to send another servant. They beat him, too, and maltreated him, and sent him away empty-handed. He went on to send a third. This one they wounded and threw out. The owner of the vineyard said, "What am I to do? I will send my beloved son. It may be they will respect him." When the tenants saw him they said to each other, "This is the heir. Let us kill him so that the inheritance will be ours." And they flung him out of the vineyard and killed him. What, then, will the owner of the vineyard do to them? He will come and he will destroy these tenants, and will give the vineyard to others.' When they heard this, they said, 'God forbid!' He looked at them and said, 'What, then, is this which stands written – "The stone which the builders rejected, this has become the head of the corner? Everyone who falls against that stone will be shattered; but if it falls on anyone it will wipe him out as the wind blows the chaff away."'

THIS is a parable whose meaning is crystal clear. The vineyard stands for the nation of Israel (cf. Isaiah 5:1–7). The tenants are the rulers of Israel into whose hands the nation was entrusted. The messengers are the prophets who were disregarded, persecuted and killed. The son is Jesus himself. And the sentence is that the place which Israel should have occupied is to be given to others.

The story itself is the kind of thing which could and did happen. Judaea in the time of Jesus was in the throes of economic trouble and labour unrest. There was many an absentee landlord who let out his lands in just such a way. The rent was seldom paid in money. It was either a fixed amount of produce, irrespective of the success or failure of the harvest, or it was a percentage of the crop, whatever it might be.

In its teaching this is one of the richest of the parables. It tells us certain things about human nature.

(1) It tells us of *human privilege*. The tenants did not make the vineyard. They entered into possession of it. The owner did not stand over them with a whip. He went away and left them to work in their own way.

(2) It tells us of *human sin*. The sin of the tenants was that they refused to give the owner his due and wished to control what it was his sole right to control. Sin consists in the failure to give God his proper place and in usurping the power which should be his.

(3) It tells us of *human responsibility*. For long enough the tenants were left to their own devices; but the day of reckoning came. Sooner or later each of us is called upon to give account for that which was committed to our charge.

The parable tells us certain things about God.

(1) It tells us of the *patience* of God. The owner did not strike at the first sign of rebellion on the part of the tenants. He gave them chance after chance to do the right thing. There is nothing so wonderful as the patience of God. If any human hand had created the world, in exasperated despair its creator would have wiped it out long ago.

(2) It tells us of the *judgment* of God. The tenants thought they could presume on the patience of the master and get away with it. But God has not abdicated. However much any individual may seem to get away with it, the day of reckoning comes. As the Romans put it, 'Justice holds the scales with an even and a scrupulous balance and in the end she will prevail.'

The parable tells us something about Jesus.

(1) It tells us that *he knew what was coming*. He did not come to Jerusalem hugging a dream that even yet he might escape the cross. Open-eyed and unafraid, he went on. When Achilles, the great Greek hero, was warned by the prophetess Cassandra that if he went out to battle he would surely die, he answered, 'Nevertheless I am for going on.' For Jesus there was to be no turning back.

(2) It tells us that *he never doubted God's ultimate triumph*. Beyond the power of the wicked stood the undefeatable majesty of God. Wickedness may seem for a time to prevail, but it cannot in the end escape its punishment. In his poem, 'The Present Crisis', the American poet J. R. Lowell wrote:

> Careless seems the great Avenger, history's pages but record
> One death grapple in the darkness, 'twixt old systems and the Word;
> Truth for ever on the scaffold, Wrong for ever on the throne,
> Yet that scaffold sways the future, and behind the dim unknown,
> Standeth God within the shadow, keeping watch above his own.

(3) It lays down most unmistakably *his claim to be the Son of God*. Deliberately he removes himself from the

succession of the prophets. They were servants; he is *the Son*. In this parable he made a claim – that none could fail to see – to be God's chosen king.

The quotation about the stone which the builders rejected comes from Psalm 118:22–3. It was a favourite quotation in the early Church as a description of the death and resurrection of Jesus (cf. Acts 4:11; 1 Peter 2:7).

CAESAR AND GOD

Luke 20:19–26

> The scribes and chief priests tried to lay hands on Jesus at that very hour; and they feared the people, for they realized that he spoke this parable to them. They watched for an opportunity, and they despatched spies, who pretended that they were genuinely concerned about the right thing to do, so that they might fasten on what he said and be able to hand him over to the power and the authority of the governor. They asked him, 'Teacher, we know that you speak and teach rightly, and you are no respecter of persons. Is it lawful for us to pay tribute to Caesar? Or not?' He saw their subtle deception and said to them, 'Show me a denarius. Whose image and inscription is on it?' They said, 'Caesar's.' 'Well then,' he said to them, 'give to Caesar what belongs to Caesar, and give to God what belongs to God.' There was nothing in this statement that they could fasten on to in the presence of the people. They were amazed at his answer, and had nothing to say.

HERE the emissaries of the Sanhedrin returned to the attack. They persuaded others to go to Jesus and ask a question as if it was really troubling their consciences. The tribute to be paid to Caesar was a poll tax of one *denarius*, that is, one day's pay, per year. Every man aged between fourteen and sixty-five and every woman aged between twelve and sixty-five had to pay that simply for the privilege of existing. This tribute was a burning issue in Palestine and had been the cause of more than one rebellion. It was not the merely financial question which was at stake. The tribute was not regarded as a heavy imposition and was in fact no real burden at all. The issue at stake was this – the fanatical Jews claimed that they had no king but God and held that it was wrong to pay tribute to anyone other than him. The question was a religious question, for which many were willing to die.

So, then, these emissaries of the Sanhedrin attempted to impale Jesus on the horns of a dilemma. If he said that the tribute should not be paid, they would at once report him to Pilate and arrest would follow as surely as the night the day. If he said that it should be paid, he would alienate many of his supporters, especially the Galilaeans, whose support was so strong.

Jesus answered them on their own grounds. He asked to be shown a *denarius*. Now, in the ancient world the sign of kingship was the issue of currency. For instance, the Maccabees had immediately issued their own currency whenever Jerusalem was freed from the Syrians. Further, it was universally admitted that to have the right to issue currency carried with it the right to impose taxation. Those who had the right to put their image and superscription on a coin *ipso facto* had acquired the right to impose taxation. So Jesus said, 'If you accept Caesar's currency and use it, you are bound to accept Caesar's right to impose taxes'; '*but*,' he went on, 'there is a domain in which Caesar's writ does not run and which belongs wholly to God.'

(1) Those who live in a state and enjoy all its privileges cannot divorce themselves from it. The more honest people

are, the better citizens they will be. There should be no better and no more conscientious citizens of any state than its Christians; and one of the tragedies of life is that Christians do not sufficiently take their part in the government of the state. If they abandon their responsibilities and leave materialistic politicians to govern, Christians cannot justifiably complain about what is done or not done.

(2) Nonetheless, it remains true that in the life of the Christian God has the last word and not the state. The voice of conscience is louder than the voice of any human laws. The Christian is at once the servant and the conscience of the state. Being the best of citizens may mean refusing to do what a Christian citizen cannot do. A Christian will at one and the same time fear God and honour the authorities.

THE SADDUCEES' QUESTION

Luke 20:27-40

> Some of the Sadducees, who say that there is no resurrection, came to Jesus and asked him, 'Teacher, Moses wrote to us that, if a man's married brother dies without leaving any children, his brother must take his wife and raise up descendants for his brother. Now there were seven brothers. The first took a wife and died childless. The second and the third also took her; and in the same way the whole seven left no children and died. Later the wife died, too. Whose wife will she be at the resurrection, for the seven had her to wife?' Jesus said to them, 'The sons of this age marry and are married. But those who are deemed worthy to obtain that age and the resurrection from the dead neither marry nor are married, for they cannot die any more, for they are like angels and they are sons of God, for they are the

295

> sons of the resurrection. That the dead are raised even
> Moses indicated in the passage about the bush, when
> he called the Lord, the God of Abraham, the God of
> Isaac and the God of Jacob. God is not the God of the
> dead but of the living, for all live to him.' Some of the
> scribes said, 'Teacher, you have spoken well'; and they
> no longer dared to ask him any question.

WHEN the emissaries of the Sanhedrin had been finally
silenced, the Sadducees appeared on the scene. The whole
point of their question depends on two things.

(1) It depends upon the levirate law of marriage
(Deuteronomy 25:5). According to that law, if a man died
childless, his brother must marry the widow and beget
children to carry on the line. It is far from likely that it was
operative in the time of Jesus, but it was included in the
Mosaic regulations and therefore the Sadducees regarded it
as binding.

(2) It depends upon the beliefs of the Sadducees.
Sadducees and Pharisees are often mentioned together but in
beliefs they were poles apart.

(a) The Pharisees were entirely a religious body. They had
no political ambitions and were content with any government
which allowed them to carry out the ceremonial law. The
Sadducees were few but very wealthy. The priests and the
aristocrats were nearly all Sadducees. They were the
governing class; and they were largely collaborationist with
Rome, being unwilling to risk losing their wealth, their
comfort and their place.

(b) The Pharisees accepted the Scriptures plus all the
thousand detailed regulations and rules of the oral and
ceremonial law, such as the Sabbath law and the laws
about handwashing. The Sadducees accepted only the written
law of the Old Testament; and in the Old Testament they

stressed only the law of Moses and set no store by the prophetic books.

(c) The Pharisees believed in the resurrection from the dead and in angels and spirits. The Sadducees held that there was no resurrection from the dead and that there were no angels or spirits.

(d) The Pharisees believed in fate; and that an individual's life was planned and ordered by God. The Sadducees believed in unrestricted free will.

(e) The Pharisees believed in and hoped for the coming of the Messiah; the Sadducees did not. For them the coming of the Messiah would have been a disturbance of their carefully ordered lives.

The Sadducees, then, came with this question about who would be the husband in heaven of the woman who was married to seven different men. They regarded such a question as the kind of thing that made belief in the resurrection of the body ridiculous. Jesus gave them an answer which has a permanently valid truth in it. He said that we must not think of heaven in terms of this earth. Life there will be quite different, because *we* will be quite different. It would save a mass of misdirected ingenuity, and not a little heartbreak, if we ceased to speculate on what heaven is like and left things to the love of God.

Jesus went further. As we have said, the Sadducees did not believe in the resurrection of the body. They declared they could not believe in it because there was no information about it, still less any proof of it, in the books of the law which Moses was held to have written. So far no Rabbi had been able to meet them on that ground; but Jesus did. He pointed out that Moses himself had heard God say, 'I am the God of your father, the God of Abraham, the God of Isaac and the God of Jacob' (Exodus 3:1-6), and that it was impossible that God should be the God of the dead. Therefore Abraham and Isaac and Jacob must be still alive. Therefore there was such a thing as the resurrection of the body. No wonder the scribes declared it to be a good answer, for Jesus had met the Sadducees on their own ground and defeated them.

It may well be that we find this an arid passage. It deals with burning questions of the time by means of arguments which a Rabbi would find completely convincing but which are not convincing to us today. But out of this very aridity there emerges a great truth for anyone who teaches or who wishes to commend Christianity to others. *Jesus used arguments that the people he was arguing with could understand.* He talked to them in their own language; he met them on their own ground; and that is precisely why the ordinary people heard him gladly.

Sometimes, when one reads religious and theological books, one feels that all this may be true but it would be quite impossible to present it to non-theologically minded people who, after all, are in the majority. Jesus used language and arguments which people could and did understand; he met people with their own vocabulary, on their own ground, and with their own ideas. We will be far better teachers of Christianity and far better witnesses for Christ when we learn to do the same.

THE WARNINGS OF JESUS

Luke 20:41-4

> Jesus said to them, 'How does David say that the Christ is his son? For David himself says in the Book of Psalms, "The Lord says to my Lord, Sit at my right hand till I make your enemies your footstool." So David calls him Lord, and how can he be his son?'

It is worth while taking this little passage by itself for it is very difficult to understand. The most popular title of the Messiah was Son of David. That is what the blind man at Jericho called Jesus (Luke 18:38, 39), and that is how the crowds addressed him at his entry into Jerusalem (Matthew 21:9). Here Jesus seems to cast doubts on the validity of that title. The quotation is from Psalm 110:1. In Jesus' time all the Psalms were attributed to David and this one was taken to refer to the Messiah. In it David says that he heard God speak to his Anointed One and tell him to sit at his right hand until his enemies became his footstool; and in it David calls the Messiah *My Lord*. How can the Messiah be at once David's son and David's Lord?

Jesus was doing here what he so often tried to do, trying to correct the popular idea of the Messiah which was that under him the golden age would come and Israel would become the greatest nation in the world. It was a dream of political power. How was that to happen? There were many ideas about it but the popular one was that some great descendant of David would come to be invincible captain and king. So then the title *Son of David* was inextricably mixed up with world dominion, with military prowess and with material conquest.

Really what Jesus was saying here was, 'You think of the coming Messiah as Son of David; so he is; *but he is far more*. He is *Lord*.' He was telling people that they must revise their ideas of what Son of David meant. They must abandon these fantastic dreams of world power and visualize the Messiah as Lord of the hearts and lives of men and women. He was implicitly blaming them for having too little an idea of God. It is always our tendency to make God in our own image, and thereby to miss his full majesty.

THE LOVE OF WORLDLY HONOUR

Luke 20:45-7

> While all the people were listening, Jesus said to his
> disciples, 'Beware of the scribes who like to walk about
> in long robes, and who love greetings in the market
> places, and the chief seats in synagogues, and the top
> place at banquets. They devour widows' houses and
> pretend to offer long prayers. These will receive the
> greater condemnation.'

THE honours which the scribes and Rabbis expected to receive
were quite extraordinary. They had rules of precedence all
carefully drawn up. In the college the most learned Rabbi
took precedence; at a banquet, the oldest. It is on record that
two Rabbis came in, after walking on the street, grieved and
bewildered because more than one person had greeted
them with, 'May your peace be great,' without adding, 'My
masters!' They claimed to rank even above parents. They
said, 'Let your esteem for your friend border on your
esteem for your teacher, and let your respect for your teacher
border on your reverence for God.' 'Respect for a teacher
should exceed respect for a father, for both father and son
owe respect to a teacher.' 'If a man's father and teacher
have lost anything, the teacher's loss has the precedence,
for a man's father only brought him into this world; his
teacher, who taught him wisdom, brought him into the life of
the world to come ... If a man's father and teacher are
carrying burdens, he must first help his teacher, and afterwards
his father. If his father and teacher are in captivity, he must
first ransom his teacher, and afterwards his father.' Such
claims are almost incredible; it was not good for anyone to
make them; it was still less good for anyone to have them

conceded. But it was claims like that the scribes and Rabbis made.

Jesus also accused the scribes of devouring widows' houses. A Rabbi was legally bound to teach for nothing. All Rabbis were supposed to have trades and to support themselves by the work of their hands, while their teaching was given free. That sounds very noble but it was deliberately taught that to support a Rabbi was an act of the greatest piety. 'Whoever', they said, 'puts part of his income into the purse of the wise is counted worthy of a seat in the heavenly academy.' 'Whosoever harbours a disciple of the wise in his house is counted as if he offered a daily sacrifice.' 'Let thy house be a place of resort to wise men.' It is by no means extraordinary that impressionable women were the legitimate prey of the less scrupulous and more comfort-loving Rabbis. At their worst, they did devour widows' houses.

The whole unhealthy business shocked and revolted Jesus. It was all the worse because these men knew so much better and held so responsible a place within the life of the community. God will always condemn those who use a position of trust to further their own ends and to pander to their own comfort.

THE PRECIOUS GIFT

Luke 21:1-4

> Jesus looked up and saw those who were putting their gifts into the treasury – rich people – and he saw a poor widow putting in two lepta. So he said, 'I tell you truly that this poor widow has put in more than all, for all these contributed to the gifts out of their abundance, but she, out of her need, has put in everything she had to live on.'

IN the Court of the Women in the Temple there were thirteen collecting boxes known as the Trumpets. They were shaped like trumpets with the narrow part at the top and the wider part at the foot. Each was assigned to offerings for a different purpose – for the wood that was used to burn the sacrifice, for the incense that was burned on the altar, for the upkeep of the golden vessels, and so on. It was near the Trumpets that Jesus was sitting.

After the strenuous debates with the emissaries of the Sanhedrin and the Sadducees he was tired and his head drooped between his hands. He looked up and he saw many people flinging their offerings into the Trumpets; and then came a poor widow. All she had in the world was two *lepta*. A lepton was the smallest of all coins both in size and in value; the name means 'the thin one'. The offering of this widow was almost as small as it could possibly be. But Jesus said that it far outvalued all the other offerings, because it was everything she had.

Two things determine the value of any gift.

(1) There is *the spirit in which it is given.* A gift which is unwillingly extracted, a gift which is given with a grudge, a gift that is given for the sake of prestige or of self-display loses more than half its value. The only real gift is that which is the inevitable outflow of the loving heart, that which is given because the giver cannot help it.

(2) There is *the sacrifice which it involves.* That which is a mere trifle to one person may be a vast sum to another. The gifts of the rich, as they flung their offerings into the Trumpets, did not really cost them much; but the two lepta of the widow cost her everything she had. They no doubt gave having nicely calculated how much they could afford; she gave with that utterly reckless generosity which could give no more.

Giving does not begin to be real giving until it hurts. A gift shows our love only when we have had to do without something or have had to work doubly hard in order to give it. How few people give to God like that! Imagine someone in church, lustily singing,

> Were the whole realm of Nature mine,
>   That were an offering far too small;
> Love so amazing, so divine
>   Demands my soul, my life, my all,

while, all the time, carefully feeling coins to make sure that it is £1 and not £2 that will go into the collection which is immediately to follow.

Only a completely insensitive person could read the story of the widow and her two lepta without searching and humiliating self-examination.

TIDINGS OF TROUBLE

Luke 21:5–24

> When some were speaking about the Temple, how it was adorned with lovely stones and offerings, Jesus said, 'As for these things at which you are looking – days will come in which not one stone here will be left upon another, which will not be pulled down.' They asked him, 'Teacher, when, then, will these things be? And what will be the sign when these things are going to happen?' He said, 'Take care that you are not led astray. Many will come in my name, saying, "I am he!" and, "The time is at hand!" Do not go after them. When you hear of wars and upheavals, do not be alarmed; for these things must happen first; but the end will not come at once.'

Then he said to them, 'Nation will rise against nation, and kingdom against kingdom. There will be great earthquakes; in some places there will be famines and pestilences; there will be terrifying things, and great signs from heaven. Before all these things, they will lay hands upon you, and they will hand you over to the synagogues and prisons, and you will be brought before kings and governors for the sake of my name. It will all be an opportunity for you to bear witness to me. So, then, make up your minds not to prepare your defence beforehand, for I will give you a mouth and wisdom against which all your opponents will be unable to stand or argue. You will be handed over even by parents, and brothers, and kinsfolk and friends; some of you will be put to death; and you will be hated by all for the sake of my name. But not one hair of your head will perish. By your endurance you will win your souls.

'When you shall see Jerusalem encircled by armies, then know that the time of the desolation is at hand. At that time let those in Jerusalem flee to the mountains; let those who are in the midst of her go out of her; and let not those in the country districts enter into her, because these are days of vengeance, to fulfil all that stands written. Woe to those who, in those days, are carrying a child in the womb, or who have a babe at the breast. For great distress will be upon the earth and wrath upon all the people. They shall fall by the edge of the sword, and they will be taken away captive to all nations. Jerusalem will be trodden underfoot by the Gentiles, until the times of Gentiles are completed.'

The Background of the Chapter

FROM verse 5 onwards this becomes a very difficult chapter. Its difficulty rests in the fact that beneath it lie four different conceptions.

(1) There is the conception of *the day of the Lord*. The
Jews regarded time as being in two ages. There was
the present age, which was altogether bad and evil, incapable
of being cured, and fit only for destruction. There was
the age to come, which was the golden age of God and of
Jewish supremacy. But in between the two there would be
the day of the Lord, which would be a terrible time of cosmic
upheaval and destruction, the desperate birth-pangs of the
new age.

It would be a day of terror. 'See the day of the Lord comes,
cruel with wrath and fierce anger, to make the earth a
desolation and to destroy its sinners from it' (Isaiah 13:9; cf.
Joel 2:1-2; Amos 5:18-20; Zephaniah 1:14-18). It would
come suddenly. 'The day of the Lord will come like a thief in
the night' (1 Thessalonians 5:2; cf. 2 Peter 3:10). It would be
a day when the world would be shattered. 'The stars of the
heavens and their constellations will not give their light; the
sun will be dark at its rising and the moon will not shed its
light . . . Therefore I will make the heavens tremble, and the
earth will be shaken out of its place, at the wrath of the Lord
of hosts in the day of his fierce anger' (Isaiah 13:10-13; cf.
Joel 2:30-1; 2 Peter 3:10).

The day of the Lord was one of the basic conceptions of
religious thought in the time of Jesus; everyone knew these
terrible pictures. In this passage verses 9, 11, 25 and 26 take
their imagery from that.

(2) There is *the prophesied fall of Jerusalem*. Jerusalem
fell to the Roman armies in AD 70 after a desperate siege in
which the inhabitants were actually reduced to cannibalism
and in which the city had to be taken literally stone by stone.
Josephus says that an incredible number of 1,100,000 people
perished in the siege and 97,000 were carried away into
captivity. The Jewish nation was obliterated; and the Temple

was set on fire and became a desolation. In this passage verses 5, 6 and 20–4 clearly refer to that event still to come.

(3) There is *the second coming of Christ*. Jesus was sure that he was to come again and the early Church waited for that coming. It will often help us to understand the New Testament passages about the second coming if we remember that much of the older imagery which had to do with the day of the Lord was taken and attached to it. In this passage verses 27 and 28 clearly refer to it. Before the second coming it was expected that many false claimants to be the Christ would arise and great upheavals take place. In this passage verses 7, 8 and 9 refer to that.

(4) There is the idea of *persecution to come*. Jesus clearly foresaw and foretold the terrible things his people would have to suffer for his sake in the days to come. In this passage verses 12–19 refer to that.

This passage will become much more intelligible and valuable if we remember that beneath it there is not one consistent idea, but these four allied conceptions.

The Passage

It was a comment on the splendour of the Temple that moved Jesus to prophesy. In the Temple the pillars of the porches and of the cloisters were columns of white marble, forty feet high, each made of one single block of stone. Of the ornaments, the most famous was the great vine made of solid gold, each of whose clusters was as tall as a man. The finest description of the Temple as it stood in the time of Jesus is in Josephus, *The Jewish Wars*, Book 5, Section 5. At one point he writes, 'The outward face of the Temple in its front wanted nothing that was likely to surprise either men's minds or their eyes, for it was covered all over with plates of gold of great weight, and, at the first rising of the sun, reflected back a very fiery splendour, and made those who forced themselves to look upon it to turn their eyes away, just as they would have done at the sun's own rays. But the Temple appeared to strangers, when they were at a distance, like a mountain covered with snow, for, as to those parts of it that were not gilt, they were exceeding white.' To the Jews it was unthinkable that the glory of the Temple should be shattered to dust.

From this passage we learn certain basic things about Jesus and about the Christian life.

(1) Jesus could read the signs of history. Others might be blind to the approaching disaster but he saw the avalanche about to descend. It is only when we see things through the eyes of God that we see them clearly.

(2) Jesus was completely honest. 'This', he said to his disciples, 'is what you must expect if you choose to follow me.' Once in the middle of a great struggle for righteousness, a heroic leader wrote to a friend, 'Heads are rolling in the sand; come and add yours.' Jesus believed in men and women enough to offer them, not an easy way, but a heroic way.

(3) Jesus promised that his disciples would never meet their tribulations alone. It is the sheer evidence of history that the great Christians have written over and over again, when their bodies were in torture and when they were awaiting death, of sweet times with Christ. A prison can be like a palace, a scaffold like a throne, the storms of life like summer weather, when Christ is with us.

(4) Jesus spoke of a safety that is beyond the threats of earth. 'Not one hair of your head', he said, 'will be harmed.' In the days of the First World War, Rupert Brooke, out of his faith and his ideal, wrote these lines in a poem entitled 'Safety':

We have found safety with all things undying,
  The winds, and morning, tears of men and mirth,
The deep night, and birds singing, and clouds flying,
  And sleep, and freedom, and the autumnal earth.
We have built a house which is not for Time's throwing,
  We have gained a peace unshaken by pain for ever.
War knows no power. Safe shall be my going,
  Secretly armed against all death's endeavour:
Safe though a safety's lost; safe where men fall;
And if these poor limbs die, safest of all.

Those who walk with Christ may lose their lives but they can never lose their souls.

WATCH!

Luke 21:25-37

'And there will be signs in sun, and moon, and stars, and on earth the nations will be in distress and will not know what to do in the roaring of the sea and of the wave, while men's hearts will swoon from fear and from foreboding of the things that are coming on the world. The power of the heavens will be shaken; and then they will see the Son of Man coming in a cloud, with power and much glory. When these things begin to happen, look up and lift up your hearts for your deliverance is near.'

And he spoke this parable to them, 'Look at the fig tree and all the trees; whenever they put out their leaves, you see it for yourselves and you know that the harvest is near. So, whenever you see these things happening, you know that the kingdom of God is near. This is the truth I tell you, that this generation will not pass away until all these things have happened. The heaven and the earth will pass away, but my words will not pass away.'

Take care lest your hearts grow heavy with dissipation and drunkenness and anxieties for the things of this life, and lest that day come suddenly upon you like a trap closing, for it will come upon all who dwell upon the face of the earth. Be watchful at all times, and keep praying that you may have strength to escape all the things that are going to happen, and to be able to stand before the Son of Man.

During the days Jesus was teaching in the Temple, but at night he went out and stayed in the Mount called the Mount of Olives; and all the people came early in the morning to listen to him in the Temple.

THERE are two main conceptions here.

(1) There is the conception of *the second coming of Jesus Christ*. There has always been much useless argument and speculation about the second coming. When it will be and what it will be like are not ours to know. But the one great truth it enshrines is this – that history is going somewhere. The Stoics regarded history as circular. They held that every 3,000 years or so the world was consumed by a great conflagration, then it started all over again and history repeated itself. That meant that history was going nowhere and human beings were tramping round on a kind of eternal treadmill. The Christian conception of history is that it has a goal and at that goal Jesus Christ will be Lord of all. That is all we know, and all we need to know.

(2) There is stressed *the need to be on the watch*. As Christians we must never come to think that we are living in a settled situation. We must live our lives in a permanent state of expectation. A novelist, in one of her books, has a character who will not stoop to certain things that others do.

'I know', she said, 'that some day the great thing will come into my life and I want to keep myself fit to take it.' We must live forever in the shadow of eternity, in the certainty that our actions will determine our fitness to appear in the presence of God. There can be nothing so thrilling as the Christian life.

(3) Jesus spent the day among the crowds of the Temple; he spent the night beneath the stars with God. He won his strength to meet the crowds through his quiet time alone; he could face the people because he came to them from God's presence.

AND SATAN ENTERED INTO JUDAS

Luke 22:1–6

> The Feast of Unleavened Bread, which is called the Passover, was near, and the chief priests and the scribes searched to find a way to destroy Jesus, for they were afraid of the people. And Satan entered into Judas, who was called Iscariot, who belonged to the number of the Twelve. So he went away and discussed with the chief priests and captains how he might betray Jesus to them. They were glad and they undertook to give him money. So he agreed, and he began to look for a suitable time to betray him, when the mob were not there.

It was at Passover time that Jesus came to Jerusalem to die. The Feast of Unleavened Bread is not, strictly speaking, the same thing as the Passover. The Feast of Unleavened Bread lasted for a week, from 15th to 21st Nisan (April), and the Passover itself was eaten on 15th Nisan. It commemorated the deliverance of the people of Israel from their slavery in Egypt (Exodus 12). On that night the angel of death smote the first-born son in every Egyptian family; but *he passed over* the homes of the Israelites, because the lintels of their doors were smeared with the blood of the lamb to distinguish them. On that night they left so quickly that, at their last meal, there was no time to bake bread with leaven. It was unleavened cakes they ate.

There were elaborate preparations for the Passover. Roads were repaired; bridges were made safe; wayside tombs were whitewashed lest the pilgrim should fail to see them, and so touch them and become unclean. For a month before, the story and meaning of the Passover was the subject of the teaching of every synagogue. Two days before the Passover there was in every house a ceremonial search for leaven. The householder took a candle and solemnly searched every nook and cranny in silence, and the last particle of leaven was thrown out.

Every male Jew, who was of age and who lived within fifteen miles of the holy city, was bound by law to attend the Passover. But it was the ambition of every Jew in every part of the world (as it is still) to come to the Passover in Jerusalem at least once in a lifetime. To this day, when Jews keep the Passover in every land they pray that they may keep it next year in Jerusalem. Because of this vast numbers came to Jerusalem at the Passover time. Cestius was governor of Palestine in the time of Nero and Nero tended to belittle the importance of the Jewish faith. To convince Nero of it, Cestius took a census of the lambs slain at one particular Passover. Josephus tells us that the number was 256,500. The law laid it down that the minimum number for a Passover celebration was ten. That means that on this occasion, if these figures are correct, there must have been more than 2,700,000 pilgrims to the Passover. It was in this crowded city that the drama of the last days of Jesus was played out.

The atmosphere of Passover time was always inflammable. The headquarters of the Roman government was at Caesarea, and normally only a small detachment of troops was stationed at Jerusalem; but for the Passover season many more were drafted in. The problem which faced the Jewish authorities was how to arrest Jesus without provoking a riot. It was solved for them by the treachery of Judas. Satan entered into Judas. Two things stand out.

(1) Just as God is always looking for people to be his instruments, so is Satan. It is possible to be the instrument of good or of evil, of God or of the devil. The Zoroastrians see this whole universe as the battle ground between the god of the light and the god of the dark, and in that battle people must take sides. We, too, know that we can be the servants of the light or of the dark.

(2) But it remains true that Satan could not have entered into Judas unless Judas had opened the door. There is no handle on the outside of the door of the human heart. It must be opened from within. In the words of John Oxenham:

> To every man there openeth
> A high way and a low;
> And every man decideth
> The way his soul shall go.

It is our own decision whether we will choose to be the instrument of Satan or a weapon in the hand of God. We can enlist in either service. God help us choose aright!

THE LAST MEAL TOGETHER

Luke 22:7-23

> There came the day of the Feast of Unleavened Bread, on which the Passover had to be sacrificed. Jesus

despatched Peter and John. 'Go,' he said, 'and make
ready the Passover for us that we may eat it.' They said
to him, 'Where do you want us to make it ready?' 'Look
you,' he said to them, 'when you have gone into the
city, a man will meet you, carrying a jar of water. Follow
him to the house into which he enters; and you will say
to the master of the house, "The Teacher says to you,
'Where is the guest room that I may eat the Passover
with my disciples?'" And he will show you a big upper
room, ready furnished. There, get things ready.' So they
went away and found everything just as he had told
them; and they made ready the Passover.

When the hour came he took his place at table, and
so did his disciples. 'I have desired with all my heart',
he said to them, 'to eat this Passover with you before I
suffer, for I tell you that I will not eat it until it is fulfilled
in the kingdom of God.' He received the cup, and gave
thanks, and said, 'Take this and divide it among
yourselves. For I tell you that from now on I will not
drink of the fruit of the vine until the kingdom of God
has come.' And he took the bread, and gave thanks,
and broke it, and gave it to them, saying, 'This is my
body which is being given for you. Do this so that you
will remember me.' In the same way, after the meal, he
took the cup saying, 'This cup is the new covenant made
at the price of my blood, which is shed for you. But –
look you – the hand of him who betrays me is on the
table with me, for the Son of Man goes as it has been
determined. But woe to that man by whom he has been
betrayed'; and they began to question one another which
of them it could be who was going to do this.

ONCE again Jesus did not leave things until the last moment;
his plans were already made. The better-class houses had two
rooms. The one room was on the top of the other; and the
house looked exactly like a small box placed on top of a

large one. The upper room was reached by an outside stair. During the Passover time all lodging in Jerusalem was free. The only pay a host might receive for letting lodgings to the pilgrims was the skin of the lamb which was eaten at the feast. A very usual use of an upper room was that it was the place where a Rabbi met with his favourite disciples to talk things over with them and to open his heart to them. Jesus had taken steps to procure such a room. He sent Peter and John into the city to look for a man bearing a jar of water. To carry water was a woman's task. A man carrying a jar of water would have been very easy to pick out. This was a pre-arranged signal between Jesus and a friend.

So the feast went on; and Jesus used the ancient symbols and gave them a new meaning.

(1) He said of the bread, 'This is my body.' Herein is exactly what we mean by a sacrament. A sacrament is something, usually a very ordinary thing, which has acquired a meaning far beyond itself for those who have eyes to see and hearts to understand. There is nothing specially theological or mysterious about this.

In the house of every one of us there is a drawer full of things which can only be called junk, and yet we will not throw them out, because when we touch and handle and look at them, they bring back this or that person, or this or that occasion. They are common things but they have a meaning far beyond themselves. That is a sacrament.

When the mother of the writer J. M. Barrie died and her belongings were being cleared, it was discovered that she had kept all the envelopes in which her famous son had posted her the cheques he so faithfully and lovingly sent. They were only old envelopes but they meant much to her. That is a sacrament.

314

When Nelson was buried in St Paul's Cathedral a party of his sailors bore his coffin to the tomb. One who saw the scene wrote, 'With reverence and with efficiency they lowered the body of the world's greatest admiral into its tomb. Then, as though answering to a sharp order from the quarterdeck, they all seized the Union Jack with which the coffin had been covered and tore it to fragments, and each took his souvenir of the illustrious dead.' All their lives that little bit of coloured cloth would speak to them of the admiral they had loved. That is a sacrament.

The bread which we eat at the sacrament is common bread, but, for anyone who has a heart to feel and understand, it is the very body of Christ.

(2) He said of the cup, 'This cup is the new covenant made at the price of my blood.' In the biblical sense, a covenant is a relationship between human beings and God. God graciously approached his people; and the people promised to obey and to keep his law. The whole matter is set out in Exodus 24:1–8. The continuance of that covenant depends on keeping that pledge and obeying this law; we could not and cannot do that; human sin interrupts our relationship with God. All the Jewish sacrificial system was designed to restore that relationship by the offering of sacrifice to God to atone for sin. What Jesus said was this – 'By my life and by my death I have made possible a new relationship between you and God. You are sinners. That is true. But because I died for you, God is no longer your enemy but your friend.' It cost the life of Christ to restore our lost relationship of friendship with God.

(3) Jesus said, 'Do this and it will make you remember me.' Jesus knew how easily the human mind forgets. The Greeks had an adjective which they used to describe time – 'time,' they said, 'which wipes all things out,' as if the human

mind were a slate and time a sponge which wiped it clean. Jesus was saying, 'In the rush and press of things you will forget me. People forget because they must, and not because they want to. Come in sometimes to the peace and stillness of my house and do this again with my people – and you will remember.'

It made the tragedy all the more tragic that at that very table there was one who was a traitor. Jesus Christ has at every communion table those who betray him, for if in his house we pledge ourselves to turn and then by our lives go out to deny him, we too are traitors to him.

STRIFE AMONG THE DISCIPLES OF CHRIST

Luke 22:24–30

> Strife arose among them about which was to be con-
> sidered greatest. Jesus said to them, 'The kings of the
> Gentiles exercise lordship over them and those who
> have authority over them claim the title of Benefactor.
> It must not be so with you; but let him who is greatest
> among you be as the youngest; and let him who is the
> leader be as him who serves. Who is the greater? He
> who sits at table, or he who serves? Is it not he who sits
> at table? But I am among you as one who serves. You
> are those who have stayed with me in my tribulations;
> and I assign to you a kingdom, just as my Father has
> assigned one to me, that you may eat and drink at my
> table in my kingdom; and you will sit upon thrones
> judging the twelve tribes of Israel.'

It is one of the most poignantly tragic things in the gospel story that the disciples could quarrel about precedence in the very shadow of the cross. The seating arrangements at a

Jewish feast were very definite. The table was arranged like a square with one side left open. At the top side of the square, in the centre, sat the host. On his right sat the guest of first honour; on his left the second guest; second on his right, the third guest; second on his left the fourth guest; and so on round the table. The disciples had been quarrelling about where they were to sit, for they had not yet rid themselves of the idea of an earthly kingdom. Jesus told them bluntly that the standards of his kingdom were not the standards of this world. A king on earth was evaluated by the power he exercised. One of the commonest titles for a king in the middle east was *Euergetes*, which is the Greek for *Benefactor.* Jesus said, 'It is not the king but the servant who obtains that title in my kingdom.'

(1) What the world needs is service. The odd thing is that the business world knows this. A familiar sight on the roadside is the sign which reads *Service Station* or *Motorway Services*. It was the claim of one company, 'We will crawl under your car oftener and get ourselves dirtier than any of our competitors.' The strange thing is that there is more argument about precedence and more concern about people's 'places' in the Church than anywhere else. The world needs and recognizes service.

(2) It is only the person who will consent to serve more than anyone else who will really rise high. It frequently happens that the ordinary worker will go home at 5.30 pm to forget his or her job until next morning, while the light will be burning in the office of the chief executive long after that. Often passers-by would see the light burning in John D. Rockefeller's office when the rest of the building was in darkness. It is a law of life that service leads to greatness; and the higher a man rises the greater the servant he must be.

(3) We can found our life either on giving or on getting; but the plain fact is that if we found it on getting we shall miss both human friendship and God's reward, for no one ever loved a person who was always bound up with self-interest.

(4) Jesus finished his warning by promising his disciples that those who had stood by him through thick and thin would in the end reign with him. God will be in no one's debt. Those who have shared in the bearing of Christ's cross will some day share in the wearing of his crown.

PETER'S TRAGEDY

Luke 22:31-8 and 54-62

'Simon, Simon,' Jesus said, 'Look you, Satan has been allowed to have you that he may sift you like wheat. But I have prayed for you that your faith may not wholly fail. And you – when you have turned again – strengthen your brothers.' He said to him, 'Lord, I am ready to go with you to prison and to death.' 'Peter,' he said, 'I tell you, the cock will not crow today before you have three times denied that you know me.'

And he said to them, 'When I sent you out without purse or wallet or shoes, did you lack for anything?' They said, 'For nothing.' But he said to them, 'But now, let him who has a purse take it, and so with a wallet; and let him who has no sword sell his cloak and buy one. For I tell you that this which stands written must be fulfilled in me – "And he was reckoned with the law-breakers" – for that which was written of me is finding its fulfilment.' They said, 'Lord, here are two swords.' He said to them, 'It is enough.' . . .

So they seized Jesus and led him away, and brought
him to the high priest's house. Peter followed a long
way away. When they had kindled a fire in the middle
of the courtyard, and were sitting there together, Peter
sat in the midst of them. A maid servant saw him as
he sat in the firelight. She looked intently at him.
'This man, too,' she said, 'was with him.' He denied
it. 'Woman,' he said, 'I do not know him.' Soon after
another man saw him and said, 'You, too, were one of
them.' Peter said, 'Man, I am not!' About an hour
elapsed and another insisted, 'Truly this man, too, was
with him. I know it for he is a Galilaean.' Peter said,
'Man, I don't know what you are talking about.' And
immediately – while he was still speaking – a cock crew.
And the Lord turned and looked at Peter. And Peter
remembered what the Lord had said, that he said to him,
'Before the cock crows today you will deny me three
times.' And he went out and wept bitterly.

WE take the story of the tragedy of Peter all in one piece.
Peter was a strange paradoxical mixture.

(1) Even in spite of his denial he was fundamentally loyal.
H. G. Wells once said, 'A man may be a bad musician, and
yet be passionately in love with music.' No matter what
Peter did, however terrible his failure, he was nonetheless
passionately devoted to Jesus. There is hope for the person
who even when sinning is still haunted by goodness.

(2) Peter was well warned. Jesus warned him both directly
and indirectly. Verses 33 to 38 with their talk of swords make
up a strange passage. But what they mean is this – Jesus was
saying, 'All the time so far you have had me with you. In a
very short time you are going to be cast upon your own
resources. What are you going to do about it? The danger in
a very short time is not that you will possess nothing; but that
you will have to fight for your very existence.' This was not

an incitement to armed force. It was simply a vivid way of telling the disciples that their very lives were at stake. No one could say that the seriousness and danger of the situation, and his own liability to collapse, were not presented to Peter.

(3) Peter was overconfident. If someone says, 'That is one thing I will never do,' that is often the very thing against which he or she must most carefully guard. Throughout history fortresses have been captured because the attackers took the route which seemed unattackable and unscalable and at that very spot the defenders were off their guard. Satan is subtle. He attacks the points at which we are too sure of ourselves, for there we are most likely to be unprepared.

(4) In all fairness it is to be noted that Peter was one of the two disciples (John 18:15) who had the courage to follow Jesus into the courtyard of the high priest's house at all. Peter fell to a temptation which could only have come to a brave man. The courageous person always runs more risks than someone who seeks a placid safety. Liability to temptation is the price paid by those who are adventurous in mind and in action. It may well be that it is better to fail in a gallant enterprise than to run away and not even to attempt it.

(5) Jesus did not speak to Peter in anger but looked at him in sorrow. Peter could have stood it if Jesus had turned and reviled him; but that voiceless, grief-laden look went to his heart like a sword and opened a fountain of tears. In one of his dialect rhymes, 'Well?', Studdert Kennedy catches that feeling:

> I think I'd sooner frizzle up,
> I' the flames of a burnin' 'ell,
> Than stand and look into 'is face,
> And 'ear 'is voice say – 'Well?'

The penalty of sin is to face, not the anger of Jesus, but the heartbreak in his eyes.

(6) Jesus said a very lovely thing to Peter. 'When you have turned,' he said, 'strengthen your brothers.' It is as if Jesus said to Peter, 'You will deny me; and you will weep bitter tears; but the result will be that you will be better able to help your brothers who are going through it.' We cannot really help others until we have been in the same furnace of affliction or the same abyss of shame as they have been. It was said of Jesus, 'He can help others who are going through it because he has been through it himself' (cf. Hebrews 2:18). To experience the shame of failure and disloyalty is not all loss, because it gives us a sympathy and an understanding that otherwise we would never have won.

YOUR WILL BE DONE

Luke 22:39–46

> Jesus went out, and, as his custom was, made his way to the Mount of Olives. The disciples, too, accompanied him. When he came to the place, he said to them, 'Pray that you may not enter into temptation.' And he was withdrawn from them, about a stone's throw, and he knelt and prayed. 'Father,' he said, 'if it is your will, take this cup from me; but not my will, but yours be done.' And an angel from heaven appeared strengthening him. He was in an agony, and he prayed still more intensely, and his sweat was as drops of blood falling upon the ground. So he rose from prayer and came to his disciples, and found them sleeping from grief. 'Why are you sleeping? 'he said to them. 'Rise and pray that you may not enter into temptation.'

THE space within Jerusalem was so limited that there was no room for gardens. Many well-to-do people, therefore, had private gardens out on the Mount of Olives. Some wealthy friend had given Jesus the privilege of using such a garden, and it was there that Jesus went to fight his lonely battle. He was only thirty-three; and no one wants to die at thirty-three. He knew what crucifixion was like; he had seen it. He was in an *agony*; the Greek word is used of someone fighting a battle with sheer fear. There is no scene like this in all history. This was the very hinge and turning point in Jesus' life. He could have turned back even yet. He could have refused the cross. The salvation of the world hung in the balance as the Son of God literally sweated it out in Gethsemane; and he won.

A famous pianist said of Chopin's nocturne in C sharp minor, 'I must tell you about it. Chopin told Liszt, and Liszt told me. In this piece all is sorrow and trouble. Oh such sorrow and trouble! – until he begins to speak to God, to pray; then it is all right.' That is the way it was with Jesus. He went into Gethsemane in the dark; he came out in the light – because he had talked with God. He went into Gethsemane in an agony; he came out with the victory won and with peace in his soul – because he had talked with God.

It makes all the difference what tone of voice is used when saying, 'Your will be done.'

(1) It may be said in a tone of helpless submission, as by one who is in the grip of a power against which it is hopeless to fight. The words may be the death-knell of hope.

(2) It may be said as by one who has been battered into submission. The words may be the admission of complete defeat.

(3) It may be said as by one who has been utterly frustrated and who sees that the dream can never come true. The

words may be those of a bleak regret or even of a bitter anger which is all the more bitter because nothing can be done about it.

(4) It may be said with the accent of perfect trust. That is how Jesus said it. He was speaking to one who was Father; he was speaking to a God whose everlasting arms were underneath and about him even on the cross. He was submitting, but he was submitting to the love that would never let him go. Life's hardest task is to accept what we cannot understand; but we can do even that if we are sure enough of the love of God. As Robert Browning wrote in 'Paracelsus':

> God, thou art love! I build my faith on that . . .
> I know thee, who has kept my path, and made
> Light for me in the darkness, tempering sorrow
> So that it reached me like a solemn joy:
> It were too strange that I should doubt thy love.

Jesus spoke like that; and when we can speak like that, we can look up and say in perfect trust, 'Your will be done.'

THE TRAITOR'S KISS

Luke 22:47–53

> While Jesus was still speaking – look you – there came a crowd, and the man called Judas, one of the Twelve, was leading them. He came up to Jesus to kiss him; but Jesus said to him, 'Judas, is it with a kiss that you would betray the Son of Man?' When those who were around him saw what was going to happen, they said, 'Lord, shall we strike with the sword?' And one of them struck the servant of the high priest and cut off his ear. Jesus answered, 'Let it come even to this!' Jesus said to the chief priests and the Temple captains, and to the elders

who had come to him, 'Have you come out with swords
and cudgels as against a brigand? When I was daily
with you in the Temple you did not lift your hand against
me; but this is your hour, and the power of darkness is
here.'

JUDAS had found a way to betray Jesus in such a way that the
authorities could come upon him when the crowd was not
there. He knew that Jesus was in the habit of going at nights
to the garden on the hill, and there he led the emissaries of
the Sanhedrin. The captain of the Temple, or the Sagan, as he
was called, was the official who was responsible for the good
order of the Temple; the captains of the Temple referred to
here were his lieutenants who were responsible for carrying
out the actual arrest of Jesus. When a disciple met a beloved
Rabbi, he laid his right hand on the Rabbi's left shoulder and
his left hand on the right shoulder and kissed him. It was the
kiss of a disciple to a beloved master that Judas used as a
sign of betrayal.

There were four different parties involved in this arrest,
and their actions and reactions are very significant.

(1) There was Judas the traitor. He was the man who had
abandoned God and entered into a league with Satan. It is
only when people have put God out of their lives and taken
Satan in, that they can sink to selling Christ.

(2) There were the Jews who had come to arrest Jesus.
They were the men who were *blind to God*. When God
incarnate came to this earth, all that they could think of was
how to hustle him to a cross. They had so long chosen their
own way and shut their ears to the voice of God and their
eyes to his guidance that in the end they could not recognize
him when he came. It is a terrible thing to be blind and deaf
to God. As Elizabeth Barrett Browning wrote:

I too have strength –
Strength to behold him and not worship him,
Strength to fall from him and not to cry to him.

God save us from a strength like that!

(3) There were the disciples. They were the men who *for the moment had forgotten God*. Their world had fallen in and they were sure the end had come. The last thing they remembered at that moment was God; the only thing they thought of was the terrible situation into which they had come. Two things happen to those who forget God and leave him out of the situation. They become utterly terrified and completely disorganized. They lose the power to face life and to cope with it. In the time of trial, life is unlivable without God.

(4) There was Jesus. And Jesus was the one person in the whole scene who *remembered God*. The amazing thing about him in the last days was his absolute serenity once Gethsemane was over. In those days, even at his arrest, it was he who seemed to be in control; and even at his trial, it was he who was the judge. When we walk with God we can cope with any situation and look any foe in the eyes, unbowed and unafraid. Then we can say with confidence, as W. E. Henley's poem 'Invictus' put it so powerfully:

In the fell clutch of circumstance,
     I have not winced nor cried aloud.
Under the bludgeonings of chance
     My head is bloody, but unbow'd.

It matters not how strait the gate,
     How charged with punishments the scroll,
I am the master of my fate:
     I am the captain of my soul.

It is only when we have bowed to God that we can talk and act like conquerors.

MOCKING AND SCOURGING
AND TRIAL

Luke 22:63–71

> The men who were holding Jesus mocked him and beat him. They blindfolded him and asked him, 'Prophesy! Who is it who hit you?' And many another insulting word they spoke to him.
>
> And when it was day, the assembly of the elders of the people came together, the chief priests and the scribes; and they led him away to the Sanhedrin, saying, 'Tell us if you are God's Anointed One.' He said to them, 'If I tell you, you will not believe me; if I ask you, you will not answer. But from now on the Son of Man will be seated at the right hand of the power of God.' They all said, 'Are you then the Son of God?' He said to them, 'You say that I am.' They said, 'What further evidence do we need? We ourselves have heard it from his own mouth.'

DURING the night Jesus had been brought before the high priest. That was a private and unofficial examination. Its purpose was for the authorities to gloat over him and, if possible, to trip him up in cross-examination so that a charge could be formulated against him. After that, he was handed over to the Temple police for safe-keeping, and they played their cruel jests upon him. When the morning came, he was taken before the Sanhedrin.

The Sanhedrin was the supreme court of the Jews. In particular it had complete jurisdiction over all religious and theological matters. It was composed of seventy members. Scribes, Rabbis and Pharisees, priests and Sadducees, and elders were all represented on it. It could not meet during the hours of darkness. That is why they held Jesus until the morning before they brought him before it. It could meet only in the Hall of Hewn Stone in the Temple court. The high priest was its president.

We possess the rules of procedure of the Sanhedrin. Perhaps they are only the ideal which was never fully carried out; but at least they allow us to see what the Jews, at their best, conceived that the Sanhedrin should be and how far their actions fell short of their own ideals in the trial of Jesus. The court sat in a semi-circle, in which every member could see every other member. Facing the court stood the prisoner dressed in mourning dress. Behind him sat the rows of the students and disciples of the Rabbis. They might speak in defence of the prisoner but not against him. Vacancies in the court were probably filled by co-option from these students. All charges must be supported by the evidence of two witnesses independently examined. A member of the court might speak against the prisoner, and then change his mind and speak for him, but not vice versa. When a verdict was due, each member had to give his individual judgment, beginning at the youngest and going on to the most senior. For acquittal a majority of one was all that was necessary; for condemnation there must be a majority of at least two. Sentence of death could never be carried out on the day on which it was given; a night must elapse so that the court might sleep on it, so that, perhaps, their condemnation might turn to mercy. The whole procedure was designed for mercy; and, even from Luke's summary account, it is clear that the Sanhedrin, when it tried Jesus, was far from keeping its own rules and regulations.

It is to be very carefully noted that the charge the Sanhedrin finally produced against Jesus was one of blasphemy. To claim to be the Son of God was an insult to God's majesty and therefore blasphemy, and punishable by death.

It is the tragic fact that when Jesus asked for love he did not even receive simple justice. It is the glorious fact that Jesus, even when he had emerged from a night of malignant questioning, even when he had been mocked and buffeted and scourged, still had utter confidence that he would be set down at the right hand of God and that his triumph was sure. His faith defied the facts. He never for a moment believed that the purposes of God could ultimately be defeated by human actions.

TRIAL BEFORE PILATE AND
SILENCE BEFORE HEROD

Luke 23:1–12

> The whole assembly rose up and brought Jesus to Pilate. They began to accuse him. 'We found this man', they said, 'perverting our nation and trying to stop men paying taxes to Caesar, and saying that he himself is the Anointed One, a king.' Pilate asked him, 'Are you the King of the Jews?' He answered, 'You say so.' Pilate said to the chief priests and to the crowds, 'I find nothing to condemn in this man.' They were the more urgent. 'He is setting the people in turmoil,' they said, 'throughout all Judaea, beginning from Galilee to this place.' When Pilate heard this, he asked if the man was a Galilaean. When he realized that he was under Herod's jurisdiction, he referred him to Herod, who was himself in Jerusalem in these days. When Herod saw Jesus he was very glad, because for a long time he had been

wishing to see him, because he had heard about him; and he was hoping to see some sign done by him. He questioned him in many words; but he answered him nothing. The chief priests and the scribes stood by vehemently hurling their accusations against him. Herod with his soldiers treated Jesus contemptuously, and after he had mocked him and arrayed him in a gorgeous dress, he referred him back again to Pilate. And Herod and Pilate became friends with each other that same day, for previously they had been at enmity with each other.

THE Jews in the time of Jesus had no power to carry out the death sentence. Such sentence had to be passed by the Roman governor and carried out by the Roman authorities. It was for that reason that the Jews brought Jesus before Pilate. Nothing better shows their malign intention than the crime with which they charged him. In the Sanhedrin the charge had been one of blasphemy, that he had dared to call himself the Son of God. Before Pilate that charge was never even mentioned. They knew well that it would have carried no weight with him, and that he would never have proceeded on a charge which would have seemed to him a matter of Jewish religion and superstition. The charge they levelled against Jesus was entirely political, and it has all the marks of the minds and ingenuity of the Sadducees. It was really the aristocratic, collaborationist Sadducees who achieved the crucifixion of Jesus, in their terror lest he should prove a disturbing element and produce a situation in which they would lose their wealth, their comfort and their power.

Their charge before Pilate was really threefold. They charged Jesus (a) with seditious agitation; (b) with encouraging the people not to pay tribute to Caesar; (c) with assuming the title of king. Every single item of the charge was a lie, and they knew it. They resorted to the most calculated and malicious lies in their overwhelming desire to eliminate Jesus.

Pilate was not for nothing an experienced Roman official; he saw through them; and he had no desire to gratify their wishes. But neither did he wish to offend them. They had dropped the information that Jesus came from Galilee; this they had intended as further fuel for their accusations, for Galilee was notoriously 'the nurse of seditious men'. But to Pilate it seemed a way out. Galilee was under the jurisdiction of Herod Antipas, who at that very time was in Jerusalem to keep the Passover. So Pilate referred the case to Herod. Herod was one of the very few people to whom Jesus had absolutely nothing to say. Why did he believe there was nothing to be said to Herod?

(1) Herod regarded Jesus as a sight to be gazed at. To Herod, he was simply a spectacle. But Jesus was not a sight to be stared at; he was a king to be submitted to. Epictetus, the famous Greek Stoic teacher, used to complain that people came from all over the world to his lectures to stare at him, as if he had been a famous statue, but not to accept and to obey his teaching. Jesus is not a figure to be gazed at but a master to be obeyed.

(2) Herod regarded Jesus as a joke. He jested at him; he clothed him in a king's robe as an imitation king. To put it another way – he refused to take Jesus seriously. He would show him off to his court as an amusing curiosity but there his interest stopped. The plain fact is that the vast majority of people still refuse to take Jesus seriously. If they did, they would pay more attention than they do to his words and his claims.

(3) There is another possible translation of verse 11. 'Herod with his soldiers treated Jesus contemptuously.' That could be translated, 'Herod, with his soldiers behind him, thought that Jesus was of no importance.' Herod, secure in

his position as king, strong with the power of his bodyguard behind him, believed that this Galilaean carpenter did not matter. There are still those who, consciously or unconsciously, have come to the conclusion that Jesus does not matter, that he is a factor which can well be omitted from life. They give him no room in their hearts and no influence in their lives and believe they can easily do without him. To the Christian, so far from being of no importance, Jesus is the most important person in all the universe.

THE JEWS BLACKMAIL PILATE

Luke 23:13–25

Pilate summoned the chief priests and the rulers and the people, and said to them, 'You brought me this man as one who was seducing the people from their allegiance; and – look you – I have examined him in your presence, and of the accusations with which you charge him, I have found nothing in this man to condemn; and neither has Herod; for he sent him back to us. Look you – nothing deserving death has been done by him. I will therefore scourge him and release him.' All together they shouted out, 'Take this man away! And release Barabbas for us.' Barabbas had been thrown into prison because a certain disorder had arisen in the city, and because of murder. Again Pilate addressed them, because he wished to release Jesus. But they kept shouting, 'Crucify, crucify him!' The third time he said to them, 'Why? What evil has he done? I have found nothing in him which merits sentence of death. I will chastize him and release him.' But they insisted with shouts, demanding that he should be crucified; and their voices prevailed. So Pilate gave

sentence that their demand should be granted. He
released the man who had been thrown into prison for
disorder and murder, the man they asked for, and Jesus
he delivered to their will.

THIS is an amazing passage. One thing is crystal clear – Pilate
did not want to condemn Jesus. He was well aware that to do
so would be to betray that impartial justice which was the
glory of Rome. He made no fewer than four attempts to avoid
passing sentence of condemnation. He told the Jews to settle
the matter themselves (John 19:6–7). He tried to refer the
whole case to Herod. He tried to persuade the Jews to receive
Jesus as the prisoner granted release at Passover time (Mark
15:6). He tried to effect a compromise, saying he would
scourge Jesus and then release him. It is plain that Pilate was
coerced into sentencing Jesus to death.

How could a Jewish crowd coerce an experienced Roman
governor into sentencing Jesus to death? It is literally true
that the Jews blackmailed Pilate into sentencing Jesus to
death. The basic fact is that, under impartial Roman justice,
any province had the right to report a governor to Rome for
misgovernment, and such a governor would be severely dealt
with. Pilate had made two grave mistakes in his government
of Palestine.

In Judaea the Roman headquarters were not at Jerusalem
but at Caesarea. But in Jerusalem a certain number of troops
were quartered. Roman troops carried standards which were
topped by a little bust of the reigning emperor. The emperor
was at this time officially a god. The Jewish law forbade any
graven image and, in deference to Jewish principles, previous
governors had always removed the imperial images before
they marched their troops into Jerusalem. Pilate refused to
do so; he marched his soldiers in by night with the imperial

image on their standards. The Jews came in crowds to Caesarea to request Pilate to remove the images. He refused. They persisted in their entreaties for days. On the sixth day he agreed to meet them in an open space surrounded by his troops. He informed them that unless they stopped disturbing him with their continuous requests the penalty would be immediate death. 'They threw themselves on the ground, and laid their necks bare, and said they would take death very willingly rather than that the wisdom of their laws should be transgressed.' Not even Pilate could slaughter men in cold blood like that, and he had to yield. Josephus tells the whole story in *The Antiquities of the Jews*, Book 18, Chapter 3. Pilate followed this up by bringing into the city a new water supply and financing the scheme with money taken from the Temple treasury, a story which we have already told in the commentary on Luke 13:1-4.

The one thing the Roman government could not afford to tolerate in their far-flung empire was civil disorder. Had the Jews officially reported either of these incidents there is little doubt that Pilate would have been summarily dismissed. It is John who tells us of the ominous hint the Jewish officials gave Pilate when they said, 'If you release this man you are no friend of the Emperor' (John 19:12). They compelled Pilate to sentence Jesus to death by holding the threat of an official report to Rome over his head.

Here we have the grim truth that the past can rise up and confront us and paralyse us. If we have been guilty of certain actions there are certain things which we no longer have the right to say, otherwise our past will be flung in our faces. We must be careful not to allow ourselves any conduct which will some day make it impossible for us to take the stand we know we ought to take and will entitle others to say, 'You of all people have no right to speak like that.'

But if such a situation should arise, there is only one thing to do – to have the courage to face it and its consequences. That is precisely what Pilate did not possess. He sacrificed justice rather than lose his post; he sentenced Jesus to death in order that he might remain the governor of Palestine. Had he been a man of real courage he would have done what was right and taken the consequences, but his past made him a coward.

THE ROAD TO CALVARY

Luke 23:26–31

As they led Jesus away, they took Simon, a Cyrenian, who was coming in from the country, and on him they laid the cross to carry it behind Jesus.

There followed him a great crowd of the people and of women who bewailed and lamented him. Jesus turned to them. 'Daughters of Jerusalem,' he said, 'do not weep for me, but weep for yourselves, and for your children, because – look you – days are on the way in which they will say, "Happy are those who are barren, and the wombs that never bore, and the breasts which never fed a child." Then they will begin to say to the mountains, "Fall upon us!" and to the hills, "Cover us!" For if they do these things when the sap is in the wood, what will they do when the tree is dry?'

WHEN a criminal was condemned to be crucified, he was taken from the judgment hall and set in the middle of a hollow square of four Roman soldiers. His own cross was then laid upon his shoulders. And he was marched to the place of crucifixion by the longest possible route, while before him marched another soldier bearing a placard with his crime inscribed upon it, so that he might be a terrible warning to anyone else who was contemplating such a crime. That is what they did with Jesus.

He began by carrying his own cross (John 19:17); but under its weight his strength gave out and he could carry it no further. Palestine was an occupied country and any citizen could be immediately pressed into the service of the Roman government. The sign of this was a tap on the shoulder with the flat of the blade of a Roman spear. When Jesus sank beneath the weight of his cross, the Roman centurion in charge looked round for someone to carry it. Out of the country into the city there came Simon from far-off Cyrene, which is modern Tripoli. No doubt he was a Jew who all his life had scraped and saved so that he might be able to eat one Passover at Jerusalem. The flat of the Roman spear touched him on the shoulder and he found himself, suddenly without warning, carrying a criminal's cross.

Try to imagine the feelings of Simon. He had come to Jerusalem to realize the cherished ambition of a lifetime, and he found himself walking to Calvary carrying a cross. His heart was filled with bitterness towards the Romans and towards this criminal who had involved him in his crime.

But if we can read between the lines the story does not end there. The author of *Our Lord's Teaching*, J. A. Robertson, saw in it one of the hidden romances of the New Testament. Mark describes Simon as the father of Alexander and Rufus (Mark 15:21). Now you do not identify a man by the names of his sons unless these sons are well-known people in the community to which you write. There is general agreement that Mark wrote his gospel to the church at Rome. Turn to

Paul's letter to the church at Rome. Among the greetings at the end he writes, 'Greet Rufus, chosen in the Lord, and greet his mother – a mother to me also' (Romans 16:13). So in the Roman church there was Rufus, a Christian of such worth that he could be called one of God's chosen ones, with a mother so dear to Paul that he could call her his mother in the faith. It may well be that this was the same Rufus who was the son of Simon of Cyrene, and his mother was Simon's wife.

It may well be that as he looked on Jesus Simon's bitterness turned to wondering amazement and finally to faith; that he became a Christian; and that his family became some of the most worthy members of the Roman church. It may well be that Simon from Tripoli thought he was going to realize a life's ambition, to celebrate the Passover in Jerusalem at last; that he found himself sorely against his will carrying a criminal's cross; that, as he looked, his bitterness turned to wonder and to faith; and that in the thing that seemed to be his shame he found a Saviour.

Behind Jesus there came a band of women weeping for him. He turned and bade them weep, not for him, but for themselves. Days of terror were coming. In Judaea there was no tragedy like a childless marriage; in fact childlessness was a valid ground for divorce. But the day would come when the woman who had no child would be glad that it was so. Once again Jesus was seeing ahead the destruction of that city which had so often before, and which had now so finally, refused the invitation of God. Verse 31 is a proverbial phrase which could be used in many connections. Here it means, if they do this to one who is innocent, what will they some day do to those who are guilty?

THERE THEY CRUCIFIED HIM

Luke 23:32-8

> Two others who were criminals were brought to be put
> to death with Jesus. When they came to the place which
> is called the place of a skull, there they crucified him,
> and the two criminals, one on his right hand, and one
> on his left. And Jesus said, 'Father, forgive them, for
> they do not know what they are doing.' And, as they
> divided his garments, they cast lots for them. The people
> stood watching, and the rulers gibed at him. 'He saved
> others,' they said. 'Let him save himself if he really is
> the Anointed One of God, the chosen one.' The soldiers
> also mocked him, coming and offering vinegar to him,
> and saying, 'If you are the King of the Jews save
> yourself.' There was also an inscription over him, 'This
> is the King of the Jews'.

WHEN a criminal reached the place of crucifixion, his cross
was laid flat upon the ground. Usually it was a cross shaped
like a T with no top piece against which the head could rest.
It was quite low, so that the criminal's feet were only two or
three feet above the ground. There was a company of pious
women in Jerusalem who made it their practice always to go
to crucifixions and to give the victim a drink of drugged
wine which would deaden the terrible pain. That drink was
offered to Jesus and he refused it (Matthew 27:34). He was
determined to face death at its worst, with a clear mind and
senses unclouded. The victim's arms were stretched out upon
the crossbar, and it was usual for the nails to be driven through
the wrists. The feet were not nailed, but only loosely bound
to the cross. Half-way up the cross there was a projecting
piece of wood, called the saddle, which took the weight of
the criminal, for otherwise the nails would have torn through

his wrists. Then the cross was lifted and set upright in its socket. The terror of crucifixion was this – the pain of that process was terrible but it was not enough to kill, and the victim was left to die of hunger and thirst beneath the blazing noontide sun and the frosts of the night. Many a criminal was known to have hung for a week upon his cross until he died raving mad.

The clothes of the criminal were given as a 'perk' to the four soldiers among whom he marched to the cross. Every Jew wore five articles of apparel – the inner tunic, the outer robe, the girdle, the sandals and the turban. Four were divided among the four soldiers. There remained the great outer robe. It was woven in one piece without a seam (John 19:23–4). To have cut it up and divided it would have ruined it; and so the soldiers gambled for it in the shadow of the cross. It was nothing to them that another criminal was slowly dying in agony.

The inscription set upon the cross was the same placard as was carried before a man as he marched through the streets to the place of crucifixion.

Jesus said many wonderful things, but rarely anything more wonderful than, 'Father, forgive them, for they know not what they do.' Christian forgiveness is an amazing thing. When Stephen was being stoned to death he too prayed, 'Lord, do not hold this sin against them' (Acts 7:60). There is nothing so lovely and nothing so rare as Christian forgiveness. When the unforgiving spirit is threatening to turn our hearts to bitterness, let us hear again our Lord asking forgiveness for those who crucified him and his servant Paul saying to his friends, 'Be kind to one another, tenderhearted, forgiving one another, as God in Christ has forgiven you' (Ephesians 4:32).

The idea that this terrible thing was done in ignorance runs through the New Testament. Peter later said to the people, 'I know that you acted in ignorance' (Acts 3:17). Paul said that they crucified Jesus because they did not know him (Acts 13:27). Marcus Aurelius, the great Roman emperor and Stoic saint, used to say to himself every morning, 'Today you will meet all kinds of unpleasant people; they will hurt you, and injure you, and insult you; but you cannot live like that; you know better, for you are a man in whom the spirit of God dwells.' Others may have in their hearts the unforgiving spirit, others may sin in ignorance; but we know better. We are Christ's men and women; and we must forgive as he forgave.

THE PROMISE OF PARADISE

Luke 23:39–43

> One of the criminals who were hanged kept hurling insults at Jesus. 'Are you not the Anointed One?' he said. 'Save yourself and us.' The other rebuked him. 'Do you not even fear God?' he said. 'For we too are under the same sentence and justly so, for we have done things which deserve the reward that we are reaping; but this man has done nothing unseemly.' And he said, 'Jesus, remember me when you come into your kingdom.' He said to him, 'This is the truth – I tell you – today you will be with me in Paradise.'

IT was of set and deliberate purpose that the authorities crucified Jesus between two known criminals. It was deliberately so staged to humiliate Jesus in front of the crowd and to rank him with robbers.

Legend has been busy with the penitent thief. He is called variously Dismas, Demas and Dumachus. One legend makes him a Judaean Robin Hood who robbed the rich to give to the poor. The loveliest legend tells how the holy family were attacked by robbers when they fled with the child Jesus from Bethlehem to Egypt. Jesus was saved by the son of the captain of the robber band. The baby was so lovely that the young brigand could not bear to lay hands on him but set him free, saying, 'O most blessed of children, if ever there come a time for having mercy on me, then remember me and forget not this hour.' That robber youth who had saved Jesus as a baby met him again on Calvary; and this time Jesus saved him.

The word Paradise is a Persian word meaning *a walled garden*. When a Persian king wished to do one of his subjects a very special honour he made him a companion of the garden which meant he was chosen to walk in the garden with the king. It was more than immortality that Jesus promised the penitent thief. He promised him the honoured place of a companion of the garden in the courts of heaven.

Surely this story tells us above all that it is never too late to turn to Christ. There are other things of which we must say, 'The time for that is past. I am grown too old now.' But we can never say that of turning to Jesus Christ. So long as our hearts continue to beat, the invitation of Christ still stands. As the poet wrote of the man who was killed as he was thrown from his galloping horse,

> Betwixt the stirrup and the ground,
> Mercy I asked, mercy I found.

It is literally true that while there is life there is hope.

THE LONG DAY CLOSES

Luke 23:44-9

> By this time it was about 12 noon, and there was dark-ness over the whole land until 3 pm, and the light of the

340

sun failed. And the veil of the Temple was rent in the
midst. When Jesus had cried with a great voice, he said,
'Father, into your hands I commend my spirit.' When
he had said this he breathed his last. When the centurion
saw what had happened, he glorified God. 'Truly,' he
said, 'this was a good man.' All the crowds, who had
come together to see the spectacle, when they saw the
things that had happened, went home beating their
breasts. And all his acquaintances, and the women who
had accompanied him from Galilee, stood far off and
saw these things.

EVERY sentence of this passage is rich in meaning.

(1) There was a great darkness as Jesus died. It was as if
the sun itself could not bear to look upon the deed that had
been done. The world becomes a dark place indeed wherever
people seek to banish Christ.

(2) The Temple veil was rent in two. This was the veil
which hid the Holy of Holies, the place where dwelt the very
presence of God, the place where no man might ever enter
except the high priest, and he only once a year, on the great
Day of Atonement. It was as if the way to God's presence,
hitherto barred, was thrown open to all. It was as if the heart
of God, hitherto hidden, was laid bare. The birth, life and
death of Jesus tore apart the veil which had concealed God.
'Whoever has seen me', said Jesus, 'has seen the Father' (John
14:9). On the cross, as never before and never again, the love
of God was visible.

(3) Jesus cried with a great voice. Three of the gospels
tell us of this great cry (cf. Matthew 27:50; Mark 15:37).
John, on the other hand, does not mention the great cry but
tells us that Jesus died saying, 'It is finished' (John 19:30). In
Greek and Aramaic 'It is finished' is one word. *It is finished*
and the great cry are, in fact, one and the same thing. Jesus

died with a shout of triumph on his lips. He did not whisper, 'It is finished', as one who is battered to his knees and forced to admit defeat. He shouted it like a victor who has won his last engagement with the enemy and brought a tremendous task to triumphant conclusion. 'Finished!' was the cry of the Christ, crucified yet victorious.

(4) Jesus died with a prayer on his lips. 'Father, into your hand I commit my spirit.' That is Psalm 31:5 with one word added – *Father*. That verse was the prayer every Jewish mother taught her child to say last thing at night. Just as we were taught, maybe, to say, 'This night I lay me down to sleep,' so the Jewish mother taught her child to say, before the threatening dark came down, 'Into thy hands I commit my spirit.' Jesus made it even more lovely for he began it with the word *Father*. Even on a cross Jesus died like a child falling asleep in his father's arms.

(5) The centurion and the crowd were deeply moved as Jesus died. His death did what even his life could not do; it broke even the hardest of hearts. Already Jesus' saying was coming true – 'I, when I am lifted up from the earth, will draw all people to myself' (John 12:32). The magnet of the cross had begun its work, even as he breathed his last.

THE MAN WHO GAVE JESUS A TOMB

Luke 23:50–6

> Look you – there was a man named Joseph, a member of the Sanhedrin, a good and a just man. He had not consented to their counsel and their action. He came from Arimathaea, a town of the Jews, and he lived in expectation of the kingdom of God. He went to Pilate and asked for the body of Jesus. He took it down, and

wrapped it in linen, and laid it in a rock-hewn tomb
where no one had ever yet been laid. It was the day of
preparation, and the Sabbath was beginning. The
women, who had accompanied Jesus from Galilee,
followed and saw the tomb and how his body was laid
in it. Then they went back home and prepared spices
and ointments. And they rested on the Sabbath day
according to the commandment.

IT was the custom that the bodies of criminals were not buried
at all but left to the dogs and the vultures to dispose of; but
Joseph of Arimathaea saved the body of Jesus from that
indignity. There was not much time left that day. Jesus was
crucified on the Friday; the Jewish Sabbath is our Saturday.
But the Jewish day begins at 6 pm. That is to say by Friday at
6 pm the Sabbath had begun. That is why the women had
only time to see where the body was laid and go home and
prepare their spices and ointments for it and do no more, for
after 6 pm all work became illegal.

Joseph of Arimathaea is a figure of the greatest interest.

(1) Legend has it that in the year AD 61 he was sent by
Philip to Britain. He came to Glastonbury. With him he
brought the chalice that had been used at the Last Supper,
and in it the blood of Christ. That chalice became the Holy
Grail, which it was the dream of King Arthur's knights to
find and see. When Joseph arrived in Glastonbury they
say that he drove his staff into the ground to rest on it in
his weariness and the staff budded and became a bush
which blooms every Christmas Day. St Joseph's thorn still
blooms at Glastonbury and to this day slips of it are sent
all over the world. The first church in all England was
built at Glastonbury, and that church which legend links with
the name of Joseph is still a place of pilgrimage for many
Christians.

(2) There is a certain tragedy about Joseph of Arimathaea. He is the man who gave Jesus a tomb. He was a member of the Sanhedrin; we are told that he did not agree with the verdict and the sentence of that court. But there is no word that he raised his voice in disagreement. Maybe he kept silent; maybe he absented himself when he saw that he was powerless to stop a course of action with which he disagreed. What a difference it would have made if he had spoken! How it would have lifted up Jesus' heart if, in that grim assembly of bleak hatred, even one lone voice had spoken for him! But Joseph waited until Jesus was dead, and then he gave him a tomb. It is one of the tragedies of life that we place on people's graves the flowers we might have given them when they were alive. We keep, for their obituary notices and for the tributes paid to them at memorial services and in committee minutes, the praise and thanks we should have given them when they lived. Often, often we are haunted because we never spoke. A word to the living is worth a cataract of tributes to the dead.

THE WRONG PLACE TO LOOK

Luke 24:1-12

On the first day of the week, at the first streaks of dawn, the women came to the tomb, bearing the spices which they had prepared. They found the stone rolled away from the tomb. They entered in, but they did not find the body of the Lord Jesus. While they were at a loss what to make of this – look you – two men stood by them in flashing raiment. They were afraid, and they bowed their faces to the ground. But they said to them, 'Why are you looking for him who is alive among the dead? He is not here; he is risen. Remember how he

said to you, while he was still in Galilee, that the Son of
Man must be betrayed into the hands of sinful men and
that he must be crucified, and that on the third day he
would rise again.' Then they remembered his words;
and they returned from the tomb and brought the news
of all these things to the eleven and to the others. Mary
Magdalene was there, and Joanna, and Mary, the mother
of James. They, and the other women with them, kept
telling these things to the apostles. But their words
seemed to them an idle tale, and they refused to believe
them. But Peter rose up and ran to the tomb; and he
stooped down and saw the linen clothes lying all by
themselves; and he went away wondering in himself at
what had happened.

THE Jewish Sabbath, our Saturday, is the last day of the week
and commemorates the rest of God after the work of creation.
The Christian Sunday is the first day of the week and
commemorates the resurrection of Jesus. On this first
Christian Sunday the women went to the tomb in order to
carry out the last offices of love for the dear dead and to
embalm Jesus' body with their spices.

In the middle east tombs were often carved out of caves in
the rock. The body was wrapped in long linen strips like
bandages and laid on a shelf in the rock tomb. The tomb was
then closed by a great circular stone like a cartwheel which
ran in a groove across the opening. When the women came,
they found the stone rolled away.

Just here we have one of those discrepancies in the accounts
of the resurrection of which those who challenge the claims
of Christianity make so much. In Mark the messenger in the
tomb is a young man in a long white robe (Mark 16:5); in
Matthew he is the angel of the Lord (Matthew 28:2). Here it
is two men in dazzling raiment; and in John it is two angels

(John 20:12). It is true that the differences are there; but it is also true that, whatever the attendant description, *the basic fact of the empty tomb never varies*, and that is the fact that matters. No two people ever described the same episode in the same terms; nothing so wonderful as the resurrection ever escaped a certain embroidery as it was repeatedly told and retold. But at the heart of this story that all-important fact of the empty tomb remains.

The women returned with their story to the rest of the disciples but they refused to believe them. They called it an idle tale. The word used is one employed by Greek medical writers to describe the babbling of a fevered and insane mind. Only Peter went out to see if it might not possibly be true. The very fact that Peter was there says much for him. The story of his denial of his Master was not a thing that could be kept silent; and yet he had the moral courage to face those who knew his shame. There was something of the hero in Peter, as well as something of the coward. The man who was a fluttering dove is on the way to become a rock.

The all-important and challenging question in this story is that of the messengers in the tomb, 'Why are you looking for him who is alive among the dead?' Many of us still look for Jesus among the dead.

(1) There are those who regard him as the greatest man and the noblest hero who ever lived, as one who lived the loveliest life ever seen on earth; but who then died. That will not do. Jesus is not dead; he is alive. He is not merely a hero of the past; he is a living reality of the present. As the poet John Drinkwater wrote:

> Shakespeare is dust, and will not come
> To question from his Avon tomb,
> And Socrates and Shelley keep
> An Attic and Italian sleep.

They see not. But, O Christians, who
Throng Holborn and Fifth Avenue,
May you not meet in spite of death,
A traveller from Nazareth?

(2) There are those who regard Jesus simply as a man whose life must he studied, his words examined, his teaching analysed. There is a tendency to think of Christianity and Christ merely in terms of something to be studied. The tendency may be seen in the quite simple fact of the extension of the study group and the extinction of the prayer meeting. Beyond doubt study is necessary – but Jesus is not only someone to be studied; he is someone to be met and lived with every day. He is not only a figure in a book, even if that book is the greatest in the world; he is a living presence.

(3) There are those who see in Jesus the perfect pattern and example. He is that; but a perfect example can be the most heartbreaking thing in the world. For centuries the birds gave us an example of flight, and yet not till early in the twentieth century was the secret of flight learned. I remember when young being presented at school with a writing book. At the top it had a line of copperplate writing; below it had blank lines on which to copy it. How utterly discouraging were our efforts to reproduce that perfect pattern! But then the teacher came and, with her hand, guided our hands over the lines and we got nearer to the ideal. That is what Jesus does. He is not only the pattern and the example. He helps us and guides us and strengthens us to follow that pattern and example. He is not simply a model for life; he is a living presence to help us to live.

It may well be that our Christianity has lacked an essential something because we too have been looking for him who is alive among the dead.

THE SUNSET ROAD THAT TURNED TO DAWN

Luke 24:13-35

Now – look you – on that same day two of them were
on the way to a village called Emmaus, which is about
seven miles from Jerusalem; and they talked with each
other about all the things which had happened. As they
talked about them, and discussed them, Jesus himself
came up to them and joined them on their way. But
their eyes were fastened so that they did not recognize
him. He said to them, 'What words are these that you
are exchanging with each other as you walk?' And they
stood with faces twisted with grief. One of them, called
Cleopas, answered, 'Are you the only visitor in
Jerusalem who does not know the things that happened
in it in these days?' 'What kind of things?' he said to
them. They said to him, 'The story of Jesus of Nazareth,
who was a prophet mighty in deed and in word before
God and all the people; and how our chief priests and
rulers handed him over to sentence of death and how
they crucified him. As for us – we were hoping that he
was the one who was going to rescue Israel. Yes – and
to add to it all – this is the third day since these things
happened. Yes, and some women of our number
astonished us, for they went early to the tomb, and, when
they did not find his body, they came saying that they
had seen a vision of angels, who said that he was alive.
And some of our company went to the tomb and found
it just as the women had said – but they did not see
him.' He said to them, 'O foolish ones and slow in heart
to believe in all the things that the prophets said! Was it
not necessary that the Anointed One should suffer and
enter into his glory?' And beginning from Moses and
all the prophets, he expounded to them the things

concerning himself in all the Scriptures. As they came
near the village to which they were going, he made as if
he would have gone on; and they pressed him. 'Stay
with us,' they said, 'because it is towards evening, and
the day is already far spent.' So he came in to stay with
them. When he had taken his place at table with them,
he took bread, and blessed it and broke it, and gave it to
them; and their eyes were opened and they recognized
him; and he vanished out of their sight. They said to
each other, 'Was not our heart burning within us while
he was talking to us on the road, as he opened the
Scriptures to us?' And they arose that very hour and
went back to Jerusalem and found the eleven gathered
together and those with them, and found that they were
saying, 'It is a fact that the Lord has risen, and he has
appeared to Simon.' So they recounted all that had
happened on the road, and how he was known to them
in the breaking of bread.

THIS is another of the immortal short stories of the world.

(1) It tells of two people who were walking towards the
sunset. It has been suggested that that is the very reason why
they did not recognize Jesus. Emmaus was west of Jerusalem.
The sun was sinking, and the setting sun so dazzled them
that they did not know their Lord. However that may be, it is
true that the Christian is someone who walks not towards the
sunset but towards the sunrise. Long ago it was said to the
children of Israel that they journeyed in the wilderness
towards the sunrising (Numbers 21:11). The Christian goes
onwards, not to a night which falls, but to a dawn which
breaks – and that is what, in their sorrow and their dis-
appointment, the two on the Emmaus road had not realized.

(2) It tells us of the ability of Jesus to make sense of things.
The whole situation seemed to have no explanation. For these
followers of Jesus all their hopes and dreams were shattered.

There is all the poignant, wistful, bewildered regret in the world in their sorrowing words, 'We were hoping that he was the one who was going to rescue Israel.' They are the words of people whose hopes are dead and buried. Then Jesus came and talked with them, and the meaning of life became clear and the darkness became light. A storyteller makes one of his characters say to the one with whom he has fallen in love, 'I never knew what life meant until I saw it in your eyes.' It is only in Jesus that, even in the bewildering times, we learn what life means.

(3) It tells us of the courtesy of Jesus. He made as if he would have gone on. He would not force himself upon them; he awaited their invitation to come in. God gave us the greatest and the most perilous gift in the world, the gift of free will; we can use it to invite Christ to enter our lives or to allow him to pass on.

(4) It tells how he was known to them in the breaking of bread. This always sounds a little as if it meant the sacrament; but it does not. It was at an ordinary meal in an ordinary house, when an ordinary loaf was being divided, that Jesus was recognized. It has been beautifully suggested that perhaps these people had been present at the feeding of the 5,000, and, as he broke the bread in their cottage home, they recognized his hands again. It is not only at the communion table we can be with Christ; we can be with him at the dinner table too. He is not only the host in his Church; he is the guest in every home. The Christian lives always and everywhere in a Christ-filled world.

(5) It tells of two people who, when they received such great joy, hastened to share it. It was a seven-mile journey back to Jerusalem, but they could not keep the good news to themselves. The Christian message is never fully ours until we have shared it with someone else.

(6) It tells how, when they reached Jerusalem, they found others who had already shared their experience. It is the glory of any Christian to live in a fellowship of people who have all had the same experience. It has been said that true friendship begins only when people share a common memory and can say to each other, 'Do you remember?' Each of us is one of a great fellowship of people who share a common experience and a common memory of their Lord.

(7) It tells that Jesus appeared to Peter. That must remain one of the great untold stories of the world. But surely it is a lovely thing that Jesus should make one of his first appearances to the man who had denied him. It is the glory of Jesus that he can restore the penitent sinner's self-respect.

IN THE UPPER ROOM

Luke 24:36–49

> While they were still speaking, Jesus stood in the midst of them, and said to them, 'Peace to you!' They were terrified and afraid, because they thought that they were seeing a spirit. He said to them, 'Why are you troubled? And why do the questions arise in your heart? See my hands and my feet – that it is I – myself. Handle me and see, for a spirit has not flesh and bones as you see that I have.' And when he had said this he showed them his hands and his feet. When they still thought it too good to be true, and when they were astonished he said to them, 'Have you anything to eat here?' They gave him part of a cooked fish, and he took it and ate it before them.
>
> He said to them, 'These are my words which I spoke to you while I was still with you – that all the things which stand written about me in the law of Moses, and

in the prophets, and in the psalms must be fulfilled.'
Then he opened their minds so that they understood the
Scriptures; and he said to them, 'Thus it is written, that
the Anointed One should suffer and should rise from
the dead on the third day; and that repentance in his
name and forgiveness of sins should be proclaimed to
all nations, beginning from Jerusalem. And – look you
– I send out the promise of my Father upon you. But
stay in this city until you will be clothed with power
from on high.'

HERE we read of how Jesus came to his own when they were
gathered in the upper room. In this passage certain great notes
of the Christian faith are resonantly struck.

(1) It stresses *the reality of the resurrection.* The risen Lord
was no phantom or hallucination. He was real. The Jesus
who died was in truth the Christ who rose again. Christianity
is not founded on the dreams of disordered minds or the
visions of fevered eyes, but on one who in actual historical
fact faced and fought and conquered death and rose again.

(2) It stresses *the necessity of the cross.* It was to the cross
that all the Scriptures looked forward. The cross was not
forced on God; it was not an emergency measure when all
else had failed and when the scheme of things had gone
wrong. It was part of the plan of God, for it is the one place
on earth where, in a moment of time, we see his eternal love.

(3) It stresses *the urgency of the task.* Out to all people
had to go the call to repentance and the offer of forgiveness.
The Church was not left to live forever in the upper room; it
was sent out into all the world. After the upper room came
the worldwide mission of the Church. The days of sorrow
were past and the tidings of joy must be taken to everyone.

(4) It stresses *the secret of power.* They had to wait in
Jerusalem until power from on high came upon them. There

are occasions when the Christian may seem to be wasting time, waiting in a wise passivity. Action without preparation must often fail. There is a time to wait on God and a time to work for God. Fay Inchfawn writes of the days when life is a losing contest with a thousand little things.

> I wrestle – how I wrestle! – through the hours.
> Nay, not with principalities and powers –
> Dark spiritual foes of God's and man's –
> But with antagonistic pots and pans;
> With footmarks on the hall,
> With smears upon the wall,
> With doubtful ears and small unwashen hands,
> And with a babe's innumerable demands.

And then, even in the busyness, she lays aside her work to be for a moment with God.

> With leisured feet and idle hands, I sat.
> I, foolish, fussy, blind as any bat,
> Sat down to listen, and to learn. And lo,
> My thousand tasks were done the better so.

The quiet times in which we wait on God are never wasted; for it is in these times when we lay aside life's tasks that we are strengthened for the very tasks we lay aside.

THE HAPPY ENDING

Luke 24:50–3

> Jesus led them out as far as Bethany; and he raised his hands and blessed them; and as he was blessing them he parted from them, and was borne up into heaven. And when they had worshipped him they returned to

353

Jerusalem with great joy; and they were continually in
the Temple praising God.

THE ascension must always remain a mystery, for it attempts
to put into words what is beyond words and to describe
what is beyond description. But that something of this order
should happen was essential. It was unthinkable that the
appearances of Jesus should grow fewer and fewer until
finally they petered out. That would have effectively wrecked
the disciples' faith. There had to come a day of dividing when
the Jesus of earth finally became the Christ of heaven. But to
the disciples the ascension was obviously three things.

(1) It was *an ending.* The days when their faith was faith
in a flesh-and-blood person and depended on his flesh-and-
blood presence were over. Now they were linked to someone
who was forever independent of space and time.

(2) Equally it was *a beginning.* The disciples did not leave
the scene heartbroken; they left it with great joy, because now
they knew that they had a Master from whom nothing could
separate them any more. In the words of J. G. Whittier's hymn:

> I know not where his islands lift
> Their fronded palms in air;
> I only know I cannot drift
> Beyond his love and care.

'I am sure', said Paul, 'that nothing – nothing in life or death
– can separate us from the love of God in Christ Jesus our
Lord' (cf. Romans 8:38–9).

(3) Further, the ascension gave the disciples the certainty
that they had *a friend, not only on earth, but in heaven.* Surely
it is the most precious thing of all to know that in heaven
there awaits us that self-same Jesus who on earth was
wondrous kind. To die is not to go out into the dark; it is to
go to him.

So they went back to Jerusalem, and they were continually in the Temple praising God. It is not by accident that Luke's gospel ends where it began – in the house of God.

En Garde!

The Institute was getting more crowded every moment, as busloads of school kids came pouring in. Mikey maneuvered his way around the throngs into a large room that had a roped-off stage at one end. "En garde!" came the shout. Mikey jumped. He looked at the stage.

A man and woman all dressed in white and wearing big helmets lunged at each other with swords.

The amazing thing was how quiet it was. There was no clank of metal on metal. Instead, the fencers went back and forth, swords always ready. Then one would jab and the other would instantly block the blade: jab, block. Mikey tensed up. His shoulders jerked with each jab. These were real blades. This was a real sword fight. And the real thing was a zillion times more wonderful than he'd ever imagined.

PUFFIN BOOKS BY DONNA JO NAPOLI

The Bravest Thing
Jimmy, the Pickpocket of the Palace
The Magic Circle
The Prince of the Pond
Shark Shock
Soccer Shock
When the Water Closes Over My Head
Zel

ON GUARD

DONNA JO NAPOLI

PUFFIN BOOKS

Acknowledgments

Thanks go to Mark Masters, Lucia Monfried, Ramneek Pooni,
Daphne Riley, Richard Tchen, and the classes of Ed Gaynor in 1994–95
and of Sheila Marcy in 1995–96 at the Swarthmore Rutledge School.
Thanks also go to my family, especially to Nick Furrow,
who coached me through this.

PUFFIN BOOKS
Published by the Penguin Group
Penguin Putnam Books for Young Readers,
345 Hudson Street, New York, New York 10014, U.S.A.
Penguin Books Ltd, 27 Wrights Lane, London W8 5TZ, England
Penguin Books Australia Ltd, Ringwood, Victoria, Australia
Penguin Books Canada Ltd, 10 Alcorn Avenue, Toronto, Ontario, Canada M4V 3B2
Penguin Books (N.Z.) Ltd, 182-190 Wairau Road, Auckland 10, New Zealand

Penguin Books Ltd, Registered Offices: Harmondsworth, Middlesex, England

First published in the United States of America by Dutton Children's Books,
a division of Penguin Books USA Inc., 1997
Published by Puffin Books, a member of Penguin Putnam Books for Young Readers, 1999

1 3 5 7 9 10 8 6 4 2

THE LIBRARY OF CONGRESS HAS CATALOGED THE DUTTON EDITION AS FOLLOWS:
Napoli, Donna Jo.
On guard / by Donna Jo Napoli—1st ed.
p. cm.
Summary: Excited by a fencing demonstration he happens to see, fourth
grader Mikey starts taking lessons in hopes that the sport will make
him special like his brother and sisters.
ISBN 0-525-45759-3 (HC)
[1. Fencing—Fiction. 2. Brothers and sisters—Fiction. 3. Self-esteem—Fiction.] I.Title
PZ7.N150n 1997 [Fic]—dc-21 96-50155 CIP AC

Puffin Books ISBN 0-14-130118-X

Printed in the United States of America

This one's for Nick,
the Men's Foil Division II
National Champion for 1996

With love,
Mamma

Contents

ON GUARD

Bombs

Mikey pedaled fast. The wind in his face felt great. He turned the corner and raced down the next block. He was flying.

His front tire hit a rock in the road and bounced high. Mikey jerked the handlebars as the bike came down. He swerved just enough to miss crashing into a parked car. Yes!

Raymond pulled up alongside Mikey. "Nice job."

"Thanks." Mikey was surprised. He hadn't realized Raymond was there. He smiled now in happy pride. Mikey had great balance, and that made him a great bike rider. He rode to the corner and stopped. This was where he turned. "Want to come play?"

"I can't. I've got to go work on my sound effects. Listen: Rrrrooom, rrrooom." Raymond paused and coughed three times. Then, "Rrrooom, rooom, rooom." He lifted his eyebrows. "That was a motorcycle with a faulty starter. The coughs were the part where the starter doesn't work."

"Good," said Mikey. "Real good."

"Motorcycles are easy. I want to learn something hard." Raymond waved and rode on.

Mikey understood. Mr. Gaynor, their fourth-grade teacher, was handing out one Olympic medal every Friday to the kid who was best at something that week. Raymond was determined his medal would be for sound effects. Raymond loved sounds.

Mikey loved weapons. Maybe he could win an Olympic medal for making a new weapon. Something original. Something no one else had ever even dreamed of.

The bus from the middle school stopped across the street. Mikey watched his big sister Victoria get off. He gave her a quick wave, zipped up his driveway, and ran into the house.

He dropped his backpack and bike helmet on the hall floor and raced upstairs to the playroom. He knew exactly what he was going to do. He had already made a stockpile of pinecones behind the garage. Pinecones looked a lot like hand grenades. But hand grenades were too small. Mikey would make something much more spectacular. He could fasten together about five or six pinecones into balls. They'd make great bombs. Original bombs.

Calvin sat on the playroom floor surrounded by wooden building blocks. "Hi, Mikey. Want to see my scab?" He stretched out his leg and pointed below the knee.

Mikey glanced at Calvin's scab. Then he looked again. "Hey, that's long. How'd you get it?"

"At recess. We have recess in kindergarten."

"I know. I remember." Mikey searched through the mess on the art shelf. Yes, there was the glue. He grabbed the bottle.

"See how big it is. It's the biggest scab I ever got."

Mikey picked the dried glue off the tip of the bottle. "Yeah. It's great." He turned the bottle upside down. The glue ran slowly down the sides. It was still good.

"Want to know the secret of my scabs?"

"Huh?" Mikey was in a rush. But it was always easier to get away from Calvin if he gave just that one extra minute of attention. "What's the secret?"

"They're really dirt."

"Huh? You can't call dirt a scab. That's dumb." Mikey ran down the stairs before Calvin could answer.

Victoria stood at the bottom of the stairs, hanging up her jacket. "Do you have a new friend?"

"Huh?"

"You were late coming home. Did you go to someone's house?"

"No."

"Too bad." Victoria's voice was singsongy. "I have a new friend."

"Oh. That's nice." Mikey ran past her out the back door. Yippy, their dog, looked up from a hole she was digging in the middle of the chrysanthemums. She barked happily and tagged at Mikey's heels as he went around behind the garage.

The pile of pinecones was a good foot high. Mikey picked out a big one. He squeezed a glob of glue on it and jammed another against it. This was going to be a fantastic bomb. He could almost feel the weight of the Olympic medal hanging around his neck already.

Yippy sniffed at the glue bottle. It tipped over.

Mikey quickly righted the bottle. The second pinecone fell off the instant he let go of it. The wet spot from the glue got covered with dirt. Mikey wiped it off with his shirt.

Yippy sniffed at the glue on Mikey's shirt. Then she licked it.

"Woof," said Mikey. "Stay away."

"Mikey?" called Calvin. "Where are you, Mikey?"

Mikey heard the screen door swing shut. Oh, no. Things had a way of going wrong when Calvin was around. Maybe if Mikey didn't answer, Calvin would go back inside. But just in case, he'd better hurry.

He lined up five pinecones, put globs of glue on the bottoms, and pressed them together. The points stuck out and looked scary. He clutched the whole thing to his chest. He knew he had to hold it tight for a few minutes to make the pinecones stick. He imagined standing on a rooftop and dropping the bomb on the enemy. It would fly apart on impact like shrapnel. "Boom," he said softly.

Yippy barked and bit the sticky clump on Mikey's shirt.

Mikey fended off the dog with his elbows.

"There you are." Calvin came around the corner of the garage. "Oh, you're gluing. I love to glue."

"Woof," said Mikey loudly. "Grrrrr."

Yippy barked and jumped at the pinecone bomb.

Mikey fell backward, with Yippy on top of him.

Calvin laughed and jumped up and down. His arms flapped like a bird's wings.

Mikey pushed the dog aside and stood up. "It's not funny, bird wing." He looked down at the stomped mess of glue and dirt that used to be his bomb. He turned around to scold Yippy, but the dog had settled under a bush, busily chewing away at the plastic glue bottle. Mikey sighed. "There goes the Olympics."

"What's the Olympics?"

"Nothing."

Calvin stood on one foot and held his arms out to each side. "Want to teach me how to ride my bike?"

"No." Mikey kicked at the pile of pinecones.

"You said you would. Last night." Calvin stared

solemnly at Mikey. "I'd teach you. If I was the big brother, I'd teach you."

Mikey sighed again. "All right, already. Get your bike."

Mikey, Victoria, and Calvin sat bent over sheets of paper at the kitchen table. Julie sat on the floor, ripping a piece of paper into little bits and stirring them into a bowl of water.

"Look." Calvin turned his paper to show what he had drawn.

Victoria frowned. "Is that water all around the house? You don't build houses in the middle of water."

"Water," said Julie. "In de water." She held up a spoonful of soggy paper bits. "Food in de water."

"You do if it's a moat," said Mikey. Still, Calvin's house did look like it was about to sink.

"It's Hamsterdam." Calvin pointed at the bottom of the house. "See? It's a boat. They live in boat houses."

"There's no such place as Hamsterdam," said Victoria.

"There is too. In kindergarten today we read a book about Hendrika. She's a cow. She fell in a canal."

"Amsterdam," said Mamma, as she walked through the kitchen. "That's a wonderful story." She carried a laundry basket full of dirty clothes. "Finish up your homework, Victoria and Mikey. Hurry now." She went downstairs to the basement.

"Amsterdam, of course," said Victoria. "It's the capital of Holland. Some people do live in houseboats there."

"Hamter food," said Julie. She put both hands into the bowl.

Calvin smiled. "I told you so." He turned his paper back around. "Have you ever been there?"

"Amsterdam? Of course not," said Victoria. "It's across the ocean."

Mikey turned to his homework again. "I only have three words left."

"You're so lucky," said Victoria. "Your homework is easy."

"It's not easy the way I do it. I put three spelling words in each sentence."

"I used to do that, too." Victoria pulled her braid over her shoulder and picked at the ends of it. "That's the only way to make it interesting."

Mikey tapped his pencil on the paper. "Give me a sentence with *planetarium*, *breathless*, and *fixture*."

Victoria twisted her mouth. "There is no sentence with those three words."

"There has to be."

"Let me guess: Your class is going to a planetarium, isn't it?"

"It's part of our field trip to the Franklin Museum on Thursday."

"I knew it. Fourth-grade teachers are so predictable. I bet you've got words all about the sky in your spelling list."

Mikey looked down at the word *constellation*. He put one hand over the top of his paper so Victoria couldn't see. After all, Mr. Gaynor was a nice teacher. Mikey owed him that loyalty. "Just give me a sentence with those three words."

"Well, how about something deranged, like *'The bathroom fixture was shaped like a planetarium, so it left me breathless'*?"

"I can't write a sentence with *bathroom* in it."

"Of course you can. That's where you find fixtures."

"Everyone would laugh at me if I wrote *bathroom*."

Victoria sighed. "Fourth graders are so pathetic."

Mikey swallowed hard. "The sentence has to start with *M*, anyway, 'cause I already wrote an *M*."

"*Mikey* starts with *M*, right?" said Calvin. "*Calvin* starts with *C*. C-A-L-V-I-N."

Mamma came up the stairs. "That's right, Calvin. Very good. Bath time, everyone. And, Mikey, don't forget to pick up your bike helmet and put it in your cubby." Mamma scooped Julie into her arms and headed upstairs.

"I take showers now, Ma," called Victoria after her.

Lately Victoria had shifted to calling Mamma 'Ma.' Mikey felt odd every time she did it. Victoria stood up. "So it's not bath time for me. It's shower time." She gathered her papers. "Erase your *M*, Mikey. It's all messy, anyway."

"It's not messy. That's how I write."

"Just because you're left-handed doesn't mean you have to write like a monkey."

Mikey looked at his *M*. It wasn't so bad. Victoria just liked to pick on him. Like a chicken, picking at things in the chicken yard. "Kpok," said Mikey. "Kpok, kpok, kpok."

Victoria looked at him, stupefied. "You sound like a chicken."

"Kpok," said Mikey. "Someday I'll drop bombs in your bed."

"Bombs? Don't be ridiculous, Mikey." Victoria ran up the stairs.

Mikey gripped the pencil tight. He carefully wrote *My kitchen fixture was shaped like a planetarium, so it left me breathless.* He underlined *fixture, planetarium,* and *breathless.* Then he put everything away on the cupboard shelf that was his. Mamma called it his cubby, just like the cubby Mikey used to have in kindergarten when he was little. When he was as dumb and happy as Calvin. When he didn't have to worry about things like winning Olympic medals.

He climbed the stairs, pulling off his shirt as he went. Did he really write like a monkey?

Victoria deserved a bomb in her bed.

Only pinecone bombs weren't real bombs. Mikey needed to do something real. And he needed to do it well. Well enough to win the Olympic medal for it.

That would show Victoria.

Cookbooks

Mr. Gaynor cleared his throat. "We're not having guitar lessons in music class today."

"Let's do kazoos instead," said Stephen. "I'm good at kazoos."

"We're not going to music class at all." Mr. Gaynor smiled. "Instead, we're going to the library to do research."

Stephen groaned.

Research? Mikey had never done research. He leaned forward in his seat.

"What do we have to do research for?" asked Pete.

"All of you are going to do a research project on something you love and how it has changed through the ages."

"I can write about my little brother," said Jennifer Braid. "He's changed a lot through the ages."

There were three Jennifers in the class: Jennifer B., Jennifer M., and Jennifer S. Mikey had dubbed them Jennifer Braid, Jennifer Mouth, and Jennifer Snot.

Jennifer Braid had a long braid, of course. Jennifer Mouth never talked, but she did have a pretty mouth. And Jennifer Snot had a cold, and it was still as hot as summer.

Mr. Gaynor shook his head. "It's got to be something that's been around a lot longer than your brother."

Guns, thought Mikey. Of course. Guns had changed a lot over the years.

"It takes time to do research," said Mr. Gaynor. He sat on the edge of his desk and leaned forward. "That's why we're going to the library now to get books. You'll have till the end of October to do the project. Between now and then, read your books and talk to your parents about your ideas."

Parents? Oh, no. Mamma hated guns.

Pete waved his hand. "Can I do it on candy?"

"Sure, candy's a great idea."

Candy was a great idea. Mikey perked up. There were plenty of things he loved besides guns. Like baseball. Mikey was a good pitcher. He had great aim. "Can I do it on baseball?"

"Baseball hasn't been around long enough. You want something that goes back at least a thousand years."

"How do we know what goes back a thousand years?" asked Jennifer Braid.

"You don't yet. That's why you need to do research." Mr. Gaynor swung his legs. "Whoever does the best research project will get the Olympic medal that week."

A half hour later Mikey stood in line at the librarian's checkout desk. The books he held were weighty. They were about food all around the world. Mikey was going to do his research project on cooking because his parents always said he was a superb cook. Cooking was a foolproof way to win an Olympic medal.

Mikey set the books on the desk and pushed them along with him as the line moved ahead. He had already chosen the recipe he would try first: stuffed baked cucumbers. It was Chinese.

"What're you doing with those books?"

Mikey turned around and faced Bill. "Huh?"

"Food books." Bill wrinkled his nose. "Sort of like cookbooks." His cheeks were beefy red, his hair was white blond, and he was sort of chubby. Mr. Gaynor seemed to like him. In fact, Mr. Gaynor had awarded the first Olympic medal of the year to Bill. It said, "1st Prize—R." The R stood for readiness. It hung around Bill's neck on a ribbon, and Bill was pulling on it right now.

But Mikey wasn't so sure about Bill. Bill's family had just moved to town and all Mikey really knew about Bill was that he talked loud. Mikey looked down. Maybe if he acted like he was thinking about something else, Bill would forget all about him.

"The closest I've ever been to cooking," said Bill, talking louder, "was lunchtime at camp. I made mustard sandwiches every day."

Mikey looked up. "Mustard sandwiches?"

"Yeah, cheese and mustard."

"That sounds good."

Bill rubbed his stomach, as though enjoying the memory. "They were. They were delicious 'cause the cheese tasted like nothing."

Mikey liked cheese.

"But real cooking, that's different. I bet no other boys are going to choose cookbooks."

Suddenly Mikey picked up his cookbooks and walked to the shelves he'd gotten them from. He shoved them back into place. His throat felt tight. He wasn't sure Bill was calling him a sissy, but it wasn't worth finding out.

He walked to a different section of the library, sat on the floor, and picked a book off the shelf at random. This one turned out to be on boats.

Mikey didn't love boats. But he needed a research project. He opened the book. A picture of a schooner in the middle of the ocean stared back at him. Water wasn't Mikey's favorite thing. He had learned to swim just last summer—and he was okay at it. But not good enough to feel safe in a boat in the middle of the ocean. He turned the page quickly and read about Eskimo umiaks.

Mr. Gaynor came striding into the library. "Okay, class," he called softly. "Library time is over. If you haven't already checked out your books, do it fast. Then form a line silently." He held up his right hand, and Jennifer Snot quickly got into line first. Jennifer Snot loved to be first at everything.

Within minutes almost everyone in the class was in line, each one holding just the right books for their projects.

Mikey looked again at the book in his hands. His heart sank, but there was no time to pick anything else now. He took the book over to the librarian's desk. He waited while Mrs. Rowe, the librarian, typed something into her computer.

Bill came up behind him again. Bill seemed to pop up behind Mikey every time Mikey did anything. He peered over Mikey's shoulder. "Boats? You love boats?"

Mikey shrugged.

"I like boats, too." Bill moved up alongside Mikey. He smiled. "That gives me an idea." He paused.

Mikey was about to ask what Bill's idea was when he glanced at the books Bill was holding. "Hey, those are the cookbooks."

"Yeah. Why'd you put them back?"

"I thought . . . I don't know."

"Well, I'm glad you did." Bill smiled down at his books. "I love desserts." He gave a little laugh and rubbed his stomach like he'd done before. "I guess you can tell."

Mikey clutched his boat book so tight his fingers hurt. Nothing was going right. Bill had the books that Mikey really wanted. And Mikey had a boat book. A yucky boat book. He felt slightly woozy, almost as though he were seasick. He imagined an Olympic medal falling into the ocean, sinking, sinking, sinking.

Fun

Mikey walked in the front door. "Hello," he called out, yanking at the strap of his bike helmet.

Their bird, Dragon, sang out from his cage, as if in greeting. Mikey whistled to Dragon.

Calvin came running up the stairs from the basement. "Hi, Mikey." His hands were grimy, and there was dirt smeared across one cheek. "Me and Mamma are shoveling."

"Shoveling in the basement?"

"I turned over a board and wiggly things ran out." Calvin jumped in a circle. "Mamma screamed."

"Mikey," called Mamma right then. "Can you help me? I've got two big garbage cans to carry out to the driveway."

Mikey whistled to Dragon again. Dragon was a parakeet. Mikey had named him Dragon when they first got him because he was all green. Victoria had said that was the worst name she'd ever heard for a bird. But it had stuck—and Mikey was glad it had stuck. Dragon's name was one of Mikey's triumphs over Victoria.

Most of the time Dragon was full of songs. Right now Dragon's song was almost sweet enough to make Mikey forget about his boat book. He put his backpack and helmet in his cubby. Then he went down the basement stairs.

"Can you believe this mess?" Mamma looked all around, but she didn't seem upset. She seemed kind of happy. "This place has been flooded so many times, at the edges the floor was three inches deep with mud. I can't believe I've let it stay this way so long."

Mikey took one handle of a garbage can and tried to pull it. It was heavy. "Why're you cleaning it out, anyway?"

Mamma took the other handle. "I'm not just cleaning. I'm going to pound the accumulated lime off the walls with a hammer . . ."

"I'm going to help," said Calvin. "I get to pound. Kindergarteners can pound."

"And then I'm going to cement up the cracks and Thoro-seal the walls." Mamma panted as they lugged the garbage can up the steps. "I got a book from the library on how to waterproof basements. Last of all, I'll wash and paint the floor."

Calvin raced past Mamma and opened the door.

Mamma and Mikey carried the garbage can out to the driveway and set it down. "Just one more can, Mikey."

"Sure, Mamma." Mikey looked at Mamma's sweaty face. "Why're you doing all this?"

"It'll be a playroom," said Mamma. "It doesn't make sense for our basement to be nothing but a place for the washer and dryer. And if it stays dry after the first heavy rain, I'll even put a carpet on the playroom floor."

"My playroom," said Calvin.

"Everyone's playroom, dirt cheek," said Mikey to Calvin.

Mikey and Mamma carried out the second can of muck. It was just as heavy as the first. "I need a shower," said Mamma. "I'm all sticky and stinky."

"Paul threw up in kindergarten today," said Calvin. "That was sticky and stinky."

"Yuck," said Mikey.

Mamma pushed her hair out of her face. "This is sort of fun, you know? It feels good to get tired from hard labor." She smiled. "Thanks, boys." Then she went upstairs.

Mikey suddenly remembered his research project. The sooner he started it, the sooner it would be over. And the sooner it was over, the sooner he'd be able to forget all about boats and turn his attention back to winning that Olympic medal. "I've got work to do," he said.

"Work?" Calvin stood beside him. "You just got home. Let's play catch."

"You can't catch," said Mikey.

Calvin reached into his pocket and took out a giant pretzel. "Here." He gave it to Mikey. "I saved it for you. Mamma was about to finish the whole box, but I saved you that one."

Mikey loved pretzels. He wiped it off and ate it. "All right. We can play catch for a little while." He went to his cubby and got out his baseball and glove. Then he headed out the kitchen door with Calvin at his heels.

"You ready?"

Calvin nodded. He squeezed his eyes shut and thrust his hands forward.

"Open your eyes, Calvin."

Calvin opened his eyes.

"I've told you a zillion times: You can't catch with your eyes closed. I'll throw it easy, okay?"

Calvin nodded. "Okay."

Mikey tossed the ball.

Calvin shut his eyes, and the ball hit him in the chest. He opened his eyes and ran to get the ball. He threw it. It went over Mikey's head and bounced across the driveway, plopping into the raspberry brambles.

Mikey got down on his hands and knees and reached his arm carefully under the thorny canes. "Got it." He stood up. "Ready?" He tossed the ball again.

Calvin shut his eyes and waved his hands over his head. The ball hit him in the arm. He opened his eyes and ran after it.

"Look, Calvin. I think you should do something else."

Calvin picked up the ball and threw it wildly. It slammed against the side of the garage.

Mikey got the ball. "Go practice on your bike." He threw the ball up and caught it in his mitt.

"Will you help me?"

"No. I've got to get to work."

Calvin pulled on the hem of his T-shirt. "I can't do it without you."

"Then ride your tricycle."

Mikey threw the ball up in the air and caught it again. He watched Calvin come riding out of the garage on the old tricycle, which had been new with Victoria, semi-beat-up with Mikey, and now totally a wreck with Calvin. Poor Julie. By the time she got it, it probably wouldn't have any wheels left.

Calvin smiled. "You catch good."

Mikey wished Calvin hadn't said that. Calvin was always saying things to make Mikey feel guilty.

"And you pass good, too."

"Passes are in football," said Mikey.

"You throw good. That's what I meant. And you run fast."

It was true. Mikey was quick on his feet. If Calvin kept up the flattery, Mikey would have to give him a bike lesson.

The kitchen door opened. Yippy bounded out with Julie right behind, holding her rag doll by the arm. Mamma leaned out the door. Her wet hair dripped on the shoulders of her robe. "Julie woke up. Watch her while I get dressed, will you, Mikey?" She took the rag doll from Julie. "Let me put this away while you play, okay?" Then she looked back at Mikey. "And no throwing that ball while Julie's around." Mamma closed the door.

Calvin got off his tricycle. "You have to put the ball away. Want to wrestle?"

"I'm twice your size, Calvin. I'm bigger than you than Victoria is than me."

"What?" said Calvin.

"We can't wrestle."

"Yes, we can. I love to wrestle," said Calvin. He grabbed Yippy around the neck and fell to the ground with her.

Julie laughed. "Jump baby dog." She flung herself on top of Calvin and Yippy.

Mikey tossed the ball in the air and caught it. Then he thought about how Mamma would scold him for doing that around Julie. "Let's all go inside. Come on, I've got things to do."

Calvin disentangled himself from Julie and Yippy. "What are we going to do?"

"Not we—me. My research project."

"What's that?"

"It's some dumb thing about boats."

"I love boats," said Calvin. "Boats bash into each other."

"In wars. Only we can't even play war because Mamma doesn't let us point guns. Mamma doesn't let us do anything fun." Mikey thought about an enemy stalking into their yard right now and killing him and Calvin and Julie. Then Mamma would be sorry she never let them learn warfare.

"You can use seeds," said Calvin.

"Seeds? What for?"

Calvin dug around in his pocket. He brought out a handful of sunflower seeds. He threw one on the ground. "Boom!" He laughed. "Seeds are good for war."

"Calvin, that's the dumbest thing I ever heard. You get dumber every day." First Mamma thought cleaning the garage was fun; now Calvin thought throwing seeds instead of shooting guns was fun.

Julie picked up the seed. "Boom!" she screamed. She ran over and kissed Mikey on the arm. "Boom, boom, boom."

Everyone in this family was crazy.

Codes

Mikey sat on the bedroom floor and wrote carefully in fluorescent purple crayon. He carried the piece of paper over to the mirror on the closet door. The warm glow of satisfaction filled him. Maybe this project was going to be fun, after all.

"Dinnertime," said Calvin, galloping into the room. "What're you doing, Mikey?"

"It's a secret code." Mikey showed the paper to Calvin.

"I love secrets." Calvin touched it gently. "Is it magic?"

"Uh-uh. It says something, but only I know what."

"What use is a code only you know?" Victoria stood in the doorway.

"You shouldn't eavesdrop," said Mikey.

"I wasn't eavesdropping. Mamma said to get you for dinner."

"You were spying," said Mikey.

"Who would want to spy on you? Besides, I have better things to do." She tossed her braid over her shoulder.

"Like what?"

"Like finding a newspaper article for my current-events paper." Victoria leaned over Calvin's shoulder and looked at the paper. "Hmmm. That's a mirror code, isn't it?"

Mikey snatched the paper from Calvin and folded it.

"It says SHIPS," said Victoria. "All you have to do is hold it up to the mirror, and you can read it."

"You saw me, spy face."

"No, I didn't. It's obvious."

Pick pick pick, thought Mikey. "Kpok, kpok." He stuck the paper in his pocket. "If we were on a ship, I'd never write you a note in code, even if you were dying."

"But you'd write to me, wouldn't you, Mikey?" Calvin tugged on Mikey's arm. "I love codes."

"Why would I want a note in code if I was dying?" Victoria put a hand on her hip. "You're losing your mind."

"Dinner!" called Mamma from the dining room.

"You'd make a horrible pirate," said Mikey. "Calvin would be a zillion times better than you."

"Goody." Calvin slapped his chest with both hands. "I get to be a pirate." He marched around

Victoria. "And Dragon can be our parrot. He can tell us where the treasures are."

"Dragon can't even talk," said Victoria. "I'm going back to my current events paper. It's all about moon glow."

"Moon glow," murmured Calvin. "Oh, it's about moon glow."

"That's right," said Victoria. "Scientists just discovered that the light of the full moon causes the earth to heat up. Only a little bit—just point zero three degrees."

Mikey didn't know what "point zero three degrees" meant. Victoria was showing off. "The moon isn't good for anything."

"Yes, it is," said Calvin. "The moon's a lot more useful than the sun, 'cause it shines at night when you need it."

"Calvin!" Victoria looked shocked. "That is so illogical, I can't even begin to explain. You're hopeless. Both of you."

"Last call," said Mamma. "Come down or starve."

"Pass the peas, please," said Daddy. He looked meaningfully at Calvin. "Calvin, what letter did I use over and over at the beginning of the words? Listen again: *Pass the peas, please.*"

Calvin looked intently at Daddy. He put his lips together and mouthed the words slowly. *"P?"*

"You got it." Daddy smiled. "Good work."

"I love *P*," said Calvin. "*Pink* starts with *P*."

"*Pirate* starts with *P*," said Mikey.

Victoria looked at Mikey. "Unless you're deranged and spell it backward in a secret code."

Mikey took a gulp of milk. He imagined Victoria in a duel, swords flashing, backed to the edge of the ship, about to get her head cut off. He'd probably have to be the one to come to her rescue. "A terrible pirate, spy face," he said softly.

"But I'll be a good pirate," said Calvin.

Victoria lifted her chin.

"So, Victoria," said Daddy quickly, looking anxiously from Mikey to Victoria, "what did you learn in school today?"

"You can't ask a sixth grader a question like that." Victoria put a ring of purple onion on her hamburger. "We don't learn things in one day. We work on them over time."

Daddy chewed his hamburger thoughtfully. "So what are you working on?"

"Countries." Victoria spread spicy brown mustard on her bun. "We each got a country to study. Mine's Ireland. I have to learn about everything Irish. Then I'll give a class report."

"Eat," said Julie. She put her finger on a pea and squashed it. "Eat pea." She searched around her plate. "Pea all gone. Eat bun." She squished her bun in her fingers.

Mikey expected Mamma to tell Julie not to play with her food. But Mamma just kept eating. Mikey put some peas from his plate onto Julie's. Then he ate potato salad. He had made it just right—with lots of diced celery and onions. It really was a shame he wasn't doing his research project on cooking.

Julie dropped her squished bun. "Yippy," she called.

Yippy bounded out from under the table and pounced on the bun. She ate it in one bite. Then she sat at Julie's side.

"I told you not to feed her from the table, Julie. That teaches her to beg, and a begging dog is a nuisance." Mamma's voice was stern. "Please don't do it again."

"That was a good meal." Daddy smiled and pushed his empty plate forward. "Well, now, what about you, Mikey?"

"Huh?" said Mikey.

"What are you learning in school?"

"I'm doing a research project."

"Oh?" Daddy rubbed his chin. "A research project in fourth grade? What happened to good old learning about fractions and geography and all those things?"

"We're going to do fractions," said Mikey. "After

I do ships. But I didn't want to do ships. That's why I'm trying to do something with pirates—to make it more interesting. Pirates are great. I wanted to do guns." Mikey looked quickly at Mamma, who was looking at him with a blank face. "Or cooking. Chinese cooking. Baked cucumbers. I bet I could have won an Olympic medal for them. But Bill checked out my books."

Everyone looked at Mikey in silence for a moment.

"You don't need a secret code," said Victoria. "No one can understand you anyway. You talk like a madman."

Mikey looked right at Victoria. "Kpok," he said. "Kpok, kpok, kpok."

"What . . ." began Daddy.

"Wait," said Mamma softly. "Mikey, what were you saying about cooking?"

"Cook, eat." Julie put an onion ring on her nose. It fell to the floor. Yippy smelled it and sneezed. Julie clapped.

"I don't want to talk about it now." Mikey took another helping of potato salad and stuffed his mouth. It had a perfect blend of mayonnaise and mustard. The best potato salad in the world.

Mamma kept her eyes on Mikey. "I like Chinese food, too."

Daddy looked at Mikey as though he was about to try to ask something again. Then he abruptly turned to Mamma. "Where are the pretzels? Pretzels would make a fine addition to this meal."

Victoria stood up. "I'll go get the box."

"Sit down," said Mamma. "They're gone."

"Mamma ate them," said Calvin. "All except the last one. I saved the last one for Mikey."

Daddy rubbed his chin again. "You ate all the pretzels? I just bought a big box yesterday."

"Don't look at me that way," said Mamma. "I like pretzels. So, Victoria, tell us about life at your big new middle school."

"It's good," said Victoria. "There are three elementary schools that feed the middle school, so everyone began the year strangers to two-thirds of the kids. And that means you get a chance to make new friends. I know a lot of cool new people already. I must know at least half the kids in my grade."

"Good use of fractions," said Daddy. "See, Mikey?" Mikey blinked at Daddy. Daddy blinked back. "So, who have you met new in your class this year, Mikey?"

"Bill." Mikey had met a lot of new people this year—people who he'd never been in class with before—but Bill's name popped out of his mouth because Bill was newer than anyone else; after all, he had just moved to town.

"The Bill who did something with books?" said Mamma.

"Yeah, Bill."

"Bill Petrow?" asked Victoria.

"That might be his last name," said Mikey suspiciously. Victoria always managed to learn odd things, like last names, and then somehow she'd use that information against him.

Victoria finished her peas and put her fork down. "John told me his little brother Bill was in your class. John's the smartest boy in my class that I know. The rest of the boys are lame."

"I hate that word, Victoria. I wish you wouldn't use it." Mamma took Victoria's empty plate and put it on top of hers. "Are you through, Calvin?"

Calvin shoved the rest of his pickle in his mouth. "Yeth."

Mamma added Calvin's plate to the stack in front of her.

"Sarah had a birthday party in school today," said Calvin. "I'm going to have a birthday party in school soon. Aren't I?"

"Two weeks, Calvin, and you'll be five." Mamma stood up. "We have a special dessert. Julie, do you want to serve it?"

"Cake." Julie climbed out of her booster seat and off the chair. She went to the counter. Mamma handed her a basket. Julie slid it onto the table. "Eat." She beamed.

"Cupcakes," said Daddy.

"They're tiny and cute," said Victoria.

"I love them." Calvin squashed a cupcake into his mouth.

"Julie made them," said Mamma. "All by herself."

"That's impossible," said Mikey. He looked around the table. Everyone was eating cupcakes. No one paid any attention to the fact that Julie couldn't have made cupcakes all by herself. Not even Victoria. Why wasn't Victoria saying Mamma was illogical? "It's impossible," he said louder.

"No, it isn't. I bought a mix and she cracked in an egg and poured the milk and stirred."

"But you're the one who put it in the oven."

"No. I bought these little tins, see?" Mamma took a miniature cupcake tin from the cupboard. "Julie filled them and put them in the toaster oven to bake. I just stood beside her."

"They're great," said Daddy. "Julie's the best little cook."

Julie clapped her hands.

Everyone clapped.

How could they betray Mikey like this? Everyone knew he was the best cook in the family. "I made the potato salad."

Daddy looked at Mikey with wide eyes. "Oh. And it was great potato salad, too. You're a fine cook, Mikey."

A fine cook? Mikey tried to calm himself. He knew

Daddy was just praising Julie because she was only two—and for a two-year-old, making cupcakes was terrific. Daddy didn't really think Julie was a better cook than Mikey. But maybe he thought Julie was a better cook than Mikey had been at two. Maybe by the time Julie was in fourth grade, she'd be making fantastic feasts.

Mikey was stupid to think he'd have won the Olympic medal for cooking. Maybe he'd never win the Olympic medal.

Julie tapped Mikey's arm. She held up a cupcake. Her eyes stared intently from her fat little face. "Eat."

Mikey ate the cupcake. "It's good, Julie." And it was. Julie was a good cook. "Thanks," he said sadly.

Julie clapped.

Swords

The Franklin Institute was on Benjamin Franklin Parkway. That made sense. Mikey fixed the street sign in his mind so that if he got separated from his class, he could ask people how to get back to the corner of Twentieth Street and Benjamin Franklin Parkway. That's where the bus would pick the class up at noon.

The class was divided into groups, which would tour the Institute together. Mikey was in a group with Raymond and Jennifer Snot and Alison. Alison's mother was in charge. She kept looking down at an index card that had their names on it. Then she'd lock eyes with them and say things like "You're Raymond. Oh, no, you're Mikey, right? That's right." After the third time, Mikey wondered if she was all right in the head.

"I want to go through the heart first," said Alison. Mikey nodded his head in agreement. The thing he most remembered from the last time he'd been here was the giant heart that you climbed through.

Alison's mother smiled nervously. "Well, if that's what everyone wants."

"I didn't vote for the heart," said Raymond.

"Oh, come on," said Alison. "It's the best part."

"All right," said Raymond. "But I didn't vote for it." He blew air through his lips so they flapped noisily. Then he moved over close to Mikey. "That was a horse noise."

Mikey nodded.

Jennifer Snot sneezed.

Alison's mother handed Jennifer Snot a tissue.

They all followed Alison, who ran ahead, twisting her way through the masses of other kids, to the heart. Mikey went up the narrow staircase inside the heart, Raymond behind him and some unknown kid in front of him. There was a continuous flow of kids in front and behind, almost like blood cells coursing through the four chambers of the heart. Pump whoosh whoosh.

As Mikey came out of the heart, Bill bumped into him. "This is boring." He held his Olympic medal out straight from his neck and swung it hard. It circled his neck halfway and flopped on his back. He pulled on the ribbon until the medal hung down his chest again. "Want to go slide the weights?"

Mikey didn't know what Bill was talking about. "No, thanks."

"I passed a demonstration of wave effects on ships. You know, with how much you like boats and all, we should go see it."

Mikey shook his head. He didn't care about boats; he cared about pirates. He cared about hidden treasures and high adventure and, especially, wild sword fights. He glanced away. Alison's mother was looking around in a frenzy. "I've got to go." He ran and joined his group.

A voice came over the loudspeaker, announcing that the airplane would be taking off in fifteen minutes. That was the simulated flight that Mr. Gaynor had told them about.

"I get to be pilot first," said Jennifer Snot. And she sneezed.

Alison's mother unfolded the floor plan of the Institute. "Okay, I can get us there. Stay right behind me." She marched off briskly, clutching the floor plan with both hands.

Alison and Jennifer Snot held hands and skipped behind Alison's mother. They kept bumping into people and giggling.

Raymond took giant steps behind them, swinging his head to each side. He looked over his shoulder at Mikey. "Horses toss their manes."

The Institute was getting more crowded every moment, as busloads of school kids came pouring in, followed by haunted-looking mothers, and teachers shouting directions. Mikey hurried so he wouldn't lose his group. He followed Raymond's striped shirt, maneuvering his way around the throngs into a large room that had a roped-off stage at one end. "En garde!" came the shout. Mikey jumped. He looked at the stage.

A man and woman all dressed in white and wearing big helmets lunged at each other with swords. Mikey pushed his way toward them. The swords had skinny blades. But they had big, beautiful silver bell guards. Mikey held on to the rope at the edge of the stage. The fencers wore special white sneakers, and their feet moved super fast back and forth in front of him. They had on thick white socks that came up to their pants, which came down to below the knees.

The amazing thing was how quiet it was. There was no clank of metal on metal. Instead, the fencers went back and forth, swords always ready. Then one would jab and the other one would instantly block the blade: jab, block. It all happened in a couple of seconds. Mikey tensed up. His shoulders jerked with each jab. These were real blades. This was a real sword fight. And the real thing was a zillion times more wonderful than he'd ever imagined.

Something caught Mikey's eye. A man sat on the

corner of the stage and waved at him with one hand while he twirled the tip of his mustache with the other. When Mikey turned his head to him, the man lifted his eyebrows and gestured to the fencers with his thumb. He pointed at Mikey, then he pointed at a stack of pamphlets on the stage floor.

Mikey picked up a pamphlet. It read: Fencing Academy of Philadelphia. He glanced at the silent, mustached man. But the man was looking at his watch.

And suddenly Mikey was being pulled backward. He stumbled and turned. Alison's mother had him by the arm.

"Oh, I'm so glad I found you." Alison's mother's voice trembled. For one terrible moment Mikey thought she was going to hug him. He drew back. That seemed to do the trick: She blinked several times. "Now you have to stay near me. The other ones are on the flight and you're missing the whole thing. Alison is in charge of them. She's so helpful." Alison's mother's voice caught. "I didn't know where you were. I was afraid something dreadful had happened." She moved her hands as she talked, and the twisted remains of the floor plan shook from her right fist.

Mikey didn't care about the simulated flight. But he was sorry he'd worried Alison's mother. "I was watching the fencing."

Alison's mother looked bewildered, as though Mikey had spoken gibberish. "Well, we can go wait outside the airplane and then we'll all go together to learn about atomic energy. You want to know about atomic energy, don't you?" Her voice cracked.

"Sure I do." Mikey spoke soothingly. "Sure."

In the next few hours Mikey's group visited exhibits on atomic energy and virtual reality and computers. They studied demonstrations of wave effects and weather reporting and static electricity. They went on a real train that actually moved a few feet, and they played on the world's largest pinball machine, and they got cricks in their necks looking up at the long planetarium show. But Mikey saw hardly any of it. All he saw were the two figures in white dancing back and forth in his head, swords ready.

"Mamma!" Mikey clattered down the basement steps.

Mamma turned around. She held a hammer in her right hand. There was white dust in her hair and eyebrows and all over her face. Her eyes and nose and mouth looked like wet black holes. Her clothes were covered with white.

Calvin stood beside her. He was ordinary colored except for his hands, which were white with dust. He smiled. "Hi, Mikey."

"Mamma, I've got to take lessons."

Mamma rubbed the back of her hand across her nose and mouth, exposing a wide streak of skin in the white background. She put her hammer on the floor. "Lessons?"

Mikey took the fencing pamphlet out of his pocket. "Look at this."

Mamma rubbed her hands on the back of her jeans. They were still grimy. She reached for the pamphlet. Mikey didn't want his precious pamphlet to get dirty, but Mamma had to see it. He let her take it.

"Fencing?"

"It's wonderful, Mamma. They practically fly at each other. They're so fast, like snakes striking."

"Swords, Mikey . . ."

"Swords?" said Calvin. "Pirate swords?"

"It's a sport, Mamma. It's not like a weapon. See?" Mikey pointed at the words on the pamphlet. "It talks about 'the modern sport of fencing' right here."

"I'm surprised at you, Mikey. You're my cautious one. How could you want to take up a dangerous sport like fencing?"

"They wear helmets that have net wire across their faces. And a thick glove on the sword hand. And these neat padded outfits. It's safe. Plus the swords don't look like regular swords. They've got squared-off sides. You can't get hurt."

"They have tips, don't they?"

"Tips?"

"The pointed tip, Mikey. That could hurt."

"No one got hurt, Mamma."

Mamma held the pamphlet in her hand and walked slowly up the steps to the kitchen. "What do you mean, no one got hurt? Did you see fencers?"

"There was a demonstration at the Franklin Institute."

Mamma put the pamphlet on the table and washed her hands in the kitchen sink. She turned the burner on under the tea kettle. "Want some banana bread?"

"I do," said Calvin. "Can I take lessons, too?"

"No." Mamma gave Calvin a dishrag. She watched while he wiped off his hands. Then she put a plate of sliced banana bread on the table. "When are the lessons? How much do they cost?"

These were good questions. Mamma was actually thinking about it. Mikey whipped his arm to the right—now quick to the left—slashing at his imaginary foe. Then he ran to the phone. "You have to ask. Here. I can dial." Mikey dialed the number without even looking at the pamphlet. He knew it by heart.

Calvin stuffed half a slice of banana bread into his mouth. "This is different," he said as he chewed. "Mucky."

"But it tastes good, doesn't it?" said Mamma.

"Yes." Calvin picked up the other half with both hands.

"When Julie wakes up, be sure to tell her you like it," said Mamma. "She made it. And she got carried away and mushed up an extra banana. That's why it's a little wet." Mamma took a bite.

Julie made banana bread. Yesterday Mikey would have been upset by that. But right now he didn't care at all. "Hello," said Mikey into the phone. "My mother wants to talk to you." He held the phone out to Mamma.

Mamma gulped down the banana bread and talked to the man on the phone. Mikey listened intently, but half a conversation doesn't tell much. Mamma hung up.

"So?" said Mikey.

The tea kettle whistled. Mamma got the kettle and poured water over the teabag in her cup. "They have classes for beginners from eight to ten years old on Saturday mornings."

Mikey was nine. "Perfect."

"What about soccer?"

Town soccer was for third- and fourth-graders. They met on the school field every Saturday morning, starting this week. Mikey had played town soccer last fall, and he had planned to do it again this fall. But not now. "I don't care about soccer."

"You loved soccer last year."

"Watch." Mikey lunged past Mamma with his invisible sword. "See? I want to fence, Mamma."

Mamma smiled and sipped her tea, while Mikey lunged over and over, slashing the air. "It costs a lot."

Mikey stopped now. Money—always money. He stood beside Mamma's chair. "How much?"

Mamma picked up her banana bread slice, then put it down.

"Can we afford it?" asked Mikey quietly.

"Well, the man said you could have the first three lessons on a trial basis, just to make sure you really liked it before we have to fork over the rest for the ten lessons."

"It only takes ten lessons to become a fencer?"

"It takes years and years to become a fencer. It's like anything else: You have to work at it. But they only make you pay for ten lessons at a time." Mamma looked steadily at Mikey. "He said it's a sport, Mikey. Like you read. But it's swords. I don't know how I feel about this."

"I won't ever hurt anyone, Mamma. I'll be the best sportsman there ever was." Mikey stepped closer.

Mamma sighed. "Are you sure about this? It isn't easy."

No, it takes years. Years and years. Suddenly fencing wasn't just an idea anymore. It might really happen. The thought of a blade pointed at him—real steel pointed right at Mikey—made him go cold with fear. He rubbed both arms.

But then the memory of those two figures in white, quick and tight and strong, danced again in his head. He couldn't say what it was about fencing that drew him, but whatever it was, it held him fast. He had to be one of those figures in white someday. He had to. "I want to start this Saturday."

"Well, you're in luck. He always lets people in during September. That's when most school kids join. The problem is . . ." Mamma paused. She got up and took a container from the cupboard and put the banana bread in it.

Mikey could hardly bear it. He walked over beside his mother. "What?"

"The problem is that we have to get you there, and it's downtown in Philadelphia near the train station."

"You could drive me."

"I hate city driving."

"Dad could drive me."

"He works so hard all week. He should rest on Saturday."

Desperation made Mikey's chest tight. "If it's near the train station, maybe I could take a train."

"Well, that's a thought. I mean, you couldn't go alone. But I could take the train with you. And that wouldn't be any more expensive than paying for parking." Mamma looked at Mikey with thoughtful eyes. "I can bring Calvin and Julie along, and we can walk around and window-shop while you fence." She tapped her fingers on the top of the banana bread container. "Maybe I can get Victoria to watch them sometimes, too, if the weather's bad." She looked at Mikey. "Three trial lessons. Okay. It's a go."

"Yes!" Mikey hugged his mother hard. "Oh, thank you."

"And now," said Mamma, pulling a bag off the counter, "look what I have." She took out a book, *The Good Food of Szechwan*. On the cover was a picture of a cooked chicken with dark, shiny sauce on it and a plate of white cubes smothered in another delicious-looking sauce. "The woman at the bookshop said this was the best Chinese cookbook. What do you think?"

"I want to make that chicken."

"That's what I was hoping you'd say. You've been making a lot of chicken noises lately. So chicken's exactly what I bought."

Birthdays

On the way home from school the next day, Mikey felt a sense of contentment. Tomorrow was Saturday, the first day of his life as a fencer.

Victoria stood on the porch of their house and scowled as Mikey rode his bike up. "What took you so long?"

"I took the longcut."

"The longcut?" Victoria shook her head in disgust. "Mikey, there is no word *longcut*."

"Sure there is. It's the opposite of *shortcut*."

"If you cut it, it gets short, not long. Be logical."

Mikey had had lessons in logic from Victoria all his life. He was sick of Victoria's logic. "Kpok. What do you care how long I took?"

"Listen, this is Friday. My one afternoon with no homework. I want to spend it at Virginia's house. I can't spend the afternoon doing things for you."

"I didn't ask you to do anything for me."

"Mamma said I had to entertain your friend till you got home."

"What friend?"

"John's little brother."

"Bill?" Oh, no, Bill again.

"He's in the backyard playing catch with Calvin."

"Why didn't you tell him to go away?"

"What? Why would I do that?"

"Why didn't you tell him I died and moved to Hamsterdam?"

Victoria furrowed her brows. "You are so illogical."

"I knew you'd say that. You are so predictable." Mikey lifted his chin in triumph. He walked into the house, put his helmet and backpack in his cubby, and went out the kitchen door into the yard. He was just in time to see Calvin catch the ball. What? Calvin caught the ball! He actually caught it.

"What took you so long?" said Bill.

"I caught it," said Calvin. He was wearing a big pair of sunglasses that slid down his nose. He pushed them up. "Did you see? I caught the ball, Mikey."

Yippy barked hello and jumped on Mikey.

Mikey sat in the grass and scratched Yippy's neck. "That's good, Calvin."

Calvin threw the ball. It bounced halfway to Bill.

Bill ran for the ball and threw it easy to Calvin.

Calvin caught it again. He smiled and jumped in place.

How did that happen? Mikey wanted Calvin to catch the balls he threw, too.

"Want to go rafting?" said Bill to Mikey.

Mikey had never been rafting. Rafting meant water. His stomach knotted. He stood up. "Throw the ball to me, Calvin."

Calvin threw the ball. It hit Mikey in the knee and bounced off into Yippy's jaws. Mikey rubbed at his knee.

Bill wrestled the ball from Yippy and tossed it from hand to hand. "Well?"

"I don't have a raft," said Mikey.

"We only need one raft, and I've got one. I made it myself."

"I'll go rafting," said Calvin.

"You can't," said Mikey. "It's dangerous."

"It's not dangerous," said Bill. "I thought you loved boats. Your research project's on boats, right?"

Mikey didn't feel like explaining why he'd chosen boats for his topic. "Calvin can't swim." Mikey looked at Bill. Bill looked back. He was waiting. Mikey had to say something more. "Where do you raft?"

"In Crum Creek. Our neighbor told my mom that's the best spot around. Unless you know someplace better."

Mikey shook his head. "Nah, I don't know anyplace else." He thought about that creek. It was deep in spots. "I can't go, though."

Bill threw the ball to Calvin. And Calvin caught it again. "Why not?"

"I've got something important to do tomorrow," said Mikey. "I can't risk getting wet and . . ." Mikey searched for a reason. ". . . and maybe catching cold."

"It's too hot to catch cold."

"Jennifer Snot has a cold."

"Jennifer Snot? Did you call her *snot*? Wow, that's great." Bill laughed. "She'll die when she finds out."

"Don't tell her," said Mikey. He gulped. Jennifer Snot wasn't a bad sort; in fact, she was nice. He hadn't meant to hurt her feelings by naming her that. He just wanted to remember which Jennifer was *S* and which was *B* and which was *M*. He had to get Bill's mind off that fast. "You really made your raft?"

"Yeah. It's in my garage. Want to see it?"

Mikey felt trapped. "I've got to take care of Calvin."

"Calvin can come."

"I want to see the raft." Calvin turned the ball over and over in his hands. "Please, Mikey. I'll go ask Mamma."

"All right," said Mikey with a sigh.

Calvin disappeared into the kitchen. A moment later he was back. "We have to be home by six."

"I know," said Mikey. "We always have to be home by six."

They walked down the sidewalk, Bill in the lead. Calvin had Yippy by the leash. When they got to Yale Avenue, they turned left. A couple of blocks down, Bill suddenly said, "Oh, no. Quick. Follow me." He ran into the nearest yard and ducked behind a thick bush.

Calvin and Yippy ran after him.

Yippy barked.

Bill reached out and grabbed Calvin by the arm. He yanked him behind the bush. "Can't you keep the dog quiet?" he whispered.

Mikey scooted behind the bush and put his arms around Yippy's neck. "Shhh, Yippy."

"Come in close," whispered Bill. He crouched half under the bush with Calvin.

Mikey crouched beside them. "What's going on?"

Bill breathed hard. "It's this big fifth grader."

"You're as big as most fifth graders."

"Nuh-uh. Not as big as Hugh."

Hugh? Mikey had heard about Hugh. He was one of the bullies the fourth graders stayed away from. Mikey had never had a run-in with Hugh himself, but Raymond had once. Hugh had called him "shorty" and pounded him on the head.

Yippy pulled her head loose from Mikey's grip. She whined.

"Here." Calvin dug in his pocket and brought out a sandy cookie. He flashed it past Yippy's nose, then held it behind his back. Yippy went around behind Calvin and lay down. She crunched the cookie loudly.

"Good work, Calvin." Mikey leaned out just enough to see the street. Three boys walked down the center holding skateboards. They looked pretty normal for fifth graders until you watched a while. Then you could see something special about them—that ominous way they walked. They were almost even with the bush now. He pulled his head back. "There are three of them."

"Hugh's in the middle. The other two are his buddies."

"How do you know them?" asked Calvin.

"They ambush people."

"Do they ambush you?" asked Calvin.

"Yeah. They slam me up against the school yard fence and laugh the whole time. They pretend like they're playing, so if an adult walks by, they can say it's just a game."

Mikey's heart pounded at the treachery. He thought about being slammed hard against a fence—so hard that he couldn't catch his breath—slammed till he dropped, dead on the ground.

Calvin put his hand on Bill's arm. "Do they ambush you a lot?" His sunglasses slid down his nose. He pushed them back up.

"Only if they see me first. But I'm always on guard. And I can spot Hugh a block away."

On guard, thought Mikey. He remembered the fencers at the Franklin Institute shouting, "En garde." He tensed up as though for a duel.

"Yeah, I thought that was you." Hugh and his buddies came around the bush.

Mikey looked up at them from where he squatted. His mouth went dry.

Yippy barked and bounded out.

Hugh jumped back.

But the boy on his right knelt down and petted Yippy. Yippy wagged her tail. "Nice dog."

Hugh relaxed his shoulders and smirked at Bill. "Some watchdog." He laughed. "You hiding?"

Bill stood up. "Why don't you just go your own way?"

"I'll go where I want." Hugh looked at Mikey and Calvin. "So the new kid's finally making friends. Who're these dorks?"

Mikey and Calvin stood up. Mikey stepped half in front of Calvin. If anyone had to die, Mikey should be first. He was older, after all.

The third boy looked at Calvin. "What's your name, pipsqueak?"

Mikey should speak up. He should protect his brother. He opened his mouth, but no sound came out.

Calvin shook his head. "My name's not Pipsqueak. It's Calvin." He shook his head again. "I don't even like fences. Really. I'll never go near the school yard fence."

Hugh looked confused. He scratched his head. "Bunch of dweebs."

"But the dog's nice," said the first boy. Yippy rolled onto her back, and the boy scratched her chest.

Hugh moved close to Bill and squinted. "Where's your face? All I can see is a wart."

His buddies laughed.

"You're lucky I don't ring the doorbell of the house there and get you in trouble for trespassing. I could say you were taking your dog in their yard to poop. That'd be good, huh?"

His buddies laughed.

"We've got things to do. Catch you later." Hugh pointed at Bill's chest. "Get it? Catch you later."

The buddies laughed again.

Hugh walked back down the yard and out to the street. His buddies flanked him.

Yippy stood up and barked.

"He's going to catch you later," said Calvin. "Oh, Bill, he's going to catch you later."

"Not if I see him first," said Bill. "Anyway, don't worry about it. He mainly just likes to make people feel bad."

Mikey took Calvin's hand and squeezed. He wished he had said something tough to Hugh. He wished he had told him to go away. "Try to forget them, Calvin."

"That's right." Bill walked out to the sidewalk. "Let's go look at my raft."

They crossed the street and went down one more block. Mikey kept looking over his shoulder. He hoped he'd never see Hugh again in his life. Finally they turned up a driveway.

"This is it," said Bill.

Calvin and Mikey followed Bill into the garage. Propped against the rear wall was a wide board with big holes drilled into it. A huge inner tube was attached to the board with ropes that wove in and out of the holes. Bill picked up the board and carried it out to the driveway. He set it down with the inner tube on the top side. "What do you think?"

Mikey walked around it. "How does it work?"

"You have two choices. You can sit inside the tube with your legs crossed. It's like being in a regular tube, just with a board under you. But then only one person can go on it. The best way for two people is to sit back-to-back in the center of the tube with your legs hanging out over the sides."

"But then one person goes down the creek backward."

"So what?"

"I love to go backward," said Calvin.

"You're not going rafting," said Mikey. He pressed both hands down on the inner tube. It was tough and sturdy. Mikey looked at Bill with new admiration. "Did you design it yourself?"

"I drilled the holes," Bill said loudly. "And I made Dad buy the board." He crossed his arms on his chest. Then he lowered his voice. "But my big brother designed it. Everyone always thinks he's smart."

"I have a big sister," said Mikey with sympathy.

"I met her."

"Yeah, I forgot." Mikey tapped the edge of the raft lightly with the tip of his sneaker. "You did a good job drilling."

Yippy sniffed the raft where Mikey had tapped it.

"I like tools. My dad taught me how to use them. So, you want to go rafting?"

"There's no time now."

Bill picked up the raft and carried it back inside the garage. He propped it against the wall again. "How about after town soccer tomorrow?"

"I'm not doing soccer."

"What do you mean? Our neighbor said everyone does soccer." Bill frowned.

"Is this yours?" Calvin appeared beside Bill with a pink plastic rake in his hand.

"It used to be," said Bill. "It's for a sandbox. We have a whole crate of old sandbox toys in the garage. Mom saves everything, no matter how often we move."

"Do you move a lot?" asked Mikey.

"Every couple of years. 'Cause of Dad's job."

"I have a sandbox. And I had a pink rake, too." Calvin swung the rake over his head. "But I lost mine."

"You can have that one," said Bill.

"Really?" Calvin stared at Bill.

Bill laughed. "Really."

"You don't have to do that," said Mikey.

"What do I care about an old rake?" said Bill. "And Mom'll never remember."

"Oh, thank you." Calvin jumped and jumped. "I love it." His sunglasses fell off. "Oh, here." He handed the glasses to Bill. "Thanks for letting me borrow them."

Bill smiled at Calvin and put on the sunglasses. "Any time." Then he looked at Mikey. "Come to soccer tomorrow."

"I can't. Tomorrow I'm going . . ." Mikey felt stupid saying he was going to fencing. Bill would probably laugh. How could someone who didn't have the nerve to even talk back to bullies ever hope to be a fencer? "I'm going somewhere with my mother."

"I'm going, too," said Calvin. "We're taking the train to . . ."

"Tell us something about kindergarten," Mikey said quickly. He had to keep Calvin from talking about fencing. "Come on, Calvin. Tell us something that happened today."

Calvin cocked his head. "What?"

"Did anyone throw up?"

"Not today."

Bill looked surprised. "Do kids in your class throw up a lot?"

Calvin nodded. "And Sarah had a birthday today."

"But she just had one the other day," said Mikey.

"I know. She's getting old fast."

Mikey looked at Calvin's face to see if maybe he was joking. He had to be joking. Only his face was dead serious.

Calvin swung his rake. "And I cut my finger so they made me go sit in the corner and suck it."

"What?" said Bill.

"It's time to get home," said Mikey. "See you later, Bill." He took Calvin by the hand.

Calvin waved good-bye with his rake.

Bill looked confused. He waved back. "Yeah." Then he went around the corner of his house.

Mikey walked beside Calvin, with Yippy leading,

pulling at the leash. "Did Sarah really have another birthday today?"

"She likes birthdays."

"Oh." It wasn't worth talking about. "Why'd you borrow Bill's sunglasses?"

"They protect my eyes. That's what Bill said. That way I can keep my eyes open when we play catch."

So that was why Calvin could catch the ball today—he could see it. What a simple solution.

"Mikey, will those mean boys catch us, too?"

"No," said Mikey. But if they did, what would he do? He had no idea.

"Mikey, Bill's the best thrower, even if he has warts."

"Bill doesn't have warts. They only said that to hurt his feelings. Now let's just walk. I want to think about things." So many things. Tomorrow, tomorrow, tomorrow.

The First Lesson

The train rushed toward them, and Mikey's heart rushed to his throat. The huge wheels slowed and finally stopped. Mikey felt his shoulders drop in relief. He realized he'd been breathing through his mouth like a dog. He climbed onto the train behind Mamma, who had Calvin by one hand and Julie by the other.

"You've got the tickets, Mikey, don't you?" Mamma looked at Mikey's empty hands worriedly.

Mikey patted his pocket. "I've got them."

Mamma smiled. She sat down and bounced Julie on her knees.

Calvin stood at the window. "The train's going again. We're going, we're going."

"Sit down, Calvin," said Mamma.

Calvin pressed his forehead against the window and stared. Mikey knew he had no intention of sitting. After a couple of minutes, Calvin said, "Oh, look how far down the ground is."

Mikey looked. They were on a trestle over a creek. The creek was shallow. It looked better for rafting than Crum Creek.

"Oh, I love it," screamed Calvin.

"Love," shouted Julie. "Love train." She threw her arms around Mamma's neck in a giant hug.

Mamma laughed.

Mikey laughed, too. He hadn't been on the train in a long time. This was exciting. Mikey watched the houses flash by. Everything was right.

"Warm-up time. Okay, cadets, there's your path." The man in the fencing suit pointed around the perimeter of an area of floor marked off by white tape. He was the man who had sat on the stage at the Franklin Institute. The mustache man.

One boy raised his hand. "Hey, mister, when do we fence?"

Mikey's heart sped. Would he hold a sword right away?

The man twirled the tip of his mustache. "Call me Coach." He looked at each of them in turn. When he came to Mikey, he winked. "Warm up first. Run nice and slow." Coach ran in place. "When I yell 'Turn,' you run backward." He ran backward. "When I yell 'Change,' you run the other direction." He jumped around and ran off, straight into the men's changing room.

The cadets looked at each other, dumbfounded.

"That doesn't make sense," said the boy who had asked the question. " 'Turn' shouldn't mean run backward."

The boy reminded Mikey of Victoria, always looking for his own kind of logic. Mikey, for one, was glad they were going to warm up and didn't have to hold swords right away. Still, he looked forward to the thrill of the sword.

They stood there another minute. Then one of the boys ran. They all followed.

Coach appeared out of nowhere and called out, "Change."

At first Mikey didn't remember what to do, but the kid in front of him turned to face him, and Mikey quickly turned and ran the other direction.

Almost instantly, Coach called out, "Turn."

This time Mikey didn't hesitate. He ran backward.

"Change."

Mikey spun around and ran backward in the other direction.

Finally Coach called, "Enough. It's time for"—he paused, and his eyes sparkled mischievously—"power skips!"

Skips? When Mikey was in kindergarten, he had loved skipping. And just last year he had taught Calvin how to skip. But in fourth grade none of the boys skipped anymore.

"High." Coach skipped in place, higher than Mikey had ever seen anyone skip before. He looked like a kangaroo. "Once around the area, then on the second time skip two forward and one backward, two forward and one backward." He skipped forward and backward. He stopped and, with both hands, he twirled both tips of his mustache. "Got it?"

The cadets skipped.

"Higher," shouted Coach. "Faster."

Mikey skipped higher and faster. It was like being weightless. It felt great.

"Enough." Coach raised his hands and wagged his fingertips.

The cadets stared. They came forward cautiously.

Coach lifted an eyebrow. He gestured with his thumb toward a line of jump ropes that dangled from hooks on the wall. "Grab yourself a rope and stand in front of those mirrors."

The cadets got their ropes and ran to the mirrors.

"Start like this." Coach jump roped with both feet. "When you feel ready . . ." Coach jumped on his right foot. "After a while . . ." He jumped on his left foot. "Finally . . ." Coach jumped with both feet and the rope going backward. Then he stopped. He looked at his watch. He looked at the cadets.

By this time the cadets knew the routine: When Coach stopped demonstrating, they jump roped madly.

Mikey wrapped his rope around his hands to shorten it. He jumped, both feet together. After a while, he jumped on just his right foot. Then he shifted to his left.

"Enough." Coach pointed at their jump ropes; then he pointed at the hooks on the wall.

The boys hung up their jumpropes.

Coach went to the center of the floor and sat down.

The cadets sat on the floor in an arc in front of him.

Coach put his legs out straight to each side. He set his hands flat on the floor in front of him and walked them outward until his chest was close to the floor. He reached both hands over his right leg. Then over his left. Then his arms made big circles.

The cadets did the same.

Coach stretched one leg straight and forward and the other bent and backward. He pulled on his toes. He switched legs and pulled his toes again. Then he stood up.

Mikey stood up, too. He felt dizzy for a second, they'd been working so fast.

Coach put his hands on his hips. "Looking good." He cracked a smile.

Mikey smiled back. They looked good. He looked good. Wow.

"Next time you're sitting around," said Coach,

"do your stretching exercises. Always behave as though you're in training." He gave a quick nod. "Because you are." He jerked his thumb toward the mirrored wall.

The boys lined up in front of the mirrors in silence.

Coach planted one foot facing forward and the other facing to the side, heels together. "Assume starting position." Mikey recognized the stance from the fencers at the Institute. "En garde." Coach reached his front foot forward, so his heels were now about a foot apart.

The cadets did the same.

"Tiptoe." Coach balanced on tiptoe.

The cadets balanced on tiptoe.

Coach slowly bent his knees. "Advance." He moved forward, keeping his feet pointed that same way.

The cadets advanced.

"Retreat." Coach moved backward, holding the stance steady.

The cadets retreated. Advance, retreat. Over and over.

"Enough." Coach rubbed his hands together. "Judging distance is a key skill." Coach walked to a box and opened it. He took out three elastic ropes. "Who's my volunteer?"

Mikey looked at Coach. Coach was looking right at him. Mikey licked his lips anxiously.

Coach handed Mikey one end of an elastic rope. "Our job is to keep this rope taut." Coach held the other end and walked backward till the rope was tight. "We have to stay within the fencing strip." He pointed at a taped-off area. Then he looked at Mikey. "Advance."

Mikey advanced.

Coach retreated, keeping the rope taut. His eyes never left Mikey's face. Mikey looked back with equal intensity. Coach blinked and advanced. The rope went slack for an instant. Mikey quickly retreated.

Coach laughed. "Good stuff. You're fast."

Mikey flushed with pride.

Coach handed his end of the rope to a cadet. He gave out the other two ropes. The pairs of boys advanced and retreated up and down the fencing strips, keeping the elastic ropes taut.

"Now the one of each pair with your back toward me," called Coach, "that one has to close his eyes."

"What?" said one of the boys. It was exactly what Mikey wanted to say: His back was to Coach.

"Do it. Let your other senses come alive."

Mikey closed his eyes and advanced. He felt the rope go slack. He retreated. There, it was taut again.

"Switch."

What did "switch" mean? Mikey opened his eyes. His partner looked at him in panic, then jumped around to face backward. The next boy over ran in a circle, got tangled in his rope, and fell.

"Stop." Coach waved his arms. " 'Switch' means one guy opens his eyes and the other guy closes his. Got it?"

The boys quickly got back into pairs. Mikey's partner closed his eyes and advanced.

"Keep a steady distance. Be aware of any changes so you know when to lunge." Coach walked up and down through the pairs of cadets. "Switch. Focus on staying relaxed."

Relaxed? How could Mikey relax in that stance, with his eyes closed, going forward and backward on the fencing strip?

"Enough." Coach lifted both arms and wagged his fingertips.

They grouped in front of Coach instantly.

"The best strategy is staying out of attack distance. That's what you were working on today—maintaining a safe distance. Fencing is strategy. And not just strategy with your body, but with your mind. A lot of fencing happens up here." Coach tapped his temple. "You have to get your opponent into a pattern and then you break the pattern and while they're stunned, you attack." Coach collected the ropes. "That's it for today, folks."

"But when do we fence?" said the boy who had started the class with the same question.

Mikey had been totally absorbed in the workout this morning. He hadn't thought about actual fencing at all. But now he looked at Coach with a mix of fear and hope.

"When you're ready."

"Next week?"

Coach shook his head. "Not for a long time."

"Awww. So what do we do next week?"

"We work on gaining skills—speed, balance, aim . . ."

Speed, balance, aim? Mikey was fast—Coach had said that himself. And he had great balance on the bike, and no one had better aim than him at pitching baseball. Mikey already had the three skills they were going to work on. Fencing was going to be the right sport for him. Oh, yes.

"How?" said the boy.

"Warm-up, stretching, footwork, and . . ." Coach lowered his voice to a whisper and leaned forward.

The cadets leaned toward him.

". . . the Zen glove drop."

"What's that?"

Coach lifted an eyebrow. Then he looked away.

"Awww," said the boy again.

Coach came over to Mikey. "A lefty." He twirled one tip of his mustache. "I'll write that down so I don't forget to order you a lefty foil."

"A foil?" said Mikey.

"That's what I teach beginners: foil. The blade is

square and the tip is rubber. Later you can take up épée, too. You'll see." Coach walked away.

Mikey looked around, just as Mamma and Calvin and Julie came in the door. Julie clutched a bunch of wilted flowers in one hand. Mamma looked frazzled.

Calvin ran up to Mikey. "Did you stab anyone?"

"No."

"Don't ever stab me."

The ugly words took Mikey by surprise. "I won't, Calvin. I hope I never stab anyone."

Calvin looked dumbfounded. Then he smiled. "Goody."

Rafting

All the next week Mikey was in training. He sat with one leg forward and one leg bent back, and pulled on his toes when he watched TV. He maintained a steady distance from the kids near him in the lunch line. He skipped backward behind the bamboo grove at recess—checking frequently to make sure no one was near.

When Saturday's lesson came, Mikey was totally ready. This lesson had the same exercises as the first, plus, of course, the Zen glove drop. In the Zen glove drop one person holds out a glove by the fingers. The other person puts a hand on top of the first person's hand. Then the first person drops the glove and the other person quick tries to catch the glove with that same hand before it hits the ground. Mikey wasn't so hot at it, but neither was anyone else in his class. Except for Keisha. It turned out one of the cadets was a girl.

Mikey loved the lesson. He went to bed happy Saturday night and stayed happy Sunday morning. At noon he sauntered into the kitchen and found Victoria making peanut butter and jelly sandwiches. He picked one up and took a bite.

"Hey! Cut it out."

"Huh?" Mikey looked at the line of sandwiches. Six, counting the one in his hand. "You don't need this one."

"Yes I do. Now I'll have to make another." Victoria laid two more pieces of bread on the counter and went to work.

"You can't be that hungry."

"Don't be ridiculous. They're not all for me. They're for my committee."

"What committee?"

Victoria screwed the lid on the jelly jar. "I got elected to Student Council, and I have to gather the opinions of my homeroom class on what the theme should be for our fall dance. So I set up a committee. They're coming over to advise me."

Mikey didn't know what Student Council was. He wished Calvin was here so that Calvin would ask. "Does Mamma know about Student Council?"

"No. The next time Daddy asks what's new at school I'm going to announce it." Victoria cut the sandwiches in half. She arranged them in a circle on a platter. "And don't you tell before I get a chance to."

"Who elected you?"

"My homeroom class, of course. Lots of kids voted for me."

"Why?"

"What do mean, 'why'? I don't know why." Victoria set glasses on the table. "Well, I do know why John voted for me."

"How do you know John voted for you?"

"He sits across from me and I saw him write down my name."

"Oh. Why did he vote for you?"

"Because I have good handwriting."

"Huh? How do you know that?"

"I asked him. I said, 'John, why'd you vote for me?' And he said, 'Because you have good handwriting.' Just like that."

Mikey remembered how Victoria said he wrote like a monkey. He'd never get elected to anything. Maybe that was good. He wouldn't have to make a zillion peanut butter sandwiches.

"Mikey," came Daddy's voice from the front porch. "Mikey."

Mikey gulped down the last of the sandwich and ran to the door. He stopped short. Bill stood on the steps, wearing shorts and those sunglasses of his. What was Bill doing here? Mikey had avoided Bill ever since Bill had started that thing about his raft.

"Mikey," Daddy called again. He put down the

Sunday paper. "Oh, there you are. Come on outside."

Mikey opened the screen door and stepped out. "Hi, Bill."

"Hi."

Daddy smiled. "So, I hear you're going rafting."

"What? I'm not . . ."

"I worked on the raft all week," Bill said quickly. "I varnished the board and attached the tube with a new rope."

"Rafts need upkeep." Daddy nodded his head. "I was telling Bill about the creek in Iowa that I rafted on as a kid."

"Can I go, too?" Calvin came up the steps from the front yard. He carried the pink rake Bill had given him.

"Another time," said Daddy. "I'll come along, too. But not today. Today's for Mikey and Bill." He rested his arms on his knees and leaned toward Mikey with a nostalgic look on his face. "And you're both dressed just right. Keep those sneakers on in the water. You never know what's on the bottom of creeks."

Mikey looked from Bill's steady, hopeful face to Daddy's dreamy, satisfied eyes. He knew he had to go. He swallowed the lump in his throat. Maybe if Calvin asked again, Daddy would decide to come along. Mikey looked hard at Calvin.

Calvin looked back at Mikey. Then his eyes lit up. "Want to see a magic trick?" He dug in his pocket and came out with a fistful of sand. "I'll squeeze this into a rock." He shut his eyes and squeezed so hard his shoulders shook. He opened his eyes and opened his fist. The sand trickled out. "It didn't work this time."

Calvin was pitiful.

"Keep at it," said Bill. "You'll get it right eventually."

Mikey looked fast at Bill. Was he making fun of Calvin? But he didn't seem to be. He seemed to genuinely like Calvin.

"You better get going if you want a full afternoon of it." Daddy stretched. "Calvin, want to take Yippy on a walk with me?"

"Goody." Calvin dropped the rest of the sand on the porch and grabbed Daddy's hand. They walked around to the backyard.

"Well, let's go." Bill led the way to his house. He took off his sunglasses and put them on a window ledge in his garage. "That way I won't lose them in the white water," he said to Mikey with a smile.

Mikey smiled back hesitantly. That was a joke, right? There was no white water in Crum Creek.

They carried the raft along the sidewalk. "You keep a lookout for Hugh on the right side and behind," said Bill. "I'll cover the front and the left."

"Okay," said Mikey. He thought about what Hugh had said that other day. "Has he caught you lately?"

"Yeah, once. But it was nothing big. Just the usual."

The usual. Mikey's stomach did a small, sick flip. He looked around nervously. No one was in sight. The afternoon was sunny and lazy and quiet. After a little while, it was almost fun to keep watch like that. Mikey pretended he and Bill were a team, traveling secretly through enemy territory, on a dangerous mission. It was exciting—as long as Hugh didn't really show up.

Finally, they veered off the sidewalk and marched across the field to the creek.

"So what've you been doing in fencing?" said Bill.

"How'd you know about fencing?"

"Your father told me."

"Oh. Not much."

Bill stopped and turned to Mikey. "Show me."

Mikey put down his end of the raft. He assumed stance. He advanced and retreated. "It's footwork."

Bill let the raft fall on the ground. He mimicked Mikey, pulling his heels together, one foot facing forward, one sideways. He advanced.

"Not bad," said Mikey.

Bill smiled a little.

"Now bend your knees, like this." Mikey advanced a full circle around the raft.

Bill bent his knees and advanced.

"Good," said Mikey, nodding.

Bill grinned.

"Now rise up on your tiptoes."

Bill got on tiptoe. He licked his top lip in concentration.

Mikey demonstrated again, paying special attention to his balance. "See? It's all a matter of weight."

"Weight?" Bill dropped down to his flat feet again. "Weight?" He shook his head and frowned. "It looks like a lot of stupid exercise to me." He retied his sneakers.

Mikey felt confused at the sudden change in Bill's mood. "It gets us ready," he said softly. "And footwork's fun."

Bill walked into the water, dragging the raft. "Feet don't have anything to do with swords. Foot exercise can't get you ready for anything, except maybe football or soccer." He held on to the raft with one hand. "You made a mistake not to come to town soccer. It was great yesterday."

"Fencing was good, too," said Mikey.

"How many sword fights have you been in?"

"None."

"None? How can you like it when you've never even been in a sword fight?"

"I will. Coach ordered me a special lefty foil. That's what you call the sword, a foil."

Bill fingered his Olympic medal. Mikey had never seen him without it since the day Mr. Gaynor had awarded it to him. Bill slipped the medal inside his shirt. "You left-handed?"

"Yeah."

"Then you better put a bullet-proof patch over your heart."

"Huh? Why?"

"Left-handed fencers die more."

"What?"

"You know. You hold your sword with your left hand and the other guy stabs at your heart. Your heart's on your left side."

Mikey knew exactly where his heart was. It was beating so hard now his shirt went up and down. "I bet you're making that up."

"No, I'm not. I heard it once. You know, if you do soccer, you won't die." Bill stared at Mikey.

Mikey knew this was a showdown. He tried not to blink. "I like fencing better."

Bill shook his head again. "Well, it's your heart." He pulled the raft toward him. "We both have to climb on at once, so grab hold."

Mikey took one end of the raft. The water was cool, but the late September air was still warm. His shoes sank a little into the creek bottom. He felt sloggy. And his chest felt all prickly near his heart, as though something were trying to poke its way through the skin.

"When I say 'Jump,' get on backward." Bill pressed down on his end of the raft. "Jump!" Bill jumped on.

Mikey's end of the raft flew up. And so did he. He fell onto his bottom, his head underwater. He scrambled to his feet.

Bill floated along on the raft, already at least ten feet away. "Are you okay?" he called over his shoulder.

"Sure."

"Well, come on. Run."

Mikey did a splash-run. The mud sucked at his shoes. The water rippled by slowly as Mikey gained on the raft. Then he stopped. Why was he doing this? Bill wasn't even nice to him. Bill talked calmly about the idea of a blade slicing into Mikey's chest, as though he didn't care.

"Come on. There's a surprise ahead. Hurry," shouted Bill.

Mikey watched the raft bob away.

Bill jumped off. "You coming?"

"I don't think so." There, he'd said it.

Bill hooked an arm through the raft tube and pushed his way up the current. "Don't quit." He put a hand over the Olympic medal, whose shape showed clearly through his wet shirt. "It's 'cause I weigh more than you. Hugh says I should go on a diet."

Mikey thought of Hugh smashing Bill into the fence and saying mean things. "I don't think you need to go on a diet."

"You don't?" Bill looked at Mikey as though he was making up his mind. Then he plucked at the front of his wet shirt. "Here, I'll hold the raft steady and you get on first."

"You said we had to get on at the same time."

"Nah. I'm strong enough to hold it. You face forward. I've seen it all before. I did a practice run to make sure we'd have fun." He turned the raft as he spoke.

Mikey hesitated.

"Let's go."

Mikey climbed on. Bill got on behind. They moved, back to back, down the creek. The tube was hot from the sun, and it felt good under Mikey's knees. This was kind of peaceful. Pleasant, almost. They floated a long time without saying anything.

Bill twisted around. "Get ready," he said.

"For what?"

"The rapids."

Rapids? So there really was white water here. Mikey's blood thumped in his ears. "What are we supposed to do?"

"Stay on."

Mikey leaned forward and hooked both arms over the tube. The water rushed faster. It splashed up his nose.

"Here we go," called Bill.

The raft slid down a tiny waterfall right toward a rock.

Bill twisted to face forward, looking over Mikey's shoulder. "Lean left," he shouted.

But Mikey couldn't lean left without letting go of the tube with his right arm. And he wasn't about to let go.

They smashed into the rock and bounced off in a spin. Mikey was facing backward now. They had made it. "This raft really works!"

"Yeah, I know."

The water sloshed in Mikey's face, cool and sweet. He kicked his feet in the rushing water.

"Lean right," shouted Bill.

Mikey's whole body tensed for the impact. They slammed into a rock and flipped over. Arms and legs thrashed everywhere. Water rushed in his eyes and nose. He scraped a knee on the now-pebbly bottom. The current tossed him onto his back and carried him downstream.

Mikey tried to swim to the surface, but the water moved too fast. It raced wildly. His chest hurt. He was drowning! He straightened his legs, hoping to shoot up for a gulp of air, and found himself standing. Actually standing.

He looked around. The raft was turned over on a rock.

Bill came up to Mikey, dripping and grinning. "Great, right?"

Mikey panted. The water was only waist deep. He couldn't drown, as long as he didn't panic. He could zoom along and he could capsize and he could get soaked, and he'd live through it all. "Yeah," he said, amazed at his own words, "not bad."

Bill walked backward toward the raft. "I told you."

Mikey thought about all of it. If he could learn to lean the right way, if he could readjust his weight fast to the changes in the water, maybe the raft wouldn't capsize. And rafting would actually help him learn about balance. He laughed. "Rafting is good practice for fencing."

"Fencing? Rafting is nothing like fencing."

"Yes it is. Want to go again next Sunday?"

"I don't know," said Bill slowly. "I'll think about it."

Strategy

"C ome on, Victoria, I need the practice. Just try it." Mikey gave Victoria one of Calvin's wooden building blocks.

Victoria held the block and looked at Mikey. "What's a wooden block got to do with fencing?"

"Put it in your armpit." Mikey put a block in his left armpit. "Like this."

Victoria scratched her chin. "You swear this is what you're supposed to do?"

"I swear."

"You better not be tricking me."

"Just do it."

Victoria put the block under her right arm.

Mikey picked up the ball. "We have to hold this ball between us with the backs of our fists and we have to move forward and backward without letting either the tennis ball or the wooden blocks fall." Mikey put the ball in place between the back of his left fist and the back of Victoria's right fist.

Mikey advanced. Victoria retreated. The ball fell.

"You have to back up only a little, so the tension on the ball stays steady. Do you understand?"

"Of course I understand."

Mikey put the ball in place. Victoria advanced. Her block fell.

"Make sure your arm doesn't move faster than your body. You have to . . ."

"Shut up," said Victoria. She picked up the wooden block and stuck it under her arm. "Put the stupid ball back in place."

Calvin sat on the floor watching them. "When I grow up, I'm going to fence with Daddy."

"When you grow up," said Victoria, "Daddy'll be decrepit."

"What's *decrepit?*" said Calvin.

"Too old to move around."

"Oh, no," cried Calvin. "Daddy's going to be decrepit."

Victoria sighed. "No, he's not, Calvin. I just said that because I'm annoyed." She glared at Mikey. "Put the ball back."

Mikey put the ball in place. Victoria advanced. Mikey retreated. Then he advanced. She retreated. The ball fell.

"I hate this, Mikey. Six weeks of fencing and this is all you have to show for it?"

"It's important. Keeping distance is half the job."

"Well, it's not my job. I tried to help you. But I'm no good at this. I'm going downstairs."

"Wait. Let's get some winter gloves to fence with."

"You fence with gloves?"

"Yeah. We try to hit each other with the gloves."

"It doesn't sound exciting."

"It is. And, to give you a head start, I'll tell you something I figured out. The ideal distance isn't just a lunge away. I bet you thought it was a lunge. The ideal distance is an advance and a lunge. The extra space keeps you safe."

"I'm safe if I don't fence at all." Victoria left.

Mikey clutched the wooden block in desperation. Tomorrow at fencing lesson they were going to use foils for the first time. Mikey had to be ready. Who could practice with him?

Bill and Mikey had gone rafting three Sundays in a row, but then the weather got cold. So for the past two weeks they'd played catch. Bill would be perfect for practicing with. But Mikey couldn't ask him. The last time they were together Bill had complained that Mikey talked too much about fencing. And all Mikey had done was try to teach him the Zen glove drop. Anyway, Bill said fencing was dumb. He almost seemed to hate it.

Mikey looked at Calvin. Calvin was blowing on his hands. Could Calvin help him? "Calvin, were you paying attention?"

Calvin looked up at Mikey. "How come when I blow on my hand like this"—Calvin rounded his lips and blew—"it's cool, but when I blow on my hand like this"—he opened his mouth wide and breathed hard—"it's warm?"

Mikey shook his head. "I don't know, Calvin." He put the blocks away and tucked the tennis ball under his pillow. Well, the practice he'd had so far would just have to be enough. And, anyway, at least he was better at keeping distance than Victoria. He smiled at the thought.

Mikey was covered with sweat. The warm-up had been long today. He patted his upper lip with his towel. He couldn't wait to hold a foil. He took a deep breath and tried to steady his wild heart.

Coach went over to the supply closet and dragged out a new carton. He raised both arms and wagged his fingertips.

The cadets trooped over obediently.

Coach handed each cadet a white jacket and knickers and a huge helmet. "This is your official outfit. Bring it with you from now on and change into it here. The shoes haven't arrived yet. I'll give them to you next week."

"Can we put on our helmets now?" asked Zach.

"Mask, not helmet. Sure. See how it feels." Coach jerked his thumb toward the changing rooms.

"When you get back, I'll give you your weapons."

Mikey slipped on the mask with shaky hands. He looked over at his family. All of them had come to see him hold a foil for the first time. But no one had told him he'd get his own fencing outfit today. And no one had told him he'd get his own weapon.

Calvin waved from Daddy's lap. Victoria and Julie rummaged around in the old juice refrigerator. Mamma leaned against a wall. She looked at him with wide eyes. She still hadn't come around to the idea that fencing was a sport. Mikey smiled reassuringly at her. Then he remembered his mask covered his face. So he squared his shoulders and tried to look sporty.

Mikey went into the locker room and changed as fast as he could. He was back in minutes.

Coach handed out foils and gloves. When he came to Mikey, he took a roll of blue tape from the shelf and cut off a short section. "You're my only lefty. You'll never confuse your glove with anyone else's, but the foil may take a while to recognize. So . . ." He wrapped the tape once around the handle.

Mikey put on the glove and watched Coach closely. This was it: his foil. He sucked in his bottom lip. Coach held the foil out to him. Mikey gripped it. His hand fit perfectly into the bell guard. He pointed the long blade up. The shine of the new metal struck awe in his heart.

"Hey, Mike." Coach tapped Mikey's mask.

Mikey put on the mask. He was totally ready.

Coach's thumb jerked toward the mirrors. "Footwork." Coach stepped back and crossed his arms at the chest.

Mikey practiced his advances. It felt different with a foil. And with that heavy mask. The balance was off. Mikey shifted his weight. There, he had it. Balance was everything. If you were even the slightest bit off balance, you couldn't retreat fast and you couldn't attack fast. You were doomed.

"Enough." Coach twirled the tips of his mustache. He pointed to the targets. Circles of different sizes were painted on them. The cadets each chose a target and went to work.

Mikey had practiced at those targets with just his fingertip before. He advanced with the foil toward the biggest circle.

He missed it. Mikey, who had terrific aim, missed that big circle. This was hard. He looked over at Nick just as Nick hit his target perfectly. Mikey hoped he'd never have to face Nick's foil. He turned to his target and tried again. And again.

"Enough." Coach raised his arms and wagged his fingertips. The cadets gathered. Coach didn't lift an eyebrow. He didn't twirl his mustache. He just looked at them with a totally serious face. Tension crept up Mikey's back and neck. "We'll try with opponents now. One pair at a time. The rest of you, take off your masks and watch while"—Coach looked from one cadet to another—"Keisha and Lloyd fence."

Mikey pointed his foil down at his side and held his mask under his arm. That's what he'd seen the older fencers do.

Keisha and Lloyd positioned themselves on a fencing strip.

Coach took Keisha's foil. He assumed starting position and held the foil point down. Then he swung it in an arc and pointed it toward Lloyd.

Lloyd jumped backward.

Coach tilted the foil to touch his own forehead, then he held it out toward Lloyd again. Then he placed the point on the ground. "That's the salute. Begin every bout with a salute." He handed Keisha her foil.

Keisha and Lloyd saluted each other.

Coach nodded. "The hit area is only the vest. Never aim for the neck or face. Never aim below the waist. Foil fencing is a duel to the death. If you get hit in the vest—the chest area—you're dead."

I don't want to die, thought Mikey.

"Your first priority," said Coach, "is don't get hit."

Right, thought Mikey.

"Your second priority," said Coach, "is hit your enemy."

Mikey gulped. He wondered if Mamma was hearing any of this.

"None of that phony TV stuff, where people try to hit each other's blades. Your goal is to hit the vest. Got it?"

Keisha nodded, silently. Lloyd nodded, silently.

Mikey wondered if maybe all the cadets were becoming like Coach, if maybe after a while none of them would talk like ordinary people, but just nod and gesture half the time.

"Back up some. Okay. When you're ready, begin."

Lloyd stood near one end of the fencing strip. He bent his legs a little and seemed to bounce in place. Keisha advanced from the other end. With a quick lunge, she hit him on the chest.

Mikey flinched automatically.

"Touch!" said Coach.

They all looked at Coach. What now? Was Lloyd dead? Mikey could barely breathe. He didn't want it to be over. Poor Lloyd.

"Usually we go till one fencer has five hits. But today we'll only go to two."

Mikey let out his breath in relief.

Lloyd went back to his end of the fencing strip. He shook his shoulders. He seemed to flap his elbows. All of a sudden he broke stance and charged Keisha.

Mikey's mouth opened in horror.

"Stop!" shouted Coach.

Keisha jumped sideways as Lloyd stumbled to a halt right where she had stood.

"Never run," said Coach. "Remember footwork. Maintain distance. Never let the other guy get in close enough for a hit. Surprise with a lunge, yes, but never with an all-out run."

"Sorry," mumbled Lloyd.

Keisha didn't say anything. If Mikey had been in Keisha's position, he might have turned tail and run. That would have been awful. How did Keisha know to jump off the strip like that?

"Start close to the center this time."

Lloyd went to the center of the strip. He bent his knees and advanced. Keisha retreated. They were close to Keisha's end of the strip now.

"If you make someone retreat so far that they back off the strip, you get a point," said Coach. "It's equal to a hit."

Keisha suddenly advanced and Lloyd retreated. Only Keisha was faster. She lunged and hit Lloyd.

Mikey felt as though he were the one who'd been jabbed. He had to work to keep himself from doubling over.

"Touch," said Coach. "Take off your masks, shake hands, and step off the strip."

Keisha and Lloyd took off their masks. Without them, their heads seemed tiny. They shook hands and got off the strip.

Coach looked at Keisha. "Fast footwork. Did you see that, cadets? Speed is a goal. Especially if you find yourself against an opponent of equal skill."

Mikey was glad that Keisha hadn't been his partner today. Usually he liked her for a partner. But today he wanted someone bad. Someone terrible at footwork and distance and everything else. Someone like Raul. He looked right at Raul.

"Mike and Raul, your turn," said Coach.

Wow. It was like Coach had read Mikey's mind. Mikey and Raul put on their masks and stood near the center of the fencing strip. Mikey swung his foil carefully in the salute, and as it circled his head, he felt a cloak of magic envelop him. He was living his dream at last.

Raul advanced, his foil pointed right at Mikey.

That's when Mikey remembered Bill's words: "Left-handed fencers die more." He instinctively covered his heart with his right hand. In that moment, Raul lunged and hit Mikey on the arm.

"Stop," called Coach. "Mike, what was your arm doing on your chest?"

It was protecting me, thought Mikey. "I don't know," he said. His arm hurt where Raul had hit him.

"If he didn't have his arm there, I would have hit him in the chest," said Raul. "So it should count as a hit anyway, shouldn't it? Shouldn't it, Coach?"

Coach lifted an eyebrow and frowned. "No." He pursed his lips. "Never put your arm up. Parry the attack with your blade, not your body. Then repost immediately—get that blade back on target." As Coach talked, he parried an imaginary attack and reposted. He was lightning fast. "And maintain distance. The best way not to get hit is to be out of range. It's just like our exercises. Footwork and distance."

Mikey nodded. But he knew Coach was wrong: This wasn't the same thing as exercising—when they fenced by hitting each other with gloves. A glove could never pierce your heart. And that's why Mikey's whole body felt jittery. And that's why sweat dripped into his eyes and his blood pumped so hard he could feel it in his temples. And that's why he wanted to be outside in the cool air without his mask, just breathing. Breathing and breathing.

Raul advanced. Mikey felt sick in his stomach. But he retreated fast to maintain distance. Raul seemed to puff out his chest a little. He advanced again. He was close now. Too close. Out of the blue came a surge of energy. Mikey lunged and hit Raul in the middle of the chest.

"Touch." Coach nodded. "Did you see that, cadets? Mike retreated fast. That emphasizes the defense and makes your opponent come in too close because he thinks you'll retreat immediately. But that's when Mike took the attack. See? He had less distance to go. That's strategy."

Mikey's ears rang with the praise. Amazing, unexpected, beautiful praise. Strategy. He hadn't even known what he was doing, but it was strategy.

Coach nodded toward them. It was time to fence again.

Raul stood motionless. Mikey realized he was waiting for Mikey to move first. Maybe he wanted to use Mikey's own strategy back on him. Well, Mikey wouldn't fall for it. He waited.

Raul didn't move.

What now? They couldn't stand there doing nothing forever. Mikey advanced with little steps.

Raul retreated with little steps.

Mikey waited for Raul to advance.

Raul stood there.

Mikey advanced a tiny bit more.

Raul retreated another tiny bit.

They both stood there, stock-still.

This was awful. Mikey advanced with teeny-tiny steps.

Raul retreated the teeniest bit possible.

And now they were close again. And again, out of nowhere, came an undeniable urge. Mikey advanced with a huge lunge.

"Touch," said Coach.

Mikey took off his mask in a daze and shook hands with Raul.

"Good strategy again. Mike took little steps on the advance so his opponent would think he had a little lunge. Then he stepped out big and struck." Coach nodded at Nick and Zach.

Nick and Zach took their places and saluted.

Mikey hardly saw them. It was as though Coach's praise had wrapped him in a blanket and nothing else mattered. Mikey had good strategy. He hadn't planned it, so maybe it came naturally. Mikey had heard of such things—natural athletes. Maybe he was a natural fencer.

"I deserved the first touch," hissed Raul in Mikey's ear.

Mikey looked at him, and all at once he remembered the fear that had made him put his hand over his heart. "I know."

Raul looked surprised. Then he nodded. "Next time."

Mikey swallowed hard. This was what fencing was all about. He'd probably get hit over and over. But he'd learn new strategies and he'd get better. Strategy was the key.

Supper

Victoria spun around in the old desk chair that they all loved because it could go in a full circle. Finally she stopped. "I feel sick."

"Just watching you made me sick," said Mikey. He sat on the den floor with a chessboard. He was reading in a book to figure out how each piece moved. Coach had told Mamma and Daddy that Mikey should take up chess because it would make his strategy even better.

"I want to spin," said Calvin. He climbed up on Victoria's lap and they spun together once around.

Then Victoria got up and left the chair to Calvin. "I have to stop fooling around; it's time for me to make supper."

"Supper?" said Calvin. "I thought you were making dinner."

"Supper's the same as dinner," said Mikey. "Just a fancy name for it, 'cause she feels so important."

"I don't feel important," said Victoria. "I'm doing

a job, so Mamma and Daddy can go out. You're the one who thinks you're so important. The strategist." She drew the last word out, as though it was the funniest thing in the world.

"Kpok," said Mikey.

"I love this chair," said Calvin.

"There's an even better one at school," said Victoria. "In keyboarding class I get to sit in a computer chair that goes up and down. But I'm not heavy enough to make it go down, so everyone has to come over and help push down on me."

"I'd love to sit in a chair that went up and down," said Calvin.

"You will someday." Victoria walked toward the door. "Time for work."

Mikey swept the chess pieces into their box. "I'll help."

"Oh, no, you won't. Mamma said I was to be the cook tonight. You just want to be the only one in the limelight."

"Is a limelight green?" said Calvin.

"I don't want to be in the limelight. I'll do whatever you tell me."

"Okay, then get a can of dog food for Yippy."

"Sure. And I'll even set the table."

Victoria looked thoughtful. "Oh, all right. I guess you can set the table."

"Let's have oatmeal." Calvin jumped off the chair.

Victoria made a face. "No one wants oatmeal."

"I do." Calvin stood on one foot.

"I do, too." Mikey closed the chess book. "I like breakfast for dinner."

"No. I'm cooking. I'll make something good."

"Let's vote," said Mikey. "Calvin and I vote for oatmeal."

"You just don't want me to cook because you want to be the only one that gets praised today for your two big hits."

"I should have lost the first touch," said Mikey softly.

"What did you say?"

"You heard me."

"Say it again."

"Raul hit me on the arm, so it didn't count. But he only hit me there because my arm was on my chest where it wasn't supposed to be. Otherwise he would have killed me."

Calvin's eyes opened wide. "Who would have killed you?"

"It's not real killing," said Victoria quickly. "In lessons, a touch with the sword is called killing."

"*Foil*," said Mikey, "not *sword*."

"Foil," said Victoria. She looked at Mikey. "Why was your arm on your chest?"

"To protect my heart."

"An arm can't protect against a foil."

"I know." Mikey looked down at his hands. Then he looked at Victoria. "I panicked."

Victoria nodded slowly. "If someone pointed one of those things at me, I guess I'd panic, too."

"You?" Mikey could hardly believe his ears. "You're never afraid of anything. I bet you weren't even afraid of the fifth-grade bullies when you were in fourth grade."

Victoria knitted her brows. "Are there jerks bothering you at school?"

"No. But some of them bother other kids."

"Well, they better not bother you or I'll kick their butts."

Victoria's words made Mikey feel good. Then he looked at her skinny legs and arms. "Have you ever kicked a big bully really?"

Victoria crossed her arms at the chest. "Actually, no. But it's a matter of attitude, Mikey. You have to feel like you can kick butt. Don't think about size. Stand up to a bully and use your head. Use that famous strategy of yours."

How could strategy put a bully in his place? "I'm going to learn chess," said Mikey doubtfully.

"Chess? What's chess got to do with it?"

"Chess teaches strategy. That's what Coach says. If I learn chess, maybe I'll never have to act dumb or afraid again."

"I know how to play chess," said Victoria quietly.

"You do?"

"I used to play it at Jilly's house. I'll teach you if you promise never to make chicken noises at me again."

Jilly was Victoria's best friend, who moved away last year. Mikey knew Victoria missed her. He stepped closer to his sister. "Thanks."

Victoria gave a small smile. "I suppose oatmeal could be fun. We can put bowls of raisins and walnuts on the table, for anyone who wants to add them."

"And chocolate chips," said Calvin.

"That's disgusting." Victoria walked into the kitchen.

"And popcorn," said Calvin.

"No."

Mikey set the table while Victoria boiled the water for the oatmeal and Calvin filled bowls with walnuts and raisins and chocolate chips.

Mamma came in carrying Julie on her hip. She had on a light blue wool skirt and a big blue sweater. Julie fingered Mamma's pearl necklace with one hand and clutched her rag doll with the other.

"You look pretty," said Calvin.

"That's just what I was thinking," said Mikey.

"Really? With all the physical labor I've been doing, my hands are a mess of callouses and I had to wash my hair twice to feel clean." Mamma set Julie in her booster seat and her rag doll on the edge of the table, leaning against the wall. "You can get your dolly again after you eat, Julie."

Yippy walked over and licked Julie's feet. Julie laughed.

Mamma scratched Yippy behind the ears. "Are you sure you can manage things, Victoria?"

"Of course I can. I'm in middle school, Ma."

Mamma nodded, but the worry didn't leave her face. "The Kirbys are home and they said you could call if you wanted."

The Kirbys lived next door, and their only son was grown and off at college. They had tons of worms in their vegetable garden every summer. Mikey liked them.

"I won't need to call anyone," said Victoria. "Don't worry. Just have a nice time with your new friends. What're their names?"

"Tom and Susan. Susan's nice. I started talking to her in the grocery line. She noticed the paint on my clothes. She'd like to have her basement redone, like I did ours." Mamma looked at the pot on the stove. "What are you making?"

"They wanted oatmeal," said Victoria. "They're crazy."

"We voted," said Calvin.

Mamma looked across the table. "With raisins and

walnuts and even chocolate chips." She smiled. "You're well prepared. And, Mikey, don't forget to let Yippy out in the yard a few minutes before putting her to bed."

"I won't, Mamma."

"And put the cover over Dragon's cage for the night."

"I will, Mamma."

Mamma kissed each child on the cheek. Then she took a piece of paper from her pocket and attached it to the magnetic clip on the refrigerator. "Here's the phone number of the restaurant."

Daddy came into the kitchen. "Everything okay?"

"I can handle things," said Victoria. "Leave already."

"Of course you can," said Daddy.

"Oh," said Victoria casually, "my friend said she might stop by later for a little while."

"What friend?" said Daddy.

That's what Mikey wanted to know, too. "I thought you were going to teach me chess tonight."

"I'll teach you tomorrow. Virginia's coming over tonight."

Daddy looked at the box on the counter by the stove. "Oatmeal? I love a good bowl of oatmeal."

"You're all crazy," said Victoria.

Daddy smiled. He took Mamma by the arm, and they left.

Victoria poured the dry oatmeal into the now-boiling water and stirred.

Julie looked around. "Mamma all gone. Daddy all gone."

"That's right," said Victoria. "They're going to have a good time and so are we. You'll like Virginia."

"Want chocolate chips?" said Calvin.

"Chip," said Julie. "Want chip."

Calvin put a handful of chips on the table in front of Julie. "Brock lost a tooth in kindergarten today."

Mikey remembered losing his first tooth. It was in an apple at lunch in first grade. "He's young to be losing a tooth."

"He's going to be rich. He's five like me, and he's going to be rich." Calvin had been in the habit of reminding everyone he was five ever since his birthday a few weeks ago.

"Rich," said Julie. She stuck a fistful of chocolate chips in her mouth.

"He gets twenty-five cents for his tooth."

"Twenty-five cents!" said Mikey. How could Calvin think twenty-five cents was a lot of money?

Victoria put a bowl in front of each child's place. "Blow on it, Julie. Blow with me." Victoria blew on Julie's oatmeal.

Julie blew hard. Oatmeal splattered across the table.

Mikey looked at Calvin. He expected Calvin to ask his question about why air was cool when you blew with round lips. He wanted to hear Victoria's answer. But Calvin just blew noisily on his oatmeal.

Victoria sat down. "Okay, let's have a conversation. Mikey, why don't you talk?"

"Huh? What should I talk about?"

"I don't care. Anything."

"We're almost through with guitar lessons. We have them every Monday, Wednesday, and Friday. But we're almost through."

"I want to play guitar," said Calvin.

"Blow," said Julie. She blew again on her oatmeal.

Calvin put a handful of raisins in front of Julie.

"Guitar is fun," said Mikey. "And Monday is the last day, so Raymond gets to do his horse imitations."

"What?" Victoria looked at Mikey. "What an absurd thing to say."

"It's true," said Mikey. "He's good at horse imitations."

"But that's ridiculous," said Victoria. "What's the last guitar lesson got to do with horse imitations?"

Mikey broke walnuts into his oatmeal. "Mr. Shankweiler likes horse imitations. He's the music teacher."

"Then the music teacher's nuts."

"My teacher made us taste salsa," said Calvin. "She's not nuts."

"Nut," said Julie. She stuffed raisins in her mouth.

"No, those are raisins, Julie. You know that." Victoria looked at Calvin. "Your teacher gave you salsa? Like the stuff people eat on corn chips?"

"Chip," said Julie. "Eat chip."

"No, eat your oatmeal now, Julie." Victoria put Julie's spoon into her hand. "You had enough chocolate chips."

"And we get to wear costumes on Halloween. I love my teacher," said Calvin.

Victoria sighed again. "Can't we have a normal conversation?"

Mikey thought about Victoria's question. She loved logic and everything normal. But sometimes life wasn't logical or normal. Mikey wanted life to be different and wonderful. So far in school Mr. Gaynor had handed out eight Olympic medals, and none of them had gone to Mikey. But today at fencing lesson Mikey had learned that he was a natural fencer. Yes, that was it: Mikey would change the topic of his research project to fencing. Oh, yes. Now he would have a real chance at the Olympic medal. He could do a fencing demonstration as part of his research project. Everyone would be amazed. "I'm going to win an Olympic medal," he blurted out with loud determination. "I'm going to win for my research project on how sword fighting has changed through the ages. And when the medal hangs around my neck, all of you will be proud of me."

"An Olympic medal for a research project? Mikey, do you even know what the Olympics are? That's it," said Victoria. "You're all demented. Let's just eat in silence."

The Fort

The next weekend Mikey watched his mother tie her hair up in a kerchief. "You're going to do their basement all by yourself?"

"All by myself," said Mamma with a smile. "It'll take weeks and weeks. And they're paying me." She went out the door, happy as could be in her old jeans and paint-stained sweatshirt. Mamma's friend Susan had hired her and now she was going off, all on her own. How could a mother abandon her family on a Sunday?

Mikey walked through the kitchen past Calvin.

"How do you spell *love?*" asked Calvin.

Mikey took a piece of scrap paper and printed *love* on it. He put the paper on the table beside Calvin and started down the steps to the basement.

"Stop right there," Victoria called up.

"Huh?" Mikey bent so he could see into the basement. "I want to come down."

"Virginia and I are doing something private. No one else is allowed in the basement."

"That's not fair."

"Mamma said."

Virginia appeared at the bottom of the stairs. "Anyway, your name doesn't start with *V*. The basement is for *V*-people."

"Since when?"

"Since today," said Victoria firmly. "Go help Calvin with his stupid note."

Mikey stood up straight. "Who wants to be a *V*-people anyway?" He went back into the kitchen.

Calvin pushed his note forward proudly. "I finished. Look how good my letters are."

Calvin's letters were neat. Mikey couldn't believe it, but they were actually neater than his. "Why would you care? First Victoria, then John, and now you." Mikey walked around the table, his arms flying, his voice rising. "I have perfectly good handwriting. Everyone's crazy to care about handwriting."

Calvin looked up worriedly. "Are you mad at me, Mikey? Don't be mad. Please don't be mad."

Victoria came upstairs. "So, how do I look?"

Mikey and Calvin stared. Victoria's hair was cut short, right below the ears. Her long braid was gone!

"Virginia did it for me. Well?"

Calvin smiled. "You look just like Mikey."

"Like Mikey!" Victoria gasped and shook her head. "No, I don't. How could you say such a thing, Calvin? How could you?" She ran back down the basement stairs.

"What did I do?" Calvin was practically in tears. "What did I do, Mikey?"

"She doesn't want to look like me."

"Why not? You look good. Why's everyone mad at me all of a sudden?"

The front doorbell rang. Mikey ran to answer it.

A woman smiled at him. "I'm Brock's mother. Is Calvin ready?"

"I'm ready." Calvin came racing from the kitchen. "I'm ready." He flew past Mikey with a wave. "I'm going to Brock's house. You can tell me why everyone's mad later."

Brock's mother looked at Mikey quizzically.

Mikey flashed her a quick smile. He watched as Calvin climbed into the car and it pulled out of the driveway.

Calvin waved again and shouted, "Bye, Mikey, bye."

Mikey stood on the front porch and looked down the road. No one was in sight. A peal of laughter came up from the basement. Mikey felt cold and alone.

Well, so what? He had plenty to do. He could go in the backyard and practice fencing exercises. He walked quickly around the side of the house.

Daddy stood by the kitchen door, looking up at the gutters. He pointed at a joint. "If I change the angle a little, the rain will get channeled over to here." He tapped his shoe on a spot on the ground. "What do you think, Mikey?"

"I think the gutters look good the way they are, Dad."

"We don't want an ice slick near the door like we had last winter. So that's what I'll do." Daddy picked up a pad of paper from the ground and drew a design. He rubbed his chin and mumbled.

Julie pressed leaves on Yippy's back. "Leaf for ween," she said happily to Mikey. Julie had been talking about Halloween ever since the family discussion about costumes at dinner last night.

"Leaves won't stick to fur," said Mikey.

Julie seemed to think about that. "Okay." She pulled off her shirt. Then she wrestled it over Yippy's head.

Yippy stood up. Julie's shirt hung around the dog's neck in a clump.

"Come, baby dog," said Julie. She went to the door. "Help, Mikey."

Mikey opened the door.

"Socks," said Julie happily. She went inside, followed by Yippy.

Mikey imagined Yippy with socks on. He smiled in spite of himself. Then he went to the middle of the yard. He stretched one leg forward and one leg backward. He jumped and switched legs. He did that over and over. Then he ran backward in a circle. Then he hopped on one foot.

Daddy came over and smiled. "You seem restless, Mikey. Where's your friend?"

"I don't have a friend."

"What about that boy you went rafting with?"

"That's Bill. He doesn't really like me."

"Mamma told me he comes over to play ball every day."

"Mamma's crazy. He hasn't come over all week." That wasn't exactly true. Bill had come on Monday. But when Mikey told him about holding his new foil, Bill had left suddenly. "He says I talk too much about fencing."

"Maybe you do."

"I don't talk about it half as much as I think about it."

"You probably still talk about it a lot." Daddy clicked his tongue against the roof of his mouth. "Maybe you should talk about things you can enjoy together. Why don't you go play with him?"

"I don't know where he is, and I don't care."

"Oh." Daddy put his pad and pencil on the lawn chair. "I think I'll take Julie and Yippy to the park. Want to come?"

The park was a few blocks away. It was fenced in, and it had swings and a slide that wasn't even as tall as Daddy and wooden animals on huge springs for little kids to ride on. No one over five would be caught dead in that park.

"No, thanks."

"What're you going to do?"

"I'll take my own walk."

Daddy rubbed his chin again. "Well, all right. See you later." He went inside, calling, "Julie."

Mikey slowly walked down the driveway and out toward Yale Avenue. He didn't think about where he was going; he just turned left automatically.

Within minutes, he was standing outside Bill's house. He waited. Who knew, Bill might just happen to come out the door. But no one came out. Finally, Mikey rang the bell.

A woman in a flowery shirt and black pants opened the door. "Yes?"

"I'm Mikey. Is Bill home?"

"Mikey? You're the great fencer, aren't you?"

Mikey couldn't believe his ears. "I've only taken a few lessons."

The woman smiled wide. "Go on around back. He's working on some construction project. He'll be so glad to see you." She waited. "Go on."

"Thanks." Mikey backed off the step. Then he walked around the house. Bill would be glad to see him? Had Bill's mother confused Mikey with someone else? But who else took fencing?

As Mikey rounded the back corner of the house, he heard a hammer. He followed the noise to a shed behind the garage. Mikey peeked in. "Hi."

Bill put down his hammer. "Hi." He looked surprised.

Mikey glanced around the shed. A stack of boards was propped against one wall. "What're you doing?"

"Building a fort."

"Oh, yeah?" Mikey ran his hand along a board. "What kind of fort?"

Bill took a folded piece of paper from his pocket. He spread it out on the workbench.

Mikey looked at the sketch of a small, square building with a pointed roof. "Wow."

"I designed it without my brother."

"It's great. Where're you going to put it?"

"It'll be a tree fort." Bill pointed to a tree in the corner of his yard.

Mikey looked at the tree with longing. "The first crook there, that's a perfect spot."

"That's what I think, too."

"It's high enough that it could be like a lookout," said Mikey. "You know. Like pirates had."

"You like to play pirates?"

"Well, yeah. I guess I was sort of thinking about pirates when I first decided to start fencing."

"Everything's fencing to you." Bill rubbed the Olympic medal around his neck. The ribbon it hung on was dirty and frayed by now. He heaved a sigh. Then he folded up the design of the fort and stuck it in his back pocket.

Mikey tried again. "It could be a great lookout."

"I've stood up there in the tree. If Hugh's anywhere within two blocks, I can see him. I can even see all the way into Jennifer M.'s backyard from there." Bill looked quickly at Mikey. "Do you have a nickname for Jennifer M.?"

"Jennifer Mouth."

"Oh." Bill looked stumped. "Why?"

"She has a mouth."

"So does everyone."

Mikey smiled. "So tell me it's not logical. My sister says I'm not logical all the time. I don't care."

Bill gave a small laugh. "I don't care what my brother says, either." He picked up the hammer and pounded a nail halfway into a board. The head stuck out about an inch. Then he pounded a second one in beside it, the same way.

"Why are you leaving the nails sticking halfway out?"

"I do this to all the boards. I put a couple of nails near each end, like these. Then when I go to hammer the boards to something, I don't have to worry about trying to hold the nails in place. All I have to do is hold the board in place and the nails are ready."

"Good system." Mikey nodded appreciatively. Then he searched the shelves with his eyes. He spied another hammer. He walked over and picked it up. "You going to build it all alone?" He stood beside Bill at the workbench.

Bill looked at the hammer in Mikey's hand. He put another board on the bench and marked two spots near each end with a pencil. Then he shoved the board over in front of Mikey. "I could use some help."

Mikey took a nail and held it in place with his right hand. He swung at it and hit his thumb. Tears stung his eyes.

"It takes a while to get the hang of it."

"I have an idea." Mikey picked up the nail again. His thumb throbbed, but he held the nail steady. This time he tapped lightly. It stuck. He tapped again and again, until the head stuck out about the same amount that Bill's nails stuck out.

"I never saw anyone hammer like that," said Bill.

"Strategy," said Mikey. "You pound. I tap. But the nail gets in either way. Like in fencing. Fencing strategy is . . ."

"I don't want to hear about fencing strategy. I don't want to hear about fencing anything. I told you that." Bill put a box of nails between them. "Let's see who can get the most nails in place the fastest. Ready?"

Mikey gripped his hammer tight. "All right, but only if we can have a second contest, and I get to choose what."

"I don't fence," said Bill.

"It won't be fencing. It'll be . . . chess."

"Chess?"

Victoria had taught Mikey the moves last Sunday, and he'd played with her every night this week. He'd won one game so far, and that may have been only because Victoria got a phone call in the middle and seemed to lose her sense of concentration. Probably he wasn't good enough to beat Bill. But he had to challenge Bill to something, and he couldn't think of anything else. "Know how to play?"

"A little."

"Then we're even. I know a little hammering, you know a little chess. Deal?"

"Deal."

Rules and Rulers

Raymond stood in front of the class and held a poster about horses pulling plows. His research project was on how people's use of horses had changed over the years. It was a good project, but Mikey knew Raymond couldn't win this week's Olympic medal. He had won last week's medal because of his horse imitations during guitar lesson, and no one yet had won two medals. Mikey was sure that Mr. Gaynor would let everyone in the class win one Olympic medal before he let anyone win a second one.

Mikey drummed his fingers on his desk.

Alison tapped him on the shoulder from behind. "Shhh!"

Mikey stopped drumming and moved his knees out and together, out and together. His project was next. They'd been having project presentations during the last half hour of school all week, and now it was Thursday and Mikey knew his project could beat any of the ones he had seen so far. He had notes on index cards, like everyone else. And he had a poster, like everyone else. But he also had something no one else had: a real exhibit. Daddy had dropped Mikey off at school this morning with his fencing bag. In it were his knickers; his jacket; his mask; his fencing shoes; and, best of all, his foil. He was amazed when Mamma had said he could bring his foil. There was a hitch, though. He was allowed to show all that stuff, but he had had to promise that if he did a demonstration, he would use a ruler instead of his foil in the classroom. Mamma was adamant about it. A stupid little plastic ruler. But it didn't matter. Everyone would be impressed with the foil.

Raymond finished talking and took his seat.

"Your turn, Mikey," said Mr. Gaynor.

Mikey lifted the lid of his desk and pulled out his poster. He flattened out the folds and went up to the front of the room. "My project is on swords." He held up the poster and showed the class his drawings. "These swords here"—he pointed to the thick, wide blades—"were used for hacking people apart in wars. They're so heavy, you had to hold them with two hands." Mikey looked around the class.

All eyes were glued to his poster.

"Only knights in the Crusades used the two-handed swords, because they were expensive to make and ordinary people couldn't afford them."

Pete sat in the back of the room and gripped an imaginary sword with both hands. He slashed the air again and again. Mikey smiled at him.

"And these are rapiers. They're lighter and thinner. They used them for duels. Like in Spain and France and Italy." Mikey pointed lower. "These short, heavy ones are cutlasses. They're for chopping at your enemy."

"Those are the kinds pirates used," said Jennifer Snot. She smiled sweetly at Mikey. Then she pulled a handkerchief out of her desk and blew her nose.

Mikey flushed. "That's right."

"Pirates!" Pete hit Stephen on the arm. Stephen turned to Pete, and they did an imaginary duel in the air, complete with cries of rage and pain. By this time most of the class's eyes had turned to the back of the room.

"Pay attention back there," said Mr. Gaynor. He cleared his throat. "Go on, Mikey."

"The ones with the curved hilts are sabers. People fought with them on horseback. And this one over here is a long sword. It's the best kind of battle sword, and it was used through the ages, with the sword in one hand and a shield in the other." Mikey held up the poster so everyone could see.

"But today people don't sword fight anymore; they fence. Fencing is a sport. The two kinds of fencing I know about are called foil and épée. Both of them are duels. That means it's just you and your opponent." Mikey pointed to the poster. "This is an épée blade. See how it's thick and triangular? The duel in épée is to the first blood. So if you knick your opponent before your opponent stabs you, then you get the point. And you can hit anywhere, on the chest or leg or even the hand. That's why the bell guard is so big, to protect your hand, because your hand's a target."

A few heads in the class were nodding as if in agreement. Everyone was paying attention again now.

"Foil uses a different blade, but I didn't draw one."

Pete groaned.

"I brought one."

Pete stood up. "Wow!"

"Sit down, Pete," said Mr. Gaynor.

Mikey grinned. He went to the closet in the corner where Mr. Gaynor had told him to stash his fencing bag until his turn to present his project. He took out the black bag and unzipped it. "These are knickers. They go down to just below your knees. And this is the jacket. See how it's thick all over, to protect you? And these are the official shoes. They look a lot like normal sneakers, but they're lighter, so you can move fast. And this"—Mikey put on his mask—"this is my mask."

Everyone laughed.

"You look like a spaceman," said Raymond.

"You look like one of those guys that go underwater," said Alison.

Mikey took off his mask. "And this is a foil." He pulled out the blade.

Everyone stared.

"See how the blade is square? In foil fencing, the duel is to the death."

Everyone gasped.

"That just means you have to hit someone on the vest area. It doesn't count if you hit on the leg or arm. You have to aim for a killing strike, and you don't get a point unless you hit in the right place. So the bell guard is smaller, 'cause no one aims for the hand."

"Let's see you fence," came a voice. "Give a demonstration."

Mikey looked around.

It was Bill. "Come on. Show us what you can do."

Mikey couldn't tell if Bill meant it in a friendly way or not. Last Sunday Bill had won the hammering contest, of course. But Mikey had actually won the chess game. And neither of them had mentioned the contests since. So Mikey didn't know how Bill felt about the contests—and he wasn't sure how Bill felt about him in this moment, when all he was talking about was fencing. Bill hated fencing. Why would he want Mikey to show the class? But Mikey had planned to show the class a bit of fencing any-way. So it was fine that Bill asked for a demonstra-tion now. "Okay. Let me put all this away first." He stuck the foil in the bag.

"Wait," said Pete. "You can't put your sword away if you're going to fight."

"I'll use a ruler," said Mikey. He took out the ruler.

"A ruler?" said Pete. "How dumb."

"A ruler's a good idea," said Mr. Gaynor. "Other-wise it's too dangerous."

"Well, if he's going to use a ruler," said Pete, "then let me fight him. I've got a ruler, too." Pete held up a ruler and stood in the aisle beside his desk, ready.

"Great," said Raymond.

"Well . . ." said Mr. Gaynor.

"Come on, Mr. Gaynor," said Jennifer Braid.

"Come on," came many voices.

"Okay," said Mr. Gaynor. "If that's all right with you, Mikey."

Mikey had folded his knickers and put them in the bag. Now he stood there with his jacket in his hands and hesitated. "I don't know. There's sort of a lot to it." Mikey kept his eyes down. He didn't want to sound like he was bragging. "You kind of need to take lessons." He folded his jacket as he talked.

"I don't care about lessons," said Pete. "Let's fight."

"Duel," said Mikey. He put his fencing shoes in the bag. "I don't know."

"Wussy."

Mikey looked around. He didn't know who had said that. His breath came dry and his chest hurt. But whoever said that was wrong. Mikey wasn't afraid. No one could get hurt with a ruler. It wasn't that at all.

"That's enough," said Mr. Gaynor. "Mikey's right. You need lessons to fence."

"Awww," said Pete.

The word *wussy* kept whispering in Mikey's ears. Everyone would think he was afraid if he didn't fence. "I guess we could fence a little," said Mikey softly. He'd just go easy on Pete, so that he didn't embarrass him.

"Okay!" Pete ran up the aisle. "Let's go."

Mikey zipped up his fencing bag and stuck it back in the closet. He assumed proper position and held up his ruler. He balanced his weight exactly right. He was poised for action. He hardly noticed all the admiring eyes on him.

Pete swung his ruler in a circle over his head and shouted, "Die!" He chopped at Mikey's left arm from the outside. The pain came in a burst. Mikey's ruler flew out of his hand. Pete jabbed Mikey in the chest. "I killed you!"

"Ha!" said Stephen. "Pete won! How many lessons did you have, Mikey?"

Mikey picked up his ruler and blinked hard. It had all happened so fast he had trouble believing it. His face was hot and his head buzzed and the place where Pete had chopped his arm hurt horribly. He wanted to run away. He wanted to run away and never come back. "You didn't fence by the rules," he said in a half daze.

"I stabbed you in the heart. I killed you. So I won," said Pete. "Those are the rules, right?"

"You're supposed to hit in the vest area and watch your footwork and position and . . ." Mikey looked at Pete. Pete looked at him hard. Everyone was looking at him hard. It was no use. No one would understand. ". . . things like that." Mikey swallowed. "It doesn't matter. You won." He held out his hand to shake.

Pete looked at Mikey's hand in wonder. Then he slapped it. "Hurrah for me."

"Hurrah for Pete," shouted Stephen.

"Hurrah!" came the shouts.

"Okay, there's just enough time for one more project today," said Mr. Gaynor. "Jennifer M., it's your turn."

Special

Mikey practically ran all the way home. He longed for his bike, so that he could pedal faster than ever and get away from everyone. So that he could escape. What an awful day to have been driven to school. He wished Daddy could have left work early and picked him up, too. Anything, anything would be better than having to walk home now.

Mikey kept his eyes on the sidewalk so that he wouldn't have to look people in the face. He had lost the duel. Pete had killed him. So what did it matter if Pete hadn't followed the rules? If it had been a real duel in real life, Mikey would be dead now. Pierced through the heart. Like Bill had said would happen.

Mikey would never win an Olympic medal. And he'd never be a good fencer. That's why he had left his fencing bag at school. He didn't know if he ever wanted to see it again.

The front porch of Mikey's house was empty.

Good. At least Calvin wasn't there to chatter at him right away. Mikey walked quietly through the house, stashing his backpack in his cubby and leaving through the back door. He walked quickly behind the garage. There was his old pile of pinecones, the ones he'd gathered in September. He tunneled a path into the middle of them and lay down on his back.

The pine tree behind the garage stood twice as tall as Mikey's house. He stared up through the needles, looking at nothing. He could hear nothing. He felt nothing. It was almost as though Mikey were nothing.

"Mikey!" came Mamma's voice.

Mikey shook himself out of the trance and sat up. He rubbed at the back of his neck. Then he went inside.

"Oh, hi, sweetie." Mamma and Julie were setting the table. "I was wondering where you were. I wanted to ask you about your big day. But it's almost time to eat now, so you can save it to tell all of us together at the dinner table." She smiled.

Mikey's heart fell. His big day. His catastrophic day.

"Could you get Calvin, please?"

"Where is he?"

"Upstairs, I think."

Mikey climbed the stairs and checked in the playroom. It was empty. He went into the bedroom. "There you are, Calvin. It's dinnertime."

Calvin was holding on to the windowsill with both hands and looking out. His favorite sleep blanket was tucked under his arm. "Shhh."

Mikey walked up behind him. "What is it?"

"There's a cougar in the yard."

"A cougar? A mountain lion?"

"Yes."

Mikey almost said how dumb that was. Then he thought of the voice calling out "wussy" in school today. Mikey had had enough of name-calling for one day. He decided to try to reason Calvin out of this. He looked down at the yard. "Where?"

"It's hiding."

"How do you know it's hiding?"

"That's what cougars do."

"But how do you know it's there?"

"What?"

Mikey shook his head. This tack wasn't working. His brother was a mental case. On the other hand, Mikey understood that kind of worry. In fact, he was surprised that Calvin thought about scary things like cougars. Calvin always seemed so carefree. Mikey felt a pang of sympathy. "Listen, Calvin, if there was a cougar in the yard, Yippy would growl and go nuts. But, see, Yippy's just digging holes in the chrysanthemum bed, like she always does."

"Oh."

"So, see, there's no cougar out there."

"He must have left."

"Sure, Calvin. He left." Mikey closed the blind. He didn't have the energy to talk Calvin out of his crazy cougar idea. He had his own problems. Mamma expected him to tell about his day at the dinner table. He could try diverting her. He could talk about something that would upset her—like that bully Hugh. Mamma went nuts over things like that.

But even if he managed to get Mamma to forget, his problems wouldn't be over. Everyone in the family knew he had brought his fencing gear to school today. So if Mamma didn't ask what had happened, someone else was bound to. Probably Daddy. Daddy always asked that kind of question.

Mikey would have to tell all of them the horrible truth. He tapped Calvin on the shoulder sadly. "Come on, cougar cub. Let's go eat."

"Okay."

Mikey twirled his spaghetti on his fork. Spaghetti was probably his favorite meal of all, but he could hardly taste it.

"So, did anyone have anything unusual happen to them today?" asked Daddy. He looked right at Mikey with a knowing smile. Then he opened a bottle of beer and filled his glass.

Mikey jammed a huge forkful of spaghetti in his mouth, so no one could expect him to talk. It dismayed him how predictable Daddy was.

"We had a standardized test today," said Victoria. She sprinkled cheese in her bowl.

"Oh, poor you," said Mamma.

"No, it was easy. It was about bats."

"Bats?" said Daddy.

"Bat," said Julie. "All bout bat." She jammed her fork into her spaghetti. "Bat bat bat."

Mikey couldn't resist. "Victoria's batty," he said.

"I am not." Victoria tossed her head. She had taken to sleeping with curlers in her hair ever since she'd cut it, and her ringlets bounced now. "We had to read this long thing about bats and answer questions. It was interesting." She took a sip of milk and patted the edges of her hair.

"I really like your hair that way," said Mamma. "It's sophisticated."

Daddy glanced at Victoria's hair; then he looked around. "Could someone please pass me another piece of garlic toast?"

Calvin stood on his chair and pushed the basket of toast toward Daddy.

"Please sit down, Calvin," said Mamma.

Calvin sat down. "Me next."

"So what happened to you today, Calvin?" asked Daddy.

Mikey wondered if Calvin would tell about the cougar and if everyone would laugh at him. He didn't want everyone to laugh at Calvin. He was sick of humiliation. "Tell about kindergarten, Calvin," he said softly.

"We had an assembly about butterflies."

"Oh, how nice." Mamma smiled. "Was the assembly for the whole school?"

Calvin nodded. "Everyone but the people who were absent."

Mamma and Daddy and Victoria laughed.

"You shouldn't laugh," said Mikey defiantly. "Especially not you, Victoria. What Calvin said was logical."

Victoria looked at Mikey. "Yes, but it was obvious. That's why it was funny."

"I didn't think it was funny," said Mikey.

"You'll understand when you're as old as I am."

"I'll never be as old as you are. That's illogical," said Mikey.

Daddy gave a muffled laugh and exchanged glances with Mamma.

"Don't be stupid, Mikey. You know that's not what I meant."

"Mikey," said Daddy loudly, "tell us about your day."

"It's Julie's turn," said Mikey.

Daddy looked surprised. Then he nodded. "Okay,

we'll save the best for last. So, Julie, what good thing happened to you today?"

"Paint," said Julie. She held up both hands, fingers spread. Her hands were red with tomato sauce. "Paint day."

Mamma smiled. "We finger painted. Julie's very good at it. We painted half the morning away. Till Yippy begged us for a walk. But tomorrow we're going to bake again, because Julie wants to make pie."

Mikey stared at his plate the whole time Mamma talked. He knew when she stopped talking, it would be his turn. He had wanted her to talk forever. But now she had stopped. His heart clutched.

"Oh, that reminds me," said Victoria. "Virginia wants to take Yippy overnight tonight."

For an instant Mikey adored Victoria. Please, let her keep talking, please, he said inside his head.

"Overnight?" said Mamma.

"What for?" said Daddy.

"Well, Virginia's never had a pet except a mouse. And it got cancer so they had to have it put to sleep." She shook her head. "Horrible. So she loves Yippy and she wants to borrow her."

"They had a mouse put to sleep?" said Daddy.

"Of course. It's the only humane way," said Victoria.

"Mouse sleep," said Julie. "Mouse sleep. Mouse eat." She put both hands in her spaghetti at once.

"Use your fork, please, Julie," said Mamma. She reached over and put the fork in Julie's fist.

Yes, said Mikey in his head, yes, everyone, keep talking. Keep talking.

"So can she?" said Victoria.

"Well," said Mamma, "I guess that depends on Yippy. Does Yippy like Virginia?"

"Yippy likes anyone who feeds her." Victoria held out a piece of garlic toast to Yippy. Yippy sniffed at it, then took it in her teeth. "See? She's a pig. She'll be perfectly happy at Virginia's for the night."

"I really wish you wouldn't feed the dog from the table. You know better than that, Victoria."

"Sorry. But, anyway, Virginia even bought Yippy a package of cherry licorice sticks, because I told her Yippy loves them. I'll walk her over after dinner."

"You can't go walking alone with the cougar out," said Calvin.

Mikey looked around the table fast. He expected all of them to hoot and howl at Calvin.

"What cougar?" said Victoria.

"Didn't you hear?" said Mamma. "Someone spotted a cougar in Fairmont Park last night. At first they thought it was a prank call or some kind of mistake. But then today there were several sightings, and the latest one was in Delaware County. It's been on the radio all day long."

"Really?" said Mikey. "I thought Calvin was making things up, like he always does."

Mamma laughed. "No, it's true. But Calvin does have a wonderful imagination. It's a gift. It makes him special. Let's all hope he can hold on to it."

Calvin smiled happily. "I'm special."

Mikey stared at Mamma. All of Calvin's stupid little made-up things made him special? The words hit him with a sharp ping of envy. Everything was so easy for Calvin. Things happened right for him without him even trying.

Daddy finished off his beer and sat back. "I can't imagine how a cougar got all the way to eastern Pennsylvania without getting killed by a car. It has to have come from as far as upstate New York, at the closest."

"Maybe it was someone's pet that escaped." Victoria put her fork and glass on her plate and carried it all to the counter by the sink. "Some people are inhumane enough to keep wild animals like that for pets."

"You're probably right," said Mamma.

Mikey thought about how he had spent the afternoon lying in the middle of the pinecone pile, completely unaware of the danger. He looked at Calvin. "You didn't really see the cougar in our backyard, Calvin. You didn't, did you?"

Calvin nodded. "He was hiding."

That couldn't be true. But Mikey shivered in spite of himself.

Mamma pursed her lips. "I doubt that. They said that it's likely to head for the golf course or a park. It'll stay as far away from houses as it can."

"It was far away," said Calvin. "It was in the bushes."

Mamma looked at Calvin and hesitated. Then she turned to Victoria. "Anyway, I'll drive Yippy over to Virginia's house after we've cleaned up from dinner." She picked up the serving bowl. "Does anyone want more spaghetti?"

Mikey put his glass and fork into his plate and pushed back his chair. The meal was over and he'd actually escaped, all because of the excitement about the cougar. He couldn't believe his luck.

"Wait," said Daddy. "We haven't heard about everyone's day yet."

"That's right," said Mamma. "How could I forget?"

There was no escape after all. Dread filled Mikey's throat.

Daddy smiled. "Victoria, come back and sit down. It was a very special day for Mikey. So, Mikey, let's hear about it."

Mikey waited while Victoria sat back down. He looked around the table. They were all looking at him. Julie's eyes were adoring. Calvin's eyes were happy. Victoria's eyes were impatient. Mamma's eyes were expectant. Daddy's eyes were proud.

Mikey's eyes burned. He blinked and blinked. "I can't stand it," he said at last.

Mamma looked alarmed. "What can't you stand, Mikey?"

"I can't stand any of it. Victoria's on the Student Council and I have bad handwriting."

Daddy looked at Mikey blankly. "What?"

"Don't you see? Calvin has imagination. And Julie bakes all the time. And that's all I wanted. I just wanted to be special, like everyone else."

"Mikey, if everyone were special, then it wouldn't be special," said Victoria. "That's illogical."

"Not now, Victoria," said Mamma. She reached her hand across the table and put it over Mikey's. "You are special, Mikey. Very special. Just wanting to do something as unusual and difficult as fencing proves how special you are." She squeezed Mikey's hand. "Did something bad happen?"

Daddy leaned forward. "What happened, Mikey?" he asked gently.

"I fenced Pete." Mikey looked quickly at Mamma. "Just with rulers, like I promised. And . . . he beat me."

"Oh, no," said Calvin.

"Oh, poor Mikey," said Victoria.

"I'm sorry," said Mamma slowly. "I'm so sorry." She got out of her chair and came around the table. She hugged him. "But you know it, Mikey, that's how sports are. Sometimes you win and sometimes you lose."

"But it wasn't fair. He fenced all wrong. He didn't do anything like it's supposed to be done. He broke all the rules."

"Lots of things aren't fair," said Daddy. "You can't control that. What you can do is work and learn and get better at it. Fencing isn't like riding a bike or swimming, where one day you can't do it and the next day you can. It's something you gain skills in gradually." Daddy put both elbows on the table and leaned toward Mikey. "Keep at it. And maybe next time you'll win."

Mikey looked hard at his father. Daddy sounded right. Mikey wanted him to be right.

"Or I could kick Pete's shins in," said Victoria.

"Victoria!" Mamma looked shocked.

"Kick," said Julie. "Kick kick."

"No one's going to kick anyone," said Mamma.

Mikey smiled at his sisters. "Thanks for the thought, anyway."

The Medal

The clock read 2:50. School would be out in a half hour. It was time for the last few research projects. But Mr. Gaynor didn't seem to notice. He had given the class math work sheets and he now sat at his desk, scribbling on a pad of paper.

Eileen raised her hand. "Isn't it time for projects?"

Mr. Gaynor looked up. "Actually, I want you to finish your math now, and we'll have the rest of the projects next week."

"But I was scheduled for today," said Eileen.

"So was I," said Stephen.

Jennifer Mouth nodded her head vehemently, but she didn't say a thing. She clutched a set of index cards in both hands.

"Well, sometimes things come up. Get back to work. There's barely enough time to finish the work sheets as it is."

"What about this week's Olympic medal?" asked Stephen. "How can you give an Olympic medal for the best research project if you haven't seen all the projects yet?"

"You're right," said Mr. Gaynor. "I can't. That's why next week's Olympic medal will be for the best research project."

"So there's no medal this week?" said Pete. "What a cheat."

"Oh, yes, there's a medal." Mr. Gaynor smiled. "There's always a medal on Friday."

"Who gets it?" asked Jennifer Snot.

Mr. Gaynor opened his drawer and held up the medal. It said, "1st Prize—S." Mr. Gaynor cleared his throat. He looked around the room. Then his eyes settled on Mikey. "First prize goes to Mikey, for sportsmanship."

"But I'm the one who won the fight," said Pete.

That was exactly Mikey's thought. He didn't want a medal for losing. He didn't want the booby prize.

"That's not what *sportsmanship* means," said Mr. Gaynor. "Sportsmanship is whether you behave with honor while you play the sport. It has to do with appreciating the sport for itself and not caring only about winning. And it has to do with whether you congratulate your opponent if he wins. For this Mikey earns first prize." He dangled the medal toward Mikey.

Mikey got up while everyone clapped. He took his medal and slipped it into his pocket. Sportsmanship.

It sounded like the sort of thing Mamma would want him to win first prize for—not the sort of thing a kid would want to win. Mikey wanted to win first prize for a skill—for being the best at something that everyone else would recognize as a skill. He sat back down in his seat and looked at Mr. Gaynor. Was that a flicker of pity in Mr. Gaynor's eyes? Mikey looked down and waited for his cheeks to stop burning.

Mikey went down the stairs and out to the bike racks. He balanced his fencing bag across the handlebars and walked the bike slowly. He was taking his fencing bag home today, even though he wasn't sure why.

Mikey reached the first corner and bounced the bike off the curb. His fencing bag slid to one side. He reached for it quickly, and the whole bike and bag and Mikey fell in the street.

"Get up." Bill appeared out of nowhere and straightened Mikey's bike.

Mikey grabbed his fencing bag.

"I'll walk the bike for you," said Bill.

"I didn't know you were here. I didn't see you." Mikey stood up. Suddenly he remembered the word *wussy* when he was giving his project presentation the day before. Had Bill said it? The whole awful event replayed itself in his head. It was all so unfair —the way he'd been led into the duel, the way Pete fenced, the humiliation of it all. Rage filled his chest. "If you think I didn't want to fence because I was afraid, you're a jerk."

"What are you talking about?"

Mikey swallowed. "Well, somebody called me wussy."

"It wasn't me."

"I don't care. If you thought it, you were wrong."

"I didn't think it. I swear. But it was my fault, anyway."

Mikey gripped his fencing bag tight. "What was your fault?"

"That you lost. You wouldn't have even dueled if I hadn't said you should give a demonstration."

Mikey looked at the ground again. "It doesn't matter." What was the point of fighting over it? He stepped on a stick and snapped it in two. "I lost and that's that."

Bill shook his head. "Pete did everything wrong."

Mikey looked up quickly. "What?"

"His footwork was all wrong. Totally. And he hit you on the arm. That's not a fair hit. He only won because he didn't play by the rules."

"How'd you know that?"

Bill laughed. "That's all you talk about, proper fencing form, all the rules and regulations. I know so much it makes me sick." He stood silent for a moment. Then he said, "I'm sorry."

"Thanks." Mikey looked around. The lines were filing onto the school buses, and the kids who walked home were wandering off. Everyone was going about business as usual. But nothing was usual anymore. Everything was terrible. "Now they all think I'm an idiot, taking lessons and everything and not even being able to beat Pete. And they think Mr. Gaynor gave me the Olympic medal because he feels sorry for me."

"No one thinks that. You got it for sportsmanship."

"Sure," Mikey said in a sarcastic tone.

Bill cleared his throat. "Who cares about the dumb Olympic medals, anyway?"

"You do." Mikey twisted the cloth handle of the fencing bag. "You wear yours every day. You got the very first medal of the year."

"I didn't deserve it."

Mikey looked at Bill in astonishment. "Why not?"

"Mr. Gaynor didn't know me yet. It was the first week of school."

"So what?"

"So he felt sorry for me because I was the new kid. He just gave it to be nice. Teachers do that sort of thing. I know." Bill reached inside his sweater and took off his medal. "I hate it. It's a big lie." He threw it up hard.

Mikey watched in horror as the medal disappeared

in a maple tree. He waited for it to come tumbling down. It didn't. The school buses took off down the street, passing under the branches of the big maple. Mikey was sure the rumble of the buses would shake the medal out of the tree. But no. "You shouldn't have done that."

"What does it matter?"

"It matters a lot." Mikey thought about how Bill tucked the medal inside his shirt when he went rafting and how he tugged on it when he was talking. "You deserved the medal for readiness. You're always ready. Every time I turn around, there you are, ready."

Bill laughed. "Are you trying to be funny?"

Mikey spoke fast. He could hardly catch his breath. The pain of Bill losing his precious medal filled his heart. "Look at how you varnished the raft and put a new rope on it so it would be ready. You even pound in nails halfway so they'll be ready. If anyone deserves a medal for readiness, you do."

"Yeah, well, Mr. Gaynor didn't know that when he gave it to me."

"So what? You still earned it."

Bill nodded. "Maybe you're right." He looked up at the maple tree. "Well, it's gone now."

"I can get it." Mikey put his fencing bag on the ground. It made him anxious to let it out of his hands, but most of the kids had already gone home and no one would bother it. Besides, Bill would watch it.

Mikey climbed the tree. The medal had disappeared into the side that hung over the street. Mikey got to the first thick branch in that direction and shimmied his way out.

"Did you find it?"

Mikey looked down. Bill was peering up at him. "Not yet." The afternoon sun glinted off the yellow and orange leaves. With every bounce of the branch, leaves fell. Where was that medal? Was that it, way, way up there? Bill sure had a good arm for throwing. Mikey studied the situation. He could only walk on really thick branches. And the closest thick branch to the medal was more than five feet below it. Mikey couldn't reach that far. He needed a longer arm.

Mikey climbed back to the lower crook and called to Bill. "Pass me my foil."

"What?"

"My foil. It'll give me extra reach."

"Oh." Bill put the bike on its side, unzipped the fencing bag, and passed Mikey the foil. "Be careful."

Mikey shimmied out on the branch again. Then he stood up, gripping a smaller branch on one side, his foil clutched in the other hand. He reached over his head and held on to the wide branch above. He jammed the foil into a cluster of smaller branches and let go of it long enough to swing himself up onto the next higher branch.

"Hey, you're not climbing higher, are you? Get down. The medal doesn't matter that much. You'll fall."

Mikey took the foil in hand again and made his way out on the branch toward the medal.

"Get down. I mean it. I don't even want the stupid medal."

Mikey looked down at Bill's worried face. If Mikey fell, he'd go twenty feet down onto the street and he'd probably break his neck—and impale himself in the process. But he'd been working on balance in fencing lessons for the past seven weeks. If he didn't have good balance by now, he deserved to fall.

And now he was within reach. Mikey slid the tip of the foil through the ribbon of the medal and yanked down hard. The medal didn't budge. That frayed old ribbon was stronger than he'd thought. He worked the foil back and around so that the ribbon was looped around it twice. He yanked down with all his might. The branches shook so hard, Mikey stumbled backward. His breath stuck in his throat. He caught himself and stood on the branch panting, his heart pounding. Then he pulled on the foil once more, harder than ever, and the ribbon finally gave; Bill's Olympic medal fell somewhere below.

"Hey, fatso, that you?"

Mikey looked down. A tall boy came up beside Bill. "You trying to sneak out the front of the school?"

It was Hugh. Horrible Hugh.

Bill's voice cracked. "I'm not bothering you."

"That a new bike?" Hugh kicked at the front tire. "Let me take it for a ride."

Bill raised the bike and stood gripping it by the handles. "Go away."

"I want to take it for a ride." Hugh stood in front of the bike now. "What's this bag here?" He kicked the fencing bag.

"None of your business," said Bill.

Hugh leaned over the bag and put his hand on the zipper.

"Hey," Mikey called down, surprising himself with his own voice. It sounded strong, a lot stronger than he felt.

Hugh looked up. "What're you doing up there?"

Mikey repeated Victoria's advice to himself: Use your head—use strategy. "Hey, Bill," he said, acting as though Hugh weren't even there, "I'm coming down. Get ready to catch my fo . . . my sword."

"Your sword?" Hugh stood up straight.

Bill opened his mouth. Then he shut it. He put the bike down on the ground and stood ready at the foot of the tree.

Mikey climbed down with care. He handed Bill

146

the foil, then jumped from the lowest branch to the ground.

"Hey, that's a real sword." Hugh took a step back. "What were you doing with a real sword in the tree?"

"Sometimes when fencers get carried away, the swords just sort of fly out of their hands," said Mikey.

"What?" said Hugh.

"Bill's a pretty wild fencer. They don't call him Killer Bill for nothing."

Hugh looked at Mikey. Then he looked at Bill. Bill shrugged. Hugh looked back at Mikey. "Is that blood on your shirt?"

Bill gasped.

Mikey looked down. He must have scraped himself when he stumbled; blood had seeped through his shirt. He tried not to think about it—now was the moment to focus on strategy. "It can take a long time to heal. But every fencer knows those are the risks."

"I've got things to do." Hugh walked away toward the school playground, looking back over his shoulder every few seconds. Then he ran.

Mikey put his foil in the fencing bag.

"Are you okay?" said Bill. "We better get that cut cleaned up."

"It's not as bad as it looks," Mikey said, hoping his words were true. "I didn't even know I had it."

Bill walked to the street and picked up his Olympic medal. "Thanks." He dropped it in his pocket.

The boys walked side by side, Bill holding on to the bike and Mikey holding on to the fencing bag.

After a while Bill said, "I was thinking . . . when you were up there on that high branch, I saw how good you were on your feet. Did you learn that in fencing?"

"Yeah."

Bill chewed on his bottom lip. "You know, even a fencer could fall. Don't climb that high again, okay? Not for anything."

"I won't."

"That was crazy."

"I know."

Bill stopped. He ran his jacket zipper up and down, up and down. "Fencing must be easy for a thin guy like you."

"Huh? It doesn't matter at all whether you're thin or not. Fencers come in all shapes."

"They do? I thought you said weight mattered. You know, when you showed me your footwork the first time. I figured I was too fat to fence."

A light went on in Mikey's head—that was why Bill hated fencing. "Well, sure, weight matters. But it's not how much weight you have. It's how you balance it. You have to balance everything." Mikey thought about Daddy's words last night at the dinner table. He spoke half to himself. "Anyone can get good at fencing. All you have to do is work at it."

Bill took a deep breath and started walking again. "I have soccer every Saturday for another month. But if you feel like it, maybe we could do some fencing stuff on Sundays. I mean, you could sort of give me lessons. Maybe. If you feel like it."

"I feel like it," said Mikey slowly. But did he really? After losing to Pete, he wasn't sure he ever wanted to fence again.

"And then, after a while, when I know the moves, maybe we can do a real demonstration in front of the class. You know, with the right footwork. Following all the rules."

"That's a good idea," said Mikey. It would be a second chance—a chance to set the record straight. Oh, yes. "A great idea."

"Yeah." Bill laughed and shook his head. "Did you see Hugh run?"

Mikey laughed, too. "My sister told me to use strategy. I can't believe it worked."

Bill stopped again. "Let me see your Olympic medal."

Mikey handed Bill his medal.

Bill nodded. "Mr. Gaynor was right to give you the Olympic medal this week. But he made a mistake." Bill slipped the ribbon over Mikey's head so that the medal hung down to the middle of his chest. "The *S* isn't for *sportsmanship*. It's for *strategy*. You've got the best strategy of anyone I ever met."

Mikey's ears burned. "Ever?"

"Ever, in my whole life."

Mikey put his hand over the medal and pressed it against his chest. And he knew now for sure, for dead sure, why he was taking his fencing bag home. Tomorrow he would be at the Fencing Academy of Philadelphia, jumping rope and doing the Zen glove drop and stretching. He would advance and retreat up and down the fencing strips with all the other cadets. He would improve his speed and his balance and his aim and his strategy. All those skills. And the greatest of them was strategy. He smiled. That was what he really loved, after all. Figuring out how to do it and then getting better and better and better at it. Oh, it would be sweet to win, too. Sweeter than sweet. But fencing itself was sweet enough.

Donna Jo Napoli teaches linguistics and is the author of several novels for middle graders and young adults, including *The Bravest Thing*, *Shark Shock*, *Soccer Shock*, *When the Water Closes Over My Head*, *The Magic Circle* (an ALA Best Book for Young Adults), and *Zel*. She lives in Swarthmore, Pennsylvania, with her family.